Human Development

Human Development

T. G. R. BOWER
UNIVERSITY OF EDINBURGH

W. H. FREEMAN AND COMPANY

San Francisco

Sponsoring Editor: W. Hayward Rogers
Project Editor: Betsy Dilernia
Manuscript Editor: Howard Beckman
Designer: Marie Carluccio
Production Coordinator: Linda Jupiter
Illustration Coordinator: Batyah Janowski
Artists: Evan Gillespie, Cyndie Jo Clark
Compositor: Typesetting Services of Glasgow
Printer and Binder: The Maple-Vail Book Manufacturing Group

Library of Congress Cataloging in Publication Data

Bower, T.G.R.   1941–
    Human development.

    (A Series of books in psychology)
    Bibliography: p.
    Includes index.
    1. Child psychology.   I. Title.   [DNLM: 1. Growth.
2. Child development.   3. Cognition.   WS105.3 B786h]
BF721.B64   155.4   78–27223
ISBN 0–7167–0058–1

Printed in the United States of America

1 2 3 4 5 6 7 8 9

Contents

Preface

I began to write this book with one aim—to present a theoretically coherent basic outline of human development. My own reading of textbooks on human development revealed that they had increasingly become catalogues of facts, with no overall framework for interpreting these facts, no overall theory of change, and no guidelines for thinking about possible therapeutic application. My own students tended to become discouraged by the "empirical" nature of the field and to take refuge in segments of study where there was a coherent theory, such as psycholinguistics, object permanence, or stranger fear. No one, as far as I could tell, was thinking about a general theory of development that would encompass all the facts generated by the diverse body of research workers who call themselves developmental psychologists.

I set off with the aim of finding a theoretically coherent line of exposition for developmental psychology. I had no idea what that line was going to be. During the course of writing, new inputs of data and new results uncovered totally new (to me) lines of explanation. The fact that I concluded by presenting a differentiation model of development is not surprising. In the terms presented in this book, I may have been influenced by my early experiences.

I hope the theoretical outline presented here is clear enough that informed dissent will be possible. I trust it is clear enough that its applicability to the large body of data not reviewed in the book will be obvious. I hope that it will serve as a framework that students can use to organize the data they encounter.

In writing this book I was assisted by a great many people. Without the help of my wife, Jane, who is a molecular biologist, I doubt if I would have understood the biological principles on which the account given here is founded. The bulk of the book was completed at the Center for Advanced Study in the Behavioral Sciences, Stanford University, to which I owe a great debt. My attempts at theorizing were greatly helped by the other Fellows at the Center, in particular, Michael Dempster, Karl Heider, Gillian Sankoff, Bob Shaw, and Tony Tanner. That only one of these is a psychologist is a tribute to the interdisciplinary spirit that flourishes there. John Watson was also an important source of ideas during that year. The book benefited greatly from critical readings by Joe Campos, Wendell Jeffrey, and Alan Sroufe. Most of all, Jane Dunkeld and Jennifer Wishart helped with everything, from data collection to rewriting. The efforts of all these people, including myself, were transmuted into immaculate typescript by Agnes Paige and Janet Panther. I would like to thank all of these people for their help.

I dedicate the book to my own four children, Nick, Elanor, and the twins, Clio and Penelope, who helped as well, as the reader will find out.

November 1978   T. G. R. BOWER

Human Development

I

In this section we shall look at the basic biological processes that shape development. Traditionally we have thought two quite distinct processes were involved in development—gene expression and learning. The genes contain the information that converts a fertilized egg into a fully grown human. They are specialized programs that have been built up through the millenia of evolution. Learning, on the other hand, refers to information acquired by the individual in the course of a life. The combination of these two processes, gene expression and learning, presents an attractively simple picture of how development can proceed. Nonetheless, this picture has been thrown into some disarray by recent research showing that gene expression itself can be modified by events occurring in the life of the individual. These epigenetic processes are the subject of Chapter 3. That chapter introduces a central theme of this

1

book, the idea that many of the most important effects in development are the result of events in the psychological environment that affect the process of gene expression, thereby producing irreversible changes in the structure of the organism. Development is thus to be seen as the result of three processes: gene expression, learning, and epigenesis.

1

Growth and
Development

We enter this world small and helpless, with few capacities and few behaviors. Within two decades, however, we have the full range of human skills at our disposal, for whatever purposes we desire. Within another two decades the inexorable decline in powers and skills through aging begins, and will continue until death. The human adult is the lord of creation, the most successful organism ever evolved. Yet no other primate—indeed, no other mammal—is as dependent as we are at birth. How does anything as helpless as a human baby become something as competent as an adult? The purpose of this book is to examine the processes that produce the changes illustrated in Figure 1–1. Many biologists have suspected that our eventual accomplishments are linked to our initial dependence. During this period of dependence we forge the skills that assure our eventual success in coping with the world around us.

THE STUDY OF DEVELOPMENT

A human life is characterized by a series of changes interspersed with periods of stability. The study of these changes is the subject matter of developmental psychology. The most obvious change, at least at first, is in size. However, along with changes in size go drastic changes in the way we

FIGURE *1–1*

The problem of development in outline. As the child grows in size, the range and flexibility of his behaviors grows too, in a way that seems cumulative.

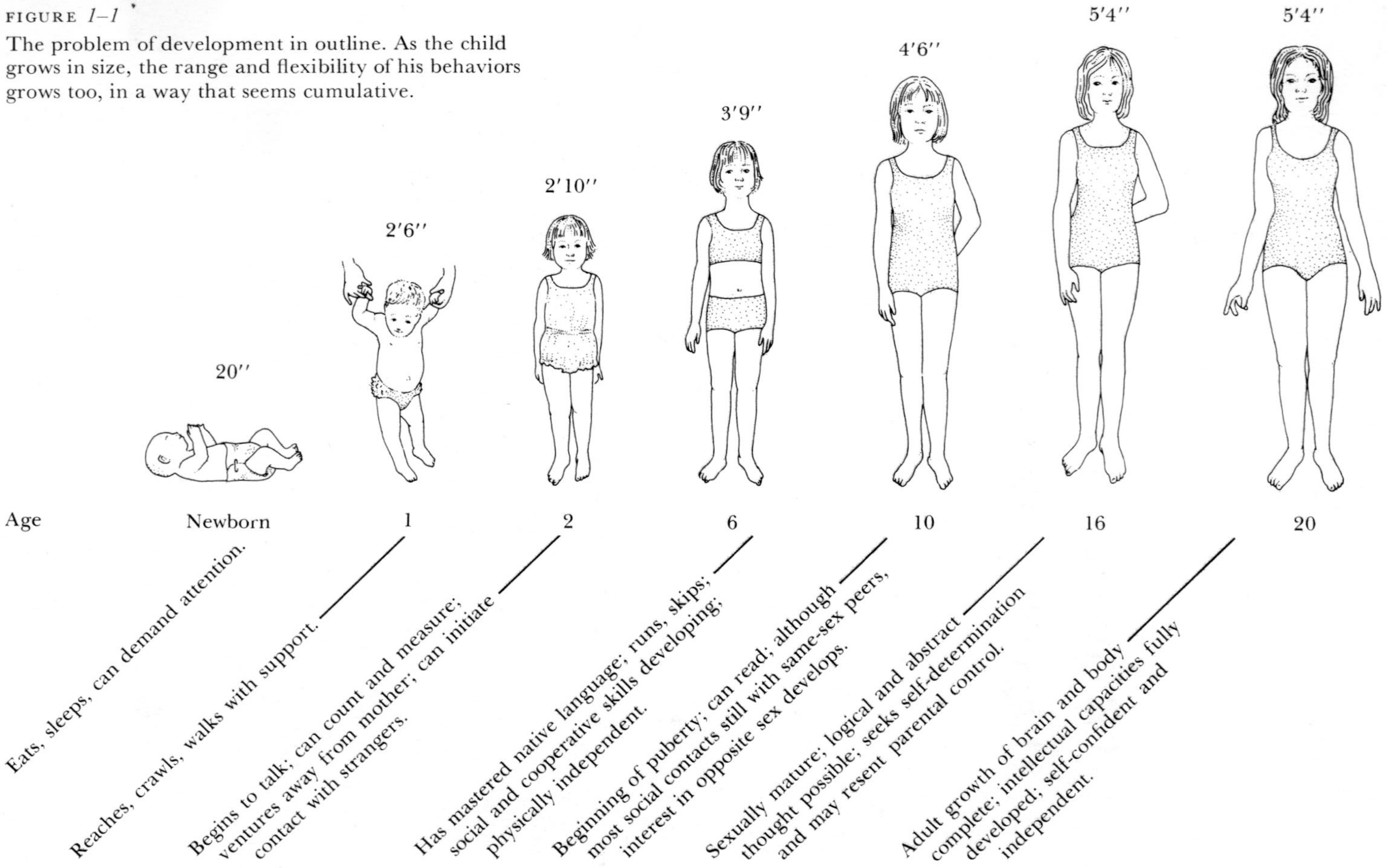

20″
2′6″
2′10″
3′9″
4′6″
5′4″
5′4″
Age
Newborn
1
2
6
10
16
20
Eats, sleeps, can demand attention.
Reaches, crawls, walks with support.
Begins to talk; can count and measure; ventures away from mother; can initiate contact with strangers.
Has mastered native language; runs, skips; social and cooperative skills developing; physically independent.
Beginning of puberty; can read; although most social contacts still with same-sex peers, interest in opposite sex develops.
Sexually mature; logical and abstract thought possible; seeks self-determination and may resent parental control.
Adult growth of brain and body complete; intellectual capacities fully developed; self-confident and independent.

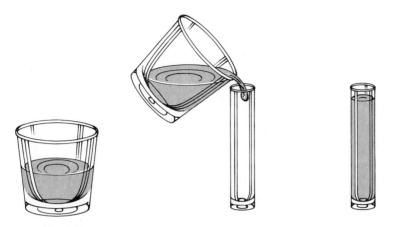

FIGURE *1–2*

When shown this sequence and asked if there is as much liquid in the thin glass as in the short one, a four- or five-year-old will typically say there is not. Because of the difference in appearance, the child believes that the volume is different.

view the world. Suppose we show a five-month-old baby three images of his mother, an easy enough trick using mirrors (see p. 153). The five-month-old will be quite delighted, happily babbling, smiling, and waving to all three in turn. A week later the situation is very different. The same baby will look soberly at each mother, then burst into tears. Why this change? Is it that the baby has only just learned he has only one mother, as I have suggested elsewhere (Bower, 1971)? Or is it something else?

Consider the sequence in Figure 1–2. When a four- or five-year-old is asked if there is the same amount in the two glasses, he will typically reply that there is more in the tall thin glass because it is higher. A six- or seven-year-old will typically say that the two are the same because nothing has been added and nothing has been taken away (Piaget and Szeminska, 1941). What produces this change? Or take this example. If we get a child of six to agree that two balls of plasticine weigh the same, and then roll one out into a sausage, he will typically say that the longer one has become heavier. An eight-year-old, by contrast, will say they weigh the same. But an 11-year-old will say the longer one is heavier! The 11-year-old will thus probably make the same mistake as the six-year-old (Piaget and Inhelder, 1941). Why?

Consider the following paradox. A child is brought up by warm and loving parents until the age of two. Some disaster results in the child spending the rest of his growing time in institutions with not much love and no consistent mother or father figure, only a succession of caretakers.

On leaving the institution, such a child is likely to engage in normal social interactions, raise children, and, generally, live a happy life. By contrast, another child spends the first two years of life in an institution, with a succession of caretakers, and then moves in with a family in which he enjoys warm, consistent care through the rest of childhood. When grown, that child is not likely to ever enjoy a normal social life, with normal loving and sharing. Why is the early experience so much more critical than the later one?

The above three problems are all from the vast field of developmental psychology. Basically, the field is concerned with all of the changes that occur during a human life. It seeks to explain why some individuals change in one direction and some in another. From a practical standpoint, it should come up with ways of altering the direction of development if the direction is abnormal, or facilitating development if it is slow. This might sound like a description of the work of the whole field of psychology, but the special tasks of developmental psychology should become clearer in succeeding chapters.

This book is organized around the assumption that we must cope with two worlds. One is the physical world—the world of sun, storms, ships, energy, and of things in general. The other is the world of people, of interaction between individuals, including cooperation in coping with the world of things. The latter world is more important to humans. Without it we could never have evolved to our present state, where we now have such close control over the physical world that our control over the interpersonal world seems primitive by comparison. Nevertheless, it is our performance in the world of objects that has historically engaged the attention of developmental psychologists. The study of development has traditionally concentrated on the child's developing comprehension of the physical world, on ways to measure the development of that comprehension, and more recently, on ways to facilitate that development. However, recent years have also seen a surge of interest in social development. This book follows the historical sequence of interest, from comprehension of the physical world to the development of social behaviors. But as we shall see, development in the world of people is increasingly being regarded as a necessary condition of development in the world of objects.

ENVIRONMENTALIST AND NATIVIST MODELS OF DEVELOPMENT

Child psychology has a long ancestry as a practical understanding but a short history as a science. Parents today manifestly treat their children in ways they think reflect the child's basic capacities, motives, and desires. It seems likely that throughout history parents have had firm ideas about how children should be raised.

The Bushmen of the Kalahari, the most primitive parents studied to date, are strong *environmentalists*, which is to say that they believe that training and practice are necessary in order for a child to grow into an adult.

> Teaching the child to walk is a group activity, greatly enjoyed by women and older children. Bushmen children do not go through a proper crawling stage, probably because the child is always held standing on its feet when playing with it. Physically they are certainly most precocious and between their sixth or eighth months are taught to walk. This consists of passing the infant from one side to another of a circle of women and children, holding him in an upright position and, at first, gently allowing him to fall forward into the hand of the person opposite in the circle. Later, children are allowed to fall forward onto their hands, but are encouraged to stand up again. The rhythms of the dances are instilled into the children at about the same age by taking their hands and beating time with them. By the time they are able to walk, they are able to keep closely approximate time with the complex rhythms of G/wi dances. (Silberbauer, 1965)

Bushmen "teach" their children to reach, grasp, walk, and talk, as well as other more obviously acquired skills, such as hunting and finding water. The Bushmen believe that if children were not trained, they simply would not acquire adult skills (Konner, 1971).

The attitude of the Bushmen is directly opposite to that which has prevailed in Western civilization. In the Western world children were traditionally regarded as simply miniature adults (Figure 1–3). Of course, they were not expected to do all the things that adults could, but that was simply because they were physically smaller. Once grown, however, they were expected to cope naturally with the grownup world, without special training or preparation. This view was expressed in the educational philosophy that we need only allow children to develop what they know *innately*—that education is not a "putting in" but a "drawing out." This position, the *nativist* position, argues then that all human skills and capacities are natural attainments for us, as natural as our ability to breathe in air and our inability to breathe in water. It was most clearly argued by Plato, more than 2,000 years ago, with an eloquence and experimental elegance that has rarely been matched since then.

In large part the history of child psychology is the history of the debate between these two extreme positions. Because the issues involved are socially important, the debate has often been acrimonious and bitter, as indeed it still is.

The issues in the debate between environmentalists and nativists have gradually become clarified over the last 500 years. Physical growth has often been used as a convenient metaphor for explicating these issues; although it may be convenient, this metaphor is highly misleading, as we shall see later. Human beings have a characteristic height and weight; very tall and very short people are relatively uncommon (Figure 1–4). At

FIGURE *1–3*

When Velasquez painted the Infanta Margarita of Austria in
1659 he portrayed her as a miniature adult, a view of children
prevalent in Western society at that time.

the same time, however, there is a characteristic height difference between
populations; the Welsh are shorter than the neighboring English. Short
parents tend to have short children, and tall parents tend to have tall
children. The nativistic interpretation of these facts is that height is *inherited*,
that the height of one's parents determines one's own height, and that
environmental factors have little influence. An environmentalist explanation of the same phenomenon might be that since tall parents eat more,
they tend to feed their children in accordance with their own requirements.
Not a great deal of research has been done on the determination of height.
Nonetheless, data have been gathered which indicate that *both* inherited
and environmental factors are involved. One study investigated Japanese
youths raised in three different environments. The first group lived in an
impoverished environment. These children did most of their growing in
Japan during World War II and the immediate postwar years when food
was in short supply in Japan. The second group lived in a normal Japanese
environment, unaffected by war or famine. The third group comprised of
children of Japanese emigrants to the United States, a nutritionally rich

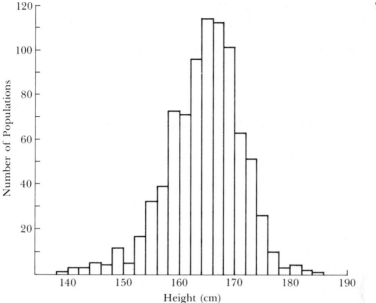

FIGURE *1–4*

Distribution of average heights of adult males in the world's populations. Middle-size people are most common. Very tall and very short people are relatively uncommon.

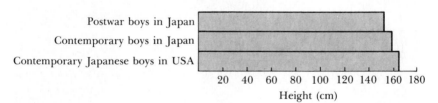

FIGURE *1–5*

Height is affected by nutrition. (After Gottesman, 1974.)

environment. We would expect that all three groups would inherit the same potential height, and that any differences between the groups would thus be a function of their environment. Figure 1–5 shows that there are in fact differences, with the enhanced environments producing taller children. However, a comparison of children of Japanese descent in the United States and white American children shows that environmental effects are not all-important, for the American children are taller. Further evidence for the role of inheritance comes from observations of the height of children born to Japanese mothers and white American fathers. The average height of these children lies midway between that of children of two Japanese parents and the children of two American parents (Gottesman, 1974).

THE GENETIC BASIS OF HEREDITY

To understand the results discussed above we must make a brief excursion into genetics. The human body is made up of a very large number of cells. Cells are remarkably complex structures. They have the important property that they can grow and then divide into two identical cells. The process of division is shown in Figure 1–6. Note that a critical step in cell division is the formation of a second set of *chromosomes*, the structures in the cell nucleus that carry the information that controls growth and development. Thus every cell of our body has an identical copy of the chromosomes in the original cell, the fertilized egg. Humans have 46 chromosomes (the number of chromosomes varies between species). Half of these are contributed by the sperm cell from the father and half from the mother's egg during fertilization, when the sperm and egg cells merge.

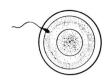 Fertilization—the sperm penetrates the ovum

 Nuclei of sperm and ovum fuse

 The 46 chromosomes begin to pair up

 Each chromosome divides into two and the pairs line up opposite each other; the nuclear membrane dissolves

 Two spindles form and the chromosomes are drawn to opposite ends of the cell

FIGURE *1–6*

In human fertilization a sperm cell with its 23 chromosomes penetrates an egg cell with its 23 chromosomes, resulting in a fertilized egg with 46 chromosomes. Identical twins, like those pictured on the opposite page, are formed from a single fertilized egg. Nonidentical twins are formed from separate eggs.

Single baby

 The original cell divides but the two new cells remain joined

 Each of these cells then divides as before

 The process of division continues

Identical twins

  The original cell divides and the two new cells become separated

  Each of these cells divides normally

  The process of division continues

The classic studies that demonstrated the genetic mechanisms of inheritance were carried out by Thomas Hunt Morgan (1927) on various strains of the fruit fly *Drosophila*. Some fruit flies in a population will inherit abnormal characteristics of appearance. Each abnormality in appearance corresponds to a chromosomal abnormality (Figure 1–7). If two abnormal flies are mated, all the progeny will have the abnormality. If an abnormal fly is mated with a normal fly, half the progeny will be abnormal and half normal; the half that are abnormal have the abnormal chromosome. This shows clearly that it is the inherited chromosomes that carry the information that generates, in development, an inherited characteristic. Thus, to the extent that height is inherited, Japanese–American children should be intermediate in height between purely Japanese and purely American children.

Although we know that height is determined in part by inheritance and in part by environmental circumstances, suppose we wished to go further and determine precisely the relative contributions of these two factors? One of the simplest ways of doing this might be to make use of identical twins. Identical twins result from an accident in early development. A single fertilized egg becomes separated into independently growing cell aggregations, giving rise to two individuals of the same sex and identical genetic constitutions (Figure 1–6). Presumably, if two identical twins were given exactly the same diet from birth, they should finish up exactly the same height. That is, if both inheritance and environment were exactly the same in two individuals, their height should be exactly the same. Now, however, let us put one twin on a rich diet and the other on a poor diet. Suppose in fact we have an identified population of people with an identified range of diets. If one twin were put on the best diet found in that population and the other on the worst, their mature heights would almost certainly be different. A comparison of the height differences of the twins with the *range* of height differences found in the population would give us an estimate of the relative importance of inheritance and diet in the determination of height in that population. Suppose that the tallest man in the population was 6′ 5″ and the shortest 5′ 7″; the height range in that population would be the difference between these extremes, or 10 inches. Suppose that the greatest height difference we could get between identical twins raised on the two extremes of that population's diet was 8 inches. We could then say that of the 10-inch range of height found in that population, probably 8 inches was accounted for by dietary differences and the remainder by inherited differences.

Although such a study is conceivable, it is not very likely that anyone would carry it out. Apart from the immorality of such a study on humans, there would be the difficulty of deciding what a "rich" or "poor" diet was— and unless one could do that the whole thing would be pointless. Second, there are profound conceptual difficulties in understanding what the

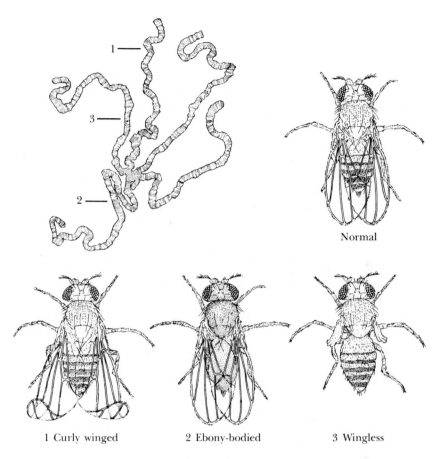

1 ——

3 ——

2 ——

Normal

1 Curly winged   2 Ebony-bodied   3 Wingless

FIGURE 1–7

Genes damaged at the points indicated on the fruit fly's four chromosomes produce the abnormal flies shown below.

statement "height is inherited" really means. Height is not inherited in the same way as money. Six-foot tall parents may have equally tall children, but they do not produce six-foot tall babies! What we inherit from our parents is a set of chromosomes, and to understand how this specific inheritance can lead to effects years later we must return to the science of genetics. It has been determined that chromosomes are in fact strings of *genes*, thousands and thousands of them. It has been estimated that the nucleus of every human cell contains about 70,000 genes. What is a gene? This is a question that is currently occupying the attention of thousands of molecular biologists all over the world. In one sense a gene is a complex arrangement of chemicals. In another, equally valid sense a gene is a set of instructions for the manufacture of an *enzyme*. Each gene produces one and only one enzyme. Enzymes are responsible for the construction of the proteins of which all cells are made. The nutrients we take in are converted into specific proteins by specific enzymes produced by specific genes. It is this process that allows cells to divide, differentiate, and increase in number.

There are many variant forms of the same gene, which explains in part the differences between people. These variants, called *alleles*, are usually functionally equivalent. Sometimes they are not, and the inheritance of one or two nonfunctional alleles can have drastic and severe effects. Consider the human disorder phenylketonuria, or PKU. This disease produces a severe mental defect—feeblemindedness of the most extreme sort. In the 1930s the suspicion arose that PKU was an inherited disorder. The disease was more frequent among the brothers and sisters of affected individuals than one would have expected on a chance basis. It was also more common in the children of parents who were themselves closely related, such as first cousins. The pattern of incidence in families suggested that a single variant allele was involved. It was then discovered that individuals afflicted with PKU were unable to produce the enzyme that converts one protein, phenylalanine, to another, tyrosine. Phenylalanine is present in a normal diet. If it is not converted to tyrosine it is changed into phenylpyruvic acid, which causes neural damage and thus leads to irreversible brain damage. The discovery of the deleterious effects of loss of a single enzyme led to one of the most spectacular successes of human biochemical genetics. Production of phenylpyruvic acid in the body could be avoided simply by cutting phenylalanine from the diet of individuals with PKU. This has been done with great success.

PKU is a dramatic instance of how the mechanisms of inheritance work. What we inherit is a complement of genes. Genes make enzymes, and enzymes make the proteins of which we are built. Loss of one enzyme—just one among the thousands we normally produce—can have severe consequences. The normal functioning of the genes permits the conversion of nutrients to cells and more cells; it is the functioning or expression of the genes that is responsible for growth.

PHYSICAL GROWTH AND PSYCHOLOGICAL DEVELOPMENT

Here perhaps we can see the connection between physical growth and psychological development that many people have wished to make. Human behavior depends on a functioning input system (eyes, ears, and so on), a functioning output system (hands, lips and tongue for speech, and so on), and a very large brain that mediates between the input and output and controls both. At birth none of these systems are fully mature physically.

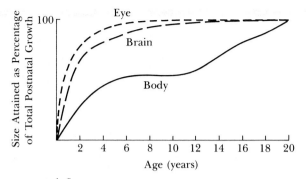

FIGURE *1–8*

Typical growth curves for the human eye, brain, and body.

Figure 1–8 shows the typical relative growth curves of the eye, brain, and body in humans. The most important link in the input-output process of human behavior is obviously the human brain. The brain, in adults, can be viewed as a number of semi-independent functional regions, each controlling a different class of human function. Damage or destruction of any one of these areas results in impairment or loss of specific skills and abilities. Figure 1–9 shows a functional map of the adult human brain, which is notably larger and more defined than the brain of a baby. Is it not possible that straightforward processes of growth, straightforward gene expression, build the complex structure of the human brain piece by piece, and that as the structure grows new behavioral capabilities arise? For example, newborn babies cannot use language. Does straightforward growth of the speech area "create" the capability of language? Newborns also cannot walk. Does straightforward gene expression result in the emergence of a part of the brain that "produces" walking? Many psychologists have answered this question with a resounding yes. They argue that, given an adequate supply of nutrients, processes of gene expression alone will result in full development of the individual, including behavioral and psychological growth, with no special input from the environment being really necessary.

Such a position is an extreme form of nativism. As we shall see in the following pages, it is a position that is held for at least some aspects of development. Is it open to many objections? Although physical growth is continuous, it is clear that behavioral development is discontinuous. For example, a baby's first step is a sudden discrete change in capacity—one week the baby can only crawl, the next it can walk. But can the manifestations of development be discontinuous if the underlying causes

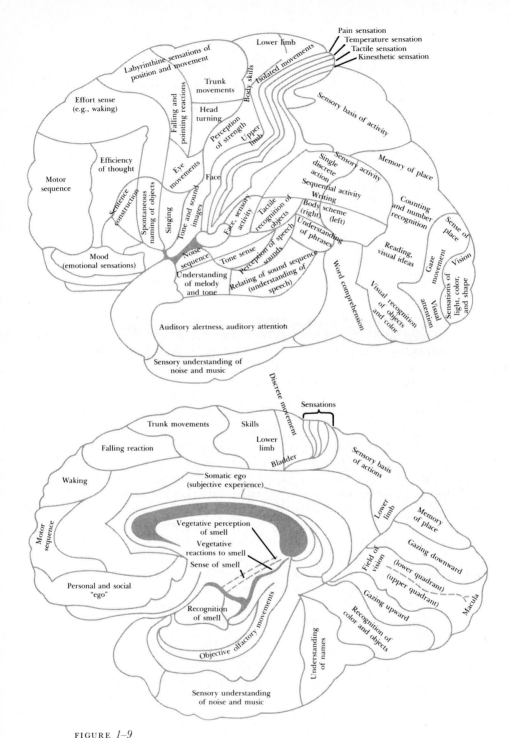

FIGURE *1–9*

A functional map of the adult human brain. The upper map shows the left lateral surface, the lower map the medial surface. (After Kleist, 1934.)

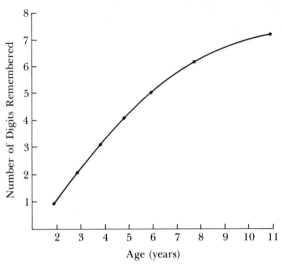

FIGURE *1–10*

Short-term memory for numbers increases steadily
with age.

are continuous? Yes, although it is perfectly true that comprehending the
formal relationship between continuous and discontinuous processes is
quite difficult.* It is surely obvious that continuous change in size can
produce quite sudden changes in capabilities. To give a trivial example,
no one shorter than 3′ 6″ can play a standard American pinball machine.
However, the condition that makes pinball playing possible, the attainment
of a height of 3′ 6″, is the result of the continuous process of growth.

A more serious objection to nativism as a general theory of development
is that there are, as we all know, certain processes of learning that can
modify and change our capacities. Let us consider a very simple example,
the ability to remember a string of numbers or letters. The number of digits
that can be recalled grows steadily with age (Figure 1–10). Moreover, the
strings can be presented faster and faster as we grow older with no drop in
performance. This is the kind of change that has led many psychologists to
think of development as a change in *information-processing capacity*. According
to this view, the continuous process of physical growth is accompanied by
a continuous increase in our ability to handle information presented in the
world around us. As with purely physical changes, e.g., height, this
continuous change in the capacity for information-processing can lead to

---

*The recent development of catastrophe theory is intended to create a mathematical language
to describe such relationships and should remove many of the difficulties (Zeeman, 1976).

TABLE *1–1*

The top row is a string of 18 binary numbers presented to subjects in a recall experiment. There are far too many digits to remember as a set. But one subject learned to group the digits into pairs and represent each pair by a single number: 10 as 2, 01 as 1, and 00 as 0. The string thus became only nine digits long, which is just about possible to remember. Further regrouping into even longer bits and assigning a new number to each allowed the subject to reduce the original 18-digit string to only three or four digits. Since it is possible to remember sets of seven or eight digits, the subject could recall strings of up to 40 binary numbers. (G. A. Miller, 1956.)

	1	0	1	0	0	0	1	0	0	1	1	1	0	0	1	1	1	0
Regrouping	10		10		00		10		01		11		00		11		10	
Code	2		2		0		2		1		3		0		3		2	
Regrouping	101			000			100			111			001			110		
Code	5			0			4			7			1			6		
Regrouping	1010				0010				0111				0011				10	
Code	10				2				7				3					
Regrouping	10100					01001					11001					110		
Code	20					9					25							

quite discontinuous changes in behavior. I have myself always believed, and still do believe, that growth in information-processing capacity is truly one of the most significant factors underlying behavioral development. However, I have no doubt that the capacity for information-processing is modifiable independently of physical growth. Consider the task described above—remembering a string of numbers or letters. The average adult is doing well if he can recall strings with as many as seven units. It is particularly difficult to remember long strings with only two elements, e.g., the numbers 1 and 0 or the letters *a* and *b*. Some years ago George Miller described a subject who could remember no less than 40 binary numbers. Does this mean the subject had a truly enormous information-processing capacity, a truly complex brain? It does not. The subject had simply devised an efficient way to recall a long string of binary numbers (Table 1–1). There is some support for the information-processing model of development in the fact that having processed the information, the subject was dealing with the same number of recoded items (eight) as he was able to remember before the experiment started. The fact that learning quintupled the efficiency of his performance is sobering to anyone who believes that information-processing capacity is fixed by the number of cells or thickness of the fibers in our brains. Any complete theory of development, even a nativistic one, must come to terms with the changes in capacity produced by processes of learning. We shall now turn to those processes in the next chapter.

2

Learning

The elucidation of the principles of learning and their use in the control of behavior has been psychology's most significant accomplishment in this century. Many psychologists have taken the position that the processes of learning alone account for all human skills and all human variation, and that the only unlearned capacity is the capacity to learn. While such an extreme argument is hard to support, the fact that it could be made at all is an indication of the power of the principles involved. We all know in some sense what learning is—we may remember how we learned to read or drive or speak a second language. Most of us believe we know what sort of things facilitate our own learning of such skills, but we are less aware of the simpler forms of learning that affect our behavior. Studies of these elementary forms, simplified to a point where they may seem far removed from everyday human life, have advanced our comprehension of learning processes, which can be defined generally as any relatively long-lasting alteration in performance consequent on specific experience. There are two standard paradigms for the study of learning: *classical conditioning* and *operant conditioning*. The two are very different, despite the fact that both are called "conditioning."

CLASSICAL CONDITIONING

Classical conditioning was first described by the great Russian physiologist
Ivan Pavlov (1849–1936), who was awarded the Nobel Prize in 1904 for
his work on the physiology of digestion. Pavlov found that while, not
unexpectedly, a great variety of substances elicit the salivation response
when placed in the mouth, a whole class of stimuli that do not come in
contact with the mouth can also elicit salivation if they are presented
in association with the stimuli in the mouth. Pavlov studied this process of
association systematically.* A standard experimental setup is shown in
Figure 2–1. The basic experiment requires a stimulus (e.g., meat powder
in the mouth) referred to as the *unconditioned stimulus* or UCS, which elicits a
natural response (salivation) referred to as the *unconditioned response* or UCR.
The UCS is presented in association with a second, neutral stimulus, (the
noise of a bell) referred to as the *conditioned* stimulus or CS. The CS is
typically presented before or concurrently with the presentation of the
UCS (Figure 2–2). After a few presentations of this sort, the CS will elicit
the UCR, even when the UCS is not presented at all. When a UCR is
elicited by the CS alone, it is called a *conditioned response* or CR. With
increased number of pairings, the likelihood and magnitude of the CR
increases (Figure 2–3).

---

*For Pavlov's early summary of his studies, see *Conditioned Reflexes*, Oxford University Press,
1927.

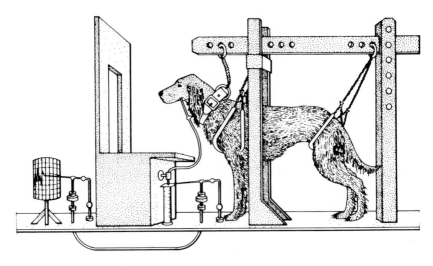

FIGURE *2–1*

Pavlov's famous apparatus for testing the salivation response of dogs. Saliva is
collected directly via the tube inserted into the animal's face.

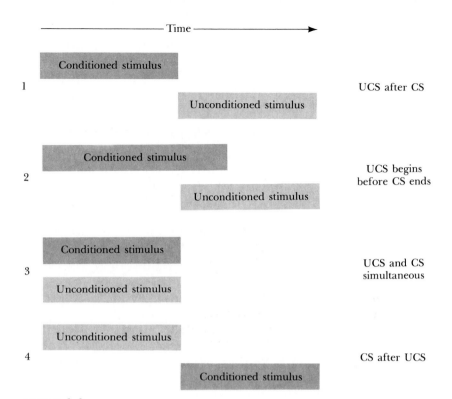

FIGURE *2–2*

Possible time relations between conditioned and unconditioned stimuli in Pavlovian learning experiments. The first three lead to learning; the fourth does not.

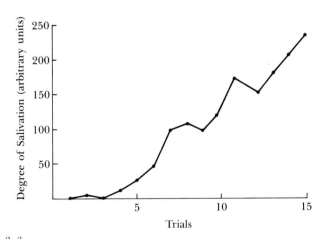

FIGURE *2–3*

In a Pavlovian experiment learning increases with the number of trials, as evidenced by an increase in the amount of salivation. (Kleitman and Creisler, 1927.)

22

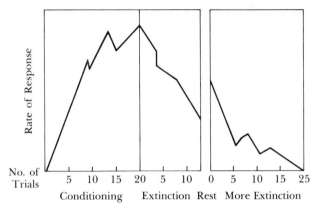

FIGURE 2-4

Rates of acquisition and extinction of a classically
conditioned behavior. Note the spontaneous recovery
immediately following the rest period.

Extinction

Classical conditioning can be reversed, i.e., the likelihood of the CR
occurring in response to the CS, as well as its magnitude, can be diminished
with repeated presentations of the CS without the UCS. This process is
called *extinction*. However, a CR that has been extinguished may be elicited
subsequently with no additional reinforcements. This phenomenon is
known as *spontaneous recovery*, and experimentation so far suggests that
complete and total extinction of a conditioned response may be a very
unusual event (Figure 2-4).

Generalization and discrimination

Classically conditioned responses can be elicited by stimuli other than the
original CS. The probability of such *generalization* seems to depend on the
similarity of the new stimulus to the CS. Figure 2-5 gives a typical
generalization gradient for pitch. There it is clear that the more similar the
tested tones are to the conditioned tone, the more likely the subject will
respond to them. Generalization is not only determined by the physical
similarity of the CS and the generalization test stimulus, but by their
psychological similarity as well. The most striking instances of this can be
seen in experiments with humans when words are used as the conditioned
stimuli. Here generalization seems to be a function of the similarity of
meaning rather than of the sound of the conditioned stimuli. Physical and

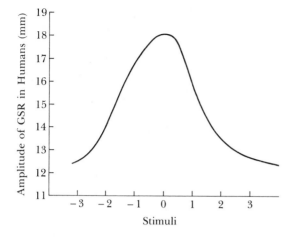

FIGURE 2–5
Curve of generalization of the galvanic skin response (GSR) to tones of different pitch. Zero is the conditioned tone. The graph shows the response to several tones varying in frequency from the conditioned tone. The closer a test tone is to the conditioned tone, the more likely the subject will respond to it. (Hovland, 1937.)

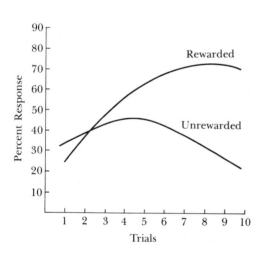

FIGURE 2–6
Discriminative learning. Neonates were rewarded when they turned their heads in response to a certain stimulus. They were not rewarded for turning their heads in response to another similar stimulus. Although on the first trial the infants were nearly as likely to turn their heads in response to either stimulus, by the tenth trial they showed discrimination between the two stimuli and were far more likely to turn their heads in response to the rewarded stimulus. (Siqueland and Lipsitt, 1966.)

psychological similarity are nevertheless often highly correlated; when they are not, the latter dominates.

An organism can learn to respond to one CS and not to generalize to another, similar stimulus. A typical curve for *discriminative learning* is shown in Figure 2–6.

It has been shown that very many unconditioned responses can be subjected to classical conditioning. For students of development the most interesting responses are those that underlie the emotional responses, such as hope, fear, anger, anxiety. There is evidence that emotional responses are easily conditioned and hard to extinguish. In one famous, or perhaps

I should say infamous, experiment on conditioned fear, a young child was taught to fear furry objects—rabbits, white rats, and the like. Prior to the experiment the child showed no sign of fear of such things. In the experiment, each time the child was presented with a furry object a loud bang occurred. The bang was an unconditioned stimulus for the unconditioned response of fear; the furry object was the CS. The child soon became afraid of furry things, and even generalized his response to the fur on the collar of his mother's coat.

Habituation

In the course of his research on classical conditioning Pavlov discovered another extremely interesting form of learning. When a novel stimulus is presented to any organism, the first response is an orienting, investigative response—what Pavlov called the "orienting reflex." All the sensory equipment, such as eyes and ears, turn towards the stimulus. Particular patterns of brain activity also occur. But with repeated presentations of the stimulus the probability of an orienting reflex declines to zero. This decline is called *habituation*. Habituation is like classical conditioning in that some form of generalization occurs. The more a novel stimulus resembles a previously encountered, habituated stimulus, the less likely the novel stimulus is to elicit an orienting response. What is the function of habituation? Habituation is not simply the result of fatigue of the relevant sensory receptors. If an organism has habituated to a particular sound, an orienting response to that sound can still be elicited by increasing or decreasing the volume of the sound. If habituation simply meant "tired ears," the latter would not work at all. Pavlov noticed that an organism must first habituate to a stimulus before that stimulus can serve as a CS. But this was merely a clue to the more general biological significance of habituation, which is that it seems to concentrate our attention on those stimuli that are novel or important. Recurring stimuli with no signal value can safely be ignored without endangering the organism through habituation.

OPERANT CONDITIONING

The second classic paradigm for the study of learning is operant conditioning, which is very different from classical conditioning. The most famous of all operant-conditioning studies was done by B. F. Skinner (1938). His apparatus and techniques have since been used extensively to study the processes of learning in humans as well as in animals. In the original experiment Skinner used pigeons. A pigeon is first starved to 80 percent of its normal weight. The bird is then placed in a box containing a key like the ones used in a telegraph setup. Because the pigeon naturally pecks, it will eventually, by chance, peck the key. Pecking the key is the *operant*. Any voluntary action of an organism can serve as an operant, which is the behavior selected for *reinforcement*. In this experiment the presentation of food is the reinforcement. Whenever the pigeon pecks the key, food is presented for a brief period. What typically happens in this situation is that the pigeon will peck more frequently at the key than it would if food were not delivered as a result. This increase in frequency of a behavior is the basic measure of learning under operant conditioning.

Reinforcement

In the experiment just described reinforcement is delivered every time the pigeon pecks the key, a condition known as *continuous reinforcement*. Operant conditioning normally begins with continuous reinforcement. However, once the basic conditioning is established any of four basic schedules of *partial reinforcement* can be initiated. Two of these are based on preestablished intervals between instances of the operant behavior, without regard to clock time. The simpler of the two is the *fixed-ratio* schedule, in which the subject receives reinforcement on every xth operant response, where x is any number larger than one. For example, the pigeon might receive food every 5th, 10th, or 50th peck. The more complex schedule is a *variable-ratio* schedule, in which reinforcement is delivered *on the average* after every xth response, where x is greater than one. Suppose $x = 5$. The pigeon might receive reinforcement after two pecks, then after eight, then after six, then after four, then after five, then after seven, then after three, then after one, then after nine. Over a total of 45 pecks $(2+8+6+4+5+7+3+1+9)$ the pigeon has received nine reinforcements. The average number of operant responses per reinforcement is thus five, but the animal is not able to predict the specific number required and must therefore maintain a very high rate of pecking.

The other two schedules are based on clock time. The simpler one is the *fixed-interval* schedule, in which the time interval between reinforcements is constant. Rewards are presented at the first occurrence of an operant response after a specified time, say 10 minutes; operant behavior during the intervals is not rewarded. The more complex schedule based on time is the *variable-interval* schedule. Here only the *average* interval between reinforcements is established; specific intervals vary in a way analogous to the variability found with variable-interval schedules.

Each of the four types of schedules produces characteristic patterns of

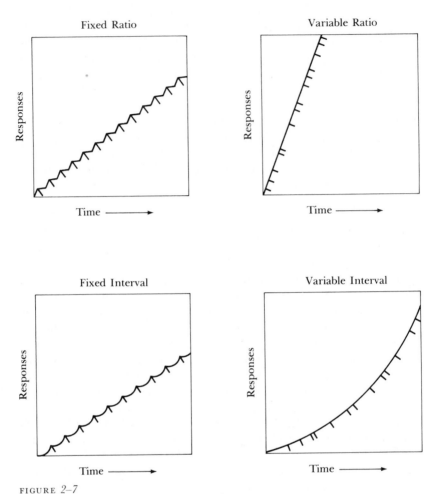

FIGURE *2–7*

Typical response records for the four types of schedules of partial reinforcement. The ticks indicate when reinforcement was given. The variable schedules result in much higher rates of response than the fixed schedules. Note the "scalloping" effect of fixed-interval reinforcement. The response rate increases in frequency as the time for reinforcement approaches and then decreases after reinforcement.

response (Figure 2–7). The resistance of the operant to extinction also varies with each type of schedule. The variable schedules take much longer to extinguish than do the fixed schedules. This may be of some practical importance to development, since it seems that much of the behavior of children is reinforced on a variable-ratio schedule.

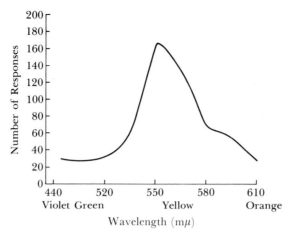

FIGURE *2–8*

Typical generalization gradient for operant
conditioning. Pigeons were trained to peck at a key
when shown a light stimulus of wavelength 550 mμ.
Later, when shown light of other wavelengths, they
responded most frequently to those wavelengths closest
to the one that had been reinforced. (Guttmann, 1963.)

Stimulus control and generalization

Suppose the operant behavior of pecking by the pigeon in the box is only
reinforced when light of a certain wavelength is present. Eventually the
pigeon will peck *only* in the presence of that wavelength. The behavior is
then said to be under *stimulus control*, since the pigeon responds only when a
certain stimulus is present. The stimulus functions like the CS in classical
conditioning. This process is not inflexible, however, since generalization
operates in operant conditioning just as it does in classical conditioning
and habituation. The more like the designated control stimulus a novel
stimulus is, the more likely it will be to elicit operant responses. Figure 2–8
shows a typical generalization gradient for operant behavior. At the same
time, operants may become discriminative, so that one and only one
stimulus will elicit the behavior.

For all of my professional life I have been fascinated by operant
conditioning. I often find it difficult, however, to communicate this enthusi-
asm to students because to most people operant conditioning seems remote
from everyday human affairs. In fact, however, it is extremely relevant, as
I hope will become clear later in the book. Here I will only describe one
experiment that indicates the relevance of operant conditioning to everyday
life. The subjects in this experiment were college students. The operant

behavior was the assertion of personal opinion, as evidenced by sentences beginning "I think," "I believe," "it seems obvious to me that," and so on. Reinforcement was verbal confirmation by the experimenter. The experimenter always said "you're right" or "I agree" whenever subjects made self-assertive statements. The frequency of such statements then increased during the course of the experiment (Verplanck, 1958). The subjects seemed quite unaware of how they were being manipulated by the experimenter. Suppose the experimenter had then gone on to a variable-ratio schedule. What would have happened? Self-assertive statements would still have occurred at a high rate and would have been very hard to extinguish. Think of how often situations like those in this experiment occur in everyday life. A few reinforcements are enough to get a behavior started, after which intermittent reinforcement is sufficient to maintain a high rate of response.

Because operant conditioning is an important form of learning, it is very important in the analysis of development, as we shall see later (Chapter 6). For the moment, one instance of its application to a practical problem will suffice. An institutionalized baby cried and fussed virtually all the time. Analysis of the situation indicated that crying and fussing usually resulted in the presence of an attendant checking to see what was wrong. The crying was being reinforced basically on a variable-interval schedule. The situation was changed in the following way. Crying for attention was never reinforced. Smiling and cooing were continually reinforced at first, then later on an interval schedule. Because the crying was no longer reinforced, it was eventually extinguished (smiling and crying are incompatible responses). The result was a rapid extension of smiling to other social behaviors of the same sort (Etzel and Gewirtz, 1967).

One puzzling factor in the description of operant conditioning just offered is the use of the word "reinforcement." The word has been used to refer to presentation of food, verbal agreement, and the presence of an adult attendant. What is the common factor? At first sight there is none. In fact, the search for a common factor has been so discouraging that many psychologists define reinforcement simply as any event that affects the rate of occurrence of a preceding behavior. This definition is basically circular. However, as we shall see later, it is possible to define reinforcement in a way that is not circular.

TRANSFER OF TRAINING

Transfer is a process of learning in which learning one thing facilitates the learning of something else. Generalization is a form of transfer: a response elicited by one stimulus becomes, through learning, elicited by other, similar stimuli. Transfer is of especial importance in development, or

TABLE *2–1*
The control group learned list B only, while the experimental group
learned list B after having two repetitions of list A. The number of trials
the experimental group took to learn list B is expressed as a percentage
of the number of trials the control group took to learn it. In (1) the
experimental group took 16 percent fewer trials than the control group,
showing a high positive transfer between lists A and B. In (3) the
experimental group took longer than controls because of high negative
transfer, while in (2) there was no real difference between the two
groups. (Bruce, 1933.)

			TRIALS		
PARADIGM	SAMPLE OF LIST A	SAMPLE OF LIST B	CONTROL	EXPERIMENTAL	SAVINGS
	S R	S R			
1. Stimuli similar, responses identical	REQ KIV	REB KIV	100%	84%	+ 16
2. Stimuli identical, responses similar	REQ KIV	REQ KIB	100	102	− 2
3. Stimuli identical, responses different	REQ KIV	REQ YOR	100	117	− 17

indeed in any real-life situation, since we rarely encounter the same
situation over and over again and yet we manifestly do not have to learn to
cope with every similar situation as if each were entirely new. Transfer has
been studied in the laboratory, where it is possible to manipulate the
similarity of stimuli and responses. One can use words as stimuli and
responses. The subjects first learn one set of word pairs and then another,
which resembles the first in some fashion. Their performance is then
compared to that of control subjects who learn the second list without
having to learn the first. If the experimental subjects learn the second list
faster than control subjects, we have *positive* transfer; if they learn it more
slowly, we have *negative* transfer. In one experiment subjects learned pairs
of nonsense syllables. They were then tested by being given the first syllable
of the pair and required to respond with the correct second syllable. The
subjects were then given a second set of pairs to learn. If the stimulus
syllables (the first of each pair) in the second set were similar to those in the
first and the response syllables (the second of each pair) remained identical,
a high degree of positive transfer occurred, with experimental subjects
learning much faster than control subjects. If the stimuli were identical
and the responses different, a high degree of negative transfer occurred,
with experimental subjects learning more slowly than control subjects. In
intermediate cases there was not much change (Table 2–1). As we shall see
later, these principles of transfer are relevant to many aspects of cognitive
development.

LEARNING AND DEVELOPMENT

In the last chapter I pointed out that although development is usually viewed as a continuous, incremental process, it actually is not. Learning, too, has traditionally been viewed as a continuous, incremental process, with associations between stimuli and responses becoming gradually stronger. However, it now appears that learning is most probably an all-or-none affair. The most important experiments on this problem were those of Rock (1958). In his experiments subjects were required to learn pairs of nonsense syllables. The procedure was to present a set of pairs, then to test recall by presenting the first of each pair alone. For control subjects this procedure was repeated as many times as it took to learn the entire set, but each time the set was presented the pairs were arranged in a different order. For the experimental subjects, successive presentations of the list differed in the following way. Any pair not correctly recalled from the list was deleted and a new pair substituted (Table 2–2). Thus the experimental subjects had one and only one chance to learn each pair—they either did or did not learn a pair. The measure of learning was the number of trials required to learn eight pairs of words. On that measure there was no difference between the two groups. These experiments have been extended and the theoretical basis of all-or-none learning greatly expanded in recent years. While there is still some controversy in the field, the bulk of the evidence seems to favor the hypothesis that learning is a discontinuous, all-or-none process. Since many developmental phenomena are all-or-none, this characteristic of learning is important. If learning were necessarily a continuous, incremental process, it is unlikely that we could have invoked it to account for the step-wise changes in performance observed in development.

At the beginning of this chapter I said that an extreme argument would maintain that learning would account for the development of all skills save the ability to learn itself. It should be obvious from the brief review of learning processes here that learning theory in fact assumes many more capacities than the simple ability to learn. Learning theory thus far has said nothing about the emergence of new behaviors. It has nothing to say about the perceptual mechanisms that underlie discrimination and generalization. For many learning theorists new behaviors and perceptual mechanisms could perfectly well emerge as a result of purely maturational processes, a conclusion others (including myself) are reluctant to accept.

More significantly, many developmental effects are different in one important way from the effects of learning: the effects of learning are *reversible*, while many developmental effects are *irreversible*. Extinction is not a characteristic of developmental processes as it is of learning processes. This is most often apparent in those tragic cases where development has gone wrong—among blind, deaf, and other handicapped children. As we

TABLE 2–2

For the control group all pairs of nonsense syllables were repeated, learned or not, in a different order until the subject had learned all pairs. For the experimental group only learned pairs (italic) were repeated; unlearned pairs were replaced with new ones and the list was presented in a different order. (From "Repetition and Learning" by Irving Rock, *Scientific American*, 1958.)

CONTROL GROUP

1	2	3
GAC QET	BIH XIR	CEZ MUN
BIH XIR	FAX SOQ	BIH XIR
TOF LAH	GAC QET	TOF LAH
FAX SOQ	CEZ MUN	DUP TEZ
GEY NUR	TOF LAH	KAR WEH
DUP TEZ	GEY NUR	GEY NUR
KAR WEH	DUP TEZ	FAX SOQ
CEZ MUN	KAR WEH	GAC QET

EXPERIMENTAL GROUP

1	2	3
POY CES	*QOZ YAT*	BOP YIT
KOB RUV	XAN NAC	*QOZ YAT*
QAT BUP	CEG YOW	*JEP BOZ*
WEM NIR	*JEP BOZ*	NOH FEJ
FAH VAQ	ROF FAZ	LUJ ZEN
JEP BOZ	YOB FAP	*QAT BUP*
ZAM VOM	*QAT BUP*	DAF VUT
XUN BEW	TIS KED	*FEC RIQ*

shall see in later chapters, the techniques of behavior modification derived from learning theory are often powerless to redirect such abnormal development. This sad fact has led some psychologists to argue that, since the behaviors consequent on the handicap are immune to modification, they must result from unalterable processes of gene expression. This is unnecessarily pessimistic. In fact, the environment operates on development in ways other than through learning. This is the central concern of our next chapter.

3

The Role of Environment in Gene Expression

In this chapter we shall look at ways in which the environment affects the expression of the genes other than through learning. To understand these effects we must again turn to the science of genetics itself. In the first chapter it was explained that identical hereditary material—in the form of long strings of genes, long strings of instructions for the construction of specific proteins—is carried in the nucleus of every cell in our body. At first sight this seems impossible. The cells in every organ of our body are manifestly different one from another, in both structure and function. The cells in our brain are different from those in our eyes, which are different from the cells in our muscles, which are different from the cells in our livers, and so on. Is it sensible to say that all these cells are produced by the same set of genes?

For a long time it seemed more plausible that specific genes each produced specific types of cell within each organ of the body. In the 1950s, however, it became apparent that this hypothesis was wrong. The most dramatic proof that it was wrong was provided by the experiments of Gurdon (1968). Gurdon first extracted the nucleus from a cell taken from an adult frog. He then inserted this nucleus into an unfertilized egg whose own nucleus had been removed. Now if the cell of the adult frog contained only the genes necessary for production of cells in the organ from which the cell was taken, say the liver, we would expect only production of a liver—if that. What actually happened was that the "rebuilt" egg grew into a *complete, intact frog*. This result shows that every cell in the body of an adult contains enough genetic information to produce an entire animal. Every organism so produced is genetically identical, a *clone* of the original frog. It is theoretically possible to produce an unlimited number of genetically

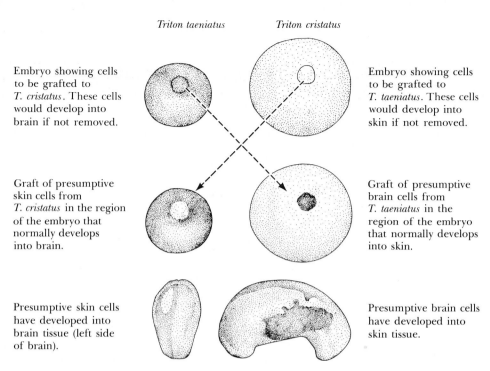

Triton taeniatus   *Triton cristatus*

Embryo showing cells to be grafted to *T. cristatus*. These cells would develop into brain if not removed.

Embryo showing cells to be grafted to *T. taeniatus*. These cells would develop into skin if not removed.

Graft of presumptive skin cells from *T. cristatus* in the region of the embryo that normally develops into brain.

Graft of presumptive brain cells from *T. taeniatus* in the region of the embryo that normally develops into skin.

Presumptive skin cells have developed into brain tissue (left side of brain).

Presumptive brain cells have developed into skin tissue.

FIGURE *3–1*

The results of exchanging parts of the embryos of two closely related species of the mollusk *Triton*. *Top*: the situation prior to grafting. *Middle*: After grafts between embryos. *Bottom*: A later stage of development. The drawings are schematic. (After Spemann, 1938.)

identical organisms. Were the technique ever perfected for man, as some have predicted will happen, any one of us could attain the god-like state of creating other humans in our own image, the ultimate narcissism.

THE EFFECT OF ENVIRONMENT ON GENE EXPRESSION

Let us leave aside these speculations. Consider instead the problems this discovery raises for geneticists. How is it that the same set of genes produces completely different effects in different parts of the body? The answer seems to be that what the genes do depends on where they are, that is, the expression of the genes depends on their specific environment, on what is around them. This can be shown very directly early in development by transplanting tissue from one region of an embryo to another. Embryonic tissue is formed of agglomerations of nonspecified cells that develop into specific functional tissue depending on their location in the organism. Thus, the transplanted tissue will take on the characteristics appropriate to its new location in the embryo (Figure 3–1). Left where it was, it would have developed in one way; in its new location it develops in a completely

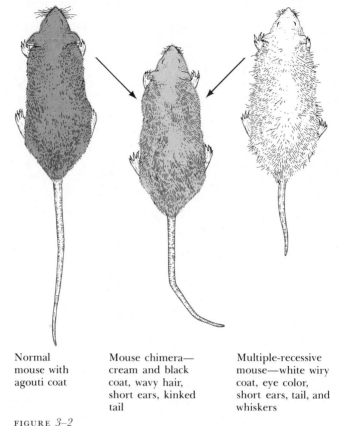

| Normal mouse with agouti coat | Mouse chimera— cream and black coat, wavy hair, short ears, kinked tail | Multiple-recessive mouse—white wiry coat, eye color, short ears, tail, and whiskers |

FIGURE *3–2*

The parents of a chimera and the chimera itself. A chimera in genetic terminology is an individual formed from tissues of different animals with different genetic constitutions. (After McLaren and Bowman, 1969.)

different way. The extreme demonstration of such environmental determination of gene expression is the construction of *chimeras*. Thus far only mouse chimeras have been made. Chimeras are constructed by removing two embryos from different wombs at a very early stage of development and squashing them together. They fuse, and the fused pair is then placed in one womb. What develops then is one organism, made of bits of each of the two mice that would have developed singly had the fusion not taken place. If mice that look very different are used, it is easy to identify which bit comes from which mouse (Figure 3–2). Chimeras possess two sets of genes, which ordinarily would produce two very different mice. But because of environmental circumstances only one-half of each set of genes is expressed, producing one mouse.

There is thus compelling evidence that the nucleus of every cell contains enough information to create a whole organism. There is also good evidence that where a cell is determines which of its genes will be expressed. But there is also evidence that at some point in development cells lose this capacity for changing development according to their location. Once cells have gone far enough toward becoming liver, brain, or whatever, they cannot be *redirected* by being put in a new location in the body. At this point they are *determined*. The nucleus of each cell retains its general competence, but the cells themselves have lost it. The processes involved in determination are probably also responsible for switching off gene activity whenever an organ (or organism) reaches mature size. The termination of development is thus probably environmentally determined.

DEVELOPMENTAL TIME AND GENE EXPRESSION

It is clear that location of a cell (and thus of genes) within an organism determines what a particular set of genes will do. Biological time is perhaps equally important. By this I am referring to the fact that some genes operate at very specific times in development. A clear case of this is sex determination in humans. Men differ from women in their possession of the so-called Y chromosome at a location where women have an X chromosome. The very large number of genes coded onto this chromosome exert their major influence before birth and at puberty and menopause.

Biological time also affects the developmental consequences of certain environmental events, and may even determine whether an event has any effect on development. Naturally, if the cells of some part of an animal have been determined, an environmental effect that would have had a critical effect before determination will have no effect at all. The wing pattern of fruit flies (*Drosophila*) is an example. If larval flies are exposed to heat shock, the veination of their wings is significantly altered from normal. Exposure of adults does not produce this result (Figure 3–3). Knowing whether or not this environmental event has occurred during development allows one to predict with perfect accuracy whether or not alterations in wing veination will appear. The effect is completely determined by the environmental event.

Single effects are not the only possibility we must consider in looking at the effects of the environment on development. There can be interactions between particular genotypes and particular environments. For example, in one experiment two genetically different types of *Drosophila* flies were reared at three different temperatures. After development was complete, the number of eye facets in each fly was counted. Figure 3–4 shows the number of eye facets for the two types of flies at each of the three temperatures. It is clear that the genes interacted with the rearing

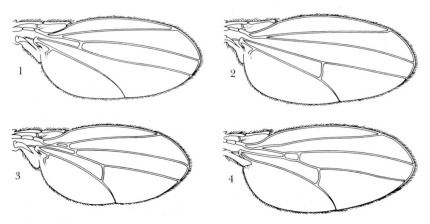

FIGURE *3–3*

The effects of heat shock on the development of the pattern of wing veination in *Drosophila* flies. The normal posterior cross vein is lost and extra anterior cross veins are present. (After Bateman, 1959.)

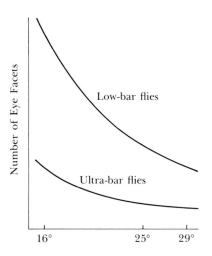

FIGURE *3–4*

The effects of seven temperatures (15°–29°C) at the larval stage on the eventual number of eye facets in two genotypes of the bar-eyed mutant of *Drosophila*. The difference between the two genotypes in number of eye facets is much greater at the lower than at the higher temperatures. There was differential sensitivity in the development of the two genotypes to temperature change. (After Gottesman, 1974.)

temperature. The two genotypes produced different effects at the same rearing temperature.

One point should be made relevant to the psychological studies that will be described in later chapters. It is much easier to do research on the origins of specific features that are present or absent, such as wing veins and eye facets, than on the origins of continuously variable characteristics, like intelligence or height, which are due to the interaction of many genes and many environmental factors.

Let us summarize what we have established thus far. The environment determines which genes will be switched on and when they will be switched on. It determines when they will be switched off. In the case of organs like the brain, once a particular set of genes has been expressed, that structure is determined, unless of course the resultant cells are later destroyed by accident, in which case no new cells of that sort grow. The essence of the *epigenetic* processes I have been describing is that their contribution to the structure of the organism is permanent and irreversible. Epigenetic effects are thus quite different from the effects of learning. As I pointed out in the last chapter, the results of learning are essentially reversible.

It may be protested at this point that while this discussion of epigenetic processes may be of conceptual interest to the student of human development, there is not much *practical* contact between genetic studies of development and the psychology of human development. I believe this apparent lack of contact lies in the fact that the term "environment" has two meanings. The environment we have been discussing in this chapter is a physicochemical environment. The environment of major interest to this book is the psychological environment, the environment of "seeing," "hearing," "understanding," the environment of rewards and punishments, successes and failures. A central contention of this book is that the psychological environment can produce effects like those produced by the physicochemical environment.

EPIGENETIC PROCESSES
AND NEURAL DEVELOPMENT

The similarity between the effects of the psychological and the physicochemical environments may be clarified by looking at studies of the development of neural connections. The most important organ for human behavior is the human brain. The formation of the brain is a developmental process. A number of studies in recent years have shown that development of the brain is an epigenetic process, that is, one in which gene expression is modified by the environment.

The brain consists primarily of nerve cells or neurons, which are connected to one another, to the sensory receptors, and to the effector system of muscles in complex ways. Research on the epigenetic development of the brain has focused on the pattern of connections between the eye and the brain, largely because that pathway is complex enough to be interesting yet accessible enough for experimentation.

Regeneration studies

Some of the most interesting work on eye–brain connections has been done on frogs and toads. These animals are robust enough to withstand a variety of experimental manipulations that would kill other animals. For example, it is possible to remove the eyes from a frog or toad and then reinsert them without destroying either the eyes or the animal. The existing eye–brain nerve connections are destroyed, but after some time the nerves regenerate and reconnect. In a classic series of experiments initiated by Sperry (1956) the effects of rotating the eye and transposing it to the other orbit were studied. When the eye is rotated, that part of the sensitive surface of the eye that is normally at the top relative to the animal's head is shifted to the bottom, and vice versa (Figure 3–5). This means that stimuli above the animal will project onto the part of the eye that normally would be stimulated only by stimuli below it (Figure 3–6). Similarly, if a frog eye is removed from one orbit and transposed to the other, stimuli in front of the frog stimulate the part of the eye that normally would be stimulated only by stimuli behind it (Figure 3–6). The results, whether measured behaviorally

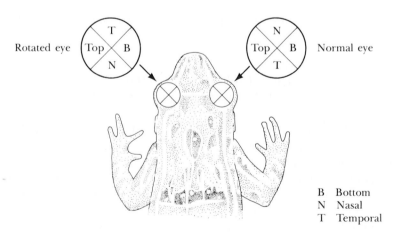

FIGURE 3–5
A normal and rotated eye in the same frog. (After Sperry, 1951.)

or in the underlying neural structures, are indeed dramatic. The frog acts as if its eye were still in its normal position. When shown a fly in front of it, it acts as if the fly were behind it. The same inversion is true for all other retinal positions. The neural substructure of this is diagrammed in Figure 3–7. The frog's eye connects with the frog's brain in a very orderly way. After rotation exactly the same orderly connections reform, regardless of the fact that the relation between the eye and the brain and between the eye and the outside world is completely reversed. No amount of practice, failure, or punishment will correct the bizarre behavior that results from it.

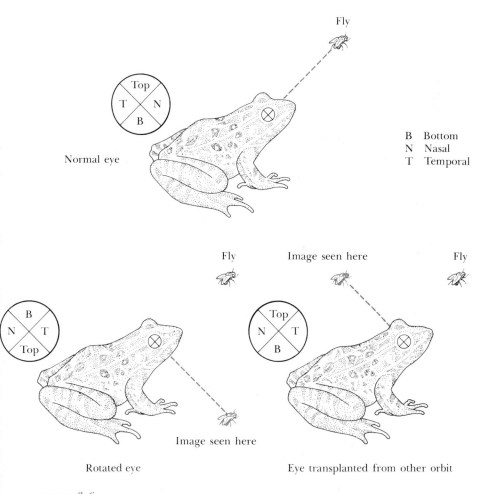

FIGURE 3–6

A frog with a rotated eye sees the fly above as if it were below him, while a frog with an eye transplanted from one orbit to another sees the fly in front as if it were behind. (After Sperry, 1951.)

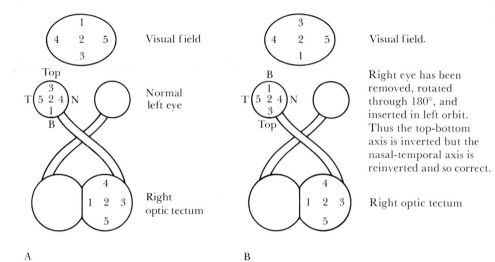

FIGURE 3–7

A. The retinotectal connections in a normal frog eye. Electrodes are inserted into the frog's brain—in this case the right optic tectum, the area of the brain connected to the left eye of the animal. Stimuli are then presented to the eye in different positions in the visual field. Thus it can be shown that position 1 in the visual field projects from the retina through the optic nerve to position 1 on the contralateral optic tectum. Other positions in the visual field are also represented onto the optic tectum in an orderly and systematic way. B. If the right eye is removed from its orbit, rotated 180°, and transplanted to the left orbit, the same orderly connections reform. However, whereas the nasal-temporal axis is the same as in the normal eye, the top-bottom axis is reversed. (Beazley, 1975.)

Developmental studies

At one time it was thought that the above experiments showed that the pattern of eye–brain connections in frogs and toads is wholly genetically controlled. However, subsequent developmental research has shown that this is not the case. If eye rotation or transposition is performed before the frog reaches the age of 35 hours (Stage 30 in its development) the pattern of eye–brain connections will be functional and appropriate, with none of the reversals found in adult animals. The animal will behave as if rotation and transposition had not taken place. Rotation after that will result in the bizarre, nonfunctional connections. Thus the retinal cells become specified at the 35th hour of life, after which they are completely determined and will only grow connections to one particular part of the brain (Jacobson, 1968). Something in the environment of the eye must produce this irreversible specification.

One can find other examples of environmental effects in the development of the nervous system of the frog. By cutting a frog's eyes in half and rearranging the halves, it is possible to produce compound eyes. Thus the frog might have an eye made up of two nasal or two temporal halves (Figure 3–8A). The rotation experiment described above shows that once

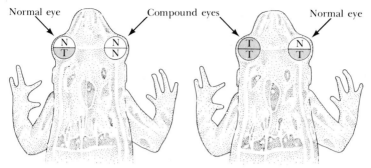

T   Temporal half
N   Nasal half

A

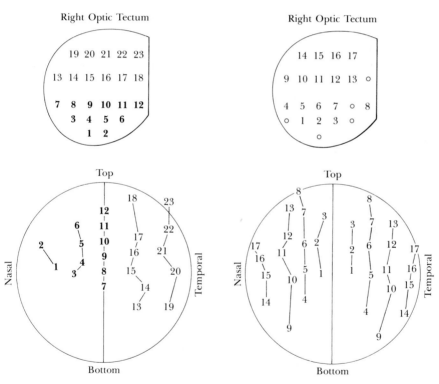

Left Visual Field in Normal Eye

Left Visual Field in
Nasal-Nasal Compound Eye

B

FIGURE 3–8

A. To make a compound eye in a frog, two eyes are cut in half and transposed as shown. B. Using the same procedure described in Figure 3–7, it is possible to map the retinotectal connections of a compound nasal-nasal eye. Comparison with the normal projections shows that in the compound eye each half connects with the whole of the contralateral tectum. (After Gaze, Jacobson, and Székely, 1963.)

the retinal cells become specified in the frog, each part of the retina grows connections to one and only one point on the brain. This would lead one to expect that the "compound eye" would grow connections to only one half of the available brain, with each unit there receiving two inputs. In fact, the input from the experimental compound eye spreads over more than half of the available brain, but the eye still does not make use of all of it (Figure 3–8B). This would seem to indicate the possibility of partial respecification of some but not all of the connections.

Complete environmental determination of at least one set of connections in the visual system of the frog has been demonstrated—those connecting the two halves of the brain. In the normal frog the sites in the two halves of the brain that "see" the same point in the world are connected. What of the frog with one rotated eye? In that half of the brain connected to the rotated eye, the representation of the world is of course reversed. But the connections between the brain halves are still such that points on the two halves that "see" the same point in the world are connected. The neural anatomy thus adapts to ensure functional connections. It is clear from other experiments that actually "seeing" the same point with both eyes is essential if these functional connections are going to grow. I emphasize this last point because *seeing* something is clearly an event that belongs in the psychological environment more directly than to the physicochemical environment. I shall return to this distinction later.

Research with primates

The visual system of primates, including man, is far more complex than that of the frog. The bulk of its specification takes place inside the womb, at which time the organism is not accessible to experimental observation. We do not know what environmental effects are involved in the specification of the visual system, although we know they could not be events in the psychological environment because vision before birth is not possible. At birth the primate visual system has the same basic structure as the adult visual system. It contains certain units that respond selectively to contours in specific orientations, others that respond to movement in specific directions, and still others that respond to stimuli of a specific size. It also contains binocular receptor units, units that respond only when both eyes are stimulated. Although these units are present at birth, they are not completely determined at birth. It appears that the visual experience available after birth determines whether or not the pattern of connections that makes these units functional will become determined or not. For example, lack of binocular visual experience can result in loss of binocular connections, in monkeys and in man. Experience of contours in one orientation only results in loss of the pattern of interconnections that permits response to contours in other orientations, and so on. It appears that the units present at birth are specified to make them more functional in the particular environment the animal finds itself in. This means that the *functional requirements* of the animal's environment after birth switch off one set of genes and switch on another. The phrase "functional requirements" again emphasizes the psychological environment. Functional requirements, in this sense, can only have an effect early in development, within the first few months after birth.

There is also evidence that large parts of the brain only become specified after birth. These data have been gathered by observing the consequences of brain damage early in development. The behavioral consequences of specific brain damage in adults has been well documented, so that we can identify behavioral "areas" of the brain. What happens if these areas are destroyed early in development? Consider the speech area. Destruction of that area in adults results in the loss of ability to speak or use language. What happens if that area is destroyed early in development? Is the ability to use language lost forever? It is not. This function takes over another part of the brain. Conversely, in the case of profound deafness from birth the lack of opportunity to hear and use language means that the potential to speak is lost, and the normal speech area is used for other purposes. Perhaps the most spectacular instance of the brain's ability to adapt to injury is found in the development of one individual lacking a corpus callosum. Most behaviors are governed by one side of the brain only. The two halves of the brain communicate via the corpus callosum, so that, for example, the left side of the brain can "talk" about an object "seen" by the right side of the brain. Destruction of the corpus callosum in adults results in the loss of certain abilities that depend on communication between the brain halves. (Destruction of the corpus callosum may result accidentally, e.g., from a bullet wound, and in the past it has been used surgically to alleviate the symptoms of epilepsy.) Amazingly enough, however, the individual who grew up with no corpus callosum suffers no disabilities at all. Both halves of her brain developed the capacity to function as an otherwise whole brain does—both halves have a speech area, both halves control both hands, and so on. A more extreme instance of functional determination can hardly be imagined.

THE PSYCHOLOGICAL ENVIRONMENT AND GENE EXPRESSION

Let us recapitulate what has been said so far.

1. The structural basis of all development is synthesis of proteins by the genes.
2. Every cell in our body contains the same complement of genes.

3. The location of a cell in part determines *which* genes will be switched on to make the very different tissues we are made of.

4. External events can determine *when* genes are switched on and switched off.

5. When a particular set of genes is switched on, they make a permanent contribution to the structure of the organism.

6. The same cells can be used for different functions. After a time they lose this capacity and become determined, and will only produce, via the genes, the proteins required for that function.

7. The triggering events that switch specific sets of genes on and off include events in the psychological environment—seeing, hearing, and so on.

This last statement is the most important statement made thus far. A great deal of development is done in the physicochemical environment, and goes on whether the organism is asleep or awake. Some aspects of psychological development may be determined solely by the physico-chemical environment. However, segments of it are certainly determined by events in the psychological environment, i.e., events in the world of experience, events like reward, punishment, conflict, communication. Because there is no experience prior to birth, and thus no psychological environment, development up to that point is entirely a function of gene expression in a physicochemical environment. Therefore, from a psycho-logical point of view, any capacities present at birth are *innate*. After birth the growing child has a physicochemical environment and a psychological environment. Our task, the task of developmental psychology, is to find the *psychological* events that influence development.

II

In deciding the relative contributions of gene expression, learning, and epigenesis to development, we rely heavily on observation of the newborn infant. Prior to birth there is no psychological environment—no rewards, punishment, successes, or failures. Any abilities the newborn has must depend on gene expression, and so may be viewed as the purest indication of the potential limits of gene expression. On examination, the world of the newborn appears to be much richer than we might have thought, although still very different from our own. Immediately after birth, however, development in a psychological world begins. The experimental paradigms that psychologists have used to separate out the causes of that development are best understood by examining the development of motor behavior. As we might expect, all three processes of development—gene expression, learning, and epigenesis—play a role.

4

The World
of the Newborn

I hope that the first part of this book has made clear the critical role that the newborn infant must play in any satisfactory theory of human development. The world inside the womb is as uniform and neutral as any environment could be. There are no rewards or punishments, so the fetus's actions have no real consequences. There can be very, very little sensory input in the womb. Since the newborn has no exposure history, no history of reinforcements of any sort, any capacities demonstrated at birth must have been formed under genetic control. Because the *psychological* environment prior to birth is so bland as to be nonexistent, it is to the expression of genetic information that we must look for an explanation of the capacities of the newborn.

PROBLEMS OF WORKING
WITH NEWBORNS

To the casual eye the newborn does little except eat, sleep, and excrete. But this perception is completely wrong. The human newborn is an extremely competent organism, perhaps even more competent than older humans in some ways. However, he does suffer from a large number of

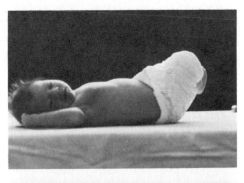

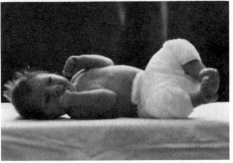

FIGURE *4–1*

A neonate lying unsupported on a table top uses his head and arms to support himself (top photo). If the baby moves his arms, he is unable to maintain a stable position (bottom photo).

limitations that make it difficult for us to assess his true level of competence. Some of these limitations are obvious. The newborn is fully awake for only brief periods, a few minutes at a time. At other times, even though his eyes may be open, the baby is probably drifting off to sleep, and that is not a good time to try to get a baby to demonstrate how intelligent he is. A second limitation, equally obvious, stems from the shape and arrangement of the baby's skeleton. If we place a baby on his back, a standard position for examination, the baby is effectively prevented from doing much with his head or arms because he needs his head and arms to maintain a posture (Figure 4–1). If we want the baby to be free to use these members, we must prop him up with cushions, so that he is free to use his head and arms for other pursuits.

In addition to these and other obvious limitations, such as very weak muscles, the newborn seems to have a strange or, more accurately, surprising motivational structure. Presentations that might well fascinate an adult or an older baby often leave the newborn cold. Since many experimental paradigms depend on at least catching the attention of the baby, these motivational differences do cause problems. Consider, for example, the paradigm of *fixation preference*, in which a baby is simultaneously shown two things that differ in some dimension. The hypothesis is that if the baby shows more attention to one thing than the other, he must prefer that one to the other. It is assumed that in order to have a preference, the baby must perceive the dimension that differentiates the two things. When the baby shows a clear-cut preference for one thing, the logic of the experiment is clear and compelling. It is not so clear when the baby attends equally to the two items. This could imply that the baby cannot tell the two things apart, or it could mean that he can tell them apart and simply does not care to look at one or the other in particular. Very similar problems arise in learning experiments. Learning, as we saw in Chapter 2, depends on reinforcement. If the baby does not find the experimenter's reinforcer actually reinforcing, then he is not going to demonstrate that he can learn. Deciding whether a baby cannot learn or is not motivated to learn is not a particularly easy question.

All of these qualifications should warn you against easy acceptance of statements of the form, "Newborn infants cannot or do not do X." Any such statement should be qualified with the statement "under the conditions of this study." There are some other precautions that I must mention before launching into a description of the findings on newborns. The major precaution is over the use of the word "newborn." With very few exceptions, psychologists have not been able to study babies who were literally *new*born. Their subjects are a few hours old or a few days old, occasionally even a few weeks old. Investigators often claim that a particular capacity shown soon after birth must have developed under genetic control because the environment after birth could not have produced the capacity. All such arguments can be examined on their own merits.

More problematic is the argument that if babies of a certain age cannot do something, then newborns also cannot. This is in fact a very dangerous inference. It is dangerous because development is not a simple linear progression. As we shall see throughout this book, older children are often unable to do something that younger children can do with perfect facility, for reasons that are sometimes obvious but more often obscure. The inference is especially dangerous when applied to the behavior of newborns because of our dependence on capturing their interest.

Nothing is easier than to show that an organism is *incapable* of something or another, especially if the organism is a human newborn, relatively helpless, apt to doze off at critical points, and ethically shielded from the sharper probes of psychological science. In accord with these warnings, I shall emphasize the positive capacities of newborns, paying more attention to what they can do than to what they cannot do.

AUDITORY CAPABILITIES:
LOCALIZATION

Auditory localization exemplifies many of the tangles touched on above, particularly those associated with growth. The term "auditory localization" refers to our ability as adults to localize the source of a sound to our right or left, front or back. We adults seem to localize sounds so automatically that we do not think of this ability as anything special. In fact, the process of auditory localization exemplifies most of the classic problems of perceptual development, problems that I have referred to elsewhere as the problems of the missing dimensions. When we hear a sound, we hear it quite clearly coming from the right or left, front or back. The experience is quite clear and unmistakable. The problem is that there are no structures within the ear for discriminating between right and left or front and back. The ear is a marvelously constructed instrument for registering some properties of sounds, but nowhere within a single ear is there any structure that can *locate* the source of a sound. It appears that two ears are necessary for registering position. Determining the position of a sound source relative to the head seems to depend on the time of arrival of the sound signal at the two ears. If a sound source lies straight ahead in the midline plane its signals will reach both ears simultaneously. If the sound source is on the right it will reach the right ear first; the more "to the right" it is, the greater will be the separation between the arrival of the sound signal at the right ear and its arrival at the left ear (Figure 4–2A). The converse is true for sounds on the left. Front–back discrimination requires head movement (Figure 4–2B). The effect of head movement on stimuli coming from a sound source in front of the listener is the exact opposite of the effect of the same movement on stimuli coming from a sound source behind the listener.

Differences in the time of arrival of sounds at the two ears specify position of a sound source because they are correlated with its position. However, these differences are not exact replicas of the position of the sound source; they must be interpreted. What happens when an infant is exposed to a sound source? At one extreme one could say that when a baby is presented with a sound from say his right, that he hears *two* sounds: one in his right ear, closely followed by one in his left ear. Only with experience and learning would the baby come to realize that this particular con-figuration of events signified a single sound source on the right. At the opposite extreme one could assume that babies can localize sounds in exactly the same way as adults. Between these two extremes lie a variety of possibilities. One of these, which I have discussed at length elsewhere (Bower, 1974a), is based on the assumption that any perceptual capability that depends on stimuli and structures that do *not* change during growth is probably present at birth, and conversely, any perceptual capability that

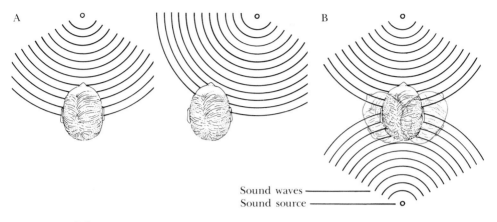

Sound waves ─────────────
Sound source ─────────────○

FIGURE 4–2

A. If the sound source is straight ahead, sound will reach both ears simultaneously. If the source is on the right, sound will reach the right ear first. B. Head movement is required to discriminate front and back locations. This movement varies the time of arrival of sound at the two ears.

depends on stimuli or structures that do change during growth is probably absent at birth. For example, in both the newborn and adult, sound sources that lie straight ahead in the midline plane reach both ears simultaneously. The specification of position in the midline by a zero difference in arrival at the two ears is thus *invariant* with age. Also invariant with age is the fact that a sound on the right always reaches the right ear before it reaches the left ear, and vice-versa. However, precise specification of the location of a sound source is not invariant with age because localization depends on a certain right-before-left time difference. Since the distance between the ears changes during growth, the time difference associated with a particular position also changes (Figure 4–3). Although the genes could specify structures that would detect the two invariants, it would be greatly inefficient to build in information that would allow the newborn to localize sounds more precisely simply because processes of growth would outdate that information relatively quickly.

The study of the development of auditory localization must begin with one of the few experiments to study a genuinely newborn baby. Wertheimer (1961) obtained access to a delivery room and began his experiment when his subject was but seconds old. His procedure was simplicity itself. He presented a sound to the right or left of the baby and looked to see if the baby turned her eyes in the direction of the sound. Note that this procedure in fact demands two things of the baby: auditory localization and an expectation that there will be something to *see* at the source of the sound. Despite this higher-order demand, the results of the experiment were

FIGURE *4-3*
The difference in arrival time of a
sound at the two ears is less for an
infant than for an adult because of
the smaller head size.

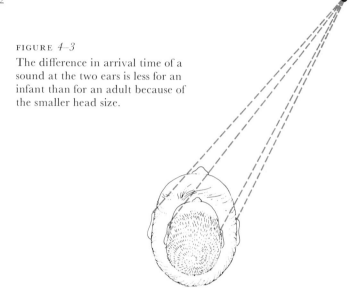

positive. The baby was sensitive to the growth-invariant information (that
a sound on the right reaches the right ear first, and vice-versa); she turned
her eyes reliably in the correct direction.

This very simple experiment demonstrates some of the problems of
research on newborns. The whole success of the experiment depends on the
infant believing that there will be something to see at the source of a sound,
and having sufficient interest in that something to turn his eyes towards it.
Wertheimer's newborn certainly met those conditions, and it seems that
six-hour-old infants do as well (Turkewitz *et al.*, 1966). However, by the
age of 28 days the experiment is unlikely to work, because infants at that
age simply do not turn their eyes when presented with a sound (Gesell and
Thompson, 1934). It seems likely that this occurs because they have lost
interest in looking at the sorts of sound sources usually used by psychologists.
If, however, one were to infer the behavior of newborns from that of
28-day-olds, one would certainly come to an erroneous conclusion.

The eye-movement experiment was not sufficiently accurate to say
whether or not newborns localize off-midline sound sources with a high
degree of accuracy. However, data gathered on much older infants imply
that newborns do not (Wishart, Bower, and Dunkeld, 1978). Despite the
dangers of backward inference that I have so insisted upon, I will present
these data. Infants were seated in darkness and presented with a noise-
making toy. The accuracy of their reaching for the toy was used as an
index of the accuracy of their auditory localization. To make sure inaccuracy was not due to possible difficulties of reaching in darkness, e.g.,
not being able to watch their hands, the infants were shown a noiseless toy,

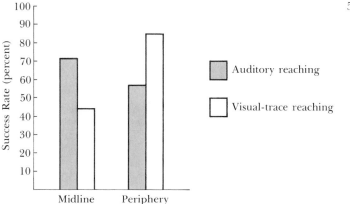

FIGURE 4-4

Infants under 20 weeks are able to locate the source of sounds with considerable accuracy in the midline but less accurately in the periphery. The accuracy of auditorily guided reaching in the midline is in fact greater than that shown in reaching for an object in the dark that had previously been seen in the light.

the lights were put out, and they were then allowed to reach for it (visual-trace reaching). Even the youngest infants studied (under 20 weeks) were able to locate audible toys in the dark with a high degree of accuracy as long as the toys were presented in the midline (Figure 4-4). Indeed, their accuracy was greater in locating the audible toys than in locating the inaudible toys first presented in the light. The reverse was true for objects presented on the periphery; the accuracy of reaching for the audible toys was much lower than the accuracy of reaching for the inaudible toys whose position had been specified visually, although there did not seem to be any confusion between right and left. For targets in the periphery, it is not until six months of age that reaching based on auditory cues attains the same level of accuracy as visual-trace reaching. One could tentatively conclude that auditory localization of peripheral sources is relatively imprecise in newborns.

VISUAL CAPABILITIES

Perception of the third dimension

The "missing dimensions" of the ear are as nothing compared to those of the eye. The human eye is an incomparable perceptual instrument. With it we can pick up positions to the right or left, gauge the distance of objects, their size, shape, color, texture, hardness, and so on. We do all of this with a flat retina that registers variables that are correlated with all of these

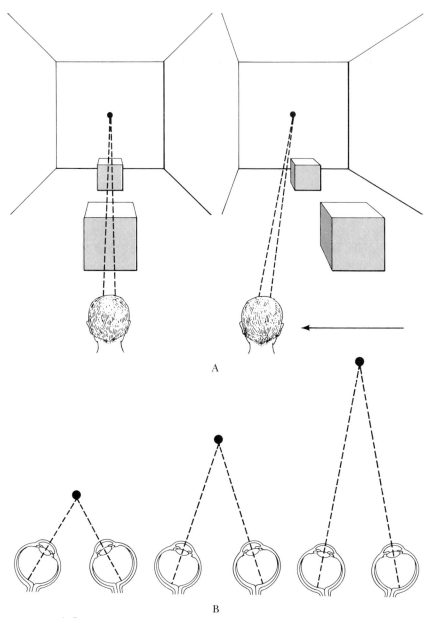

A

B

FIGURE 4-5

Retinal cues to distance perception. A. Motion parallax. If the head moves left and the eyes are kept fixed on the horizon, the nearer object appears to move further and faster to the right than the more distant object does. B. Convergence angle declines with distance. (From "The Visual World of Infants" by T. G. R. Bower, copyright© 1966 by Scientific American, Inc. All rights reserved.)

physical dimensions but that are certainly not like them in any literal sense. Figure 4–5 shows some of the retinal variables that specify distance, another "missing dimension." One question that has intrigued psychologists, and philosophers before them, is whether infants perceive distance or whether they simply see a two-dimensional world with no arrangement in depth at all. Although the issue is by no means settled, it would appear that infants from a very early age do perceive a three-dimensional world. No one has studied the visual perception of a truly newborn infant. However, very young infants, only days old, do show responses that indicate they live in a three-dimensional world. The 10-day-old baby in Figure 4–6A, for example, shows the defensive response to an approaching object that is typical of young babies. Obviously, the baby must be fully awake for this to happen. Also, for complex reasons that are not entirely understood, the baby must be in an upright or semi-upright position. Given that these conditions are met, the response is easy to elicit (Bower, Broughton, and Moore, 1970a). The response is specific to the distance traveled by the object, not to the object's size. Infants will defend themselves against a small object that approaches until it is close to them. A large object that does not come near will not elicit a defensive response, even though it projects as large an image on the retina (Figure 4–6B).

What of the possibility that the baby is simply responding to the movement against his face of the air displaced by the approaching object? Experiments have been conducted using a shadow-caster device like that shown in Figure 4–7A. While infants were not as distressed by the approach of the shadow as by the approach of a real object, a very similar defense response occurred, indicating that the response is primarily a reaction to visual information (Bower, Broughton, and Moore, 1970a).

Several other interesting results have been gathered in experiments using a shadow-caster. Ball and Tronick (1971) found that infants could discriminate between a shadow of an object that appeared to be headed directly at them and one that appeared to be on a "miss" course. The babies defended themselves against the former but not the latter (Figure 4–7B). A second finding, which may be of more general importance, is that the speed of the approaching object affects the likelihood of the defensive response. It seems babies cannot register visual information if it is coming in too fast, i.e., they appear to have a very limited *information-processing rate*. Many everyday events may occur at a rate too high for babies to register all the relevant information.

These experiments show that infants do process three-dimensional information, at least as regards the relative distances of an approaching object. Adults of course can do much better than that. They can perceive the distance of objects in quite specific terms, as so many feet or so many paces away, or at least within reach or out of reach. The latter capacity can be tested with newborns, for they do show a kind of very crude

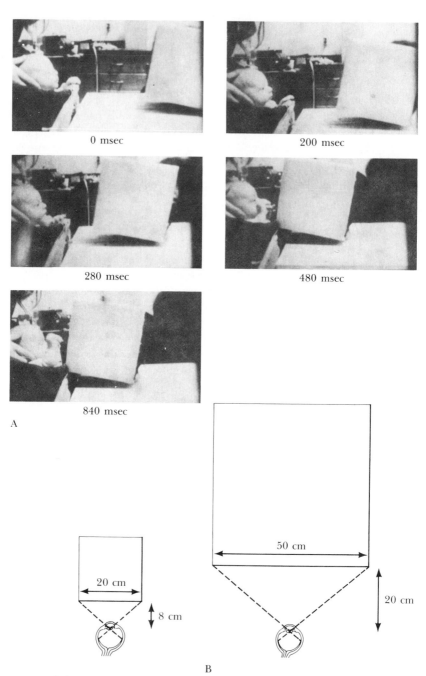

0 msec

200 msec

280 msec

480 msec

840 msec

A

20 cm

8 cm

50 cm

20 cm

B

FIGURE 4-6

A. A newborn baby will defend itself against an approaching object. The defensive behavior has three clear components: a widening of the eyes, head retraction, and interposition of the hands between the face and object. This response is specific to the distance traveled by the object and not its size. B. The retinal image of a large object at a distance is the same as that of a smaller object closer to the eye.

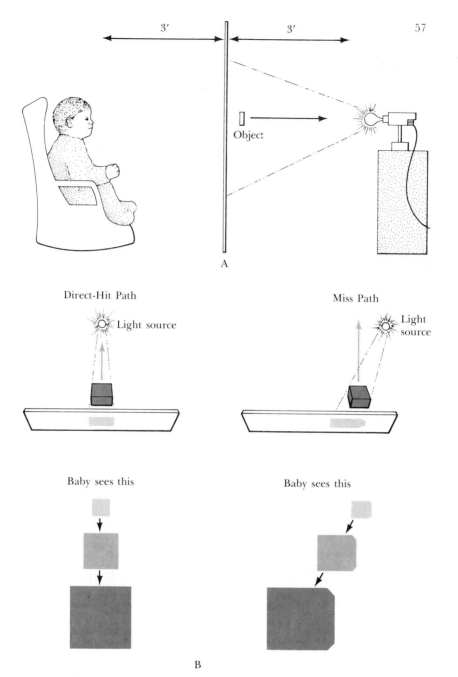

A. The defensive response of infants to approaching objects can be studied with a shadow-casting device. When an object is moved away from the screen and toward the point-source lamp, the shadow of the object increases in size.
B. Infants only a few days old are able to discriminate between objects approaching them on a "direct-hit" path and a "miss" path. They defend themselves against the former but apparently are not frightened by the latter.

FIGURE 4-7

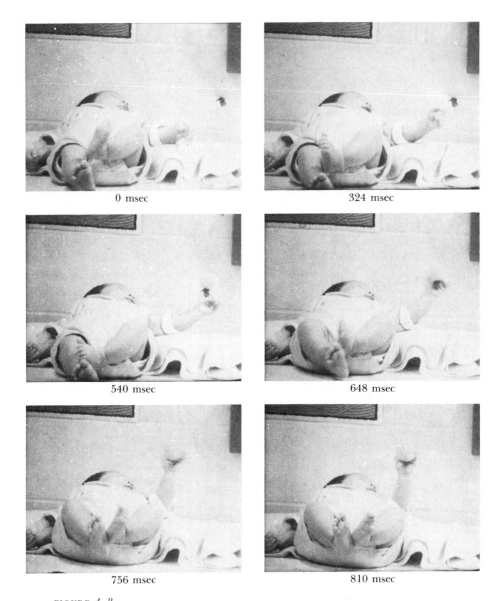

0 msec

324 msec

540 msec

648 msec

756 msec

810 msec

FIGURE *4–8*

This baby is less than two weeks old but is obviously reaching out for the object and grasping it.

reaching behavior (Figure 4–8). The nearer an object is, the more likely newborns are to reach for it (Bower, 1972). However, they do not show the sharp discrimination that adults or even older babies show. This could be because they do not perceive the different distances with any accuracy, or because they do not know how long their arm is, or some combination of the two. There is no way of knowing at this time.

Perception of things and holes

Although distance is an important "missing dimension" in visual perception, it is not the only one. For some psychologists the most important missing dimension of vision is the dimension or feature that allows us to differentiate things or objects from the spaces between objects. There are circumstances in which this is not easy (Figure 4–9), but adults usually are in no doubt about what is object and what is space between objects. Gibson (1966) has suggested a series of variables that would allow us to make this discrimination. One of these variables is progressive textural occlusion/disocclusion. Progressive occlusion specifies approach of or toward an object; progressive disocclusion specifies approach of or toward an aperture or empty space. There is evidence that newborns are sensitive to this variable. In one experiment infants were presented with a visual simulation of the approach of an object, in the form of progressive occlusion; they were also shown the approach of an aperture, in the form of progressive disocclusion (Figure 4–10A). The experimenters looked for a defensive response, specifically head retraction. The results clearly showed that the infants were more inclined to withdraw from the approaching object than from the approaching aperture (Figure 4–10B). Since an object in the real world can hurt if it hits you, whereas an aperture (empty space) cannot, this difference makes sense if the babies see textural disocclusion as approach of an aperture. In other words, infants in the second week of life can discriminate between things and the spaces between them. Given their

FIGURE 4–9

A classic example of ambiguous visual information. The picture can be seen as two faces or as a vase.

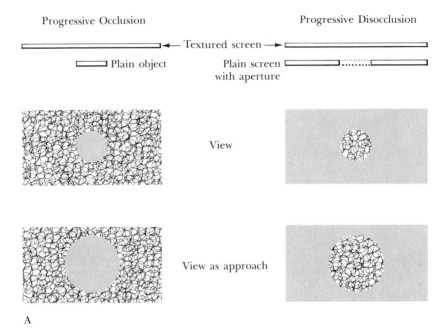

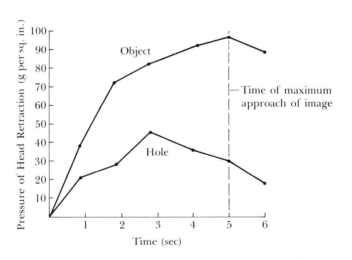

FIGURE 4-10

A. As this figure shows, an object approaching or being approached progressively occludes the background, whereas an aperture progressively disoccludes the background. B. Comparison of the amounts of backward head movement of babies presented with an approaching object (progressive occlusion) and an approaching hole (progressive disocclusion) using a shadow caster. (Bower and Dunkeld, unpubl.)

lack of opportunity to learn about such things—how many infants in their second week of life have banged into or been struck by objects?—it seems plausible to assume that the capacity is unlearned, i.e., present at birth.

INTERSENSORY COORDINATION

The results of the last experiment and of some of the other experiments described suggest that newborns are aware of the *intermodal* properties of objects, i.e., seen objects are also tangible, heard objects can be seen and touched, and so on. Interestingly enough, newborns may have a stronger belief in the necessary intermodality of objects than do older babies or adults. In an experiment testing the response of infants to discordant visual and auditory input, mothers talked to their babies through a stereo system from behind a window. When the system was in balance the mother's voice seemed to come from her mouth (Figure 4–11). By adjusting the balance of the speakers, the source of the voice could be shifted from the midline, thus in effect "separating" the mother's voice from her mouth. Infants less than three weeks of age are distressed by this change—they seem to expect voices to come from mouths—but older babies and adults

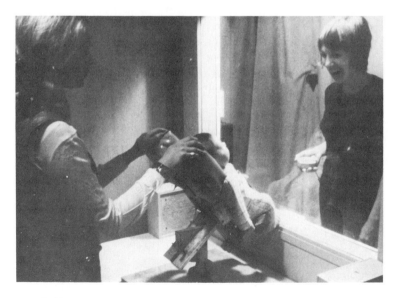

FIGURE *4–11*

A mother talks to her baby through a stereo amplification system. By shifting the balance of the speakers, the mother's voice can be made to appear to come from a source other than her mouth. (Aronson and Rosenbloom, 1971.)

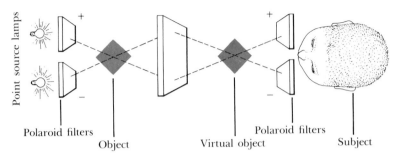

Point source lamps

Polaroid filters

Object

Virtual object

Polaroid filters

Subject

FIGURE *4–12*

Two projection lamps produce two oppositely polarized images on a screen. The baby wears polarized goggles, so that his left eye sees one image and his right eye the other. The perceptual result is a three-dimensional object seen between the baby and the screen. Such virtual objects, although perceptually convincing, are of course completely intangible.

are not distressed. Indeed, adults typically do not even notice it. If we did, watching movies or listening to a speaker through an amplification system would be a bizarre experience.

Similar developmental changes seem to occur in the coordination between vision and touch. Objects that look completely real but are in fact intangible can be created using a rear-projection screen and Polaroid filters (Figure 4–12). When presented with such *virtual objects*, young infants display stress. This, however, declines with age (Bower, Broughton, and Moore, 1970b). Older infants and adults seem able to accept the separate existence of the visible and tangible domains, whereas younger babies behave as if the two *must* be linked. One experiment found evidence of distress in infants as young as two weeks (Bower, Broughton, and Moore, 1970c). Although drawing inferences about newborns from these results is precarious, extrapolation from the decline in responsiveness back to the newborn stage would suggest that infants are born with a belief in the unity of the visible and the tangible, a belief that they gradually lose with experience in the world.

PERCEPTUAL CONSTANCIES

An important aspect of the perceptual world of adults is its *constancy*. Objects appear to stay the same size as we approach them, even though their retinal image gets much bigger. They also appear to remain the same shape as we move around them, even though their retinal image changes drastically.

The world of the newborn would indeed be a "blooming, buzzing confusion" if the constant aspects of our world were inconstant in his.

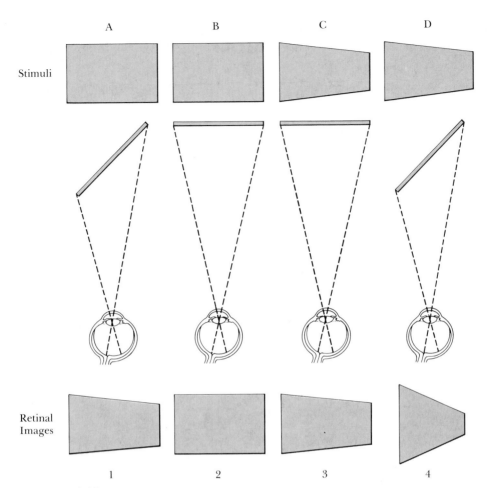

A   B   C   D

Stimuli

Retinal
Images

1   2   3   4

FIGURE 4-13

Having been trained to respond with a head turn to a rectangle in the orientation shown in A, infants were tested for generalization with this and three other displays (B–D). The retinal image produced by each display is shown at the bottom. Infants generalized most to displays A and B, those with the same real shape as the original training stimulus. Little generalization was shown to either C (although the retinal image produced by C was identical to that of the original training stimulus) or D.

Unfortunately, direct evidence on this point is not available. Among the indirect evidence are two studies of shape constancy in six-week-old infants. In one study infants were trained to respond with a head turn to a rectangle in one orientation. After they had reached a criterial rate of response, they were given generalization trials (p. 27) with four stimuli: (1) the rectangle in its original orientation; (2) the rectangle in a new orientation; (3) a trapezoidal figure placed in the same orientation as (2), and which thus projected a retinal image identical in shape with that produced by (1); and (4) the trapezoid in the same orientation as the rectangle in (1), thereby producing a completely novel retinal shape (Figure 4–13). The results

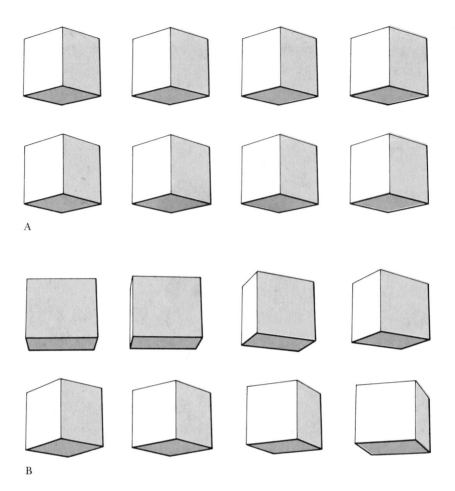

A

B

indicated quite clearly that the infants generalized most to the displays with the same real shape as the rectangle with which they were originally trained (displays 1 and 2). That is, the change in orientation in display 2 did not depress their responses, but they generalized very few responses to display 3 or 4. The responses to displays 1 and 2 were so alike that the infants seemed not to have noticed the orientation change at all. The few responses to display 3 show that the babies were not fooled by the identical retinal images of 1 and 3 (Bower, 1966).

Very similar results were obtained in a study using habituation rather than learning as a probe technique (Day and Mackenzie, 1973). Infants were first shown a cube with a complex irregular pattern on it for 20 seconds. Then they were shown either a series of 20-second presentations of a plain cube in a constant orientation (Figure 4–14A) or a series of presentations in which the orientation of the plain cube was changed with each presentation (Figure 4–14B). In the situation where the infants saw a cube in a constant orientation we would expect a decline in attention.

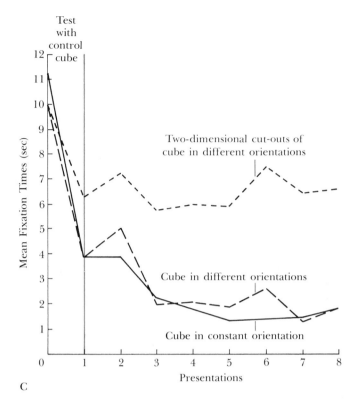

Test
with
control
cube

FIGURE 4-14

A and B. Presentations used in an experiment to test shape constancy. C. Results of the experiment. (Day and Mackenzie, 1973.)

This is a straightforward case of habituation to a constant stimulus (see p. 24). The other display was more interesting. If the infants were capable of shape constancy they would see the series as the same cube in different orientations and thus would show decreasing attention to it, although the change in orientation might be expected to arrest the decline to some extent. If, on the other hand, the babies were in fact incapable of recognizing the identity of the cube in different orientations, attention would not decline. In fact, the results showed that attention to both types of presentation declined in exactly the same way (Figure 4–14C). That the decline in attention was not merely produced by boredom with the whole experimental situation was shown by a third condition. The babies were shown a series of presentations of different two-dimensional cutouts, each of which produced the same retinal image as the cube in one of its orientations. In that situation there was no decline in attention. We are therefore safe in asserting that, in the other conditions, the babies could recognize the identity of the cube in each presentation, even when it was in different orientations. Real shape, rather than retinal image, was being attended to.

The most puzzling feature of both of these experiments was the way the babies seemed to ignore the different orientations of the shapes presented to them. Psychologists have always assumed that shape constancy is attained by combining retinal shape information with information about orientation. In neither of these experiments was there any indication that the infants even noticed the changes in orientation. This result was strange enough that it provoked a third experiment designed to see if infants could respond to changes in orientation of an object. The basic method used was to examine the responses of two-week-old infants to a rectangle that was rotated so that its upper edge approached the face; a shadow-caster device

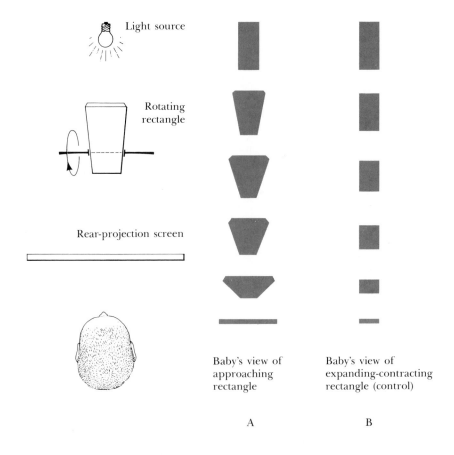

Light source

Rotating rectangle

Rear-projection screen

Baby's view of approaching rectangle

Baby's view of expanding-contracting rectangle (control)

A   B

was used (Figure 4–15). To make sure the infants were responding only to changes in the orientation of the rectangle, the same babies were shown the display illustrated in Figure 4–15B, an event that would normally be produced by a rectangle expanding and contracting like a concertina but not by a rectangle changing orientation. The response measured was head withdrawal. If the babies perceived the changes as changes in orientation of a rectangle they should withdraw their heads to protect themselves from contact as it "approached" their faces. This in fact occurred for the object-rotation event but not for the expansion–contraction display (Figure 4–15C). One could argue that the infants who perceived the change in orientation as something threatening must have shape constancy of a sort, for the one implies the other. An argument of this sort cannot be conclusive.

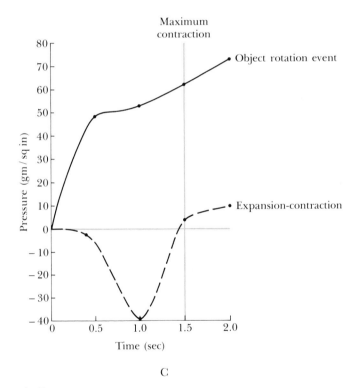

FIGURE 4–15
A shadow caster was used to simulate rotation of a rectangle toward the baby's face. A and B. What the baby saw in the experiment. C. Results of the experiment. (Dunkeld and Bower, 1978a.)

However, taken together, the results of the above experiments suggest that the world of the newborn is as constant as our own, and is not the confusing flux it would otherwise be.

MOTOR CAPACITIES

Thus far we have emphasized the capacity of newborn infants to pick up information from the world around them. Is there any evidence that newborns can act in the world? Do they have a repertory of motor behaviors? The best-developed system of movements is the head-eye system. The newborn has relatively refined control of head movements and eye movements. But the eyes or head are normally only moved to permit better registration of available information and do not result in any changes in the outside world. However, the newborn does show other motor behaviors. For example, a newborn who is correctly supported can "walk," marching boldly across any flat surface (Figure 4–16). This behavior normally disappears about the age of eight weeks. Also, as described earlier, newborns will "reach" out to seen objects, a true effector behavior. They manage to contact the objects about half the time, but successful grasping occurs much less often. Even when grasped, the object is normally dropped after a few seconds. Moreover, grasping is never integrated with other behavior, such as putting the grasped object in the mouth. This kind of reaching normally disappears about the age of four weeks.

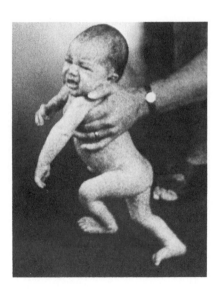

FIGURE *4–16*
A neonate (six days old) "walking."

This brief list does not exhaust the behavioral repertory of the newborn. We shall return to it in Chapter 14, where we will discuss the social behavior of the newborn.

LEARNING ABILITIES

The newborn then can pick up information about the world and he can act in limited ways in the world. Is there any evidence then that the newborn can learn? It is quite clear now that newborns come into the world with a very high ability to learn. Indeed, one expert on infant learning has gone so far as to say that the newborn can learn better then than he will be able to at any later age (Lipsitt, 1969). All three basic types of learning described in Chapter 2 are within the capacity of the newborn. Classical conditioning has been demonstrated using the Babkin reflex (Figure 4–17). In the conditioning procedure the reflex was elicited after presentation of a sound. After 25 such pairings the sound alone was sufficient to elicit the reflex (Kaye, 1965).

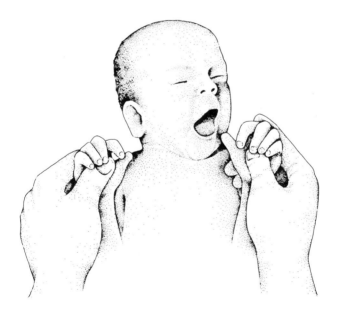

FIGURE 4–17

The Babkin reflex. When a baby's palms are pressed back, its mouth opens and its head moves to the midline.

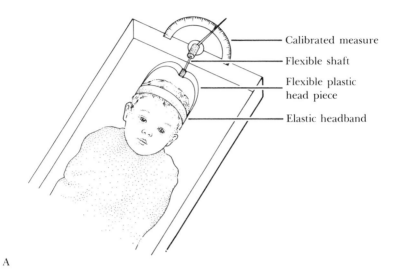

A

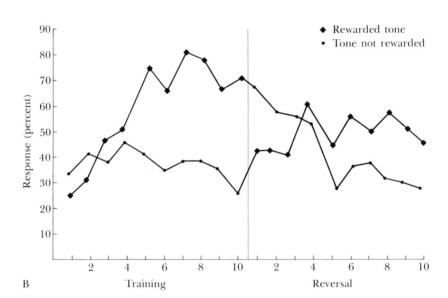

B   Training   Reversal

FIGURE 4-18

A. Apparatus for a study of conditioned head-turning in babies. When a bell was rung, infants were to turn their heads right to obtain reinforcement; they were not to turn their heads when a buzzer sounded. When the procedure was reversed, the infants quickly learned to turn their heads right when the buzzer sounded and not to turn their heads when the bell was rung. B. Results of the experiment. (Siqueland and Lipsitt, 1966.)

Habituation has been demonstrated in numerous studies. One of the most ingenious of these examined habituation to odor (Engen and Lipsitt, 1965). Babies were first presented with a compound odor (a solution of amyl acetate, heptanal, and diethyl phthalate) that resulted in a change in breathing rate. This diminished after a few trials, and breathing became regular again. The babies were then presented with a weaker solution, in which one of the original chemicals was replaced with more of the diluent (diethyl phthalate). Again the babies' breathing rates changed, thus showing a clear recovery from habituation and indicating that the earlier decline in responsiveness (return to normal breathing) resulted from habituation and not merely from sensory fatigue.

The most spectacular demonstrations of the learning ability of the newborn involve various forms of operant learning. In one of the most striking examples of a learning task that newborns can solve, babies were required to discriminate between two stimuli and to respond to only one (Siqueland and Lipsitt, 1966). When a bell sounded the head was to be turned right to obtain reinforcement (sugar solution); when a buzzer sounded the head was not to be turned. The experimenters then reversed the contingencies, so that the bell sound meant no head turn and the buzzer a right turn. The babies were able to cope with this *discrimination reversal* very easily, more easily than most other organisms would (Figure 4–18).

Contrary to common belief, then, the human newborn is an extremely competent organism. He is built to take in information about the world, he has a few motor behaviors, and he can learn. He is sensitive to success and failure, reward and punishment. How does this psychological world affect his development?

5

Motor Development

One of the most obvious aspects of development after birth is motor development. Throughout infancy new motor skills pop into the baby's repertory at a great rate. The emergence of these skills is gloriously easy to observe—one can never be in any doubt about what is developing when one studies motor development. At the same time, these changes pose the classic problem of developmental psychology, namely the relative contributions of genes and environment to the emergence of new behaviors. Some psychologists have viewed the rapid succession of new motor skills in infancy as the expression of information coded in the genes, a process largely independent of environmental influences. Others argue that it is the demands of the environment acting on a reactive organism that produce novel behaviors and coordinations. The familiar dilemma that we have seen before, and will see again, is sharply focused in the study of motor development.

SCHEDULES OF DEVELOPMENT

A considerable amount of effort has been invested in describing the basic steps in motor development during infancy. Although the newborn does not have a large repertory of motor behaviors, new behaviors begin to emerge very rapidly. Figure 5-1 presents a typical schedule of development

Age (months)

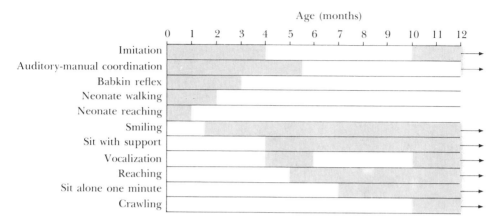

FIGURE 5-1

A typical schedule of motor development to the age of 12 months. Note that some behaviors disappear never to reappear, while others disappear but reappear at a later point in development.

of new behavior during infancy. The ages given are typical of the average child, as is the sequence of emergence. New behaviors arise all the time during infancy, a point that has intrigued many psychologists. These new behaviors do not typically seem to be the result of a combination of pre-existing behaviors. The sequence of emergence is not always invariant—some children walk before they crawl. In such cases behaviors other than those that normally precede a particular behavior are obviously associated with its appearance, a fact that argues against any analysis based on straightforward learning theory. As we saw in Chapter 2, learning theory can account for the emergence of a new combination of old behaviors; it can also account in principle for changes in the frequency of a given behavior. It has, however, nothing to say about the emergence of totally new behaviors. This fact has led many psychologists to assume that the psychological environment is quite unimportant, and that new behaviors emerge as a consequence of new sections of the genome coming into operation—thereby creating new brain structures, larger bones, more muscles. Walking, for example, usually emerges at the end of a fairly invariant sequence of behaviors (Figure 5–2). The development of walking after the first step with support could possibly be explained by learning theory. However, learning theory would be hard pressed to explain that *first step* from the behavior that preceded it. It is a long way, of course, from saying this to making the claim that development of this kind occurs

Chin up — 1 mo.

Chest up — 2 mo.

Sit with support — 4 mo.

Sit alone — 7 mo.

Stand with help — 8 mo.

Stand holding furniture — 9 mo.

Creep — 10 mo.

Walk when led — 11 mo.

Pull to stand by furniture — 12 mo.

Climb stair steps — 13 mo.

Stand alone — 14 mo.

Walk alone — 15 mo.

FIGURE 5–2
The sequence of behaviors that normally precede walking.

entirely under genetic control. Many psychologists have wanted to make this leap and have developed a number of experimental paradigms to allow them to do so. We shall now examine some of these paradigms in detail.

Twin studies in the natural environment

A favorite paradigm for elucidating the relative roles of genes and environment is the comparison of identical with nonidentical twins, where both twins are raised in the same family. One study of this sort (Wilson, 1972) used the Bayley scales for mental and motor development (Table 5–1). The sample consisted of 261 pairs of twins, of whom 100 were identical. As can be seen in Table 5–2, the correlations of scores on the Bayley scales were higher for monozygotic twins than for dizygotic twins, indicating that genetic identity produces virtually identical patterning in motor development. These results are extremely interesting, but they are virtually irrelevant to the problem of determining the relative contribution of genetic and environmental factors to motor development. All of the twins in this study, at some time in the course of their development, developed the abilities measured. The important fact was that the identical twins exhibited new behaviors virtually simultaneously. However, identical twins are not only genetically identical, they also have identical environments if they grow up together. This environmental overlap could equally well explain the high correlation of motor development in identical twins

TABLE 5–1

Some behaviors characteristic of the second year in Bayley's scales of psychomotor development.

	AVERAGE AGE OF ACHIEVEMENT (MONTHS)
Walks alone	11.7
Throws a ball	13.3
Walks sideways	14.1
Walks backward	14.6
Walks upstairs with help	16.1
Walks downstairs with help	16.4
Tries to stand on walking board	17.8
Walks with one foot on walking board	20.6
Walks upstairs alone; marks time	25.1

76

TABLE 5-2

Identical (monozygotic) twins are more alike in motor
development throughout infancy than are nonidentical
(dizygotic) twins. The data are correlations of
performance scores on Bayley's scales of psychomotor
development. (Wilson, 1972.)

AGE (MONTHS)	WITHIN-PAIR CORRELATIONS	
	MONOZYGOTIC	DIZYGOTIC
3	.84	.67
6	.82	.74
9	.81	.69
12	.82	.61
18	.76	.72
24	.87	.75

raised together. Identity of environment of identical twins is something
that is hard to appreciate if one has not had direct experience with a pair.
The fact that their parents often cannot tell twins apart enough to treat
them differently—even if they want to, which most parents of twins do
not—is an indication of how identical the environments can be. The
correlation between environmental overlap and genetic overlap makes
data on such identical twins virtually useless in measuring the relative
weight of genetic and environmental factors in motor development.

Comparison of premature and full-term babies

Another experimental paradigm is to control the environment in some
way. The environment is enriched in some way, or impoverished; the
effects of a normal, enriched, or impoverished environment are then
compared. Nature has provided us with a seemingly easy and natural way
to do this. Humans are normally born 40 weeks after conception. Thus, at
birth, when chronological age is zero, the *conceptual age* is normally 40 weeks.
Premature infants may survive when born at a conceptual age of only
28 weeks. At the other extreme, some infants remain in the womb as long
as four weeks past term, and thus have a conceptual age of 44 weeks at
birth. If behavior development is determined entirely by experience
outside the womb, then chronological age should be our most reliable
predictor of the onset of any particular behavior. Further, we should find
no differences between premature, term, and post-term infants of the same

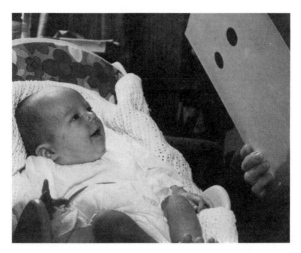

FIGURE 5–3
Smiling emerges around six weeks of age, and can be
elicited by a wide range of stimuli.

chronological age. On the other hand, if behavior is primarily determined
genetically and is largely unaffected by events in the environment, then
conceptual age should be our best predictor of the onset of a particular
behavior, and we should find no differences between premature, term, and
post-term babies of the same *conceptual* age. The logic of such studies is very
clear. It allows us to decide between two extreme theories of the
development of motor behavior.

Smiling is one behavior that has been studied in this way. Normal
infants will smile in response to a visual stimulus, such as that shown in
Figure 5–3, at a chronological age of six weeks, at which time their
conceptual age is 46 weeks. The question is whether premature and post-
term babies will also smile at a chronological age of six weeks or if smiling
will begin at the conceptual age of 46 weeks, regardless of chronological
age. The results are quite unambiguous: all infants smile at a conceptual
age of 46 weeks, regardless of their chronological age. In this case at
least, a longer time outside the womb does not accelerate the development
of premature infants, nor does the longer time inside the womb retard
development of post-term infants. Is it fair, therefore, to conclude that
smiling is primarily determined by processes of maturation? The answer
must be no. This study shows us quite unambiguously that the different
exposure times of premature, normal, and post-term babies to the environment do not change the conceptual age at which smiling begins. Nevertheless, environmental stimulation may still be critical for the development

of smiling. The study itself does not exclude the possibility. It only implies that stimulation from the environment can have no effect *until* the conceptual age of 44 weeks. It is entirely possible that a given level of maturation is necessary before environmental stimulation can have any effect. Thus the above study could be pointing to a very specific genotype–environment interaction, one that only occurs within a very restricted time span. Much more research would be necessary to decide the precise implications of these studies.

Reliance on premature or post-term babies as a source of data is complicated by the unusual or difficult deliveries and variety of health problems generally associated with such births. Despite the additional environmental stimulation that such babies have, the majority of studies of premature babies have found them to be somewhat disadvantaged in comparison with full-term babies, not altogether surprising given the difficult circumstances of their birth and early physical growth.

Cross-cultural comparisons

An alternative source of information about the effects of environmental inhibition or facilitation of development is cross-cultural comparisons. Babies are treated in different ways in different cultures, and a comparison of the rates of motor development under diverse conditions may give us some clues about the relative contribution of environment to such development. A classic study of this sort was carried out by Wayne Dennis (1940), who studied the development of walking in Hopi Indian babies. Hopi Indians have traditionally bound their infants to cradle boards during the first months of life (Figure 5–4). Infants on the cradle board are unwrapped only once or twice a day to be cleaned and have their clothes changed. An infant on a cradle board thus has a very restricted range of possible movement. The infant cannot sit up or roll over, and only the slightest arm and leg movements are possible. Even nursing and feeding are carried out on the board. These traditionally reared infants were compared with other Hopi babies whose parents, affected by European practices, did not restrict their infants at all. The results were quite surprising. There was no difference at all between the two groups of infants; both groups walked unaided around the age of 15 months. This finding seems to lend strong support to the hypothesis that walking is primarily determined by maturational processes and thus is under genetic control.

On the face of it, this study seems to show that the onset of walking is determined entirely by processes of maturation. But, again, it is not impossible that it is only the case that a critical point in maturation must be reached before environmental stimuli can have an effect. Another

FIGURE 5-4
A hopi cradle board.

objection that could be laid against this study is that it did not control for possible genetic differences between the two groups. It is possible that the restricted group were simply faster developers than the unrestricted infants and might even have walked *sooner* than the unrestricted infants if they had been allowed freer movement earlier. In any comparison of the effects of environment on development, we always face some uncertainty over whether or not the two groups given the two treatments are genetically equivalent.

There are ways to minimize such uncertainties. One obvious way is to use identical twins as subjects, one twin receiving one environmental exposure, his co-twin the other. Since identical twins are genetically identical, any differences in their rate of development could only result from their different environments. A number of studies of this sort have been carried out.

Manipulation of the environment: co-twin control

A typical, and deservedly famous, comparative study of identical twins whose environments differed was that carried out by Arnold Gesell and his co-workers (Gesell and Thompson, 1929). Gesell worked with a pair of identical twin girls. The twins' mother had died shortly after their birth and so they were raised in a nursery home under very similar living

TABLE *5–3*

Observations of cube play by identical twins at 52 weeks of age in an experiment in which one twin (T) had been given six weeks of training in cube manipulation. No significant differences in performance were observable. (See Table 5–4 for an analysis of cube play by these twins at various ages.) (Gesell and Thompson, 1929.)

TWIN T	TWIN C
1st cube: Secures in right hand; bangs on table top. Transfers to left hand, taps on table top.	*1st cube*: Approaches with right hand; transfers to left; holds up to experimenter; transfers back to right hand, hits against side panel with right hand, then with left, after transfer.
2nd cube: Transfers 1st to right hand, approaches with right, secures, drops.	*2nd cube*: Transfers 1st to right hand; picks up second with left hand.
3rd cube: Drops left-hand cube; secures, holds 2nd. Rocks back and forth.	*3rd cube*: Drops left-hand cube; picks it up; holds 2nd. Considerable brushing instead of rocking; hitting cubes.
Bangs cubes, transfers, drops, picks up again. Shoves it back and forth. Drops one to secure 3rd. Heeds but one cube at a time. Holds two cubes. Hits side rail. Drops over side rail. No definite combining activity. Considerable lateral brushing.	Transfers; bangs with left hand on table top. Hits against side rail. Puts on platform, picks up again. Throws cube to platform. Heeds but one cube at a time. Drops one to secure third. Holds two cubes. No definite combining activity. Considerable lateral brushing.

conditions. They were given the same food and the same clothes and were put on the same sleep schedule. From the published paper it would seem that the twins were virtually identical in appearance and were treated in identical ways by the staff of the nursery home. When the twins reached the age of 46 weeks, however, one of them was given special training in two motor skills: stair climbing and cube manipulation. The trained twin was identified as T; her sister, the control twin, was called C. Prior to the training period the twins were given a prolonged and simultaneous developmental examination to ensure that they had reached comparable stages of development. The correspondence in skill was very striking. Even more striking was the similarity of their behavior in free situations. Gesell and Thompson write that when they were each given a spoon to play with "a chain of four or five behavior events occurred in almost simultaneous sequence in both children. This kind of correspondence . . . takes on a weirdly astonishing aspect." This observation reinforces the point made earlier, that identical twins reared in the same environment are virtually two versions of the same individual.

TABLE 5–4

Analysis of cube play (with the second of three cubes) by identical twins at various ages. The experimenter's observational account of the twins' performance at 52 weeks is given in Table 5–3. (Gesell and Thompson, 1929.)

SECOND CUBE	52 WEEKS		63 WEEKS		79 WEEKS	
	TWIN T	TWIN C	TWIN T	TWIN C	TWIN T	TWIN C
Total prehension time	3 sec	5 sec	1 sec	3 sec	2 sec	$1\frac{1}{2}$ sec
Approach time	$\frac{13}{16}$ sec	$\frac{14}{16}$ sec	$\frac{11}{16}$ sec	$\frac{9}{16}$ sec	$\frac{11}{16}$ sec	$\frac{22}{16}$ sec
Closure time	$\frac{6}{16}$ sec	$\frac{10}{16}$ sec	$\frac{17}{16}$ sec	$\frac{37}{16}$ sec	$\frac{4}{16}$ sec	$\frac{22}{16}$ sec
Amount cube displacement	1″	1″	2″	$1\frac{1}{2}$″	1″	$2\frac{1}{2}$″
Approach height (maximum)	$2\frac{1}{2}$″	$2\frac{1}{4}$″	2″	3″ +	2″	2″
Forward angular displacement of						
Body	15°	15°	15°	10°	10°	10°
Head	30°	35°	30°	35°	10°	10°

The training program for the one twin consisted of daily 20-minute sessions, six days a week for six weeks. The 20-minute sessions were equally divided between cube play and locomotor activity, particularly stair climbing. The cube play was free, but if the baby did not play with the cubes the experimenter would attempt to stimulate the activity in a variety of ways, e.g., by giving the baby blocks, building a tower of blocks himself, and so on. The stair-climbing training was more stereotyped. The baby was placed at the bottom of the stairs and a desirable toy placed at the top. If T made no attempt to get up the stairs, she was moved by the experimenter from tread to tread and allowed to play with the toy when she got to the top. When the two twins were compared at the age of 53 weeks, one week after the end of T's special training, T could climb the staircase in 17 seconds. C, who had had no practice with the staircase at all, still succeeded in climbing it, although it took her 40 seconds. After this, C was given two weeks of training on the staircase, at the end of which she was as skilled as her sister had been after six weeks of training. At the age of 56 weeks there was virtually no difference between the two.

There was even less difference in cube manipulation. At the age of 52 weeks C was given cubes for the first time; T at this time had had six weeks of practice. The record of their performance at this time shows very similar cube play by both twins (Table 5–3). This similarity was even more pronounced at later ages and extended even to the fine grain of the behavior (Table 5–4). Save for a slight speed advantage, the performance

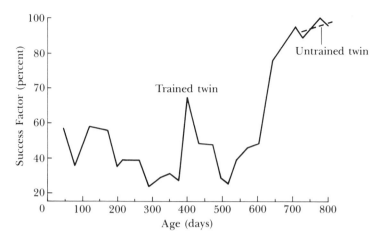

FIGURE 5–5

One twin was not introduced to toilet training until the age of two years, yet he rapidly became as well trained as the twin with 23 months of training. (McGraw, 1940.)

of T, with six weeks of practice, was no different from that of C, with no practice at all. As Gesell and Thompson conclude, these findings "point consistently to the preponderant importance of maturational factors in the determination of infant behavior. . . . The time of appearance is fundamentally determined by the ripeness of the neural structures." At best, practice produces only fine-tuning of behavior already established by maturation.

McGraw (1940) came to a similar conclusion at the end of her study of the effects of toilet training. In this study one twin was introduced to toilet training at a relatively early age and given daily training for no less than 23 months, after which the child had become effectively toilet trained. The completely untrained twin was then introduced to toilet training and achieved the same level of success right away (Figure 5–5). This result, so contrary to conventional wisdom, again seems to point to the primary role of maturation in early motor development. Or does it?

There are severe difficulties in the way of a straightforward interpretation of such results. If one is very strict in interpreting the above studies, what do they in fact show? They show that some selective manipulations of a baby's environment do not accelerate or retard the appearance of a certain behavior. However, they do not provide evidence that *no* environmental event is critical for the emergence of the behavior in question; they show only that the environmental events that have been *controlled* are not critical. This is a much more restricted conclusion than the experimenters would wish, and some may feel that such caution is unnecessary. Nevertheless, there are considerable problems in the analysis of development that no studies of the kind so far reviewed have confronted. The question at issue is the *origin* of behaviors that appear to arise all of a sudden throughout infancy. We are really asking whether behaviors have an ancestry, whether they are derived from temporally prior behavior or experiences.

It seems to me that this should impel us to consider carefully whether or not the selective environmental controls applied in the two studies described above were likely to be ancestral to the particular behavior under investigation. For example, there is some evidence that the key element in toilet training is the awareness of a full bladder (Mowrer and Mowrer, 1938). McGraw did not focus at all on this aspect of training. Similarly, the training given by Gesell and Thompson does not seem too relevant to the behaviors to be developed. For the first few weeks T's "practice" consisted in her being lifted from tread to tread up the stairs. She was quite passive and took no part in the proceedings. Why should such an experience—for we can hardly call it behavior—be thought of as critical for the development of stair climbing? Surely, active crawling on a flat surface, to take but one obvious example, is more likely to be the ancestor of crawling up a stairway. Both twins were free to crawl as they wished; that activity was not controlled in the experiment. Similarly, in the cube experiment only T was given access to cubes, but both twins had perfectly free access to other objects that could be handled. Why should we assume that other handling behavior was not relevant to cube handling? Plainly, we cannot make such assumptions.

THE PROBLEM OF
BEHAVIORAL ANTECEDENTS

The problem of defining the antecedents of a behavior is a considerable one. A possible model for enabling identification of the antecedents of behavior comes from embryology, the study of the genesis of structure. Embryology attempts, among other things, to trace the *cell lineage* of structures of the mature system, e.g., to discover what cells in the early stages of cell division develop into the eyes. To do so, a cell is stained in the early stages of development; all of its descendants will then carry the stain and thus can be readily identified later. An even more obvious method is possible in the case of mosaic systems; by destroying a cell we can discover its descendants by looking to see what is missing in the developed organism (Figure 5–6). In studying the genesis of behavior, however, we have no recourse to such direct physical techniques. We cannot stain or ablate behaviors—even less can we stain or ablate experience. The problem of establishing a relation between an environmental event and some later behavior is even more severe than that of establishing a relation between an early and a later behavior. The studies cited thus far have all concluded

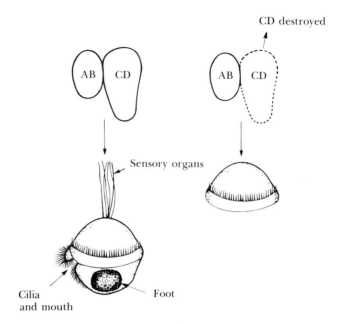

CD destroyed

AB CD

AB CD

Sensory organs

Cilia
and mouth

Foot

FIGURE 5-6

In the case of mosaic systems, e.g., mollusks, it is possible to trace the cell origins
of body parts by destroying individual cells at an early stage of development and
then observing what part of the developed organism is missing. A normal
trochophore larva is shown on the left. If the CD cell is destroyed at the two-cell
stage, one obtains the part organism shown on the right, indicating that all of the
missing parts develop from the destroyed CD cell and all of the existing parts
develop from the AB cell.

that environment was not involved in the development of a particular
behavior. However, all of the babies studied were open to environmental
stimulation at all times. For all we know, some other unsuspected (and
therefore uncontrolled) stimulus may have been critical.

Motor development in the absence of an environment

There is one clinical case that avoids such criticism. Wolff (1969) studied
an infant who suffered from, in addition to other neural disorders,
holotelencephaly (failure of separation of the hemispheres of the brain). A
consequence of this condition was that the infant experienced continuous
random seizures; in adults this condition is known to prevent perception of
external events. If this infant was similarly affected, then she too would
have had no awareness of the events in her environment. Nonetheless,
some development did occur: the infant developed the ability to raise her
head in a prone position, to support herself on her elbows, and to make
coordinated creeping movements. Although these behaviors hardly

measure up to anything approaching successful development, they apparently resulted without any external environmental support.

Although such an extreme example can hardly serve as a paradigm for research, the study of infants with more selective sensory handicaps could obviously be informative about the effects of missing categories of experience on the development of behavior. Infants who lack one sensory modality can be used to study the development of behavior in much the same way that experimental organisms subjected to cell destruction are used to study structural development. If infants who lack one or another sensory modality fail to develop certain behaviors, we can argue that there is a causal connection between input through that modality and development of the behaviors in question. The causal connection need not be direct, but some causal connection would be hard to deny.

Can we find a marking technique for the study of behavioral development analogous to cell staining? I think we can. Suppose we have two behaviors we think might be connected. If we introduce some environmental modification that changes the earlier behavior, then, if the two behaviors are connected, there should be some trace of that change in the later behavior. We could then conclude that the behaviors are at least ancestrally connected.

Walking

Walking is an example of a behavior whose development is susceptible to the second kind of analysis. Newborn infants will "walk" after a fashion if supported. This behavior normally disappears, and true walking begins many months later. Is the early walking an ancestor of the later walking? The two behaviors are separated by many months, yet they are commonly referred to as "primary" walking and "secondary" walking. It is argued that primary walking disappears because of an active inhibition that is necessary for secondary walking to appear. Such theorizing is purely speculative, however; it is quite possible that the two behaviors are independent of one another. What evidence would convince us that the two behaviors are connected? If the earlier behavior is an ancestor of the later behavior, surely environmental modifications that affect the first would also affect the later behavior; this would be comparable to introducing a stain into a primordial cell and tracing the stain in the cell's descendants. In one experiment the primary walking of a group of infants was exercised on a daily basis rather than being ignored as is commonly done.* As a result, the appearance of secondary walking in these infants

---

* It is worth noting that the duration of primary walking was much longer in these infants than in normal infants, a fact that rules out the inhibition hypothesis mentioned above.

was greatly accelerated (Andre-Thomas and St.A. Dargassies, 1952). Since the early training produced effects on the later behavior, this study demonstrated that primary walking is indeed the ancestor of secondary walking. If the early training had produced no effects, we would be forced to conclude that the two behaviors were unrelated. If one accepts this criterion for establishing a connection between earlier and later behaviors, then one must assume that studies in which practice of one behavior has no effect on some later behavior in fact show that the practiced behavior is unrelated to the criterion behavior—a conclusion that vitiates the basis on which the co-twin studies described above were conducted.

This study also is an example of yet another approach to motor development. Numerous other behaviors disappear in the course of development (see Figure 5–1). This fact is quite contrary to commonsense conceptions of development. Common sense tells us that development is a process of cumulative acquisition, with older children having all of the behavior and capacities of younger children, plus some more. Nonetheless, behaviors do disappear in the course of development. Behavior loss is as much a developmental phenomenon as behavior acquisition, but is more amenable to study than the latter. While a behavior may disappear as suddenly as another appears, at least the disappearing behavior is there until it disappears, and so is available for study, practice, etc., until it disappears—a gift to observation that we should not neglect. The question whether or not the appearance of a new behavior is primarily determined by maturational or environmental influences could equally apply to the *disappearance* of an existing behavior.

Vocalization

The development of vocal behavior is one area where all of these techniques discussed so far are applicable. It is characterized by both the loss of early behaviors and the constant acquisition of new behaviors. It is also clearly affected by sensory handicaps, such as deafness and exemplifies some principles of motor development that appear to be quite general. Vocalization shows two phases of development. Normal infants develop highly differentiated babbling behavior in the first five months. The range of sounds that infants of this age can produce is indeed very wide; some have claimed that it includes the sounds of all human languages. Babbling wanes during the second half of the first year. The next phase of vocalization begins when the infant begins to reproduce the speech sounds of his own particular environment. This involves a loss of many sounds that were produced during the babbling phase. It is noteworthy that these sounds, perfectly available to the child in the first half-year of his life, disappear from his repertory and cannot be produced again without considerable training and practice. It is small consolation to those of us who struggle to recreate a French *r* or German *ö* to realize that we could make these noises perfectly well when we were babies.

The development of vocalization has been studied in deaf infants. Infants who are profoundly deaf go through the same initial phase of babbling as do hearing infants. At five months their range of sound production is as extensive as that of hearing infants, despite the fact that they have never heard a spoken word and cannot even hear their own babbling. This would seem to indicate that the initial phase of vocalization does not require auditory input. The second phase of vocal production, the reproduction of the speech sounds in the child's environment, does not occur in deaf children. It thus seems that this second phase does require auditory input for its establishment. It appears, too, that in order for speech sounds to be maintained and speech to develop, continued auditory input is required for some time after the initial onset of this phase of development. The vocal production of children who are deafened during childhood may regress in extreme cases to the level of congenitally deaf children. The later the deafening occurs the less likely this is, however. After the age of six or so deafening has no effect on vocal production; at this point it seems that vocal production has become completely independent of supporting auditory feedback. If children born deaf are given hearing aids at some point in development, they can develop normal vocalization. The earlier the aid is introduced, the better the results; if the introduction of the hearing aid is postponed too long, language may never be acquired (Lenneberg, 1967, 1969). The critical point again seems to be about age six. There have been a few cases of normal hearing children so criminally neglected that they were never exposed to language, and who thus did not develop vocalization. One exception, Genie, was able to develop language although she was 13 years old before being exposed to it (Curtiss *et al.*, 1974).

What then does development of vocalization tell us about motor development? It is clear that the first phase of babbling develops under genetic control and does not require auditory input from the environment. Deaf children show the same sequence and range of vocalization as do hearing children. It is also clear that the child is genetically prepared for all possible linguistic environments, since he can produce a much wider range of sounds than any one environment will require of him. The selective disappearance of this wide range of sounds from the child's repertory is a more complex problem. Obviously, the child retains those sounds that he hears in the world around him. Bilingual children retain the sounds of both of their languages (Leopold, 1947). The retention of sounds and their combination into speech is thus obviously environmentally determined. There is some evidence that the loss of the ability to produce language may be environmentally determined as well, although in a very

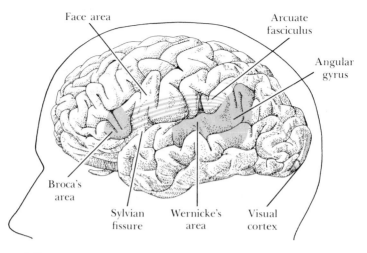

Face area

Arcuate
fasciculus

Angular
gyrus

Broca's
area

Sylvian
fissure

Wernicke's
area

Visual
cortex

FIGURE 5–7

Primary language areas of the human brain are thought to be located in the left
hemisphere because only rarely does damage to the right hemisphere cause
language disorders. Broca's area is adjacent to the region of the motor cortex that
controls the movement of the muscles of the lips, the jaw, the tongue, the soft
palate, and the vocal cords, and apparently incorporates programs for the
coordination of these muscles in speech. Damage to Broca's area results in slow
and labored speech, but comprehension of language remains intact. Wernicke's
area lies between Heschl's gyrus, which is the primary receiver of auditory
stimuli, and the angular gyrus, which acts as a way station between the auditory
and the visual regions. When Wernicke's area is damaged, speech is fluent but
has little content and comprehension is usually lost. Wernicke's and Broca's areas
are joined by a nerve bundle called the arcuate fasciculus. When it is damaged,
speech is fluent but abnormal, and patients can comprehend words but cannot
repeat them. (From "Language and the Brain" by Norman Geschwind.
Copyright © 1972 by Scientific American, Inc. All rights reserved.)

complex way. The production of language, like every other motor act,
depends on patterned discharges in the brain. Rather large areas of the
normal human brain are involved in language comprehension and production, but the most important area is the left side of the brain, the side
that is normally dominant (Figure 5–7). When this area is destroyed in
adults, there is a tendency for most speech functions to disappear. Other
evidence that the left hemisphere is important to language comes from
studies that show that if information is fed to the right side of the brain via
the left ear, an appropriate response takes much longer to emerge than it
does if the information is fed to the left side of the brain via the right ear
(Table 5–5). In infancy large areas of the brain appear to be available to
control language, but in the course of development these areas are taken
over by other behavioral functions. This takeover seems to be responsible
for the increased difficulty in establishing speech in older children. Parts of
the brain that are available in infancy are simply not available later in

TABLE 5–5

Most subjects respond faster to verbal inputs if they are fed directly to the left hemisphere of the brain through the right ear. (Springer, 1971.)

SUBJECT	REACTION TIME DIFFERENCE* (msec)
1	+87
2	−19
3	+75
4	+18
5	+18
6	+60
7	+94
8	+44
9	+29
10	+38
11	+41
12	+122
	Mean: +50

* Reaction time to input in the left ear *minus* the reaction time to input in the right ear.

development. The case of Genie, the child who was not exposed to language until she was nearly 14 years old, is extremely interesting in this connection, as the following observations show (Curtiss *et al.*, 1974).

In an effort to establish whether or not lateralization was complete, specially devised dichotic listening tests were administered to Genie. In such tests the subject hears simultaneous differing stimuli, one to each ear. In right-handed normal subjects, the right ear excels for verbal stimuli (nonsense syllables, words, etc.), the left ear excels for certain non-verbal stimuli (musical chords, environmental sounds, etc.). Genie is right-handed; hence if lateralization for language had occurred, it was anticipated that verbal stimuli presented to her right ear would be "preferred" to those received by the left ear. . . .

The results of these tests are surprising, since her verbal dichotic scores show an extreme left-ear advantage; this points to right-hemisphere dominance for language, unusual in a right-handed subject. The right ear performed at a chance level. Such extreme ear differences have been found only in split-brain and hemispherectomized subjects. The results of the dichotic tests using environmental sounds also show a left-ear advantage, but only to a degree found in normal subjects. This "normal" result shows that

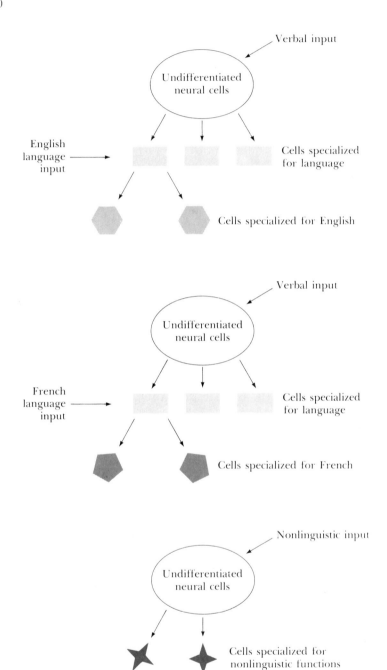

FIGURE 5-8
Equivalent neural structures may develop very differently if given different inputs.

Genie is not simply one of those rare individuals with reversed dominance, but instead is one in whom all auditory processing currently appears to be taking place in the right hemisphere.

It seems that areas of Genie's brain that had been available for language functions became specialized for other purposes and were no longer available for language. The fact that Genie's environment and developmental possibilities had been so restricted may, however, explain why she was able to acquire language at such a late age. In a more demanding environment, she, like other children deprived of auditory input, might have lost the capacity completely at an earlier age.

We can thus tentatively conclude that the emergence of vocalization is genetically controlled but that subsequent development is environmentally determined. The course of that development is determined by a switching process; the environment does not simply add to the results of genetic expression, but actually switches them into different channels. Neural structures that could be used for specific language functions can be switched to other functions, if the environment does not keep them on a linguistic track. Figure 5–8 is an attempt to represent this kind of process. In effect, the genotype proposes and the environment disposes. The creative role of the environment in the process of vocalization is restricted to reinforcing certain combinations of elements created by genetic processes. Neither alone can create speech. The finished product, however, is not a simple summation or multiplication of two sources of influence.

Vocal behavior is too important a part of human behavior for it to be submitted to the full range of possible experimental variations. Deliberate restriction or modification of auditory input would be an unacceptable experimental variation in all but the very shortest of experiments—speech is too great a part of the definition of what is human for that. We have, however, considerably more information about the development of other skills that are almost as important to the definition of what is human—the skills of the human hand.

Prehensile skills

The whole society of modern man depends on the refined manual skills that we humans share with no other primate. This superior skill in large part depends on man's superior skeletal equipment (Figure 5–9). The question of psychological interest is whether the ability to *use* this superior equipment is, like the development of the equipment itself, maturationally determined, or whether interaction with the environment is necessary for its development. Reaching begins well before birth. The components of mature reaching—arm extension and hand closure—can be elicited from

The human hand shows perfect
opposability of the thumb.

An orangutan can only grasp
a grape within its hand.

FIGURE 5–9

The human hand is the only one that permits perfect finger-thumb opposition.

fetuses with a conceptual age of 14 to 16 weeks (Humphrey, 1969). At birth the newborn already has some reaching skills in his repertory of behaviors. Newborns can reach out and grasp seen objects under the circumstances described in Chapter 4 (p. 48). Although this early eye-hand coordination is crude and inaccurate, it is nevertheless present and functional. It disappears from the repertory of the normal infant around the age of four weeks. Reaching and grasping for seen objects is not seen again in the normal infant until the age of 16–18 weeks. The behavior at this time is like early reaching. Soon, however, there are major changes. Close analysis shows that the early and later behaviors are very different, both quantitatively and qualitatively. The quantitative difference, in terms of the sheer success of the behavior, is very striking. Phase I reaching (normally found between 0–4 weeks and 16–20 weeks, approximately) results in the hand contacting the object of interest about 40 percent of the time; successful grasping is even rarer, occurring about 6 percent of the time. In Phase II (which usually begins around 20 weeks) the contact rate is virtually 100 percent, and success in grasping is almost as high. On the face of it, it would appear that the later behavior is simply more skillful, presumably the result of practice. However, more detailed observation reveals more profound, qualitative differences. Successful capture of a seen object involves two actions: *transport* of the hand to the object and *closure* of the hand on the object. In Phase II reaching these two actions are separated by about 450 msec (Bower, 1974a; Bruner and Koslowski, 1972). Twenty-week-old infants transport their hand to an object and then after a short pause close their hand on the object (Figure 5–10). This pattern is much less common in Phase I reaching. The data on reaching patterns in Phase I could in fact be interpreted to mean that the Phase II pattern never truly occurs in Phase I infants. The problem is laid

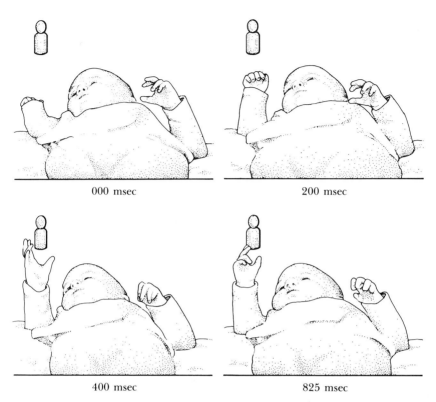

000 msec

200 msec

400 msec

825 msec

FIGURE 5–10
When an older baby's hand reaches an object he will pause for approximately half a second before closing on the object. This pattern of closure occurs at about the age of 20 weeks. (Drawn from video records.)

out in Figure 5–11, which shows the distribution of offset-times between hand transport and hand closure. These times are computed by determining the point at which the hand has been transported to a position where it *could* close on the object. The offset time is the time between arrival of the hand in this position and actual closure on the object. Offset times can be zero, i.e., the hand could close just as it reaches the object— a perfectly timed reach and grasp. Offset times can equally well be negative, with the hand closing before it reaches the object (in which case the reacher will fail to grasp the object) or positive, with the hand closing after it has reached the object. The latter pattern of reach-then-grasp is the prevailing one in Phase II reaching, whereas all three patterns *seem* to occur in Phase I reaching. The average offset time in Phase I is zero, which is more common than any specific positive or negative offset time.

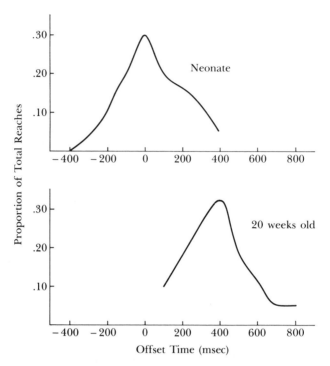

FIGURE 5-11
Distribution of offset times for hand closure of neonates and 20-week-old infants. Offset time is the time difference between arrival of the hand at the position where it could close on an object and actual closure on the object. The offset times are greater for older babies.

Looking at such data, we have a choice of two interpretations. We could say that Phase I reaching is characterized by the zero offset pattern, with the positive and negative patterns simply resulting from errors in the perceptual-motor system. Alternatively, we could say that Phase I reaching is characterized by a variety of patterns, with no one predominant. The choice is crucial for theory but cannot be made on the data thus far presented. For the moment, we should note that the offset time difference between Phase I and Phase II reaching can in part account for the greater success of the latter. Reaching and grasping with negative offset time can only lead to failures of grasping. Reaching and grasping with zero offset can be successful but must be perfectly executed to be successful; a slight mistiming of the grasp will result in failure. The long positive offsets characteristic of Phase II reaching are a safety-first way of capturing a seen object.

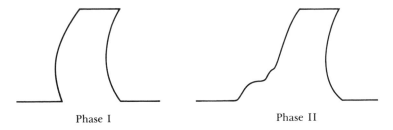

Phase I   Phase II

FIGURE 5–12

Sample traces of the pressures applied to an object during Phase I and Phase II reaching. Any contact with the object produces an upward trace.

In addition to the change in the relation between hand transport and closure, there are qualitative differences in the component acts themselves between Phase I and Phase II. The change in the hand closure component is a change in the stimuli that control closure. Closure during Phase I (and even at the beginning of Phase II) is visually controlled. The sight of an object is sufficient to elicit the entire reaching-grasping sequence. This is not the case in Phase II. Hand closure in Phase II is determined by tactual input; only the actual contact of an object with the skin of the hand elicits hand closure. This is something that the naked eye cannot tell us. However, by placing sensitive pressure transducers inside an object one can observe different patterns of grasping in the two phases. As Figure 5–12 shows, Phase II grasping is preceded by contact with the object; Phase I closure happens all at once, with maximum pressure applied straight away.

Additional and more convincing evidence of the change from visual to tactual elicitation of hand closure comes from studies using the virtual-object device described in Chapter 4. The virtual object is a visual projection that appears to be substantial but is actually quite intangible— when the hand reaches the seen "object" there is nothing there to touch. Nonetheless, during Phase I reaching the hand invariably closes at the object locus; during Phase II this is very rare indeed (Figure 5–13). It seems that in Phase II actual contact with the object is required to elicit hand closure, whereas in Phase I the sight of the object is sufficient. In Phase I, if an object contacts the hand it will in fact elicit grasping. However, physical contact is not necessary for grasping in this stage.

The changes that occur in the pattern of hand transport toward an object are more obvious. Figure 5–14 shows the paths of hand transport for three babies of different ages. As can be seen there, the path becomes less and less direct with increasing age, until, in the oldest babies studied, hand transport is made up of two discernible paths. Observation of these paths suggests that older (Phase II) babies first extend their hand into the visual

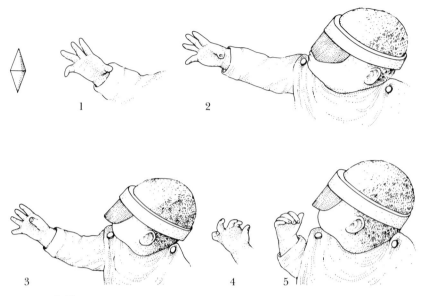

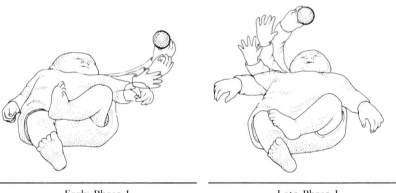

FIGURE *5–13*

A 28-week-old baby reaching for a virtual object (see Figure 4–12). Rather than closing the hand, the baby stops, withdraws it, and then looks at it.

Early Phase I

Late Phase I

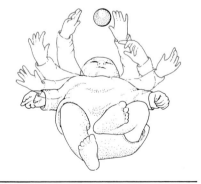

Phase II

FIGURE *5–14*

Changes in the pattern of hand transport and reaching. In both early and late Phase I, reaching is direct, whereas Phase II reaching is less direct and visually controlled. (Drawn from video records.)

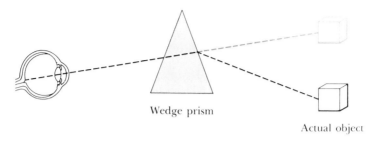

Wedge prism

Actual object

FIGURE 5–15
A prism bends light so that objects are seen in incorrect locations.

field and then bring it to the object. Younger babies, by contrast, seem to bring their hand directly to the object from wherever it happens to be. Closer inspection further suggests that the older babies visually guide their hand to the target object, which would explain why their reaching is so much more accurate than that of younger babies, whose behavior does not seem to be corrected by visual feedback in the same way. These conclusions are supported by two experimental studies of reaching in two abnormal situations.

The first of these used prism spectacles (Dunkeld and Bower, 1978b). Prism spectacles displace objects in the visual field in systematic ways (Figure 5–15). What should be the consequences for reaching? In Phase II, accuracy should hardly be affected if transport of the hand is under visual control; the hand and object would both be displaced by the same amount and visual monitoring of hand transport would allow the infant to correct the path of his reach. In Phase I, by contrast, if such visual control is not yet available, accuracy should be greatly disrupted. The hand would go to where the object is seen to be rather than where it is; without visual control of hand transport the infant cannot make use of visual feedback to correct this error. A comparison of Phase I and Phase II performance in this experiment shows that Phase II performance is indeed virtually unaffected by the prism (suffering only a 14 percent drop in accuracy) whereas Phase I performance is drastically affected (a 50 percent drop in accuracy) (see also McDonnell, 1975; von Hofsten, 1977).

If Phase II reaching does incorporate visual control, there are circumstances in which Phase II reaches should do less well than Phase I reaches, namely circumstances in which visual control is not possible. One experiment tested this possibility (Bower and Wishart, 1972; see also Wishart, Bower, and Dunkeld, 1978). Babies were seated in a light-tight room. They were shown an object with the room lights on, and then, before they could reach for it, the lights were switched out, so that reaching had to take place in darkness. There was thus no possibility of visual control of hand transport. As the data below show, the performance of older babies was considerably poorer than that of younger babies.

Age (months)	5	7	9	11
Probability of accurate first reach	.50	.30	.16	.16

Observation of their behavior, via an infrared television system, showed quite clearly that the younger babies were able to maintain this direct hand transport in darkness, whereas the older babies simply groped around in the dark, seemingly finding the objects almost as a result of chance contacts. In this admittedly rather unusual case, processes of development in fact resulted in a decrement in performance with increasing age.

It thus seems that there are two qualitative differences between Phase I and Phase II reaching. In Phase I, hand closure is visually controlled, whereas hand transport is not. In Phase II, hand closure is tactually rather than visually controlled, while hand transport has become visually controlled. The net effect of the two qualitative changes in reaching and grasping is to improve the success of reaching, even though under some circumstances, e.g., deprivation of visual control, the reverse may occur. What is the nature of the developmental effect that produces these changes?

A number of painstaking studies have examined the transition between Phase I and Phase II reaching under different environmental circumstances. One study produced data that seems to suggest that environmental factors are largely responsible for the transition (Bower, 1977a). A group of infants was given daily practice in reaching from the age of one week. Every day the infants were presented with a dangling object, placed so as to be within their reach. Once a week their behavior was filmed for analysis. The most striking thing was that there was not, as is usual, any clear cessation of reaching behavior during the 20 weeks of the study—the infants were always willing and able to move their hand towards the presented object. In the early weeks of the study, however, hand transport did not always follow the usual Phase I pattern of terminating in hand closure. As Figure 5-16 shows, hand closures (attempted grasping) declined to a low frequency by the age of four weeks. Whereas reaching behavior typically disappears at four weeks, these babies continued to reach out toward the presented object but with no attempt to close the hand on it until around the age of 17 weeks, when grasping attempts resumed. These were typical of Phase II grasping: the hand was brought to the object and then closed, with a clear gap in time between the end of hand transport and the onset of hand closure. Some of the babies were then tested with a virtual object; none of them showed any inclination at all to close their

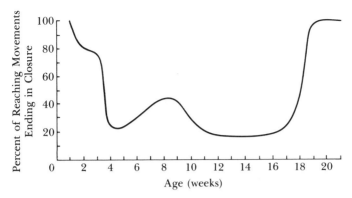

FIGURE 5–16

In an experiment infants were presented with a dangling object
daily for 20 weeks. The proportion of reaching movements that
ended with attempts to grasp the object changed as a function of
age. (Bower, 1977a.)

hand on it. The pattern of development seen here suggests that the
disappearance of reaching in normal infants between four and 16 weeks of
age results from a lack of opportunity for reaching. Infants in the first four
months of life frequently spend long periods lying on their sides or stomach.
As we have already seen (Chapter 4) reaching cannot occur unless the
baby is supine and supported appropriately. It is also necessary that the
objects be within reach. If, as in the above study, such opportunities are
given, reaching behavior does not disappear at four weeks, as is usual. The
early disappearance of visually initiated grasping in this study suggests
another environmental effect. It seems plausible that visually initiated
grasping may have been *extinguished* due to the difficulty of grasping the
dangling objects used in this study. These objects simply flew away on
contact with the hand unless the grasp was perfectly timed (zero offset
time), a rare occurrence in the early weeks of the study. Premature closure
of the hand (negative offset time) or closure of the hand after reaching the
object (positive offset time) would not allow for successful grasping of a
dangling object.

That failure to seize the object was responsible for the disappearance of
the visually initiated grasping is suggested by another study in which
failure was made pretty much impossible (White and Held, 1966). The
subjects were infants in a somewhat impoverished institution. Their
movements were restricted by the ancient, hollowed out mattresses on
which they lay. The visual surroundings were a homogeneous white, with
few contours. Objects for reaching were not normally available. The
experimenters introduced two modifications into the life of some of these
infants. Between the ages of 37 and 68 days the selected babies had in their

cribs two pacifiers attached to discs close to their eyes and within reach. In addition, between the ages of 68 and 124 days an elaborate multicolored stabile was hung over their heads, in a position again designed to elicit hand transport. The babies were also given frequent opportunities to reach for and grasp an object held in one place by the experimenter. The notable thing about all these targets was that they were rigidly fixed in one place. If the baby banged them with his hand, these objects would not move, unlike the freely dangling objects used in the previously cited study. If visually initiated grasping disappeared in the previous study as a result of a lack of success in capturing freely moving objects, it should hardly have disappeared in this study, since the objects would remain in place for a second try.

The results in fact confirmed these expectations. The babies had been given nothing to reach for prior to the beginning of the experiment. As these babies were over five weeks old, we can assume that any early Phase I reaching would have died away by the time the experiment began, as a result of lack of use or opportunity for reinforcement. However, as we saw in Chapter 2, extinguished responses can be regenerated, whether or not they are again reinforced. This happened in this study. Phase I reaching and grasping appeared again at nine weeks of age. Indeed, in this study the Phase I pattern of reach-and-grasp persisted from nine until 14 weeks of age—much longer than this pattern would continue in more "normal" environments. The striking thing is that even in this artificial world of immovable objects the mature Phase II pattern of reach-then-grasp did force its way through at this point. Although the Phase I behavior pattern was successful with immovable objects, it was nevertheless replaced by the Phase II pattern. Unless White and Held did not have the tight control over the environments that they claim, we must concede there is some maturational influence on the development of reaching.

Leaving aside the question of the maturational component, what picture of the development of reaching do we get? Babies are born with the Phase I reaching abilities that we described above. The sight alone of an object elicits hand transport to the object and hand closure, but hand transport is not yet under visual control. To be successful, such reaching-and-grasping needs extremely accurate timing in its execution. This means that the grasping component will rarely be successful in a world of reachable objects and we would therefore expect it to be extinguished. Hand transport, on the other hand, since it often results in the displacement of the object eliciting reaching, at least produces an interesting event for the baby. And since interesting events are presumably reinforcing, this visually elicited reaching should continue. Meantime, of course, grasping elicited by physical contact will continue to be reinforced. Every time an object of a graspable size contacts the baby's palm or fingers it will be grasped, whether it be a bottle, a finger, one of the bars of his crib, or whatever.

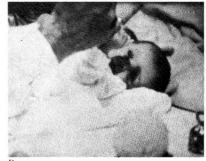

A

B

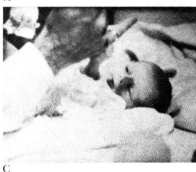

FIGURE 5–17
Hand regard in a 12-day-old infant.
This neonate, when given a finger to
reach for, looks at her hand when it
comes into the visual field (A). She
looks back at the finger as she raises
her hand to it (B), but the reach stops
as she again catches sight of her own
hand (C).

C

Thus, since both are reinforced, hand transport to seen objects and hand closure due to physical contact should continue. This sequence, as we have seen, is one of the defining characteristics of Phase II reaching. In a normal environment principles of reinforcement could thus account for part of the development of Phase II out of Phase I reaching.

There remains, however, a variety of maturational effects to be explained. Maturational effects seem to account for the emergence of Phase II reaching in a world of rigid objects (regardless of its success, Phase I reaching was replaced in White and Held's study). They also must account for development of reaching in an environment in which *no* objects are given to stimulate reaching. This is a very rare environment, but the institutional environment studied by White and Held came close. A control group of babies from the same institution who were not included in the above experiment had no reachable objects in their environment but still they developed reaching. The event that made such development possible was the onset of *hand regard*. Hand regard first emerges in the neonate period (Figure 5–17) but occurs in a more obvious fashion around 12 weeks of age. Around this time the baby will bring his hand into the visual field and then move it around, tracking it with head and eye movements. Because the hand in the visual field is also an object in the visual field, the unoccupied hand can and does reach out and grasp it.

Thus, even in the absence of real objects one hand can serve as a substitute object for the other hand, thereby maintaining reaching behavior. Hand regard is almost certainly maturationally generated in its entirety. My reason for saying this is that the same behavior is observed in blind infants; they too will raise a hand into the "visual" field and track it with their unseeing eyes (Urwin, 1973; Freedman, 1964). Of course, since they cannot see the hand, they do not attempt to grasp it. Nevertheless, since hand regard occurs in these tragic circumstances, where no visual event from the environment could possibly trigger it, we can safely concede that the behavior has a maturational origin.

Hand regard, although maturationally determined, only allows for the maintenance of reaching behavior; it is not a direct ancestor of that behavior. Its role in the determination of reaching behavior is facilitative rather than determining. A similar facilitative event may underlie the emergence of Phase II reaching in those babies in White and Held's study who spent their early weeks of life in a world of rigid objects. This possibility emerged from studies of a somewhat unique form of reaching: reaching for noise-making targets that cannot be seen. This form of reaching, or *auditory-manual coordination*, can be conveniently studied in sighted babies. One places a baby in a totally dark room and then introduces a noise-making toy. The baby's behavior can be observed with an infrared TV system, which does not introduce any visible light into the room. Of course, auditory-manual coordination can be observed directly in infants born blind. The two sources of data yield similar results. Like visually guided reaching, auditorally guided reaching shows a biphasic pattern of development. Up to about the age of 20 weeks a sighted infant in darkness will reach out for a noise-making toy. The reaching is direct and accurate within the limits of the auditory system; it becomes quite accurate around 20 weeks of age, as Figure 5–18 shows. Shortly after this, the behavior disappears completely; infants sit limply with no hand or arm movements at all when noise-making toys are presented in darkness. This sequence was first described in sighted babies (Wishart, Bower, and Dunkeld, 1978). At first it was thought that the extinction of this behavior could also be accounted for by the lack of opportunity to exercise it. Since sighted babies ordinarily rely on vision to get to objects and seldom need to rely on sound alone, we might expect the behavior to fade away through lack of use. This explanation has turned out to be untenable. The extinction of the behavior is not prevented in sighted infants who are given intensive practice in reaching for noise-making objects in darkness. More-over, a blind infant who was intensively coached to use auditory-manual coordination nonetheless lost the coordination at about the same age sighted infants typically do (Urwin, 1973). In this case there could be no possibility that a developing reliance on vision led to the decline and eventual disappearance of this behavior—the baby simply had no sight to

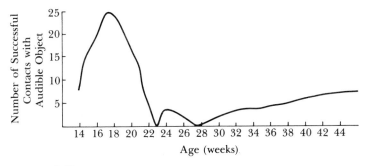

FIGURE 5-18

The ability to reach accurately for a noise-making object in darkness peaks at around 20 weeks of age and then declines precipitously. (Bower, 1974a.)

rely on. Since practice and reinforcement cannot arrest the disappearance of the behavior, it would seem that maturational processes must be responsible for the loss (but see p. 108).

The disappearance of auditory-manual coordination roughly coincides with the emergence of Phase II reaching and with the ending of attempts to grasp a virtual object. Is it possible that these three events reflect a common underlying process? As we saw in Chapter 4, the newborn lives in a very unified perceptual world. Events that can be heard must also be visible; events that can be seen must be touchable; and so on. This unified perceptual world seems to be innate and independent of experience for some considerable time. What is more striking evidence for this than the blind baby "looking" at his hand? This kind of unity of the senses disappears around five months of age when the senses become dissociated. A sound no longer denotes something to be seen or touched. As sounds begin to represent communication, they gradually become an object of interest in themselves and so are more likely to elicit listening than any other behavior. The sight of an object is no longer automatically followed by an attempt to grasp it; the specification of "graspability" falls to the sense of touch (Bower, Broughton, and Moore, 1970b). The dissociation of the senses would allow for the appearance of Phase II reaching, in which vision and touch are separately controlled. It would also ensure the disappearance of auditory-manual coordination. Although there are neural changes going on at this age that could underlie this change in behavior, such changes do not explain the shift. Indeed, they themselves must be explained. What sort of explanation could we offer then?

We obviously cannot invoke events in the individual experience of the child. It is the apparent irrelevance of environmental events that led us to explore maturational causes. We are therefore looking for functional explanations of a genetic process, i.e., for the adaptive significance of the development or loss of a particular capacity. It is not hard to find functional explanations for the shift from perceptual unity to sensory independence. The specialization of audition for sound reception will obviously facilitate the learning of language. Similarly, as seen objects become things to be looked at, the impulse to reach and grasp will decline, with the possibility of "thought" preceding action. The shift from a unified reach-*and*-grasp behavior to the sequence reach-*then*-grasp obviously also allows for the reverse sequence, grasp-then-reach. This in turn allows for tool use, one of man's most distinctive skills. It is far harder to understand why perceptual unity is built in in the first place. One could conclude that the evolutionary process simply has not yet got rid of it (Bower, 1974b). Alternatively, one can seek a functional explanation for it. One possible function would be to provide for the possibility of selective *re*connection of neural pathways, if the environment demands it. The opportunity to use the coordination while it is there may program subsequent development so that the coordination could be regenerated whereas lack of such opportunity may result in the deletion of the capacity from subsequent developmental channeling. If this is the case, it would be an instance of the environment operating like points in a railway line, switching development from one path to another, quite different path. Such a process could explain the fact that sight-restoration operations have different effects according to the age at which they are performed, a topic we shall discuss in Chapter 8.

What of our main concern—prehensile skills in a normal environment? As Figure 5–19 illustrates, the development of the aspects of visually guided reaching that we have been considering is an overdetermined process. Both environmental events and maturational events seem to change the behavior in precisely the same direction. The environment may accelerate or retard the process but its role is minimal.

The same seems to be true of the shift to visual control of hand transport, which we have not yet considered. Since in the early stages of development of visually controlled reaching the hand competes with objects in the visual field for attention, such reaching requires greater information-processing capacity than reaching that is merely visually elicited (the hand being brought directly to the object without visual control of its path). Hand regard, as we have seen, is maturational in origin. Although information-handling capacity grows maturationally, it also grows as a result of familiarity with an object to be attended to, since identification of that object requires less attention. Here again, maturational processes dovetail with environmental events to produce the same effect.

Throughout the last few pages I have been discussing the *development* of reaching. But does reaching in fact develop? On the basis of the account given here we must conclude that one type of reaching replaces another by a process of selective reinforcement and extinction. In other words, standard processes of learning could explain these alterations in behavior. What I am asking then is whether or not learning can produce development. In Chapter 3 I argued that the essence of development—gene

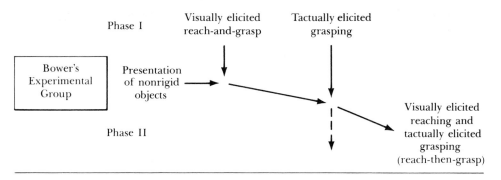

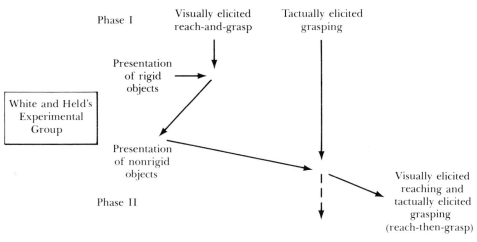

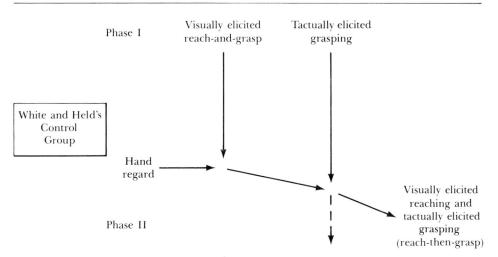

FIGURE 5–19

The development of Phase II reaching is an over-determined process.
Environmental events and motivational events push the development of reaching
in the same direction. The occurrence of maturationally generated hand regard
makes reaching relatively buffered from environmental deprivation since one
hand can serve as an object for the other to reach for.

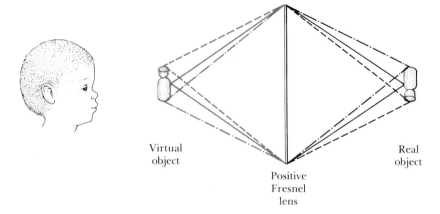

FIGURE 5–20

Virtual objects can be produced by using a positive Fresnel lens. Virtual objects produced in this way are visually indistinguishable from real objects.

expression under environmental control— is that it results in *irreversible* changes in the structure of the organism. Learning, by contrast, produces *reversible* changes in behavior. Are the changes in reaching behavior that we have described genuine developmental changes, or are the changes in fact reversible? Put this way, the changes in reaching that we have been discussing are not in fact developmental changes. The behavior that is replaced, Phase I reaching, remains in the individual's repertoire and can be elicited in appropriate environmental circumstances. Admittedly, the evidence for this contention is not overwhelming. However, in one study of reaching for virtual objects at different ages it was found that Phase I reaching could be elicited from babies as old as 11 months (Bower, 1977b). In this experiment virtual objects were produced with a Fresnel lens (Figure 5–20); such "objects" are visually indistinguishable from real objects. Because grasping is visually rather than tactually elicited in Phase I, the young babies kept trying to grasp the virtual object, even though it was intangible. Toward the end of an experimental session, however, even the older babies would typically let fly with a few Phase I reach-and-grasp attempts before quitting completely. The fact that they could do this implies that the shift from Phase I to Phase II reaching is not in fact a structural change, i.e., a truly developmental change, but rather a change in the relative probability of two different and mutually exclusive behaviors. Therefore, while the psychological events we described above (reinforcement, success) do change motor behavior, the changes do not qualify as genuine developmental changes.

MOTOR DEVELOPMENT IN BLIND BABIES

Is there any evidence that psychological events do produce genuine motor development? It does appear that there can be long-term, irreversible changes in motor capacity in blind children, namely in their auditory-manual coordination (p. 102). Blind and sighted children are equally able and willing to reach out and grasp an unseen, noise-making object in darkness. Performance is constrained only by the limitations of accuracy of the auditory system (pp. 50ff). The behavior becomes quite accurate by the age of 5–6 months, at which point it drops out of the repertory of both blind and sighted infants. Recovery of auditory-manual coordination is difficult and sometimes never happens. Fraiberg (1968) has described blind teenagers who cannot reach at all, even for an object auditorily defined.*

> The behavior of the hand is striking. While many of the children can use the hand for self-feeding and can even use spoons and forks, the hand appears to have no autonomy of its own. It can serve the mouth; it can bring objects to the mouth; but it is not employed for examination or manipulation of objects. Discrimination of objects remains centered in the mouth; however, as already seen, objects are important not for their own characteristics but for their qualities in stimulating the mouth.

Blind children as old as 13 years will hold their hands in a stereotyped shoulder-high position while they engage in stereotyped finger and hand movements quite unrelated to events in the external world. Differentiated reaching and grasping simply have not developed. It is possible that such children have failed to redevelop a capacity for auditory-manual coordination they had when much younger. It is also possible that whatever deleted the capacity in the first instance produced a permanent loss. Deciding between these options is in part a question about whether the early auditory-manual coordination is the ancestor of the later behavior. It is also a question about *what* deletes the early behavior.

In my own research on these problems I took as possible models the two other behaviors that showed a biphasic pattern in development— reaching and walking. Both of these are susceptible to practice, as we have seen. Sufficient practice of the early behavior can mean that it does not drop out but rather simply merges with or turns into the later behavior. It thus seemed worthwhile practicing auditory-manual coordination to see whether that too would stop it from dropping out. A study of sighted babies reaching for noise-making objects in darkness found no beneficial effects of practice at all. Two studies of auditory-manual coordination in blind babies likewise found that practice of the early behavior did not prevent its decline. Moreover, in neither of these latter studies was there any apparent acceleration of recovery of the coordination, which would have been evidence of some connection between the early and later behaviors. These results were puzzling to say the least. The resistance of the decline to practice and reinforcement seemed to indicate a maturational origin for the decline. However, an alternative explanation may lie in the

---

*See also Fraiberg and Freedman, 1964; and Fraiberg, Seigel, and Gibson, 1966.

difference between the normal conditions of visual stimulation and those of auditory stimulation. The infant's response to visual stimulation is normally an active one. He can look at things that interest him and he can look away from things that bore or disturb him. Or he can close his eyes if he chooses. The response to auditory stimulation, on the other hand, is quite different. The infant cannot switch on sounds he likes or switch off sounds he dislikes. He cannot shut his ears as easily as he can shut his eyes. In short, he has no control over auditory input; he is necessarily passive in the face of such stimulation.

Passive situations of this type have important effects on development. The classic experiments on the effects of passivity were done on vision, using kittens as the subjects (Held, 1965). Kittens raised for as short a period as 30 hours without being allowed to respond actively to visual stimulation became functionally blind. They did not respond to any type of visual stimulation. The results of these experiments suggested the possibility that human infants lose auditory-manual coordination because they are passive in the presence of auditory stimulation. How could we present auditory information to the blind infant in such a way as to give him an active role?

After some trial and error we found that the answer was to fit the infant with an ultrasonic echo-location device (Figure 5–21). The device sends out pulses of sound waves at ultrasonic frequencies in a cone with a width of 80 degrees. Ultrasound is above the range of human hearing so the outgoing pulses are not heard. The device itself converts the ultrasonic echoes from objects into an audible range and these sounds are channeled directly into the ears of the infant. The closer the object, the lower the pitch of the sound; the larger the object, the louder the sound. Objects to the right of the infant produce a louder sound in the right ear and objects

FIGURE 5–21

This seven-month-old baby is congenitally blind. With an ultrasonic device she is able to locate a toy without having to explore tactually the space in front of her. The device is a modification of one invented by Professor Leslie Kay after extensive study of the bat's ultrasonic echo-location system. The device continuously irradiates the environment with ultrasound; echoes from objects are then converted into audible sound. Ultrasound was chosen because the size of an object that produces an echo is inversely proportional to the frequency of the sound source. Ultrasound will thus generate echoes from smaller objects than will audible sound. The conversion from ultrasound to audible sound codes the echo in three ways. The pitch indicates the *distance* of the object from which the echo came (high pitch means distant objects, low pitch near ones); the amplitude of the signal indicates the *size* of the object (loud = large, soft = small); and the clarity of the signal indicates *texture*. In addition, the audible signal is stereophonic, so the direction of the object can be perceived (by the difference in time of arrival of the signal at the two ears—see Figure 4–2A). (Photos from *New Scientist*, February 3, 1977.)

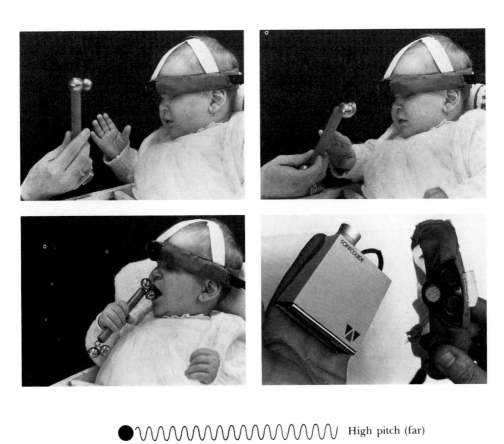

Distance	High pitch (far)
	Low pitch (near)
Size	Low volume (small)
	High volume (large)
Texture	Clear sound (hard)
	Fuzzy sound (rough)

to the left produce a louder sound in the left ear; objects that are straight ahead produce sounds of equal amplitude in both ears. Hard objects make a clear sound while soft objects make a somewhat fuzzy one.

Most important, however, is that anyone wearing the device has direct control over the sounds channeled to his ears. The wearer can focus on "interesting" objects; he can turn away from "boring" objects and thereby silence them; he can inspect objects by moving his head and thus changing the signal pattern; and so on. In other words, the wearer has active control over this particular auditory input. If our hypothesis about the extinction of normal auditory-manual coordination is correct, behavior guided by the ultrasonic device should not disappear.

The device has been tested only on a few infants who were congenitally blind. The results, however, were quite satisfactory (Bower, 1977d, 1978). Not only did auditory-manual behavior not decline with the device but the infants actually developed some skills comparable to those acquired by a normal infant of the same age. Furthermore, the experiment clearly showed the flexibility of the newborn infant's perceptual system. No humans in the history of life had ever received the type of input these infants were given, yet the babies appeared to make some sense of the sounds within seconds after the device had been put on. It thus seems possible at least that the source of the decline observed normally is the enforced passivity associated with noise-making objects. Enforced passivity seemingly can have extremely long-term, irreversible effects on motor behavior.

LIMITS OF MOTOR DEVELOPMENT

Despite this one case, it seems on balance that the emergence of new behaviors is very much a matter of gene expression, with the environment operating as accelerator or brake, rather than a switch. This should not surprise us too much, for the behavior associated with a species is as much a part of the definition of that species as its anatomy or physiology. Indeed, much of human behavior is a direct consequence of the arrangement of our bones and muscles, which is of course strictly the result of gene expression.

All of the evidence on reaching indicates that it is an over-determined behavior. Normal environmental events and maturational processes push it in the same direction. Unusual environments may slow or retard it, but it is hard to see how they could redirect it. Even in the case of auditory-manual coordination (auditorily guided reaching) the question at issue is regeneration or loss, not redirection. With vocal behavior, the environment selects which actual language will be spoken. The environment cannot, however, produce languages that have no basis in the child's genetic endowment nor can it produce new uses for vocal behavior. In other words, it cannot redirect vocal development. It appears the environment cannot even retard the emergence of walking, though it may accelerate it. The picture of the development of motor behavior that thus emerges is one of ongoing maturational processes that *use* input from the environment but do not really need it. Where a facilitative or inhibiting effect of the environment has been demonstrated, it turns out to be slight—a matter of a few weeks' gain or loss. The environment does not switch development into one path rather than another. Even in those cases where the environment has a crucial role, e.g., vocal behavior and auditory-manual coordination, the role is one of an on-off switch rather than the creation of any genuinely new pathway of development. The development of human behavior is therefore as much the expression of our genes as is the development of our bones. Indeed, the two presuppose one another. Because we would not be human if we did not have "human" behaviors, we should not be surprised that they are programmed by that particular genetic core that defines a human being.

Environmentalists can rightly object that we have thus far looked at a narrow sample of motor behavior. All of the behaviors we have looked at have precursors in the neonate period. They are also in a real sense simple instances of development in that we are dealing with changes within a single behavior. We have not looked at any dependencies between behaviors, for example, or even at the more complex expressions of the behaviors we have been discussing. Both of these seem to require more complex explanations than any we have offered so far.

Consider the issue of sequential dependency between different behaviors. Many investigators have argued that certain behaviors can emerge only after the appearance of another. Their arguments are usually based on evidence that is too narrow. The argument that crawling must precede walking collapses the first time one meets a child who walks before he or she crawls, as did two of my own children. The strongest evidence for interbehavioral dependencies comes from some of Fraiberg's data (1968) on development in blind infants. A major and severe problem for the blind child is lack of mobility. Therapists working with such children have the greatest difficulty in making them crawl or walk. Even if the child has the motor control for locomotion—like one child who could balance himself on hands and knees and move either leg forward or back—no locomotion will occur until auditory-manual coordination has been reestablished. Once the latter behavior has been reestablished, enabling the infant to reach for noise-making objects around him, locomotion follows within a very short time. Fraiberg notes that no baby in her sample ever learned to crawl before being able to reach. At first sight this would appear to indicate a dependence between reaching and crawling, a dependence that we would not observe in the normal child because reaching normally occurs well before crawling (see Figure 5–1). Such a dependence would argue against the rather simple maturational model of motor development that has been proposed thus far. If the child must gain experience with one behavior before a second behavior can appear, it would seem that that experience is necessary for the emergence of the second behavior. However, there are other clinical data that should warn us against acceptance of such surface indications.

Consider the case of the so-called thalidomide babies, who because their mothers took the drug thalidomide during pregnancy were born with severely shortened limbs or no limbs at all. Locomotion is not greatly retarded in these babies. Even those with no limbs will roll themselves over and over in order to move from place to place (Gouin-Décarie, 1969). Clearly, there can be no dependence between reaching and locomotion here. The seemingly critical behavior for the blind babies, reaching, simply cannot occur in thalidomide infants. Yet locomotion occurs. This suggests that the apparent link between reaching and crawling in blind infants is in fact a manifestation of another process that is essential for both behaviors. This other process is presumably the establishment of the idea of an "out there" to reach for or move into. The effect of the dissociation of the senses (p. 61) on the blind child is that he is left with no sensory modality to specify "out there." Not until audition has been reestablished in its role of specifying the presence and position of objects and surfaces will the blind child have any motive or direction for arm or body movements. The thalidomide infant, being sighted, obviously has no such problems. It is the establishment of a specified perceptual space that must precede any directed movement, rather than one movement serving as a prerequisite for another. A perceptual space thus seems to be a prerequisite for action in space, contrary to the conclusions of many authors (e.g., Taylor, 1962).

DEVELOPMENT OF WEIGHT CONSERVATION

The development of reaching as outlined above is far from complete. By about six months of age, which has been the limit in our discussion so far, infants can reach out and grasp objects in any direction from any posture. This is a considerable advance. Nevertheless, the behavior is still far from the adult level of competence. Although the behavior is adjusted to the size and shape of objects, it is not yet adjusted with respect to the weight of objects (Mounoud and Bower, 1974). That is to say, prior to actual contact with an object, infants do not adjust the force of their grip or the tension of their arms in anticipation of the weight of the object.

This can be shown by analyzing the force of an infant's grip following contact with an object. A six- or seven-month-old infant grips an object as tightly as possible, regardless of the weight of the object. Although this force varies between babies, it is nevertheless constant for the individual baby and independent of the weight of the object. At this age there is some accommodation of arm tension to object weight following contact, but it is not yet *anticipatory*. Infants of this age can bring objects to their mouths; they do so with a tremor at the beginning that indicates changes in the tension exerted. When infants of this age are handed an object, invariably their arm initially drops under the weight of the object. Arm tension is adjusted very quickly, and the object is pulled back up to the desired position. The initial hand drop indicates lack of anticipation of the weight of the object. Even on repeated presentations the hand drop continues, indicating that anticipatory behavior is simply not possible at this stage.

Around nine months of age the picture begins to change. The force of the grip becomes adjusted to the weight of an object presented, although this still does not happen until after the object has been grasped. The hand continues to drop on presentation of an object, even after repeated trials. At this point both the force of grasp and arm tension accommodate to different weights of objects. However, the accommodation is still after the fact; there is no anticipation of weight, even after the same object has been presented several times. Around the age of one year, a significant advance occurs. On repeated presentations of the same object, errors in the force of grasp and arm tension decline to zero. Indeed, shortly after this pattern appears, error disappears on the second presentation of *any* given object. That is, the force needed to hold an object and the required arm tension are discovered on the first presentation and are applied instantaneously on the second trial.

This anticipation represents a considerable advance, but the behavior is still very restricted. Suppose that after holding an object once a child can reach out and take it with just the right arm tension for smooth transport. If that child is then given a similar object, but twice as long and therefore twice as heavy as the first, he will be unable to infer the weight of the new object from his knowledge of the weight of the first. At this stage anticipation is possible, but only for single familiar objects. As yet the child has no predictive rule that permits anticipatory adjustments for new objects that are similar to a familiar object in some respects but different in others, such as length or width. The only predictive rule the child at this stage has would be something like, "The same object weighs the same every time it is picked up."

Toward 18 months of age anticipation of the weight of objects that have not yet been grasped is evident. Suppose we have a series of objects with proportional increases in length and therefore weight. If the infant is given the shortest (lightest) object, his initial grasp force and arm tension will probably be wrong; however, on the second presentation of this same object he will apply the right amount of force needed to grasp and hold the object. There is nothing new in this. However, on the *first* presentation of the second object he will also apply accurate force, as he will on the first presentation of all subsequent objects in the series. The infant now seems able to predict the weight of objects prior to actual interaction with them. He now seems capable of following the rule, "The longer an object is, the heavier it will be when picked up." But this rule can lead 18-month-old infants to make mistakes that younger infants would never make. Suppose we add to our series an object whose length is increased in proportion to the series but whose weight is not, i.e., a longer but lighter object. The infant will typically overestimate the weight of this trick object, gripping it too hard and applying too much arm tension. As a result, the infant's arm will fly up. The opposite is likely to happen if an object were short and also disproportionately heavy; the object would probably be dropped. The occurrence of these errors shows that weight conservation is now possible for all objects that can be serially ordered in some visible dimension that covaries with weight. The stages in the development of weight conservation may be summarized as follows:

STAGE I   : No differential response to objects of different weight.
STAGE II   : Differential response to objects of different weight after grasping.
STAGE III : Differential response after grasping, with anticipation that the same object will weigh the same on repeated presentations.
STAGE IV : Differential response after grasping, with anticipation that the same object will weigh the same on repeated presentations, and anticipation that objects similar in appearance but varying in length will be correspondingly graded in weight.

Development of weight conservation is still far from complete at this point. We have followed the infant up to a point where he can make two different kinds of estimates. He anticipates that an object will be the same weight on repeated presentations. He also anticipates that the longer an object is, the heavier it will be. What happens if we create conditions in which the two kinds of anticipation are in conflict? Suppose we present an infant with a pliable object. After the first presentation the infant will have ascertained the force required to grasp it. On the second presentation the infant should apply the same force. Suppose, though, that we elongate the object before giving it to the infant again. What should the infant do? Since it is the same object, should he apply the same force? But it is also longer—should he therefore apply more force? How should the infant resolve the conflict? At this point it is surely obvious that we are no longer talking about motor behavior at all, but rather about the rules that control behavior. The conflict between these rules can be resolved, as we shall see. The processes of resolution do not change the behavior, only the way in which the behavior is used. With increasing age *behavior* changes less and less, while the *control* processes become increasingly more complex. The study of these control processes is the subject of our next chapter. As we shall see, although these processes change the way motor behavior is used, their developmental pathway is quite different. The complex changes in motor behavior that occur late in infancy are not the consequence of motor development, but of developments in the control mechanisms operating on a developed motor system. For all practical purposes, motor development is completed in infancy. Development obviously is not.

III

The most profound changes manifested in the course of development are undoubtedly the changes in understanding of the world that occur between birth and maturity. A baby's understanding of the world is very different from that of a two-year-old, which in turn is very different from that of a six-year-old, and so on. By and large, cognitive development seems over by the end of the teenage years. The view of the world acquired then seems to persist throughout life. Indeed, some pessimists argue that our basic descriptions of the world cannot be altered after this time. Nevertheless, the world view or system of cognition that one develops is very much dependent on the culture one grows in. Cognitive development may thus be an example of epigenesis in development.

6

Cognitive
Development

The picture of cognitive development to be presented here is largely based on the work of Jean Piaget, the great Swiss psychologist whose work has dominated this field for many years. Piaget has worked out a theory of the development of cognitive skills that is drastically different in every respect from the kind of theory of intelligence development associated with investigation of IQ test performance—an approach to be discussed in Section 4 (Chapters 11 and 12). These two approaches to the analysis and description of the development of cognitive skill are different at every level—from the nature of the tasks given to the subjects to the theory underlying these tasks.

The major difference between traditional intelligence testing and testing based on Piaget's theories is that in the latter the emphasis is on testing behaviors that index very general concepts that underpin a wide range of specific cognitive skills. Traditional intelligence testing, on the other hand, makes use of any item that can be shown to differentiate reliably between older and younger children, whether it be stringing beads or reciting the days of the week in correct order. While Piagetian test items also differentiate younger from older children, they are selected primarily for their ability to test the child's level of understanding of certain basic and powerful concepts that are important to development. The main difference between Piagetian theory and the theory behind traditional IQ testing is that the latter holds that development is a progressive, continuous process, whereas Piagetian theory argues that development involves frequent repetition and even reversal, with an older child at times doing less well than a younger child on the same task.

Piaget divides development into three major stages. The first is the *sensori-motor stage*, which corresponds to the period of infancy, the period prior to the onset of language. This period covers the first 18–24 months of life. The next is the stage of *concrete operations*, which lasts until 7–10 years of age. The last stage of development is the stage of *formal operations* (occasionally referred to as the stage of propositional thought), which lasts until approximately age 16. Each of these stages may be defined in terms of the nature of the child's understanding of certain basic and generally useful concepts, such as space, number, and causality, the very concepts that underlie Western scientific thought. Each of the three stages represents an overall advance in the understanding and use of these concepts, although at times particular changes may look more like retreats than advances.

THE SENSORIMOTOR STAGE

The sensorimotor stage is an extremely busy stage for the developing child. During this stage the child acquires his first concepts of object, space, size, number, weight, volume, and causality. A brief outline of the behavioral indicators of each of these concepts will make clear what intellectual advances are being made at this stage.

The concept of an object

We adults know a great deal about objects. We know about the spatial relations objects can have to one another—things can be "in," "behind," or "on" other things. We know that inanimate objects do not move by themselves and that animate objects do. We know that when objects move from place to place they must move along some path and cannot simply dematerialize in one place and rematerialize at another. The young infant does not know any of these things. Consider the experiment illustrated in Figure 6–1. A baby of 3–4 months is shown a toy train in the center of the track. The train sits there for 10 seconds and moves slowly to a place on the right, where it sits for 10 seconds before returning to the center; after 10 seconds the train moves again to the place at the right. The train is repeatedly moved back and forth on this schedule. Suppose after a while the train simply stays at the center. What does the baby do? He turns and looks for the train at right and shows some surprise that the train is not there, even though he can see the train sitting at the center and has not

Baby sees toy train in center of track.

After 10 sec the train moves slowly right and remains at right.

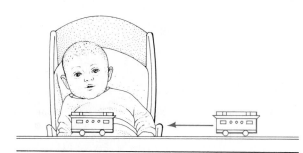

After 10 sec the train returns slowly to center and remains there.

Catch trial. After 10 sec at center the train does *not* move off to the right as usual. The baby, however, looks to the right, expecting to see the train there.

FIGURE 6–1

This experiment demonstrates that infants around 3–4 months old do not yet understand that an object must move in order to reappear in another place.

seen it move. The baby does not seem to realize that movement is necessary if the train is to appear at the right.

Although infants stop making this kind of error by the end of the first half year of life, they continue to make similarly "bizarre" errors with objects for much longer than that. Consider the simple hiding game illustrated in Figure 6–2. A toy is placed under one of two cups, say the

1. Baby sees object being hidden in left cup.

2. Baby retrieves object from cup.

3. Baby sees object being hidden again in left cup.

4. Baby again retrieves object from cup.

5. Baby now sees object being hidden in right cup.

6. Baby continues to look for object in left cup and is surprised and confused to find the cup empty. He ignores the cup under which the object is hidden.

FIGURE *6–2*

In the first six months of life an infant thinks that an object that has been hidden will always be found in the same place.

left, while the baby is watching. A baby of 6–12 months is quite able to reach out and take the object from under the cup. We take the toy back from the baby and place it again under the left cup. The baby again picks up the toy and we retrieve it from him. The toy this time is placed under the right cup, again with the baby watching. What does the baby do? He reaches for the left cup and is surprised and puzzled that there is nothing in it. He makes no attempt to grab the right hand cup. Although he had successfully retrieved the object from a cup on two occasions, his behavior when the object was placed under another cup in a different location shows that his success on the first two occasions was not due to any true understanding of the spatial relationship between object and container. Both this and the earlier error reflect an incomplete understanding of the nature of objects. Even after both these errors have disappeared, the infant will continue to make very similar errors that stem from his developing concept of space, a concept intimately related to the concept of the object.

Spatial egocentrism

What does a one-year-old do when confronted with the situation in Figure 6–3? The baby does not seem to realize that the cups have changed their relative position as a consequence of his movement. He seems to think that things that were straight in front of him will stay straight in front of him, regardless of his movements, and looks for the object under the center cup. If one does the experiment by turning the table rather than the baby, one obtains similar results. The baby again seems to think that an object straight in front of him will stay straight in front of him, regardless of its movements. This view of space and objects in space has been labeled *egocentric*—the baby seems to imagine that he is the absolute referent for spatial position. In perceptual space all positions are given relative to the self. The developmental transition from perceptual space to *conceptual* space, at about 18–24 months, marks the end of perceptual egocentrism. Around this time the child realizes that his movements bear a lawful relation to the position of objects but that the spatial referents for that position, while including him, are not centered on him, as he previously believed.

The concept of size

Egocentrism of another sort seems to underlie the difficulties the young baby has with the concept of size. Babies are exceedingly skillful at gauging the size of objects relative to their own bodies, or body parts. A six-month-old can adjust his finger-thumb separation very precisely to the size of any object he can grasp. If two hands are required, he can adjust his inter-hand separation very exactly. Despite this, one-year-olds

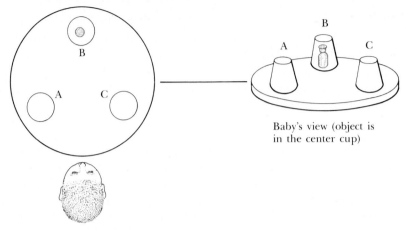

B

Baby's view (object is
in the center cup)

Object is put in cup B

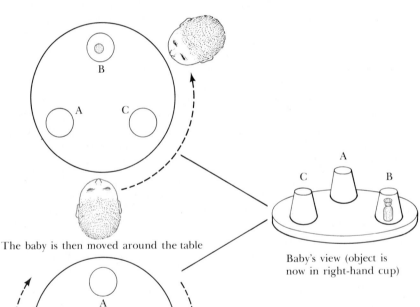

The baby is then moved around the table

Baby's view (object is
now in right-hand cup)

FIGURE 6–3
After an object is placed in the center
cup, the baby is moved around the
table or the table is turned around.
Either form of movement results in a
change of the relative position of the
object from center to right. The
baby, however, will still search under
the center cup, demonstrating the
egocentrism of his notions of space.

or the table is turned 120°

FIGURE 6-4
When presented with the cups
and shown how to make them into
a tower, one-year-olds can do no
better than construct pairs.

cannot perform the simple task shown in Figure 6–4. Although one-year-olds have no difficulty whatsoever in picking up the cups, showing that they can gauge the size of the cups relative to their bodies, they have no success at all in arranging the cups, indicating that they have no appreciation of their size relative to one another. A baby around one year of age simply makes pairs of big and little cups. With development, the baby's strategy shifts from an egocentric perceptual one to a conceptual one based on the relative sizes of the objects involved, thus enabling him to perform the task successfully. The age of attainment of success in this task is very variable, ranging from as young as 12 months to as old as 24 months.

The concept of weight

Similar processes operate in the development of the baby's concept of weight. Problems associated with the sensorimotor concept of weight were discussed in the last chapter. Babies begin by making no predictions at all about the weight of objects, and then move to a stage where the weight of any given object is assessed empirically. At this point the infant is capable only of assuming that the same object will weigh the same on repeated presentations. In the next stage in the development of the concept of weight (15–18 months) the baby is capable of predicting the weights of a series of objects whose visual dimensions covary with their weight. This is a truly significant intellectual achievement. It implies that the baby can make a deduction of the form, "That object was size 1 and weight A; this object is size 2, therefore it must weigh 2A." This discovery also implies that the baby can think about weight in terms that allow for multiplication and

126

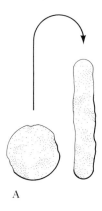

A   B

FIGURE 6–5
"Conservation" refers to our knowledge that some aspects of an object,
such as its weight, are unaffected by changes in the shape of the object (A).
The lack of such knowledge produces behavioral errors (B). Believing the
sausage to be heavier than the ball, the infant adjusts his arm tension
accordingly. Since the weight has of course not changed, this causes his
arm to fly up.

division—*twice* as heavy, *three* times as heavy.* The baby thus must have
some quantitative concepts, some concept of unit and combination of
units, i.e., number.

Further evidence of this comes in the terminal step in the development
of the sensorimotor concept of weight, namely *conservation of weight*
(Figure 6–5). Suppose we present a baby with a lump of some plastic
substance, such as Playdoh. He will have to discover the weight of it
empirically, but once this is done, the one-year-old will be able to
take, hold, and transport the object without error. He knows the weight
of that object. Suppose we then roll the ball out into a sausage shape and
hand it to the baby again. Will the baby realize that the weight of the
object is the same even though the shape of the object has changed? Or
will he think that since the shape is changed the weight has necessarily
changed as well? The evidence is that one-year-olds think that a shape
change implies a weight change. Typically, if a ball is changed into a
sausage shape, the babies think it has become heavier, and make the error
shown in Figure 6–5B. This stage of error-making is over by 18 months.
At 18 months, provided the baby can see the shape being changed, he

---

*The maximum variation used in the experiment was seven times as heavy.

shows in his behavior an awareness that the weight of an object is invariant under changes in its shape—he shows us that he has a concept of weight conservation. This represents a conceptual advance rather than a simple increase in motor skills.

The concept of volume

Drinking from a cup appears to be so simple and practical that it is hard to realize its developmental implications. It was Bruner (1968) who first pointed out the astonishing number of conceptual attainments that drinking from a cup must require.

One is discovery of the fact that the surface of the liquid in a container always remains parallel to the earth's surface. The 10-month-old does not seem to realize this. When babies of this age pick up a glass to drink, they ignore the amount of liquid in the glass and tip the glass more or less as if they were pouring jelly from a mould. The consequences are usually messy (Figure 6–6). We may assume that the baby thinks that the liquid stays in a fixed relation to the container regardless of the angle of the container. If so, the only way he can get the liquid out is to tip the container to some angle less than 90° to the force of gravity. This assumption at least makes

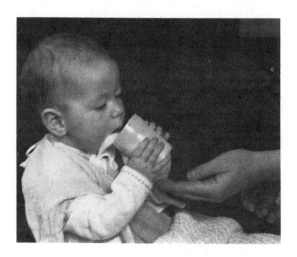

FIGURE 6–6

Lack of understanding of the relation between a liquid and its container can have messy results.

sense of the baby's rigid behavior—holding the cup at a constant angle of tip regardless of whether he is coping with a nearly full or a nearly empty glass. This unsuccessful behavior, while amusing for the baby, gives way around one year of age to skillful drinking behavior that takes into account the quantity in the glass and the constant parallel relation between the surface of the liquid and the earth's surface. The baby can then pick up a glass and tip it expertly so that a just drinkable amount passes from the glass to his mouth.

A second conceptual discovery involved in cup drinking is *conservation of volume* (Bower and Wishart, 1976). This means the baby becomes aware that a given quantity of liquid remains the same regardless of the shape of the container. To learn this is to learn that if a given quantity of liquid is poured from a wide container into a narrow one, the level of the liquid in the narrow container will be higher than in the wide one. What then will a baby do when he sees a given quantity of liquid poured from a wide transparent glass into a narrow opaque one? Of course, he cannot see the level of the liquid in the opaque glass. Can he predict the level from the transparent glass? Around one year of age babies seem to assume that the level will be the same in the narrow opaque glass and tip the glass to the angle that would be appropriate for that level—and spill liquid all over themselves (Figure 6–7). Sometime later, by about 15 months, they become very cautious in picking up the opaque glass, as if they know the level will be different but not just how different. Later yet, around 18 months,* they pick up the opaque glass and tip it to just the right angle, without trial or error, showing that they can predict the level in the new container without difficulty. Thus drinking, an everyday act for most children, relies on a substructure of conceptual knowledge that is truly astonishing.

The concept of causality

Infancy also sees the establishment of patterns of exploratory behavior that allow systematic induction or deduction of causal relations. There is less data on this than on the other sensorimotor concepts discussed so far. However, experiments by Papousek (1969) show clearly that systematic exploration is possible at an early age. The babies in these experiments, aged 3–4 months, could switch on a light with various patterns of head movements. Once they had caught on to the idea that a pattern of movements could switch on the light, they began to produce units of patterned movement (e.g., right-right-right, right-right-right, etc), check-

---

*These ages are only approximate and depend very heavily on what age the baby is introduced to cups and how much experience he is then given with them.

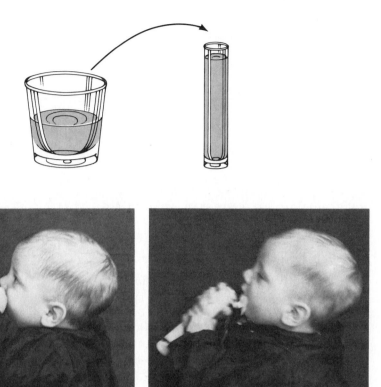

FIGURE 6-7

When liquid is tipped from one glass to another of a different shape, the quantity remains the same although it appears to be different. This *conservation of volume* is not understood by infants until around 18 months of age. The one-year-old baby in this picture was shown the contents of a wide transparent container being poured into a narrow opaque container. She assumed that the level in the narrow container would be the same as in the wide one. As a result, she misjudged the angle of tip necessary to drink successfully from the narrow one.

ing to see whether that pattern switched on the light, then systematically varying the pattern if it did not (Figure 6–8). This systematic exploration of causal possibilities is a form, albeit a primitive one, of experimentation. Here the baby is experimenting rather than merely being experimented on. Monnier (1977) has found similar results in an experiment in which it is easier to see systematic exploration. In her experiment nine-month-old babies had strings attached to both arms and legs. Movement of one limb caused movement of a mobile. The initial session usually found a high rate of activity in all four limbs, which rapidly narrowed to activity in the limb

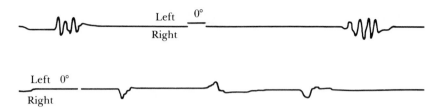

FIGURE 6–8

Polygraphic recording of head movements in a conditioning experiment in which babies could turn on a light by making various patterns of head movements. *Top:* Grouped triads of head turns to the right when every third consecutive turn to that side was reinforced (light turned on). *Bottom:* Alternating head turns to left and right when reinforcement was provided for this sequence. (Papousek, 1969.)

that could control movement of the mobile. When the effective limb was changed, the behavior became more systematic than it had been initially; the babies tended to try out each limb in succession to find which one was effective. This pattern became virtually standard on all subsequent changes.

These studies demonstrate a nascent form of experimentation, aimed at finding out just what causes a particular event to happen. There are also significant changes in the definition of cause during infancy. Briefly, young infants less than nine months old seem to define a causal relation purely on temporal terms: one event causes another if the second succeeds the first instantaneously and invariably. Spatial contiguity is not included in the early definition. This leads young infants into making certain rather peculiar errors. When an infant of six to nine months is shown a desirable object that is out of reach but placed on another object that is within reach, say a cloth, he will readily pull on the cloth to get the desirable object. If the desirable object is then placed *beside* rather than on the cloth, the baby will still pull on the cloth and will look disappointed at his failure to get the desirable object (Figure 6–9). The change in the spatial relation between the cloth and object does not inform babies of this age that the former causal connection between movement of the cloth and movement of the object no longer applies. After the age of nine months, this kind of error drops to a zero frequency.

Although the incorporation of spatial contiguity undoubtedly represents an advance in the infant's definition of causality, it can occasionally result in paradoxical declines in performance, as in a learning situation in which the reinforcing events are presented at some distance from the baby. For example, in the experimental setup in Figure 6–10 the baby's foot movements activate a photocell that causes a slide to appear on a screen several feet away. Babies working with a definition of causality that necessitates spatial contiguity between two events will be at a disadvantage because there is no obvious mechanical connection between the behavior and the reinforcement. Without knowledge of the working of photocells, they will be unable to understand how the two events could possibly be causally related. Unlike younger babies, who attend only to the temporal succession of the two events, nine-month-old babies find the task difficult (or even impossible) to learn. This difficulty does not necessarily index a decline in learning ability itself, as has been suggested, but can be explained by the infant's developing concept of causality.

This brief outline of the cognitive advances that are made during infancy may serve to justify the claim that the sensorimotor period is indeed one of the most active periods of cognitive development in the entire life span. Virtually every human intellectual capacity appears, in embryonic form at least, during infancy. We will look at the details of this developmental stage in the next chapter.

FIGURE 6–9

This baby is pulling on a cloth to get a toy that was placed out of reach on the cloth. However, when the toy was placed out of reach but *next* to the cloth, the baby still pulled on the cloth (right), fully expecting to be successful again. The use of the cloth to get an object out of reach is still "magic" to babies less than nine months old. They do not understand the spatial relations between the cloth and toy necessary for the pulling strategy to work.

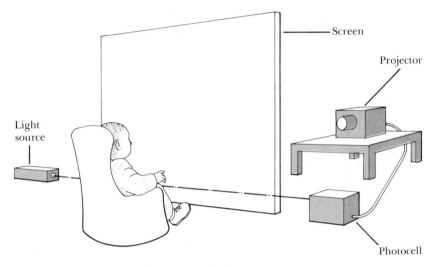

Light beam unbroken

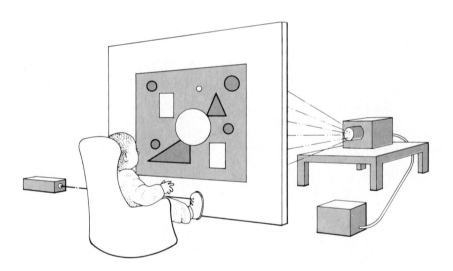

Light beam blocked by baby's boot

FIGURE *6–10*

If there is no obvious connection between an operant response and reinforcement, babies of around nine months of age will find such a learning task very difficult, apparently puzzled by the fact that their behavior appears to have some causal relation with an event at a distance. Here the baby turns on a slide projector every time his leg kicks up and blocks the light beam. Younger infants have little difficulty in learning how to control the appearance of the slide.

THE CONCRETE-OPERATIONAL STAGE

The next great stage of development in Piagetian theory is the period within which concrete operations are developed, a period that lasts from 18–24 months of age until 7–10 years of age. The beginning of this period is marked by the onset of language. Language has an importance in cognitive development that can hardly be overestimated. Its initial effects, however, seem to be disastrous; many of the attainments of infancy appear to be lost during the early years of this stage.

Conservation of weight and volume

Suppose we show a child two balls of plasticine of equal size. The child will agree that there is the same amount of plasticine in both balls. We then roll one ball out into a sausage form and ask the child if there is the same amount to play with as in the remaining ball. A child of four, five, six, or seven will say, no, that there is more in the sausage than in the ball because it is longer. He will also state that the sausage form is heavier. Or suppose we present the same child with two identical volumes of liquid in two identical wide glasses. Again, the child will agree that there is the same amount in both. We then pour the contents of one into a tall narrow glass. If the child is asked whether there is as much in the tall narrow glass as in the remaining wide glass, the answer, at least up to the age of seven, will be no, that there is more in the tall glass because it is higher. Basically, although the child appreciates conservation at the sensorimotor, preverbal level, he must reformulate the concept in order to cope with it in a communicational framework. This process of reformulation, as we shall see in Chapter 8, can also cause temporary reversals in behavioral competence with the concept. Such a child is called *pre-operational*.

Concepts of space

The child must also reformulate his concepts of space. Children between four and seven have the same egocentric concept of space at a verbal level as is seen in the motor behavior of one-year-olds. In the classic experiment demonstrating this, a child is seated before a three-dimensional model of a landscape. He is shown a series of pictures of the landscape and asked to pick out the picture that represents the view he sees. Children four to seven years old can choose correctly. The child is then asked to pick out the picture that represents the panorama seen by the experimenter sitting at right angles to the child. Without exception, children in the early phase of the concrete operations stage will choose the view seen by themselves, an egocentrism formally identical with that shown in the sensorimotor period.

The concept of size

Although infants from an early age demonstrate an appreciation of the size of objects relative to their own body, we have seen that it is not until toward the end of the sensorimotor period that they demonstrate an appreciation of the size of one object relative to another. Exactly the same problem reappears in the concrete-operational stage. When asked to arrange a set of 10 rods in a row from smallest to biggest, they fail completely, managing to form only a few pairs (Figure 6–11), the very strategy we see adopted and then replaced in infancy (see pp. 125, 172).

Class inclusion

The concrete-operational child shows several other conceptual difficulties. These may or may not also represent "declines" in conceptual ability from the sensorimotor period. We do not know because it seems impossible to present these problems without using language. One of these is the celebrated class-inclusion problem. If a child is shown a set of wooden beads, most of which are brown but with some white, and asked whether there are more brown beads or more wooden beads, he will answer that there are more brown beads. If the child is then asked if all the beads are

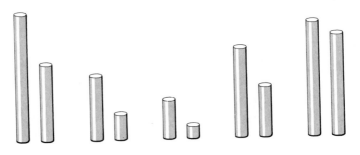

FIGURE 6–11
These rods could be arranged in a row from shortest to tallest. However, four- and five-year-olds can do no better than arrange them in pairs of "big and little."

wooden, he will reply that they are. If the original question is then asked again, "Are there more brown beads or more wooden beads?" back again will come the answer that there are more brown beads.

Advances of the concrete-operational stage

Since it seems that all of the laborious acquisitions of the sensorimotor period must be reconstructed in the concrete-operational stage, it is tempting to say that this period is one in which the child learns to report in words what he already knows but can only express in behavior. This would not be inaccurate, nor is it greatly at odds with Piaget's own conception of what happens in this period. Piaget himself points out that in the sensori-motor period the baby develops ways of behaving appropriately to certain stimulus presentations. During the concrete-operational period the child develops appropriate ways of talking about the same stimulus presentations. The fact of talking allows advances that are beyond anything that can be expressed in behavior. We have seen that by around 15–18 months the baby develops what seems like a concept of a unit. He can make anticipatory adjustments of grip and arm tension when grasping objects that are unfamiliar but ordered serially with reference to an object of known weight (pp. 113ff). The idea of a unit is fundamental to counting operations. The representation of units by numbers that can be added, subtracted, multiplied, and divided is essentially a verbal attainment. There is no way the number system can be expressed directly in behavior; it can be formalized and systematized only in words. The range of thought that can be verbally expressed far exceeds that which can be expressed in behavior. Along with this newfound ability to speak about the world goes the ability to solve a problem that is verbally presented, as long as the problem is also demonstrated in concrete ways. Thus, a child who has solved the liquid conservation problem described earlier can explain that the amount of liquid remains the same because nothing has been added and nothing taken away and that it only looks like more because the new container is narrower.

THE FORMAL-OPERATIONAL STAGE

The final step in development comes when the child can pose problems verbally as well as answer them verbally. It is no longer necessary for the elements of the problem to be presented concretely. This takes us into the development of formal thinking, the final and highest stage of development. Here again we find the reappearance (in formally equivalent form at least) of those very errors that have already been overcome twice by the child in the course of development—in the sensorimotor stage and again in the concrete-operational stage. Recall the initial inability of the baby to build a tower from a graduated set of cups, or the six-year-old's failure to arrange a series of sticks by size. Piaget cites the following problem that will trouble an 11- or 12-year-old. "Edith is fairer than Susan; Edith is darker than Lily; who is the darkest of the three?" Both the babies and the six-year-olds were only able to arrange pairs of contrasting units (big–little). According to Piaget, that is just what happens with the verbally posed problem. The children reason erroneously in the following way: "Edith and Susan are fair; Edith and Lily are dark; therefore Lily is the darkest." That is, they treat a series as a set of pairs rather than looking at relations within the entire series.

Nevertheless, the child's ability to formulate ideas independent of specific sensory inputs permits discoveries that go beyond anything that could be derived from particular experiences. This kind of advance is evident in the formulation of the concepts of weight, volume, density and specific gravity.

The concept of density

Weight and volume are always simultaneously present in experience. We never encounter an object that does not have both weight and volume. But there is no simple relationship between weight and volume. Large objects can be lighter than small objects depending on their density. The contrast between them suggests a dimension of density but does not specify it directly. A child is perfectly at home with weight and volume so long as they are correlated, but will be thrown if density variations are introduced. An eight-year-old can arrange three objects by weight so long as all three objects have the same density. However, if the densities vary, e.g., if the lightest and heaviest ones are made of wood and the middle one of lead, the eight-year-old will be unable to arrange the objects by weight, even though he is allowed to feel them and compare their weights directly. Even more puzzling to the child are *changes* in density. Suppose we have a child who understands the concept of conservation for weight, e.g., that a ball of plasticine transformed into a sausage shape does not change in weight since the increased length of the sausage shape is compensated for by its decreased width. This (European) child is shown popcorn for the first time. We invite him to check the weight of unpopped corn. One batch is then popped. What he sees is an enormous change in volume. This is not a case of a change in one dimension compensated for by a change in another— the popped corn grows in all dimensions. The transformation is totally mysterious to a child limited to the information coming through his senses. Surely the popped corn should weigh more? Children do in fact predict that the popped corn will weigh more. When shown that it does not, they become totally confused and may end up maintaining that the popped corn is lighter, even though it is neither lighter nor heavier. Children do of course solve this problem eventually, once they understand the concept of density. An object is made of an infinite number of tiny particles. The density of the object is a function of how close together these particles are. Changes in density are a function of changes in the distribution of the particles. Children thus arrive at a primitive version of the atomic hypothesis in order to make sense of the relation between weight and volume. Neither the concept of density nor the atomic hypothesis are given directly through the senses. Entry into the formal-operational stage thus finally frees the mind from the particularity of sensorimotor experience.

Development of experimental skills

The experimental abilities that were immanent in the sensorimotor period now become more refined and more frequently applied. A simple example is the ability to predict whether an object will float or not. An object will float if it is less dense than water. The set of operations that formal-operational children use to establish this includes establishing the volume of an object and then comparing its weight with that of an equivalent volume of water. Objects that are less heavy than the volume of water will float. The most notable feature of formal-operational children is their ability to juggle descriptive concepts that are not given directly in experience. To determine whether or not an object will float, they first compare the weights of equivalent volumes, thereby establishing a scale of density. They then compare the weight of a given volume of some substance with an equivalent volume of water, thereby establishing the relative density of the substance and water, the information required to predict whether or not an object will float.

DISTINCTIVE CHARACTERISTICS
OF PIAGETIAN THEORY

We will discuss the three major stages of intellectual development in greater detail in succeeding chapters. By this point, however, the essence of Piagetian theory should be clear. It is Piaget's interest in general strategies of intelligence rather than discrete items of knowledge that makes his approach unique. A great deal of effort has been spent on theoretically defining the characteristic strategies of each of the three stages. A substantial portion of any book by Piaget consists of descriptions of the general intellectual structures that underlie specific problem solutions. The most powerful structures, of course, are those that operate at the formal level. By way of example, let us consider a very simple task.

Suppose a child is presented with two switches, one pink and one quince, that can be pushed or pulled. The child is told that some action or sequence of actions on the switches will produce candy. How should he go about finding out how to get candy? Let the term p = pulling the pink switch and $\bar{p}$ = pushing the pink switch; likewise q = pulling the quince switch and $\bar{q}$ = pushing the quince switch. One possibility is that any single action, i.e., pushing or pulling either of the switches, will produce the candy. This can be written as $p \vee q \vee \bar{p} \vee \bar{q}$, where $\vee$ = or. Another is that only one of the switches, say the pink one, will produce the candy. We would write this possibility as $(p \vee \bar{p}) \sim (q \vee \bar{q})$, where $\sim$ = not. On the other hand, any sequence of the two switches might be sufficient:

p & q, or

p & $\bar{q}$, or

$\bar{p}$ & q, or

$\bar{p}$ & $\bar{q}$.

Or the sequence of actions might be more restrictive, as in the following.

$(p$ & $q) \vee (p$ & $\bar{q})$, or

$(p$ & $q) \vee (\bar{p}$ & $q)$, or

$(p$ & $q) \vee (\bar{p}$ & $\bar{q})$, or

$(p$ & $\bar{q}) \vee (\bar{p}$ & $q)$, or

$(p$ & $\bar{q}) \vee (\bar{p}$ & $\bar{q})$, or

$(\bar{p}$ & $q) \vee (\bar{p}$ & $\bar{q})$, or

$(p$ & $q) \vee (p$ & $\bar{q}) \vee (\bar{p}$ & $q)$, i.e., any sequence except $\bar{p}$ & $\bar{q}$, or

$(p$ & $q) \vee (p$ & $\bar{q}) \vee (\bar{p}$ & $\bar{q})$, i.e., any sequence except $\bar{p}$ & q, or

$(p$ & $\bar{q}) \vee (\bar{p}$ & $q) \vee (\bar{p}$ & $\bar{q})$, i.e., any sequence except p & q.

Finally *any* pair of operations might be effective:

$(p$ & $q) \vee (p$ & $\bar{q}) \vee (\bar{p}$ & $\bar{q}) \vee (\bar{p}$ & $q)$.

The ability to formulate all of these possibilities and test them is one of the characteristics of the formal-operational stage. Such a statement would seem to imply that younger children cannot formulate all possible hypotheses. Strictly speaking, this is true. The experiments of Papousek (1969) and Monnier (1977) testify, however, to a similar sort of behavior in infancy, the only major difference being the number of hypotheses that will be tested. There seems to be no real qualitative difference between hypothesis-formation in the two periods.

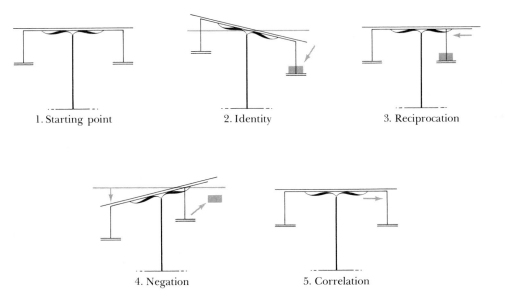

1. Starting point   2. Identity   3. Reciprocation

4. Negation   5. Correlation

FIGURE *6–12*

This simple task exemplifies the four basic operations of the formal-operational
stage and their interrelation. These four operations are known as identity,
reciprocation, negation, and correlation—the IRNC group. A stable system, the
balance pans, is perturbed by the *identity* operation. It can be brought back to
equilibrium by various operations. *Reciprocation:* By bringing the weighted pan
closer to balance point we can restore the equilibrium between the arms.
Negation: We could cancel the original operation by removing the weight. If we
negate after reciprocating, we produce a new perturbation that can be corrected
by restoring the pan to its original position; this operation is known as *correlation*.
It is always possible to restore equilibrium using some combination of these
operations. From this it can be seen that $I + N = 0$, i.e., the situation is restored
to its original equilibrium; and that $I + R + N + C = 0$, i.e., the four operations
combine to make a stable, self-canceling structure. The operations are understood
by the child when he can cancel any perturbation of a system.

More interesting than the exhaustive iterative ability of formal thinkers
is the set of general operations they have at their command. (The power or
generality of these operations will become clearer in Chapter 9, where they
are discussed more fully.) The four basic intellectual operations of the
formal-operational stage are illustrated in Figure 6–12 in the context of a
simple problem involving two pans on a balance arm. The operations
are identity, negation, reciprocation, and correlation, the INRC group.
These operations are also in the repertory of children at the end of the
sensorimotor period (Figure 6–13), a paradox I hope succeeding chapters
will illuminate.

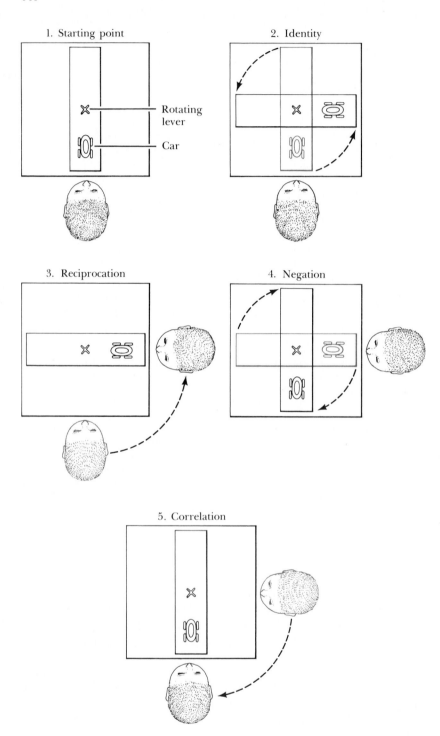

1. Starting point

Rotating lever

Car

2. Identity

3. Reciprocation

4. Negation

5. Correlation

REPETITION AND SEQUENCE
IN COGNITIVE DEVELOPMENT

Each developmental stage represents an advance over the preceding one. At the same time, however, it is almost impossible not to note the repetitive nature of development. Every intellectual capacity, even those characteristic of the most advanced cognitive development, appears in a simplified form in the sensorimotor period. Furthermore, development of these capacities seems to depend very intimately on complete development in the sensorimotor period. An example of this is the development of concepts of space. The normal child develops concepts of space during the sensorimotor stage; these concepts are then reconstructed during the concrete- and formal-operational stages. If for some reason, such as accidental blinding, the child fails to complete the sensorimotor development of his concepts of space, apparently no amount of intervention can make him able to develop the concrete- or formal-operational concepts of space (Hatwell, 1966). On the other hand, if sensorimotor development of the concepts are complete before blinding takes place, the concrete- and formal-operational concepts will develop without any special effort. At one extreme this would imply that sensorimotor development is both necessary *and sufficient* for subsequent intellectual development. Although this is an extreme claim, it is one that we must bear in mind in the following chapters.

Even if we cannot accept this extreme claim, we are still forced to accept the strong probability that development in the sensorimotor period contains, in kernel form, the groundplan for a great deal of subsequent development, even if it does not specify the whole of subsequent development. If this is in fact the case, the question to bear in mind is just what is added to the capacities for thought after the sensorimotor period. An

---

FIGURE *6–13 (Opposite)*

This task, which is within the capacities of two-year-olds, involves the same operations as those shown in Figure 6–12. The child is required to retrieve a toy that is moved out of his reach by the experimenter in the way shown (the *identity* operation). The child can cancel the effect of that operation by the *reciprocating* operation—in this case, by walking round the table to the new position of the toy. The original operation can also be *negated*, by returning the toy to its original starting position. If reciprocation and negation are combined, as shown here, the child must then use the operation of *correlation* to get the toy, i.e., he must walk back round the table to his original starting point. The child's ability to cancel the experimenter's perturbations involves the same comprehension as that shown in Figure 6–12. It can be seen again that $I + N = 0$, i.e., the original circumstances are restored (the child can reach the object), and that $I + R + N + C = 0$, i.e., the four operations combine to make a stable, self-canceling structure.

obvious answer is of course language, and language is certainly a critical factor in subsequent development, as we shall see. But what exactly is it that language adds to our capabilities? One extreme answer is nothing, that language simply reflects the attainments of sensorimotor development (Piaget, 1967a). The other extreme holds that it is language that allows us to represent the essence of particular sensorimotor events in abstract terms that have general applicability (Bruner, Olver, Greenfield, *et al.*, 1966).

My own answer lies closer to Piaget's position rather than Bruner's. Unlike either of these theorists, however, I believe that babies *begin* life as very abstract thinkers. In the sensorimotor period, prior to the acquisition of language, this abstract thought is expressed in *behavioral responses* to specific stimulus situations. Later, at the concrete-operational stage, it is expressed through language in representations of *possible responses* to specific stimulus situations. Finally, it becomes expressed in representations of *possible stimulus situations.* Just as the child in the concrete-operational stage can think about possible actions without doing them, the child in the formal-operational stage can think about possible stimulus situations without having to experience them.

THE UNITS OF THOUGHT
AT THE VARIOUS STAGES

Discussions of the role of language and the issue of the generality of thought are discussions about the "units" or elements the child thinks in or with. Despite a distaste for such notions—the result of being trained in American behaviorism—I do think that they are essential if one is to make sense of the overall progress of cognitive development throughout childhood. Accordingly, in succeeding chapters we will pay attention to the units of thought characteristic of the various phases of development.

Finally, we must of course concern ourselves with the great debate—the relative roles of maturation and experience in cognitive development. Here we will find, for the first time in this book, evidence of irreversible, directional processes in development. The development of spatial concepts in the blind, mentioned above, is an instance of this. The blind child who has failed to complete his sensorimotor concepts of space before being struck by blindness is not simply stuck with incomplete sensorimotor concepts. Rather, he develops a completely different concept of space from that of the sighted child, a concept based on temporal ordering. In some situations a temporal concept of space may even be more useful than the usual, visually determined concepts (Hatwell, 1966). The blind child thus moves down a completely *different* pathway of development. His development has not been arrested, only redirected. Theories of development based on the idea that the environment acts only as an accelerator or brake on the expression of genetic information cannot cope with redirection of development.

7

Cognitive
Development
in Infancy

The subject of this chapter is the development of intelligence in the first
18–24 months of life, or in Piagetian terms the development of sensorimotor intelligence. As we noted in the last chapter, the first two years are
one of the busiest periods of development; the total range of changes in
capacity that occur in this time is very large indeed. Piaget's three classic
books on this period brought a wealth of new insights into development in
infancy and have stimulated thousands of research papers.* It would
obviously be impossible to do justice in a book of this sort to the whole
body of knowledge that has accumulated about intelligence in infancy.
Rather than attempting such a broad summary, I shall concentrate on a
few topics that illustrate the basic processes in development.

DEVELOPMENT OF
THE OBJECT CONCEPT

The central developmental accomplishment that I wish to focus on is
development of the object concept (Bower, 1971). Adults have a great deal
of knowledge about objects. We know that objects continue to exist when
we do not see them. We know that every object in the world is unique but

---

* *The Origins of Intelligence* (original French edition 1936; English edition 1954); *The
Construction of Reality in the Child* (original French 1937; English 1955); and *Play, Dreams,
and Imitation* (original French 1946; English 1951).

that some objects look so much alike as to appear identical. We know that some objects can change drastically in appearance and yet still be the same object. We know that nonliving objects cannot change their characteristics unless some outside agency changes them. We also know about the spatial relations between objects, that one object can be on, in, behind, or underneath another. This knowledge is not completely available to the baby until the very end of infancy. In Chapter 4 we emphasized the amount of information available to the newborn child; we must now emphasize the sheer amount of information still to be acquired. In that chapter we also emphasized the efficiency of the newborn's object perception; we did not, however, point up the limited range of circumstances in which that perceptual system will in fact be used to pick up information about objects. Here, as in the discussion on motor skill, we are talking about conceptual control over an established behavior. As we shall see, there are many situations in which an object seems to become functionally invisible to a young baby, even though it is still "there," still in sight and still emitting stimulation. A great deal of research on the object concept has, however, neglected to take account of such behavior and has focused only on what the baby does and does not do when an object in fact goes "out of sight."

Out of sight, out of mind?

Many psychologists equate the object concept with the ability to locate objects that have gone out of sight. It is commonly said that objects *exist* for the baby only so long as he can see them. This view underestimates the complexities of the object concept and overestimates the importance of the visibility of objects in the behavior of young infants. Consider one of the standard object permanence tests. A six-month-old baby is shown an attractive toy, which is covered by a cup when he reaches out to take it. The baby will then stop reaching, withdraw his hand, and make no further attempt to retrieve the toy. He acts in general as if the toy no longer existed (Figure 7–1). Behavior of this kind has led to the conclusion that out of sight means out of mind for the young baby. Suppose though that instead of covering the toy with a cup we place it on top of some other object. What happens then? The baby responds exactly as he did when the toy was inside the cup: he arrests his reach, withdraws his hand, and makes no further attempt to retrieve the toy (Piaget, 1955). He acts as if the toy no longer existed, even though it is still completely visible (Figure 7–2). Two different situations—one involving disappearance, the other not—lead to exactly the same termination of behavior. If the behavior in *both* cases is due to the toy being "out of mind," this surely cannot be because the toy is "out of sight." "Out of sight" by itself need not trouble the baby at all.

Baby sees toy.

As baby starts to reach for the toy it is covered by a cup.

FIGURE *7–1*

An object-permanence test. In such tests young babies (around six months) will typically fail to search for the hidden object, acting as if it no longer existed. Such behavior clearly demonstrates the inadequacies of their understanding of objects.

Baby is baffled and makes no attempt to retrieve the toy by removing the cup.

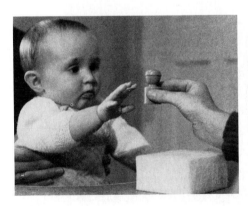

FIGURE *7–2*

Young babies have difficulty understanding the spatial relationship "on." If an object is placed on a platform they are unlikely to succeed in recovering the object, even if they are already in mid-reach.

Suppose that we show a toy to a baby but switch off all the lights in the room before the baby can reach out to take it (Bower and Wishart, 1972). The toy is then undoubtedly "out of sight" physically. Nonetheless, babies as young as 16 weeks can reach out and take the toy, even after a wait of 90 seconds (Figure 7–3). It seems clear then that the lack of visibility of an object cannot be a factor in the infant's failure to reach for an object in the standard object-permanence test.

The results described above could be interpreted as showing that the baby's real problem is one of motor skill, and not conceptual at all. It may be that the baby simply doesn't have the motor skill to retrieve an object from inside or on top of another. This consideration has led to attempts to find other behaviors to index the status of the baby's knowledge of objects, behaviors that would not require the same order of skill as the manual-search tasks described above. The simplest possible response one can ask of a baby is a startle, and various measures of startle have been used. In one study babies were first shown an object; a screen then moved in to hide the object and then moved off again, either revealing the object or revealing an empty space where the object had been (Figure 7–4). If babies think that an object no longer exists when it is no longer visible,

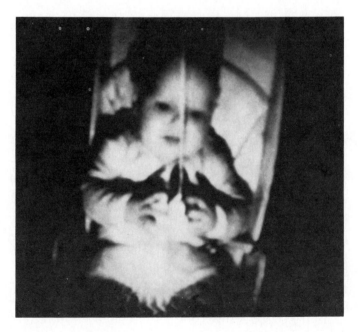

FIGURE 7–3
This infrared photo shows a 16-week-old baby reaching in the dark for an object he had seen earlier in the light.

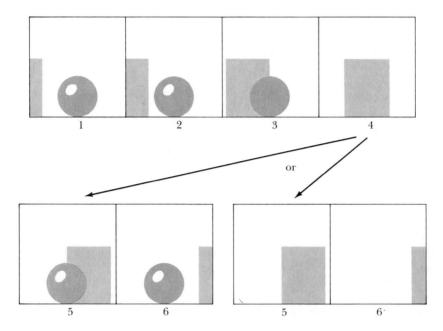

FIGURE 7-4

Even infants as young as four weeks found the sequence of events ending in disappearance (right) more surprising than reappearance (left). This indicates a very early understanding of the fact that an object still exists even though it is out of sight.

they should be more surprised to see the screen reveal an object than to see it reveal nothing. If, on the other hand, they know perfectly well that the object is still there, though out of sight behind the screen, they should be more surprised if the screen moves on to reveal nothing. In fact, disappearance proved to be much more startling than reappearance, even in babies as young as four weeks, indicating that even at four weeks babies know that an object still exists when it is out of sight behind a screen (Figure 7-5).

The problem of spatial relations

The above result seems to imply that the real problem the older babies have with the standard manual tests of object permanence is indeed one of motor skills. Other experiments, however, compel us to adopt a more complicated explanation of the babies' difficulties. Suppose we show a baby an object moving on a straight path from left to right. Babies from about 12 weeks of age are able to keep their eyes on the object all along its

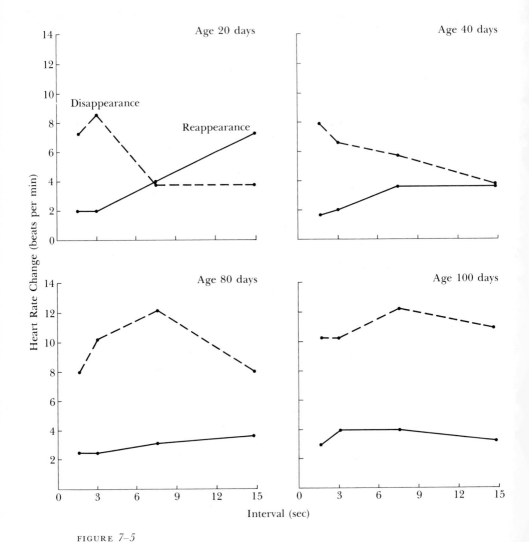

FIGURE 7–5

Changes in heart rate in infants reveal the degree of surprise at the reappearance or disappearance of an object after it has been covered by a moving screen for various intervals. Regardless of age, disappearance is much more startling than reappearance. Even the youngest infants are surprised by failure of the object to reappear when the interval is brief. However, if the time of occlusion is increased to 15 seconds, they seem to forget about the object and show surprise at its reappearance. (From "The Object in the World of the Infant" by T. G. R. Bower. Copyright © 1971 Scientific American, Inc. All rights reserved.)

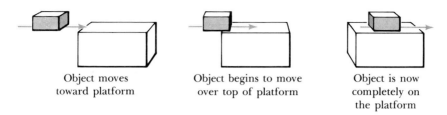

Object moves toward platform	Object begins to move over top of platform	Object is now completely on the platform

FIGURE 7–6

Although very young babies are able to track an object moving in open space, their tracking will be disrupted if the object passes over a platform.

path. Now let us put a platform in the middle of the path so that the moving object will move across the· top of the stationary platform (Figure 7–6). In this situation the baby will stop tracking the object as soon as it reaches the platform. During the time the object is over the platform, the baby's attention may remain fixed on the left side of the platform, or he may look back at the starting point of the path, as if searching for the object there. When the object moves off the right side of the platform, the baby may or may not reestablish eye contact with it. In any event, the baby's ability to track a moving object smoothly becomes disrupted by the introduction of this second object. Why? We might say that the platform simply distracts the baby, pulling his attention away from the moving object. While this explanation is plausible, it loses force if we observe the baby's tracking ability when a moving object goes behind a screen. The same babies who are so disrupted by the platform will readily track past the screen and smoothly establish eye contact with the moving object as it emerges (Figure 7–7). Surely the screen should be more disruptive than the platform if simple visual distraction were the problem. Why then does the platform disrupt smooth tracking? It would appear that for the young baby something is an object to be looked at or picked up only when it has no boundaries in common with any other object. For the baby an object is something with a top and bottom, a front and back, and a left and right. If it loses any one of these bounds, if it is placed on another object for example, it ceases to exist for the baby as a separate object and becomes *functionally* invisible, even though clearly in view. The baby's behavior when an object is placed on a platform illustrates this well (see Figure 7–2). If the baby reaches at all in this situation, his grasping will be directed at the "platform-and-object," as if these were a single object (Piaget, 1955; Bresson *et al.*, 1977). He does not realize that the object still exists as a separate object, and indeed will look astounded if the object falls off the platform during his reaching attempts.

This explanation may seem unnecessarily simpleminded. Nevertheless, adults can make similar errors. We are often unable to tell whether an

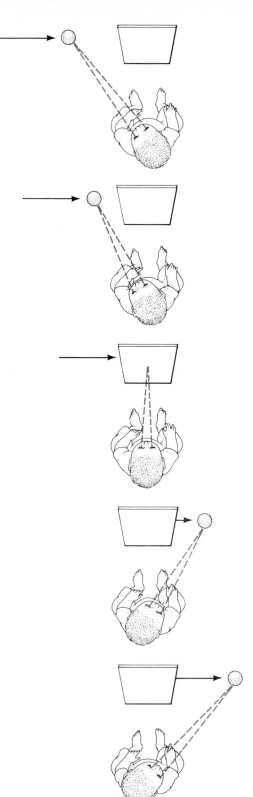

FIGURE 7–7

Babies have no difficulty
tracking an object moving in a
straight path behind a screen.

object represents a single thing or an amalgamation of several smaller things (Figure 7–8). However, if we see one object move on top of another, we then know that the resultant object is made up of two objects. The infant seemingly does not. In a sequence like that shown in Figure 7–6, the infant does not coordinate the information available in the various time frames; the information in frames 1 and 2 is not used to decode frame 3. The obvious question is why not?

Although several answers have been proposed, the correct answer is not obvious and is indeed very complicated. Basically, it seems that babies less than five months old do not realize that an object *can* move from one place to another. When such a baby sees an object in one place, A, which then moves to another place, B, and then back to A, he thinks he is dealing with four objects: "the object at A," "the object at B," "the object moving from A to B," and "the object moving from B to A." Evidence in support of this interpretation was introduced in Chapter 6 (pp. 120ff). When the movement sequence center-right-center was repeated a number of times, the infant looked for the object at the right at the time when he would normally expect to see it there, even if the object was still at the center (see Figure 6–1). What if instead of remaining in the center the object moves off in a completely new direction, to the left? The infant will again look to the right, at the time when he expects to see the object there, and will ignore its perfectly visible displacement to the left. This erroneous strategy of looking for an object in its usual position is known as the *place error*. Figure 7–9 shows another experimental setup in which babies younger than five months do not coordinate the successive appearances of an object. In particular, it seems that they do not coordinate a stationary object with itself in motion, nor the opposite, a moving object with itself when stationary. Babies of this age can efficiently track an object if it is in *continuous* motion. However, if the object stops midway through a trajectory, they will stop with the object momentarily but then continue to track along the arc the object was moving on, as if searching for the moving object. They do not seem to realize that the stationary object *is* the object

FIGURE 7–8

An adult shown the objects on the left of each pair is not able to tell that they are composed of the objects shown on the right.

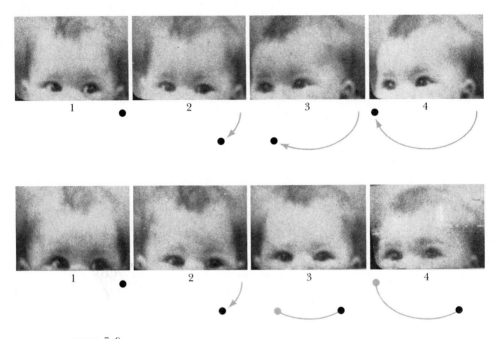

FIGURE 7–9

The upper sequence of photographs is from a videotape of behaviour in response to continuous arc movement; the lower sequence shows behavior in response to a trial in which the object stopped in mid-arc. In the latter, the standard movement error test, the infant continues to track after the object has stopped. (After Bower and Paterson, 1973.)

they had previously been tracking—that only one object is involved. This error is known as the *movement error*.

These two errors decline to a very low frequency by the age of five months, indicating that babies of that age have succeeded in realizing that a single object can move from place to place and, though seen in different places, still be the same object. Prior to that point it would appear that babies think that the same object seen in different places is in fact a series of different objects. Some dramatic evidence in favor of this hypothesis has been gathered from experiments in which the baby is presented with multiple images of a truly unique object, his own mother. A baby has only one mother and yet he sees her in many different places. Does the baby think he has many mothers? It would appear that he does. A simple optical device allows one to present the baby with three or more identical images of his mother, all looking at him, all talking and gesturing simultaneously (Figure 7–10). Babies below five months are quite delighted by this kind of presentation, interacting quite happily with each "mother" in turn. Older babies, by contrast, become quite disturbed and may be reduced to tears by the sight of three "mothers" (Bower, 1974a).

If babies of less than five months think that the same object seen in different places is in fact a series of different objects, what happens if they are shown different objects in the same place? They appear to believe that they are all the same object. Although the evidence for this is not overwhelming, it is nevertheless suggestive. Suppose a baby is shown a transformation like that in Figure 7–11. An adult might reason: "It *looks* as if the cup has changed into a vase, but I know that's impossible. The cup must still be somewhere." Babies, however, seem to lack the "but." They do not look for the original object, and may even appear somewhat surprised if it reappears in a different place. Not until after five months of age does the baby look around, as if trying to locate the original object.

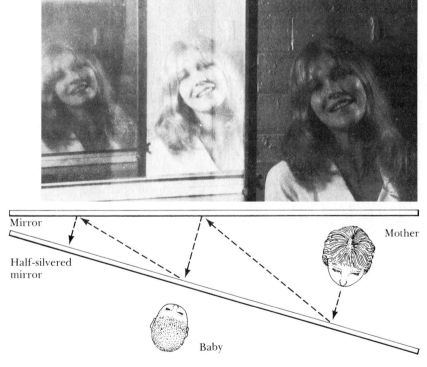

FIGURE 7–10

Babies less than five months old do not find the appearance of multiple mothers in the least disturbing and will interact with each one in turn. With increasing understanding of object identity, the simultaneous presentation of three mothers becomes most disconcerting to babies.

FIGURE *7–11*
Young babies accept a gradual visual transformation as possible and do not look for the original object as long as the transformation occurs in exactly the same place. The transformation is achieved by using a half-silvered mirror, as in Figure 7–12. The light illuminating one object is gradually dimmed as the light illuminating the other is increased.

The evidence is more convincing that young babies think that all objects on the same path of movement are the same object (Bower, Broughton, and Moore, 1971). If a baby of less than five months sees a moving object suddenly transformed in mid-track, he will continue to track the new (transformed) object even if it differs in every possible feature from the original object (Figure 7–12). The situation is quite different if only the characteristics of the *movement* change, if for example there is an abrupt deceleration or acceleration. Babies as young as 12 weeks will then look back and forth from the moving object to the place where the object would have been had the movement not changed. This shows that a lack of appropriate sensorimotor skills is not the explanation for the babies' failure to search when the visual features change. Rather, it seems that a moving object is identified only in terms of its particular speed and path of movement; its other features are unimportant.

If it is indeed the case that babies believe that only one object can be in one place, we have a ready explanation of why they act as if an object ceases to exist when it goes inside another object, as in Figure 7–1. The container is a bounded volume in space, occupying a particular place. The contained object is in the same place. If babies in fact believe that only one object can be in one place, then the contained object has simply gone out of existence. There is no place for it to exist since the place where it was is now occupied by the container. The idea that the two objects can be in the same place is completely incomprehensible to a baby struggling to interpret the world with the rules we have attributed to him.

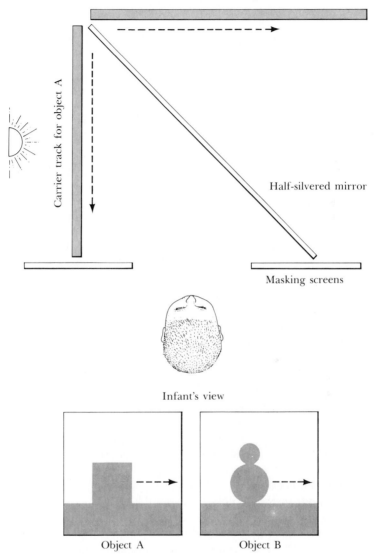

FIGURE 7–12

Babies less than five months old are not troubled by the instantaneous visual transformation of a moving object and will continue to track its path. In this experimental set up the baby's visual field is restricted to the mirror. Both objects move at the same speed and whichever object is illuminated will appear in the mirror. Thus, by switching illumination from one object to another, the image in the mirror is instantaneously transformed; the small object appears to change into a larger, completely different object on the same path of movement.

TABLE 7–1

The object concept before and after five months of age.

PRIOR TO 5 MONTHS	AFTER 5 MONTHS
An object is a bounded volume of space in a particular place.	An object is a bounded volume of space that can move from place to place.
An object is a bounded volume of space in motion.	
Two objects cannot be in the same place.	Two objects cannot be seen in the same place *simultaneously*.
Objects in the same place are one and the same object.	
Identical objects seen in different places are different objects.	Identical objects seen in different places *simultaneously* are different objects.

Table 7–1 summarizes the changes in the object concept that take place at around five months of age. The first is the realization that an object can move from place to place along trajectories and still remain the same object. This change involves the coordination of the infant's two ways of identifying objects—objects as "movements" and objects as "places"—so that neither is used for identification by itself. However, this new concept does not yet incorporate anything about the spatial relations objects can have to one another. The baby will still be puzzled when one object is placed *on* or *inside* another. Indeed, there is evidence that babies will also be flummoxed if an object is placed in *front* of or *behind* another in such a way that it loses a boundary by sharing it with the other object (Figure 7–13). It seems clear that even at six months babies still do not know how to obtain an object that is in, on, in front of, or behind another, i.e., if it shares a boundary with that other object (Wishart and Bower, 1977a; Neilson, 1978; de Schonen and Bower, 1978).

A well-established sequence of tasks can be used to demonstrate the baby's growing comprehension of the possible spatial relations between objects (Piaget, 1955; Bower, 1974a; Uzgiris and Hunt, 1975). Success with a single cup or platform does not initially indicate complete comprehension. The baby who succeeds in retrieving a toy placed under a cup or on top of a platform seems to have acquired a magical behavioral rule of the form, "To find an object that has been mysteriously amalgamated with a second object, go to the second object." Success in this task does not entail any understanding of the spatial relations involved. If the baby is faced with two cups, or two platforms, and a toy is consistently "hidden" in the same cup or on the same platform, the baby very quickly seems to learn the rule "To get the toy, go to *that* object." If, however, the toy is then put on the second platform or in the second cup, the baby will still go to the first platform or cup, and look disappointed that he does not get the toy. The behavior on this catch trial clearly demonstrates the inadequacies of the baby's comprehension of the spatial relations between the objects in this task (see Figure 6–2, p. 122).

In the stage of development of the object concept we are discussing, the baby characteristically searches for a "vanished" object where he last found it, a repetition of the erroneous strategy shown by younger babies in visual search tasks. This strategy eventually disappears, at least in these particular test situations. The change here is not likely to be due to reinforcement of a more efficient behavior and extinction of the erroneous strategy. The earlier strategy, although erroneous in these test situations,

An object loses all of its boundaries if placed *in* another object.

It loses a boundary when placed *on* another object.

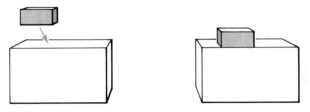

It may or may not lose a boundary when placed *in front of* (or *behind*) another object.

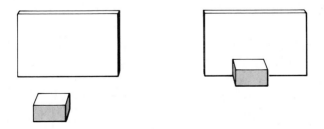

FIGURE 7–13
Babies are puzzled when two objects are placed together such that one loses some or all of its boundaries.

is too useful to be extinguished. In the real world it makes sense to look for things where they have previously been found, particularly if one has a tidy mother. Rather, what occurs is probably a differentiation and refinement of the original discovery. The baby learns a rule of the form, "An object that has vanished from its established location still exists somewhere." The baby learns in detail that one object can be on, in, or behind another and still be obtainable.

The last stage of refinement of the object concept, beginning around 12 months, involves a change in the child's concepts of spatial relations themselves. In the previous chapter we discussed how the infant shifts from an egocentric definition of spatial positions to a relativistic one. This is not a single-step process. The baby initially seems to define the location of objects egocentrically (Wishart and Bower, 1977a). If he is moved, or if objects are moved, the baby does not comprehend the change in the spatial relations between himself and the objects (see Figure 6–3, p. 124). He does not understand, for example, that an object that was on his left is now on his right. In a way the baby is repeating the error he made earlier, at around 10 months of age, when he failed to realize that a single object placed under one and then another cup has changed position (see Figure 6–2). By 12 months the baby is long past this single object error; he is no longer absolutely egocentric. He is capable of appreciating simple relational changes like that shown in Figure 7–14, where the objects change position relative to his body but not relative to each other. The child here defines "on the right" in terms of the array rather than in terms of absolute position relative to himself. This emerging relativism will not help him with the kind of change of position shown in Figure 6–3, where in addition to a change of position relative to his own body, the objects appear to change position relative to each other. Labeling an object as

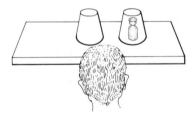 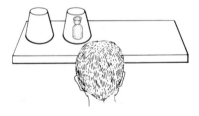

Baby sees a toy being hidden in the cup on his right.

Both cups are moved left so that the cup with the toy is to the left of the baby but still to the right of the other cup.

FIGURE 7–14
This change in position does not present a problem to the infant.

"the one on the right of the array" will not help if the spatial relations within the array are altered, as they are by the movements we are discussing. For the child to solve a problem like this he must know that spatial relations *between objects* are also changed by any change in his *own* relation to the objects. In other words, he must reinsert *himself* into the definition of spatial relations. He must realize that "in the middle" refers to his momentary perspective, and is not a property of an object. The child must realize that an object is not "in the middle" in the same way as it is "red."

How does he do this? The difference between "red" and "in the middle" may be involved. We have seen that, around six months, the baby begins to define objects in terms of their features, e.g., color and size, rather than their absolute position. As the child moves about the world he must notice that some objects change their spatial labels as he moves—the red one that was "in the middle" is now "on the left." Given that the baby's limited understanding of space at this point leads him to distrust spatial labels, he should tend to rely on the features of an object. When, however, there are no distinguishing physical features (as in Figure 6–3), he must rely on spatial relations as a way of identifying objects. The latter situation must occur often enough in the real world to keep spatial labels somewhere near the forefront of the child's mind, where they will often conflict with labels based on physical features. This kind of conflict could impel the child to change his definitions of spatial labels from egocentric to relativistic ones.

DETERMINANTS OF DEVELOPMENT OF THE OBJECT CONCEPT

How does this sequence in the development of the object concept come about? Is it wholly genetically determined, with variations in rate perhaps due to environmental variation? Or is the sequence environmentally determined, with rate variations perhaps due to genetic differences? Or is it that the pattern of development here escapes this boring pair of extreme alternatives? It is certainly a very regular sequence, one that is relatively imperturbable by even quite extreme environmental variations, as we shall see below. The standard and obvious attempts to unravel genetic factors have been made. It has been shown that identical twins develop more in step than do nonidentical twins (Wilson, 1972). It has also been found that specific practice on any part of the sequence does not necessarily speed up development of either the particular problem being practiced or the later stages of the object concept (Bower and Paterson, 1972). Piaget himself has often said that the sequence is not a result of learning, from which statement many have understood him to imply that the sequence must result from maturation. This is a misunderstanding. Although, as we shall see, the sequence cannot be explained by learning theory, neither can it be attributed to maturational processes alone. Instead, it is due to organism-environment interactions of a specific and subtle kind. If one capitalizes on these interactions, one can produce quite drastic accelerations of development, without changing the sequence of development.

Reinforcement versus conflict in the development of the object concept

Let us consider one specific step in development where these issues come into sharp focus. Above we described how young infants, less than 20 weeks old, make two specific errors in tracking tasks. One of these, the place error, consists in looking for an object where it has previously been seen, while ignoring its perfectly visible current position. The other, the movement error, consists in searching for an object along its projected path of movement after it has stopped, with only momentary attention being given to the perfectly visible object. Both errors decline to virtually zero frequency by the age of 20 weeks. A learning theory might explain the decline in the movement error by arguing that since (1) the infants do stop when the moving object stops; and (2) they are reinforced by the (presumably interesting) sight of the stationary object when they do stop; and (3) they are not reinforced for continued tracking (since there is nothing further to see), simple processes of reinforcement and nonreinforcement could account for the decline in errors. The place error would likewise not be reinforced, since it results in looking at an empty place; following the actual movement of the object would result in reinforcement, since the baby is at least looking at the moving object. This kind of account is attractively simple. It does, however, ignore the origins of the erroneous behavior, which most probably arose through the reinforcement of keeping interesting sights in view in the real world; after all, in the real world it is quite sensible to follow moving objects or to look for objects in their familiar place. It is nevertheless an attractively simple theory of these changes and could generate a number of simple procedures to accelerate development.

The Piagetian account of this segment of development is quite different. The dynamic factor in Piaget's system is not simple reinforcement. Development begins when the organism is placed in a state of *conflict*. Conflict is likely to arise when the child has two contradictory concepts, rules, or modes of coping with the same or similar environmental problems. Conflict produces processes of *equilibration*, which continue until the organism has resolved the original contradiction. Recall that we argued that the child of less than 20 weeks identifies objects as *either* places *or* movements. "Places" do not move and "movements" do not stop within this conceptual framework, whereas in the real world they do. Every time the child faces this everyday situation he is, according to Piaget, put into a state of conflict because of the contradiction between his two concepts of objects. The way out of this is to reconcile these two partially valid concepts into a new one that defines objects as "things that can move from place to place along trajectories."

Piagetian theory makes several predictions that are different from those that would be made by standard learning theory. If the two primitive, contradictory object concepts do become combined, then it follows that both the movement error and place error should disappear concurrently. It further follows that the new concept should generate new behaviors that are relatively independent of those that indexed the old concepts. Since Piaget views development as a series of conceptual revolutions rather than as gradual evolution, we should see a sudden improvement rather than a gradual change. Finally, any environmental modification that does not induce conflict should not induce development, no matter what its reinforcement properties are. There are data on all four questions, all of which support the Piagetian position.

First, the movement and place errors do in fact show a similar pattern of decline, disappearing concurrently (Figure 7–15). Also, new behaviors appear as these errors decline. One new behavior was first described by Mundy-Castle (1970). When faced with a display apparatus like that shown in Figure 7–16, infants around five months of age begin to interpolate trajectories between the disappearance and reappearance points of the

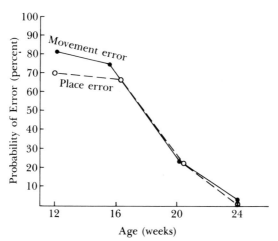

FIGURE 7–15

Two visual tracking errors of infants, the movement error and the place error, decline concurrently.

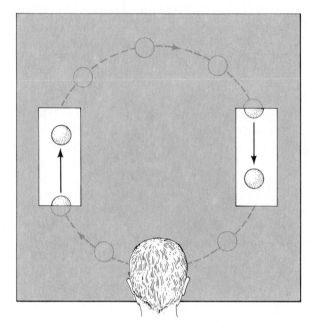

FIGURE *7–16*

The Mundy-Castle tracking apparatus is used to test whether an infant realizes that objects move from place to place along trajectories. An object moves upward in the left window and disappears. After a certain time it moves downward in the right window and disappears. After a certain time the object appears at the bottom of the left window to begin the same sequence. Around five months of age, babies will begin to interpolate a trajectory between the disappearance and reappearance points.

object, trajectories that are appropriate to the speed of movement of the object and the interval between disappearance and reappearance. This is just the sort of behavior we would expect from infants who have realized that objects move from place to place along trajectories. It is not something that a simple learning theory would predict.

One experiment was done to compare the relative efficiency of conflict and reinforcement in producing new behaviors (Bower, 1974a). The criterion behavior chosen was the same as in the above experiment, the ability to interpolate a trajectory. Two training presentations were used. In one, designed to reinforce curvilinear, up-and-over eye movements, an object moved continuously in a circle. Since the object was in constant motion, there should not have been any conflict between the baby's two definitions, "object as movement" and "object as place." In the other presentation the object simply moved back and forth in a straight line, stopping at each end of the track. The only eye movements reinforced were therefore to-and-fro movements in the horizontal plane. On the other hand, since the object in this situation did stop periodically, in Piagetian terms this situation should have introduced conflict in the mind of the infant. The findings of this experiment left no doubt that the latter presentation was more effective in inducing development, as indexed by trajectory interpolations in the Mundy-Castle task (Figure 7–16).

One last important point on which Piagetian theory differs from simple learning theory is the conditions under which we can in fact expect development. For Piaget, development can only occur after the conditions for contradiction have been met; the child must first have *two* ways of coping with or comprehending the same situation. In fact, there is an asynchrony in development of the two early, imperfect ways of coping with moving objects we described earlier (p. 151). Usually, infants will show anticipation of the pathway of a continuously moving object before showing anticipatory search for an object that moves between two stationary places. This means that, at some point in development, they will show movement errors but not place errors in certain tracking situations. At that point in development of the object concept, according to Piaget, infants cannot develop further because they have only one way of coping; there is not as yet the possibility of conflict between two alternative strategies.

In one experiment designed to test this hypothesis, the standard test for movement errors (see Figure 7–9) was presented to two groups of infants. One group began at eight weeks, the other at 12 weeks; each was tested weekly for response to an object that moved in a semicircular path and stopped occasionally. After the eight-week-old group had had four weeks of training, they did worse than the naive group (which at that point was only beginning the experiment). The experienced group would not even track the target object; indeed, they seemed to find the situation aversive. By 16 weeks, however, neither group made any errors to speak of; neither group continued tracking after the object had stopped. Apparently, then, if training is introduced to correct a behavior at a time when there is no alternative way of coping, the experience will not lead to improved behavior but rather to complete extinction of the behavior during this phase—a result quite in accord with Piaget's theory but wholly at odds with any simple learning model.

At least for this tiny segment of development, it would seem that Piaget's theory offers a more valid account than does standard learning theory. The emphasis on contradiction as the motive force in development explains why Piaget has said that simple learning theory cannot account for development. It also explains why his theory is not maturationist, for it is mainly in interaction with the outside world that the child will come across the contradictory aspects of his view of the world. Maturation alone cannot reveal these contradictions.

Later stages in the development of the object concept

This dynamic model of development can also be applied to the later stages of development of the object concept. By around 20 weeks the child believes that two objects cannot be in the same place at the same time. However, he does not yet comprehend that two objects can be in the same place at the same time if one is inside the other. Consequently, when he sees one object placed inside another, what he sees is a totally incomprehensible disappearance. When the object is brought out again, the baby sees a totally incomprehensible reappearance. At the same time, now that he is identifying objects in terms of their features rather than their place, he can at least recognize that he is dealing with the same object. This is reflected in the time he spends looking at an object before picking it up; familiar objects are picked up more readily than unfamiliar objects (Schaffer, 1971). The baby's recognition that he is dealing with the same object contradicts his belief that an object placed inside another object no longer exists anywhere: if it no longer existed anywhere it could hardly reappear, and yet it does. The only way to resolve this contradiction is to say that the object must exist somewhere. This belief would produce the poorly oriented search behavior characteristic of this stage.

ALTERNATIVE PATHS
TO AN OBJECT CONCEPT

Our account of the development of the object concept gives a heavy role to environmental inputs in generating that development. We have proposed that the sight of objects moving and stopping is critical in the first phase, that recognizing the identity of an object that disappears and then reappears is critical for the next phase, and that experience in putting things in and out of or on or behind other things is critical for the final phase (Bower, 1974a). This picture is probably valid for normal development. It is important to note that there are other paths to the attainment of a functional object concept.

The most striking finding in this regard is the discovery by Gouin-Décarie (1969) that the object concept develops normally in thalidomide infants, infants without hands or limbs. In the standard manual object-permanence tests these infants uncovered the hidden objects with their teeth. These babies could never have the manipulative experiences of normal babies. For example they could never learn about "inside" relations by putting objects in and out of other objects. Nonetheless, they developed a normal object concept, more or less on schedule. The conceptual nature of the development of the object concept and its independence of specific behaviors is clearly demonstrated here.

Speculation about the path of development of the object concept in thalidomide infants has led to a number of experiments on normal infants. These experiments are of relevance to a major developmental problem we have not so far touched on: the issue of what the "units of thought" are throughout development. The experiments were begun on the hypothesis that the only information channel the thalidomide babies could be using was their eyes, i.e., that visual input alone was responsible for their development of the object concept. This hypothesis led to a number of experiments in which normal infants were given increased exposure to tracking events that included all the information required for the object concept. It was thought if vision alone could serve as an alternative pathway for development of the object concept, the increased exposure along with normally available experience would lead to earlier success in standard manual object-permanence tests. A number of tracking events were used for this purpose. The results were both encouraging and puzzling. In all of the experiments augmented tracking experience did produce accelerated success in the tests (e.g., Bower and Paterson, 1972). However, on many occasions the experiments did not produce as much acceleration as might have seemed likely from performance on the tracking tasks.

One experiment that produced surprising and illuminating results is outlined in Figure 7–17. Infants were tested weekly between the ages of 12 and 20 weeks. At the beginning of training, when the catch trial was presented the infants would look to the right where they were used to seeing the object reappear, ignoring its change of direction and the appearance of the object on the left. Long before the end of the training this type of error disappeared. The infants could maintain contact with the object no matter what sequence of movement it went through, thus showing that they knew very well (at least as gauged by their eye movements) what was happening to the object when it disappeared. The same apparatus was used to test the object concept using reaching rather than visual tracking as the indicator behavior. The transparent screens were removed and the babies were allowed to pick up the object when it reappeared right or left. The first disappointment came on trials when the object was stopped *behind* an opaque screen. The trained babies, instead of reaching behind the screen to get the object, sat helplessly before the display, acting as if the object no longer existed. This behavior was identical to that of a control group of untrained babies. The second disappointment came when catch trials were introduced. After obtaining

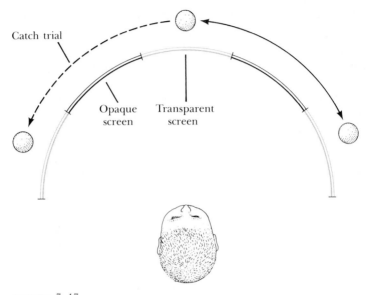

FIGURE 7–17

A visual tracking task. The object moves repeatedly between the
center and right "windows" (transparent screens). On the catch trial
the object moves to the left window. (Neilson, 1978.)

the object twice at right, the trained babies would again reach out happily
to the right on the catch trial, ignoring the fact that the object had moved
to the left. The "knowledge" that had controlled their eye movements
previously did not seem to be available to control their hand movements.
Occasionally, however, the baby would *look* in the correct direction while
reaching in the wrong direction. In other words, there was a *conflict* between
the trained (visual) and untrained (manual) response. According to
Piagetian theory, such conflicts would explain the acceleration that training
produces. Certainly, the infants in this study succeeded in resolving the
problems of the situation well before control infants.

However, another study produced far greater acceleration (Wishart
and Bower, 1977a). Between the ages of 12 and 20 weeks, each infant saw
each of the training presentations in Figure 7–18 four times. Compared
with the other experiments, the babies in this study had relatively little
practice on any one task, and this showed in the relative inefficiency of
their tracking at the end of training. Manual object-permanence tests
(Figure 7–18) were begun at 21 weeks. Note that the test situations were
quite different from the training situations. In the training situations there
was one platform, one screen, and one tunnel; in the test situations there
were two platforms, two screens, and two cups. In training the object was
moved in the horizontal plane by mechanical means; in the test situations

the object was moved vertically by hand by the experimenter. The training and test situations were thus sufficiently different that conflict of the sort described in the previous experiment was most unlikely. Nonetheless, these babies showed the greatest acceleration of development ever obtained. In fact, at 21 weeks only a few babies made errors on even the most complicated object-permanence tasks used in this experiment (those in which an object that has been successfully retrieved from one location several times is then hidden in a new location). Why should relatively little training in tasks that differ from test situations produce greater acceleration

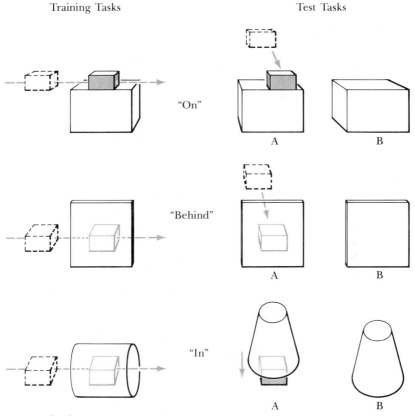

FIGURE 7–18

The visual training tasks on the left were designed to promote the babies' understanding of the spatial relationships "on," "behind," and "in." Their understanding of these relations was then tested by standard object-permanence tests (right). In these tests the object was "hidden" twice on one side (A) and then once on the other (B). Success in this situation is not normally achieved until around 10 months (see p. ●ff) ; however, the babies in this study successfully recovered the object from both locations at an age of only five months. (Wishart and Bower, 1977a.)

of development than a great deal of training in tasks that are identical to test situations? It is at this point that we must pay attention to the units of thought in infancy.

THE NATURE OF
REPRESENTATION IN INFANCY

We must ask ourselves how infants solve the problems we present to them. My own model for the process was stimulated by the results of an experiment that we have already discussed in part—the experiment on whether infants remember the presence of an object that has been hidden by a screen (p. 147). In the complete experiment one of three situations was revealed when the screen moved on: nothing, the original object, or an object completely different in size, shape, and color from the original. All of the infants in the study showed surprise when nothing was revealed. However, they were not surprised by either of the other events; so long as *an* object reappeared it did not matter if its size, shape and color were completely different. What these infants were storing in memory while the screen hid their view of the object must have been something rather abstract, a representation having neither size, shape, nor color. Such a representation cannot be construed as any kind of image or literal trace of an object. I would say that the infants must have been storing *symbolic* information. It would seem to me that with frequent exposure to an object, the abstract symbol for that object (when it goes out of sight) becomes more detailed, including such characteristics as size, shape, and color. We have already seen how any change in any one of these dimensions will be noticed by older or experienced babies but not by younger babies (see Figure 7–12). With increasing exposure to an object, the representation changes from an abstract symbol to a very specific image or icon of the object presented. I feel that such a process—in which thought progresses from abstract representations to more specific representations—can serve as a model for analysis of any problem situation that we present to the baby.

Suppose we show a baby an object passing through a tunnel. At first the presentation is totally mysterious to the baby. I would propose that the baby first of all decides that the object he sees on the two sides of the tunnel is the same object. Given that, the baby can deduce that while the moving object is out of sight, it must be inside the stationary object. In other words, the child learns that one object can be inside another. At this point, a child confronted with the standard manual object-permanence task with cups would have no difficulty. Although the behavioral response appropriate to this task is different from that for the tracking task, it nevertheless requires comprehension of the same spatial relation. This would account for the perfect transfer found in the experiment described above. The child is still coping with tracking at a level abstract enough that the information derived from the tracking task can transfer perfectly to the manual task in the object-permanence test. Suppose, though, the infant is given greater, long-term exposure to the tracking task (the object passing through the tunnel) before being presented with the manual object-permanence task. The internal description of the event would become more and more precise, so that the baby would end up with information of the form, "When the object disappears on the left, look for it to reappear on the right after x seconds." This is a very specific sensorimotor rule or schema, and very obviously would not help a child cope with standard object-permanence tests. On the other hand, it is specific enough to insure perfect contact with the object in the tracking situation, which may explain why it replaces the abstract description of the tracking event.

What evidence is there that the sensorimotor schema replaces the abstract description? The infants given intensive training in the experiment described above (Figure 7–17) had had enough exposure to the tracking event to have elaborated a sensorimotor schema of the form, "When the object moves to the right, look for it to appear x seconds later on the right-edge of the screen toward which it is moving; when the object moves to the left, look for it to appear x seconds later on the left-edge of the screen toward which it is moving." This is very specific information, containing a precise description of the stimulus and equally precise directions for behavior. When a different response is demanded, e.g., a reaching response, this very precise schema would be of no help at all. We thus have an explanation for the puzzling data presented on pp. 165–166.

I am proposing that the most efficient transfer of relevant information from a training to a test situation occurs at that point when the training has proceeded far enough for the baby to have formulated an abstract description of the training situation, a description that does not contain specific stimulus descriptions or response prescriptions. As soon as training has gone far enough for it to be schematized in precise stimulus-response terms, possibilities of transfer are minimal. This implies that the function relating amount of training to transfer of information should be of the form shown in Figure 7–19. There is one experiment that demonstrates just such a relationship (Bower, 1974a). Recall the experiment designed to accelerate trajectory interpolation with the Mundy-Castle apparatus (p. 162). Two training presentations were used. How would an infant describe these two situations in abstract terms? A preliminary, abstract description of the first presentation (simple left-right, back-and-forth movement of an object) would be, "An object moves from place to place along a trajectory." This information transferred to the Mundy-Castle situation would be just the information that would generate trajectory interpolations. A schematized description of this same presentation would have the form, "To keep the

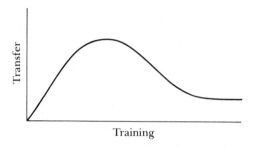

FIGURE *7–19*
The amount of transfer of
information is postulated
to be a nonlinear function
of the amount of training.

object in view, look for it along a horizontal path between place 1 and place 2." The schematized description transferred to the Mundy-Castle situation would produce port-to-port looking, with no interpolated trajectories at all, which is exactly the behavior seen in babies given training with this presentation. A preliminary, abstract description of the second presentation (continuous circular movement of an object) would be of the form, "An object continues to move along a trajectory. . . . If this description were applied to the Mundy-Castle situation it would not produce trajectory interpolation. Rather, the disappearance of an object at the top of one window would elicit visual search to the uppermost limits of the infant's gaze, and vice versa on the disappearance of the object at the bottom of the other window. A schematized description might be, "To find the object, search for it along the circumference of a circle with center straight ahead and radius x feet," a description with no applicability at all to the Mundy-Castle situation. Infants trained with this presentation should thus shift in the Mundy-Castle situation from a "heaven-hell" search pattern to performing like naive infants with no training at all. Again, this is exactly the behavior shown by infants trained with the second presentation.

There is thus some data to support the hypothesis that babies think about things in abstract terms, but will, as soon as they are able, schematize problems in terms of specific stimulus descriptions and response .prescriptions. Schematization permits efficient performance in specific situations but inhibits smooth transfer to new, conceptually related problem situations. It seems that at this stage of cognitive development the infant cannot retain both an abstract and a schematized solution to the same problem. Consequently, the schematized solution, being more efficient, will tend to drive out the abstract solution at the cost of efficient transfer. The verb in the last sentence, "drive out," is surely inaccurate. Babies who have developed highly efficient schematized solutions to visual tracking problems, and who thus do not show immediate transfer to manual search tasks, nonetheless show accelerated success in the manual tasks. Something must remain of the abstract solution to the tracking task. How can this be?

A MODEL FOR COGNITIVE
DEVELOPMENT IN INFANCY

We have concentrated on the object concept in this chapter in part because its attainment is one of the best studied attainments of infancy. Certain important ideas with general applicability to development have emerged from our study of the object concept.

1. Development does not follow a necessary sequence.
2. Conflict is important in generating development.
3. There are several *behavioral* paths to the same developmental end.
4. Each of these behavioral paths reflects the same *conceptual* path.
5. Processes of schematization make behavior highly efficient but inhibit transfer to new situations.
6. Early experience can facilitate later development.

It is these last two conclusions that make it necessary for us to think about cognitive development in terms of what is happening in the mind of the child.

The process of cognitive development in infancy as described by Piaget is attractively simple. According to Piaget, infants acquire specific S-R solutions to specific problems. These S-R solutions may conflict, in which case the process of *reflective abstraction* will result in the formation of *schemas*, higher-order rules that can control a range of behaviors. The broader the S-R experience of the child, the more general and abstract will his schemas be. However, the results of the transfer experiments place an important limit on the model. For Piaget, abstract, schematic rules are necessarily formed from earlier specific S-R solutions to particular problems. The experiments we have reviewed suggest that it is the more abstract solution that comes first. This can then be used to generate an S-R solution to a specific test or transfer situation. Babies given experience in visual search tasks show accelerated success in coping with manual search tasks. However, if the transfer task is not given soon enough, transfer will be delayed, although it will still occur.

A child stuck in the visual search situation will perfect his S-R behavior in that situation to such an extent that he need no longer call upon the abstract solution. What then does he do with the abstract solution? I would propose that the baby puts it into a "conceptual store," a memory for abstract solutions. If the baby is given a new task that requires that abstract solution, he will search through his conceptual store to find anything that might help with the problem at hand. Faced with an object-permanence task, the baby is most likely to come up with the generally useful abstract rule, "To find something that has mysteriously vanished, search for it where it normally is," a rule generally useful in any home with toy boxes and a tidy mother. Since this rule will not work in the object-permanence task, the baby will rescan his conceptual store. If there is an adequate concept or schema there, worked out in visual tracking situations, the baby will eventually find it and use it to solve the manual search problem. If there is not, the baby will have to set out to discover just how to solve the problem. This would presumably account for the advantage that trained babies have over untrained babies, even in those cases where training has continued beyond the point for greatest efficiency of transfer.

Figure 7–20 shows a path model for the development of the object concept. Can this kind of model help us understand the processes of development underlying the other attainments of infancy? It must be obvious that the weight conservation problem (pp. 125ff) is a conflict situation in the mind of the infant. The baby presented with a conservation task knows two things: the same object always weighs the same and longer objects weigh more than shorter objects. Before his very eyes he sees an object become longer, and yet there is no replacement of one object by another! The *same* object grew *longer*. This is an obvious conflict for the baby, a conflict that can only be resolved by deducing a concept of conservation. Or take the problem of arranging an array of objects according to size. The young baby arranges them in pairs—one big, one little. When faced with three cups of different sizes, what does he make of the middle-sized cup? Will he pair it with the largest and thus call it "little," or will he pair it with the smallest and thus call it "big"? The only escape from this conflict is to formulate the concept of a series to replace the simple binary concept of "big and little."

Throughout this chapter we have been speaking of the baby as thinking, deducing, reasoning. We have even argued that the baby reasons in abstract terms. "Reasoning" in our terms is what Piaget calls *equilibration*. For Piaget, equilibration is in principle a rule-bound process; given the elements of a contradiction, one should be able to deduce the solution that will be arrived at by the baby. Unfortunately, these rules have not as yet been fully elucidated by researchers in infancy. We will save our discussion of them until we have reviewed the whole field of cognitive development. One thing that we can say is that equilibration processes have been shown to occur, and occur efficiently, in even the youngest infants so far studied.

What of the formal problem-solving strategies that are most charac-teristic of adolescence but that have their precursors in infancy? These strategies are based on comprehension of a set of operations, the INRC group (see pp. 139ff). Babies also seem able to combine these operations to reach a desired end. This ability to combine operations is present at a very early age, if we take combined head and eye movements as an index (Figure 7–21). For example, the displacement of an object is equivalent to an identity operation (see Chapter 6), with head and eye movements

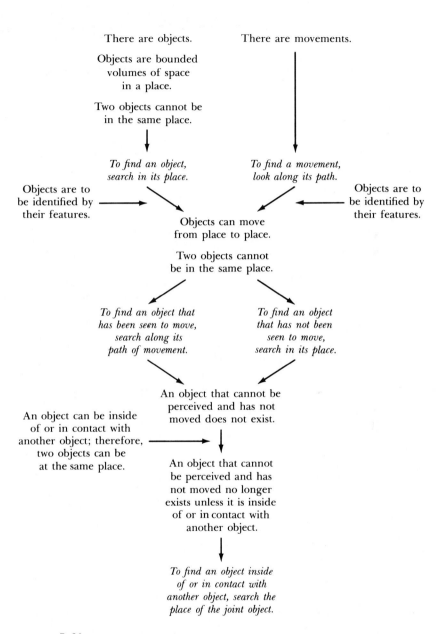

There are objects.　　　There are movements.

Objects are bounded
volumes of space
in a place.

Two objects cannot be
in the same place.

To find an object,
search in its place.

To find a movement,
look along its path.

Objects are to
be identified by
their features.

Objects are to
be identified by
their features.

Objects can move
from place to place.

Two objects cannot
be in the same place.

To find an object that
has been seen to move,
search along its
path of movement.

To find an object
that has not been
seen to move,
search in its place.

An object that cannot be
perceived and has not
moved does not exist.

An object can be inside
of or in contact with
another object; therefore,
two objects can be
at the same place.

An object that cannot
be perceived and has
not moved no longer
exists unless it is inside
of or in contact with
another object.

To find an object inside
of or in contact with
another object, search the
place of the joint object.

FIGURE *7–20*

A modified epigenetic landscape, showing the sequence of rules acquired in the
development of the object concept.

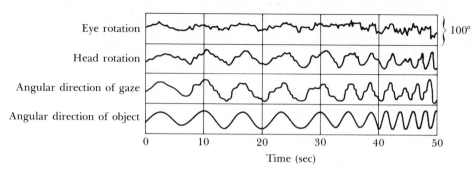

Eye rotation ⎫ 100°

FIGURE 7–21

A record of a nine-week-old infant's eye and head movements as he tracks a small target (visual angle of 1.5°) rotating in the horizontal plane 36 inches from the head axis. The angular direction of gaze is the sum of eye and head rotations. As can be seen, this correlates well with the angular direction of the object, and the eye and head movements are combined smoothly. (Trevarthen and Tursky, 1969.)

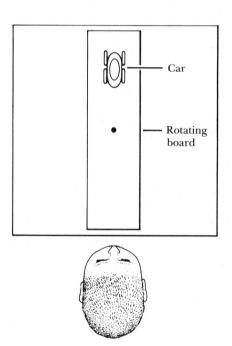

FIGURE 7–22

In order to recover the toy car, the baby must rotate the board. The solution of this problem requires understanding of the group of INRC operations (see Figure 6–13, p. 140).

equivalent to the reciprocating and correlating operations. A head movement itself can be an identity operation with eye movement a reciprocating operation. Negation of the head movement would then require a correlated eye movement. However, these operations are not automatically combined and applied to all situations. The problem shown in Figure 7–22 requires comprehension of the INRC group. The problem is not typically solved before 18 months of age, although at that age it is solved smoothly and fluently, without trial and error (Koslowski and Bruner, 1972; Monnier, 1977). This delay may be an ill effect of simpler strategies rather than a direct developmental effect; younger children typically persist in trying one of two inappropriate responses—going directly to the object or pulling on the rotating lever. It is quite understandable that these strategies should be applied, since both are reinforced in the normal course of events. Older babies do not waste their time on these unprofitable strategies. Unfortunately, we do not as yet have any data on the developmental sequence. Bruner has proposed that the critical events in solving this kind of problem are, first, the discarding of unsuccessful strategies and, second, the discovery of the INRC structure of this situation. In this connection he has made the interesting observation that children may become so pre-occupied with intellectual exploration of the task that they will ignore the toy when it comes within reach. Application of the INRC structure seems to proceed automatically in similar situations thereafter. Bruner seems to suggest that the child's difficulty is not in comprehending the INRC structure, but in applying it in a particular situation, where he cannot forecast the precise effect of the possible transformations without empirical test. In other words, to succeed the child must schematize the abstract structure he already has in his head into a more specific S-R solution. Schematization is thus not always counterproductive. Particularly in the world of the infant, solutions must be schematized to be of any use.

ENVIRONMENTAL EFFECTS, GENE EXPRESSION, AND COGNITIVE DEVELOPMENT IN INFANCY

What can we say about the role of heredity and environment in cognitive development in the sensorimotor period? The first thing to note is that rates of development are very plastic and are completely under environmental control. The differences that can be produced by environmental manipulations far exceed the individual differences that exist in "normal" groups of infants. A second point to note is that severe genetic abnormality, as in Down's syndrome (mongolism), does not preclude normal sensorimotor development. Overall development is slowed but the slowing is probably due to the way the condition isolates the child from normal environmental inputs. No gene has ever been shown to be necessary for the emergence of any aspect of sensorimotor intelligence. By contrast, specific environmental inputs are necessary. However, we should note that if and only if the organism we are dealing with is human will these inputs, in the correct order, be sufficient for the development of sensorimotor intelligence; the same inputs would accomplish little without the human genotype.

TABLE 7–2

Early learning opportunities greatly facilitate later learning. The infants in group A were subjected to conditioning procedures from birth. Those in group B were started at the age of three months. (From Papousek, 1967.)

	MEAN AGE AT START OF TEST (DAYS)	MEAN TRIALS TO CRITERION
Group A	107.54	94.63
Group B	105.92	176.23

The acquisitions we have looked at thus far all concern specific information about the world. But, as we indicated above, infants also acquire ways of finding out about the world, strategies for gaining information. Papousek (1969) described the babies in his learning experiment as "testing hypotheses" about what combination of movements would produce reinforcement. He has also presented data indicating that the more practice babies get in testing hypotheses, the better they become (Table 7–2). There is positive transfer from one learning situation to another. There is some evidence that the babies learn to learn, i.e., that they formulate strategies for finding out information. The strategies themselves have a structure that is of great interest. The initial strategies can in fact have negative effects on some aspects of learning in infancy. The experimental problem that illustrates this is familiar to us. It involves changing the effective or operant response after the child has learned to make a particular response to the given problem. A new operant response is then required for success in the same situation. As we saw earlier (p. 71), newborns can cope with this kind of problem, as can infants 3–4 months old (Siqueland and Lipsitt, 1966; Papousek, 1969). In the experiment in question the babies wore cuffs on each wrist and each ankle, attached by strings to an apparatus that switched on a motorized mobile for a few seconds at a time (Monnier, 1977). Any one cuff was in control at a given time. The younger babies at first showed a pattern of activity involving all four limbs in their attempts to discover how to control the mobile. This was then refined into separate movements of individual limbs until the controlling limb was discovered. When the contingency was changed (i.e., the mobile was to be turned on by a different limb) the babies' overall activity rate rose again, and then again narrowed down to the effective limb. The older babies were much more systematic. Suppose the effective limb was the left arm and the effective movement either upward or downward. We might expect that a baby who had switched on the mobile with an upward movement of his left arm would simply repeat that action. A younger baby would.

However, the older babies in this study did not. Instead, they typically made a *downward* movement of the effective arm, which was also effective. Did they then simply move that arm? They did not. The left arm was held still, while first the right arm, then one foot, then the other foot was moved up and down. Some of the babies even went so far as to try combined movements, before satisfying themselves that a left arm movement was in fact the effective movement. What happened then when the experimenter changed the contingency so that, say, the left foot was operative? The babies by and large gave up as soon as it became clear that the left arm was no longer effective.

What is happening in this kind of situation? The initial strategy of the babies is extremely interesting. Presumably the strapping on of the cuffs informed the babies that their arms and legs were involved in this game. It is the way they found out just exactly how they were involved that is so fascinating. The problem-solving behavior of these babies has a structure, a most important structure. Without describing it in detail we can say that the babies learned how to work systematically through all possible options in a problem situation.* A corollary to this is that they seem to have learned that the world has a consistent causal structure and does not change its rules—witness their astonishment at the breakdown of their laboriously acquired causal deduction. The neural structure that controls behavior at this stage is the root of the structures that will control systematic experimentation later in life. More systematic study of the early development of these structures would surely be worthwhile.

---

*Compare this with the formal strategies described on pp. 138–139.

$$8$$

Cognitive
Development
in Childhood

Infancy is over as soon as the child begins to use and be used by language. The acquisition of language marks the beginning of the development of the skills that are most typically human. The development of language itself is a fascinating topic; we will consider it in detail in Chapter 10. Our present concern is the effect that language has on the cognitive skills of the child. At first sight the effects seem to be disastrous. Skills that are well embedded in the behavior of infants disappear as soon as language develops. It is not simply that children cannot express in language concepts that they can express in behavior. The very formulation and expression of an erroneous verbal concept seems to be sufficient to undo the valid preverbal concept that had controlled behavior up to that point. Children thus start to repeat many of the same errors they made when younger.

CONCRETE OPERATIONS
AND SENSORIMOTOR SKILLS

Consider the object concept, whose attainment so preoccupied us in the last chapter. You will recall that around 5–6 months of age the baby discovers that he has only one mother, who is only ever in one place at a time. By this time, too, the baby knows that an object *is* where it is *seen* to be, no matter how unusual that place is for that object. The child stops looking for objects where he has been accustomed to finding them if he sees the objects elsewhere. What then happens in the following situation? A mother and her two-year-old child are in the garden of their house. The mother says to her child, "Where's mummy?" The child then points toward the kitchen, or whatever part of the house her mother is usually in. If mummy says, "Go find mummy!" the child is quite likely to toddle off to the kitchen, the place where mummy usually is. Piaget tried this experiment on his own children. The observations were repeated by Gouin-Décarie (1966), on a larger sample, and by numerous other psychologists. Given their importance in everyday life, the loss of object-concept skills is a tribute to the burgeoning importance of language in the control of behavior.

A similar take-over effect has been demonstrated for weight conservation by Sheeran (1973). Nursery school children from three to five years old played a game that involved taking a lump of plasticine from the experimenter and handing it on to someone else, who passed it back to the experimenter. After a few repetitions the shape of the plasticine was transformed by the experimenter and the game went on. This game served as a weight conservation test; the behavior of the child was observed to see whether there was any error in the judgment of the weight of the object after shape transformation. After this, a verbal interrogation procedure was begun. A series of questions were asked to find out if the child understood the use of such words as "weigh," "weight," "same," and "more." Few of the younger children did. If the child's answers indicated that he did know what these words meant, he was then given a standard weight conservation problem. The child was shown two identical lumps of plasticine and asked if they weighed the same. If the child said yes, one was transformed in shape and the question repeated. Not surprisingly, since the oldest children were five years old, the vast majority answered incorrectly; the children said that the weight changed when the shape changed. After this, the behavioral conservation test (the game described above) was repeated. Both younger and older children had performed the first behavioral test correctly; their arm movements indicated that they knew that the weight of an object did *not* change when the shape of the object did change. However, in the second behavioral test, after having *said* that the weight of the object changed when its shape was changed, the older children proceeded to *behave* as if this were true. They committed a behavioral error they had not made since they were 18 months old (Table 8–1). Some of them talked quite freely as they were doing the task and it was obvious that they described what was happening in verbal terms without prompting. Remarks like, "You're making it longer, it'll be heavier now," were not uncommon. As I said some pages back, it really seems as if the very verbal expression of an incorrect solution to a problem is enough to wipe out the behavioral expression of a correct solution, even

TABLE *8–1*

Mean change in arm position on the third presentation of a lump of plasticine and on the first presentation after the shape of the plasticine had been transformed. Change in arm position was measured from a photograph showing superimposition of the arm position on taking the object and arm position 250 msec later. Two age groups were studied.

AGE	BEFORE TRANSFORMATION	AFTER TRANSFORMATION
3 yr, 2 mo	0.3 mm	0.9 mm[a]
4 yr, 10 mo	2.4	7.8[b]

[a] Not significant
[b] $p = .03$

if that correct behavioral solution has been expressed and reinforced for years before.

While we simply do not know if such effects will occur with all of the accomplishments of infancy, it certainly seems possible that they would, particularly if the sensorimotor skill conflicted directly with the verbal formulation of the same problem. Figure 8–1 represents the major accomplishments of the concrete-operational stage. Many of them, we know, have a behavioral antecedent in infancy, an antecedent that is certainly not expressed in verbal terms until late in the development of concrete operations.

The accomplishments laid out in Figure 8–1 differ significantly from the accomplishments of infancy. So far as we know, every infant in every culture will develop the full complement of skills that make up sensorimotor intelligence. This is not true of the skills of the concrete-operational period. There are many individuals in many cultures who simply do not develop these kinds of skills. They remain *preoperational* for all of their lives, never spontaneously developing valid verbal solutions to the problems we are discussing. Since this lack of development is most marked in non-Western cultures, whose members are racially and genetically different from Europeans, the suggestion has naturally been made that attainment or nonattainment of conservation skills is directly due to specific genes or combinations of genes.

GENES VERSUS ENVIRONMENT

The most serious attempt to analyze a specific genetic effect on concrete-operational skills was made by de Lemos (1969a, b). His subjects were Australian aborigines, either pure blooded or with some proportion of

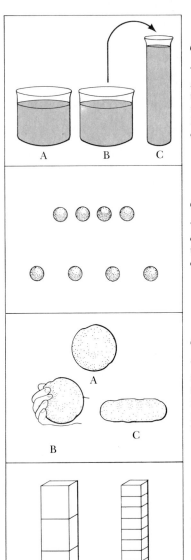

Conservation of continuous volume

The child agrees that B contains the same amount of liquid as A, and also understands that if B is poured into C there is still the same amount of liquid in C as was in B, even though the level of liquid has changed.

Conservation of discontinuous number (or quantity)

The child understands that the two rows contain the same number of items, although the length and density of the rows are different.

Conservation of continuous substance and weight

The child agrees that A and B contain the same amount of plasticine or weigh the same, and also understands that if B is squashed into C, C still has the same amount of plasticine as was in B and still weighs the same.

Conservation of discontinuous length

The child is able to make a tower the same height as A using a different number of units (B).

Conservation of objective space

The child is able to represent someone else's view of a table model. For example, he realizes that the other person would not be able to see the house he sees.

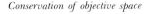

FIGURE *8–1*

Five of the major accomplishments of the concrete-operational stage.

European blood. If specific genetic effects are responsible for specific cognitive skills, this would be the ideal population in which to try to isolate the effects. Prior to colonialization, Australian aborigines were reproductively isolated from the rest of the world. The aborigines never attained any form of technology beyond a stone age level. By contrast, the European colonizers possessed most of the technology that characterizes the modern age. De Lemos tested his subjects with a set of conservation tasks and found considerable differences between the racially pure and mixed groups of aborigines. The pure-blooded aborigines were virtually incapable of the simplest conservation tasks. De Lemos concluded:

> The significance of our results lies in the fact that in this case there were no apparent differences in the environment of the two groups. . . . The differences cannot be attributed to environmental factors. It would seem reasonable to attribute the significant differences between the part and the full Aborigines . . . to genetic differences between Europeans and Aborigines.

These conclusions seem quite justifiable on the basis of the data. If generally valid they would point to the dramatic hypothesis that specific genes or combinations of genes were responsible for the genesis of specific cognitive skills. But the conclusions are very strong and would be falsified if one were to find but one full-blooded aboriginal who did possess the cognitive skills in question. A study by Dasen (1974) found many more than one full-blooded aboriginal with just these skills. Dasen's results are shown in Table 8–2. While the values are lower than would be found in western European or American samples, they are quite in line with values

TABLE *8–2*

Percentage of aboriginal subjects succeeding on conservation tasks. The Hermannsburg group had medium contact with Europeans; the Areyonga group had low contact. (From Dasen, 1974.)

	AGE	5	6	7	8	9	10	11	12	13	14	15	16	ADULT
	Hermannsburg													
	C		0	10	20	40	30	10	50		70		70	40
	T		10	10	40	10	0	30	10		10		20	20
Conservation	NC		60	80	30	50	70	60	40		20		10	40
of Quantity	F		30	10	0	0	0	0	0		0		0	0
	Areyonga													
	C				17			0		20		30		30
	T				0			0		27		10		20
	NC				75			89		40		60		50
	F				8			11		13		0		0

TABLE 8–2 *(Continued)*

		AGE	5	6	7	8	9	10	11	12	13	14	15	16	ADULT
	Hermannsburg														
Conservation of Weight		C	0	0	10	10	10	10	20		20		50		20
		T	10	20	0	20	0	20	10		40		40		0
		NC	70	50	60	70	90	70	70		40		10		80
		F	10	40	20	0	0	0	0		0		0		0
	Areyonga														
		C					8		11		13		9		10
		T					25		22		20		37		10
		NC					42		56		60		27		80
		F					25		11		7		27		0
	Hermannsburg														
Conservation of Volume		C	10	10	0	30	30	10	20		20		60		30
		T	10	20	40	30	60	20	30		30		30		0
		NC	40	40	20	40	10	70	50		50		10		70
		F	40	30	30	0	0	0	0		0		0		0
	Areyonga														
		C					25		22		13		30		0
		T					42		56		13		20		0
		NC					17		22		53		50		100
		F					17		0		20		0		0
	Hermannsburg														
	Part 1	C		20	50	40	30	50	50	60	20		70		
		T		0	0	0	10	10	20	10	10		0		
		NC		70	40	50	60	40	30	30	70		30		
		F		10	10	10	0	0	0	0	0		0		
	Part 2	C		0	10	10	10	40	40	50	20		40		
		T		0	0	0	0	10	0	0	0		0		
		NC		80	80	80	90	50	60	50	80		60		
		F		20	10	10	0	0	0	0	0		0		
	Part 3	C		0	10	20	30	30	0	10	10		20		
Conservation of Length		T		10	10	0	0	0	0	10	20		0		
		NC		70	70	70	70	70	100	80	70		80		
		F		20	10	10	0	0	0	0	0		0		
	Areyonga														
	Part 1	C					17		25.0		27		37.5		
		T					25		12.5		0		12.5		
		NC					58		62.5		67		37.5		
		F					0		0		7		12.5		
	Part 2	C					8		0		20		25.0		
		T					17		0		0		12.5		
		NC					75		87.5		73		50.0		
		F					0		12.5		7		12.5		
	Part 3	C					17		12.5		13		50.0		
		T					0		12.5		27		0		
		NC					83		75.0		53		37.5		
		F					0		0		7		12.5		

C = Conservation
T = Transitional (between conservation and nonconservation)
NC = Nonconservation
F = Failure to communicate

found in Yugoslavia, Sardinia, and other technologically less developed European cultures. It thus seems that the hypothesis of gene-specific cognitive skills is ruled out. Dasen suggests that the differences between his own and de Lemos's results are due to differences in environment. His own subjects had a rather better school environment with much more emphasis on the relation between verbal concepts and manipulative skills.

There have been many, many attempts to specify specific environmental effects that might be responsible for the transition from the preoperational stage to that of concrete operations. Indeed one author complains that the issue has become an obsession with American psychologists, filling up journals to the exclusion of other topics (Wohlwill, 1973). I must confess that I share this obsession. The skills embodied in conservation tasks, for example, are so fundamental that scientific or mathematical knowledge would be impossible without them. Western society, founded on an advanced scientific technology, would be totally impossible without the concepts of unit, measure, and invariance that are expressed in conservation skills. Also the problems seem so simple that most of us feel a genuine amazement at the responses of the preoperational child; these responses force one to acknowledge that "younger" is not just "smaller," it is also different. Finally, correct responses cannot be taught directly. Simply telling a child the correct response will not change his responses at all. The child may obediently parrot the correct response in the situation in which it has been taught, but if the situation is changed, even slightly, he will revert to a preoperational response. It appears that the child must acquire these concepts on his own.

Since there have been literally thousands of attempts to specify the factors that produce concrete operations, any summary of the kind I am attempting here must be highly tentative. Nonetheless, there are a few conclusions that one can draw without running into obvious objections. First of all, concrete operations will not develop unless the corresponding sensorimotor skills have developed. Although this has been demonstrated only for spatial abilities, extension by analogy to other abilities seems quite reasonable. The conclusion is based on comparisons of two groups of blind children: those who were blind before the end of the sensorimotor period and those who became blind thereafter. Both Drever (1962) and Hatwell (1966) found a sharp distinction in the ability of these two groups to comprehend spatial concepts (Figure 8–2). Children born blind or blinded during the sensorimotor period could not be taught spatial concepts; no amount of instruction compensated for the lack of the relevant sensorimotor attainment. Some very intelligent individuals in this group were later able to memorize the theorems of Euclid, but without understanding them one bit. Children who became blind following sensorimotor development required no special instruction at all to acquire spatial concepts. In fact, some such individuals have even become famous geometers, making

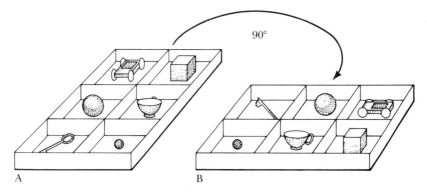

FIGURE 8–2

A child is presented with a partitioned box of toys (A). He is then given a
duplicate set of toys and asked to put these in the identical arrangement in
another box turned 90° from the position of the first box (B). The task is then
repeated, reversing the orientations of the model box and test box. Congenitally
blind children are unable to perform this apparently easy task. (Hatwell, 1966.)

original contributions to the field of geometry. It should be noted that the
child who becomes blind before sensorimotor development is complete
differs from the normal child only in his ability to use spatial concepts.
Other concepts are not significantly affected.

PARADOXICAL TRANSFER EFFECTS
AND SCHEMATIZATION

If we admit that sensorimotor concepts are necessary for the development
of operational concepts, we should beware of thinking that they are
sufficient for the development. Many children who have developed normal
sensorimotor concepts may fail to translate these to the operational level.
Understanding these failures is a task of practical as well as theoretical
importance. If we admit the importance of sensorimotor development for
operational development, an assumption central to Piagetian theory, we
still must explain the failure or delay of *transfer* of sensorimotor concepts
to the operational level.

Development of operational concepts is very much a matter of transfer.
What seems to be involved is the transfer of information from the diverse
motor systems to the unifying control of language. In the beginning, other
people's utterances control the child's behavior. But in time his own
utterances, as well as his silent verbal formulations, can come to control his

behavior. Speech is both an input and an output. Once a child reaches the developmental stage at which language can control his behavior, if he *says* that something is more, he will act accordingly. This situation, in which a new response (the verbal response) can also be the stimulus for a whole system of responses, sets the transfer between sensorimotor and operational concepts quite apart from conventional transfer situations. Despite this, it is worth looking again briefly at the characteristics of transfer within the sensorimotor period, which were discussed in the last chapter.

There we argued that transfer can be inhibited by schematization. In order for an abstract conceptual solution to be expressed in behavior, it must first be "translated" in terms of the specific S-R situation. As a result, the same problem presented with different stimuli or in such a way as to require different responses will not elicit a spontaneous transfer of the original abstract solution—the original solution has been replaced by a schematized solution that is too specific for transfer. If this also applies to the transfer from sensorimotor to operational concepts, what would we expect to find? The paradoxical answer is that younger children should be more likely to show transfer than older children. This means that younger children should do better than older children on tests of operational concepts, a prediction that seems ridiculous at first sight. However, the prediction could be correct even if the relevant experiments are hard to do. Language, after all, does not spring up instantly. It takes a long time before concepts that are expressed in behavior can be expressed, even erroneously, in words. It is possible that sensorimotor solutions are so well practiced that they are completely schematized before there is any possibility of expressing a verbal solution. If we wanted to test the prediction that younger children will do better than older children, it would be necessary to find a problem that cropped up relatively infrequently, to minimize the chances of schematization, but one that could be described in very simple language so that it could be tested at a young age.

Several problems seem to meet these criteria. Consider the counting problem outlined in Figure 8–3. Without any real evidence—save unsystematic observation of babies in their own homes—it seems to me that counting problems occur relatively rarely in the normal environment of the preschool child. At the same time, the verbal responses required in the task seem to be simple enough that two-year-olds can give consistent responses. In fact, two-year-olds not only gave consistent responses to the counting problem in Figure 8–3, they also gave many more correct responses than did three- or four-year-olds (Figure 8–4). This admittedly controversial experiment* thus confirms one of the most paradoxical predictions in our whole account of cognitive development.

---

*The experiment has been replicated five times; the results were positive in three and negative in two (see Bever, Mehler, and Epstein, 1968).

A B C

FIGURE *8–3*

A child is asked which row in each pair has more pellets. In A, both rows clearly have the same number. In B, although the top row is the longer of the two, the bottom row is denser and has more pellets. In C, the bottom row, although less dense than the top row, has more. Correct responses for B and C require the child to ignore the perceptual aspects of the display (length and density) and to respond on the basis of number only.

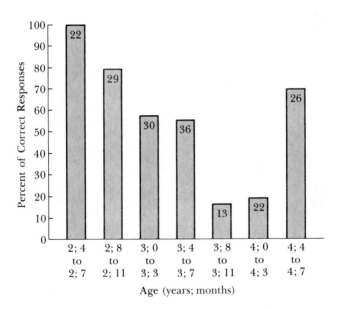

FIGURE *8–4*

Responses to the problem in Figure 8–3. Numbers inside the bars indicate total number of subjects at that age. (Mehler and Bever, 1967.)

Similar results have been obtained by Maratsos (1973). Children were shown pairs of rectangles and asked to identify the larger of a pair (Figure 8–5). Younger children accurately identified the bigger one; older children, by contrast, focused on only one dimension, height, and so made incorrect responses. There is an obvious similarity between this error and

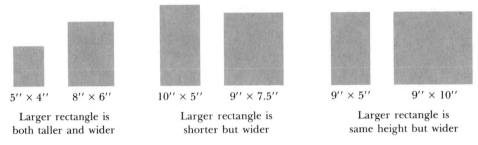

5" × 4"   8" × 6"   10" × 5"   9" × 7.5"   9" × 5"   9" × 10"

Larger rectangle is
both taller and wider

Larger rectangle is
shorter but wider

Larger rectangle is
same height but wider

FIGURE 8–5

Children were shown pairs of rectangles and asked to identify the "big" one. The correct answer in all cases shown here is the one on the right. Older children were misled by height and so gave erroneous answers. (Maratsos, 1973.)

the standard conservation errors, which would seem to imply that non-conservation develops from a form of conservation.

Why should the child shift from a strategy that produces correct responses to one that does not? Various psychologists have speculated on this question. One suggestion is that the way in which comparatives ("more," "bigger") are used encourages the child to focus on only one physical dimension. A child who asks for more orange juice sees the level rise in his glass. Since the cups and glasses used by a family are usually standard, the simplest way to see who has more is to compare levels. Thus the word "more" might become associated with increased height. It has also been suggested that focusing on one dimension is an attempt at greater precision than is possible if more than one dimension enters into the calculation. Neither of these explanations has been tested so far. Nor have any longitudinal studies been attempted that might decide whether the early transfer found in tasks such as those described above can inhibit or eliminate the subsequent appearance of the incorrect verbal formulations so typical of this period. Such experiments seem simple and are of obvious importance.

Suppose we wanted to change this odd developmental pattern of a correct response being supplanted by an incorrect one which in turn is replaced by the correct response. How would we go about it? One obvious way would be to give infants regular practice in sensorimotor behaviors in order to facilitate schematization prior to verbal formulation. This would obviously inhibit transfer and lead to the early appearance of incorrect verbal responses. This may not seem at first glance to represent an advance; it means, however, that the initial step of the three-step process has been bypassed and only one more stage lies between the child and eventual success. This was attempted in one experiment in which infants from the age of one year were practiced once a week in a behavioral version of counting (Wishart and Bower, 1977b). The babies were required to choose

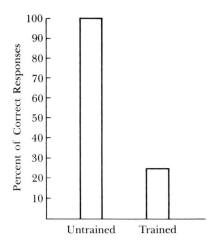

FIGURE *8–6*
The behavioral version of the counting task shown in Figure 8–3 requires the infant to choose between two sets of the same candy that differ in number. Infants trained weekly from the age of one year in this version did very poorly at 28 months on the verbal version of the task. By contrast, untrained infants responded with 100 percent accuracy. (Data for untrained group from Mehler and Bever, 1967.)

the larger of two sets of candy differing in number only. If successful they were allowed to eat the candy. Counting was required for a correct solution (see Figure 8–3). When asked at 28 months which set had more, they did much less well than control infants with no training (Figure 8–6). A year later, however, the practiced children were doing significantly better than the control infants; their performance was virtually perfect. By contrast, the control group's performance had slumped drastically (see Figure 8–4).

ACCELERATION STUDIES

Paradoxical transfer of the sort described above may help us to understand failures that normally occur at later ages. It does not help us understand later successful transfers. These occur at such a late age that it seems most unlikely that schematization would not be complete before the transfer occurs. In the last chapter we discussed an alternative transfer process, one involving conflict between the early solution to a problem and a later, differently expressed solution. The case described involved conflict between eye and hand responses (p. 165). There are many more obvious possibilities for conflict between verbal and nonverbal responses to the same problem. If the type of conflict described in the last chapter is a pervasive factor in development, any verbal–nonverbal conflict should have an accelerative effect on development of concrete operations. This conflict can only occur if the verbal utterance as response can reenter the system as an instruction. By this I mean that verbal utterances can control behavior; utterances *are* responses, but they have the additional capacity for control, absent in nonverbal responses. If erroneous, the verbal instruction will conflict with the schematized sensorimotor instruction. If, as Piaget claims, conflict is the motor of development, this should at least set off the processes of development. Given that development needs such triggers, events of this kind should accelerate development. There is indeed evidence that this verbal–nonverbal conflict does facilitate development (Bruner, Olver, and Greenfield, 1966).

It has been claimed that *any* way of introducing conflict into the mind of the child should produce acceleration of development. If so, simply telling the child that he is wrong should facilitate development. By and large, however, this does not seem to produce conceptual development. What it will do is produce correct verbal responses in relatively specific situations. A child has little difficulty in learning to say what an adult tells him to say, but there is little evidence of transfer from such training to new situations and no evidence whatsoever that such training produces comprehension of what happens in a conservation test. Subjects in such experiments parrot what they have been told. Their justifications are quite different from those given by children who have developed the concepts "spontaneously" (Strauss, 1972; Brainerd, 1973).

The word "spontaneous" in this context does not imply maturational influences. Piaget (1967a) argues that "spontaneous" development reflects the child's encounters with large numbers of events in his environment. The changes produced by such encounters are, in Piaget's view, quite different from the changes produced by simple case-by-case instruction. This is not to say that we cannot facilitate development by manipulating the environment. However, facilitation of cognitive development is not the same thing as teaching a correct verbal response in a specific situation.

Berry (1966, 1971) has made an extremely fascinating attempt to characterize those environmental features that facilitate or retard the appearance of concrete operations. In his view we must look at the kind of information that a culture requires its members to transmit from one to another if we are to understand the diverse patterns of development that occur in diverse cultures. Sensorimotor acquisitions are an entirely individual affair—the individual must pick up the relevant skills if he is to cope with the world of objects and he must do it alone, because, lacking language, there is no way he can be taught. In some cultures these skills may remain individual, for the members of the culture may never be in a situation where they must communicate such information to one another. Only when communication is required, when the individual's concept must be expressed in communicable form, will concrete operations be required. The essence of operational concepts, as opposed to sensorimotor concepts, is that they are cast in linguistic terms so as to permit efficient communication of the essential information.

Dasen (1975) has attempted to test the validity of Berry's hypotheses.

He studied two groups whose cultures impose very different communication requirements. One group was Cape Dorset Eskimos, a nomadic hunting people. Spatial information is critical to them because they must be able to communicate information about routes and locations if they are to survive at all. On Berry's model there should be a cultural demand for the development of operational concepts of space. On the other hand, there is no great requirement in their culture for communication about quantities of any sort. Game, for example, is caught and eaten by the family group; the division follows qualitative rather than quantitative rules, as it is distributed according to kinship or social relationship. It is not divided up and sold or exchanged. At the other extreme, Dasen studied Africans in Adiopodoumé (French Cameroons). These are agricultural people who do not travel; they grow food on a seasonal basis, store it, sell it, and exchange it. It would seem that in their culture there is no demand for transmission of spatial information but a very high requirement for efficient transmission of information about quantities, weights, and volumes. If cultural demand is important in generating operational concepts, the Eskimos should be far ahead of the Africans in development of spatial concepts and far behind them in development of quantitative concepts. The results of the study (Figure 8–7) fitted perfectly with the cultural demand hypothesis.

There is an even more striking demonstration of the effects of social communication requirements on cognitive development in a study by Price-Williams and his colleagues (1969). They studied the development of conservation skills in children whose families earned their living as potters in Mexico. The children helped their parents. The control group were other Mexican children living in the same town, matched in terms of age and socioeconomic variables, whose families earned their living in other ways. All of the children were aged between six and nine years of age. The hypothesis was that pottery-making families would require efficient transmission of information about amounts of clay, water, etc., and so the children should develop the relevant conservation skills more rapidly than their peers whose family activities did not demand transmission of such information. The hypothesis was resoundingly confirmed, particularly for conservation of substance, the most relevant skill in pottery-making.

The hypothesis that the communication requirements of the cultural milieu are causal factors in the generation of operational skills leads to some odd predictions. Children in a milieu in which particular types of information are not crucial, and who have therefore not developed certain operational skills, should develop the skills readily if the requirements of the milieu are changed. In the study described above, Dasen presented some evidence that this may be the case. The 10–12 year olds in his Eskimo group seemed to acquire conservation concepts simply from the cumulative questioning spread over 12 days, with no real training or instruction.

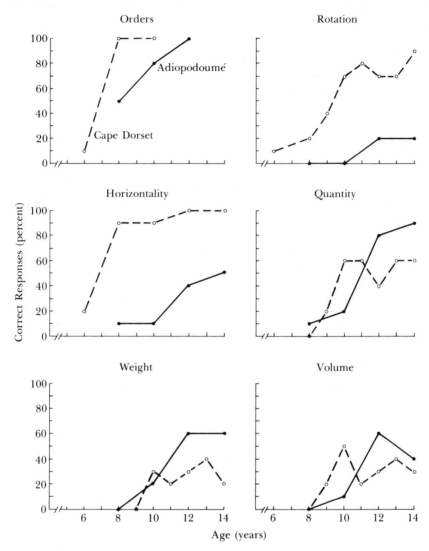

FIGURE 8–7

According to the cultural demand hypothesis, Cape Dorset Eskimos should do better on tasks requiring spatial concepts (horizontality, rotation, orders) than the African subjects from Adiopoduomé. The reverse should be true for tasks requiring quantitative concepts (quantity, weight, volume). As can be seen here, the predictions were confirmed. (Dasen, 1975.)

These results are fascinating. They make the mystery of the long period of nonconservation in Western European children even more mysterious. Why is it that a European or American child, in an environment that does demand transmission of information about quantities, persists in non-conservation?

EXPLANATIONS OF THE PROBLEM OF CONSERVATION

Standard attempts at explanation, from Piaget onward, have argued that the preoperational child does not understand the operational concepts necessary for conservation.* It is argued, for example, that the child does not comprehend compensation. Given the conservation of liquid problem (see Figure 8.1, p. 181), he does not understand that although the column of water is higher in the second glass, it is also narrower, and that the one change is *compensated* for by the other. In addition, it is assumed the child does not understand that the change is *reversible*, that by pouring the water back he could finish up with the same amount. Finally, the child is not supposed to understand the *identity* concept, i.e., if nothing is added and nothing taken away, then the quantity must remain the same. Attempts at accelerating the development of conservation skills have for the most part focused on developing these supposedly basic concepts (Strauss, 1972; Brainerd, 1973; and Wohlwill, 1973). The poor results of these attempts are evidence of the feebleness of the standard explanation of the problems of the preoperational child. Whatever these problems are, they have *nothing* to do with the operations described above.

The reasoning that goes with nonconservation is truly astonishing as the following protocol may illustrate. The child has just been presented with two equal quantities of water in two identical glasses and asked what will happen if one of them is poured into a narrow glass.

> *It will be more* — Why? — *Because this one is thinner, so the water will go higher.* — And that will mean there is more water? — *Yes.* (Pouring is then carried out. The child compares levels.) *See. It's more.* — If I pour it back what will happen? — *It'll be the same again.* — It's more now, but it'll be the same when I pour it back? — *Yes, unless you spill some.*

This child understands that the water in the narrow ("thin") glass rises to a higher level because the glass is narrower. She realizes that the pouring back will result in two equal levels and quantities again. She knows that the transformation is completely reversible unless some water is taken away during it. Nonetheless, she maintains that the initial transformation results in an *increase* in the amount of water. Thus the preoperational child uses operational concepts to explain nonconservation. The operational child uses the same operations to explain conservation. The irrelevance of the operations could hardly be clearer. Application of these operations can indeed lead to erroneous answers in some tasks.

---

* See for example Piaget and Inhelder, 1974 (orig. 1941), 1956 (orig. 1948), 1975 (orig. 1951); Piaget, Inhelder, and Szeminska, 1964 (orig. 1948).

Consider the pseudo-conservation problem shown in Figure 8–8. Here there is a change in one dimension and an opposite change in another dimension. The transformation is reversible. Nonetheless the transformed area is not equal to the untransformed area. How are children to know that this pseudo-conservation problem is different from a true conservation problem, as indeed they do (unlike child psychologists, who, by and large, get this problem wrong)? The critical point, for this as for all true conservations, lies not in the defining operations discussed thus far. What then is the critical point?

Consider the phenomenon of *horizontal decalage*, the fact that there is a considerable gap between the ages of solution to the various discontinuous conservations shown in Figure 8–9. Children may use the *same* operations to justify conservation in one case and nonconservation in another, again pointing to the irrelevance of the operations. What *is* different between the various tasks is the difficulty of the schemas of measurement required to justify conservation. Developmentally, the easiest conservation task is conservation of discontinuous quantity (Figure 8–9) because the unit in it is given; the child can therefore establish a one-to-one correspondence between the two sets. By matching each unit in one set with each unit in the other, he can find out whether the sets are equivalent. Establishing any kind of one-to-one correspondence is far more difficult for all the other conservations. Conservation of area, for example, requires a two-dimensional unit of comparison (Figure 8–9). Solving the pseudo-conservation problem in Figure 8–8 likewise requires a two-dimensional unit of measure. The equation of volume problem, the most difficult of these problems, requires a three-dimensional unit if it is to be solved (Figure 8–9). Is it any wonder we get horizontal decalage?

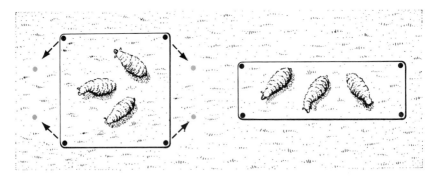

FIGURE *8–8*

In this problem the child is asked to imagine that there is an area of grass bounded by the string and the four sticks. The area is then transformed by moving the sticks, and the child is asked if there is as much grass for the sheep to eat after this transformation as before.

Conservation of Discontinuous Quantity

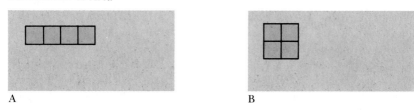

Conservation of Area

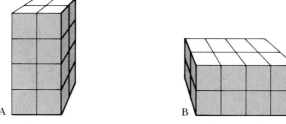

Conservation of Volume

FIGURE *8–9*

Discontinuous conservations. In the first task (conservation of quantity, or number concept) the child is asked if there are as many items in row A as row B. In the second task (conservation of area) the child is told that houses have been built in a field; each house shares the rest of the field with the others in its group. Do the two sets of houses (A and B) have the same amount of field to share? In the third task (conservation of volume) the child is shown a "house" of blocks (A) and asked to make another "house" with as much room inside but on a different base (B).

In a way, continuous conservation problems, e.g., conservation of liquid, substance, and weight (see Figure 8–1), are even more abstruse. Such problems can only be solved by comparing two temporally separated displays. Simultaneous matching of units is not therefore possible. Indeed, the only way the child can find units for these conservation tasks is to take the given quantity (e.g., the amount of water in the glass) as a unit, an algebraic unit with no specific numerical value. Once the idea of the given quantity as unit is accepted by the child, conservation must follow, for it is part of the definition of a unit that it is invariant. The steps leading up to this would have to include dissatisfaction with height as a measure; realization by the child that he knew no way other than height to measure continuous quantity; and finally, acceptance of the algebraic unit. The conservation attained thus is precarious, as we shall see.

Motor behavior would be impossible unless the concept of a unit were somehow embedded in the structure of the nervous system. Neither manipulation nor locomotion would be possible without some internal representation of size, weight, and distance—a size, weight, and distance coordinated with the size, weight, and distance of the physical world. For example, a baby who can pick up a 1″ cube can instantly make the motor adjustment necessary to pick up a 2″ cube or even a 3″ cube. However, the "units" of motor behavior are not the abstract units of conservation tasks. The conceptualization of an abstract unit is thus a genuine revolutionary discovery, an intellectual advance akin to the advance from arithmetic to algebra. Once the child discovers for himself that any amount can be taken as a unit, which is then invariant by definition, conservation is not a problem. In fact, questions about conservation are often seen by children who understand conservation as "silly."

The hypothesis outlined above receives some support from studies of spatial conservations. Conservation of length is facilitated if the child is given a ruler or other measuring unit. Conservation of volume—in the sense of ability to construct equal volumes—seems to be possible only after children have invented units. The third experimental problem shown in Figure 8–9 would seem to be easy for a child who can solve the conservation of liquid problem. In fact this is not the case. The *construction* of equal volumes with different shapes seems much more difficult than *recognition* of volume equality. When different shapes are involved, the inability to use even ready-made units is striking, as the following protocol makes clear (Piaget, Inhelder, and Szeminska, 1960):

> FLU (5; 0) (The child is told to rebuild a model of $3 \times 3 \times 4$ units on an island measuring 2×3; the "house" which he builds is $2 \times 3 \times 4$, i.e., its height is the same as that of the model.) "Is that enough? — *Yes, that's enough.* — Which of these two houses is bigger? — *That one* (the model). — Well, what are you going to do about it? (He adds another story to his building, which makes it $2 \times 3 \times 5$ units or a total of 30, against 36 in the model.) — Is that right now? — *No. Here* (pointing to his copy) *there are more bricks.* — Well, I want you to build me a house using the same number of bricks. — (He changes his house back to $2 \times 3 \times 4$ by removing the top story.) Is yours the same size now? — *Yes.* — How do you know? — *Because I put the bricks there.* — Is there the same amount of room inside it? — *It's the same because it's the same height.*" — (He is given a model half the size of the first, measuring $3 \times 3 \times 2$ units, so that it has 18 units in all and is built up of two layers. Once again he is asked to build another the same size on an "island" measuring 2×3 units: immediately FLU builds a house $2 \times 3 \times 2$ units, i.e., the same height as the model.) "Are there the same amount of rooms in both houses? — *Yes, because it has these bricks.* — Have you measured it? — *Yes* (indicating that the two heights are the same). — But what about that (pointing to the difference in breadth, 2 in the copy, 3 in the model)? —

Oh, yes! (He adds a third story). — Is that right now? — *No, that* (his copy, $2 \times 3 \times 3$) *is bigger than that* (the model, $3 \times 3 \times 2$). — Where is there more room? — *There* (pointing to his copy, the higher construction.) — Well? — (He takes the top story off again.) — Well, let's try and build a house with as much room as that one (18 bricks) on that little island (1×1). — (He puts two bricks together, one above the other, giving the same height as the model.) — Is there the same amount of room in that one? — *No, it's tiny.* — Well, what are you going to do about it? (He adds a third brick.) Is that enough? (He adds a fourth.) Is that right now? — *No, this* ($1 \times 1 \times 4$) *is bigger than that* (the model, $3 \times 3 \times 2$!) *because I've put a lot of bricks to it.*"

Successful children use units spontaneously, as the following protocol illustrates (Piaget, Inhelder, and Szeminska, 1960):

GRA (9; 6) (This child has apparently found out for himself how to evaluate volume, for bright as he is, he is [still] in the same class at school as others of his own age, and geometry has not yet been touched.) — "See if you can build me a house with the same amount of room as mine ($3 \times 3 \times 4$) but on this island (2×3). — *I can see it's a bit small* (having built $2 \times 3 \times 4$). *It's different in width, so I've got to put more on top.* — How would you do it? — *I count the bricks first* (those bricks on the model which project beyond the copy). *There are twelve of them in the row, so I simply put them over the top* ($2 \times 3 \times 6$). — All right. Now how would you build a house like this one ($2 \times 3 \times 6$) on this island (2×2)? — *If you take the bricks in this* ($2 \times 3 \times 6$) *house there are 36 of them: here* (on the 2×2 island) *you'll have 4 for each story, so there are 9 stories* ($2 \times 2 \times 9$). — What about rebuilding this ($3 \times 3 \times 4$) on this island (3×4)? — *I count them* (on the model). *All the sides are 3, which makes 9 in each story. Then there are 4 stories and that's $4 \times 9 = 36$, since each story is 9, 3×3, and there are 4 altogether.* (Whereupon he constructs $3 \times 4 \times 3$). *There, now the house is finished.* — Has it the same amount of room? — *Yes.*"

Arriving at the concept of a unit is perhaps the most significant attainment of the concrete-operational period. It is an attainment, too, that seems to be progressive from the sensorimotor period. Body referent units are readily available and readily used all through childhood—distances, for example, are spontaneously thought of as so many steps. This body reference system can be satisfactory but can also lead to errors. Young children tend to think the distance from the bottom of a mountain to the top is greater than the distance from the top to the bottom. In purely muscular terms this makes sense, since it requires much more effort to get up a mountain than to get down. In a study of (nontaught) measurement, Piaget found that body units were used spontaneously by children (Piaget, Inhelder, and Szeminska, 1960). In the task used the children were shown a tower of 12 blocks, 80 cm high, placed on a table. The child was asked to build a tower of the same height on another table, which was 90 cm shorter than the table with the model. The child was given smaller blocks to use, many more than he needed. Sticks, strips of paper, and other things, all potential measuring units, were available but not mentioned by the experimenter. The youngest children relied exclusively on visual comparison. Given the size of the towers and the height of the average four-year-old, this is not surprising. Slightly older children made errors that would suggest an over-generalization of the principle involved in conservation of quantity, the principle of one-to-one correspondence. By making a one-to-one correspondence between the bricks in the two towers, they succeeded only in building a smaller tower, since the bricks they were using were smaller than those in the original model. Other children in the same range would use their bodies as measures, marking off the height of the towers relative to their own height. As Piaget points out, the essential idea of a unit is that the sizes of two things can be compared by comparing each with a third term. Implicit in this is the idea that if $A = B$, and $B = C$, it must be true that $A = C$. Body measures are soon abandoned and the child goes on to use sticks. At first the sticks must simply match the height of one or the other tower. Later true measurement becomes possible, e.g., defining height as six times a standard unit.

All but the very youngest children studied understood the essential ideas in measurement. The children who made one-to-one correspondences were using units, albeit inappropriate ones, and did accept the reasoning that if $A = B$ and $B = C$, then $A = C$. The idea of a unit thus seems primitive in development. As we said above, any motor movement carries within it the idea of a unit. The use of motor units as third terms likewise seems very primitive, e.g., the use of steps to measure distance.

Continuous conservations can be made easier for the child if the analogy with discontinuous conservations is made more obvious. If the task is presented so that one-to-one comparisons are possible, the problem is much less difficult for the child (Figure 8–10). This kind of presentation

---

FIGURE *8–10* (*Opposite*)

A. Conservation of continuous volume can be made simpler for the child if the analogy with discontinuous conservation is made. The experimenter and the child simultaneously drop eight or 10 beads, one by one, into two identical opaque glasses and the child agrees that the number of beads in each glass is the same (1). The same procedure is again followed, this time using transparent glasses of different diameter. The child can therefore see the differences in height and width between the two collections of beads but will agree that they are still equivalent (2). The experimenter then goes back to the two identical opaque glasses and *pours* their contents into the two transparent glasses of different height and width (3). By analogy with the earlier tasks, the child may now be able to answer correctly questions on the conservation of continuous volume.
B. Conservation of weight or substance can also be presented in a discontinuous fashion. Small squares of plasticine are presented (step 1). If the child agrees that sets A and B are equivalent in substance or weight, the experiment then proceeds. Set A is transformed as shown (steps 2–8) while set B remains unchanged. The child must agree that both sets are still equivalent after each step. Again, such a presentation will facilitate success with the same problem presented in a continuous fashion.

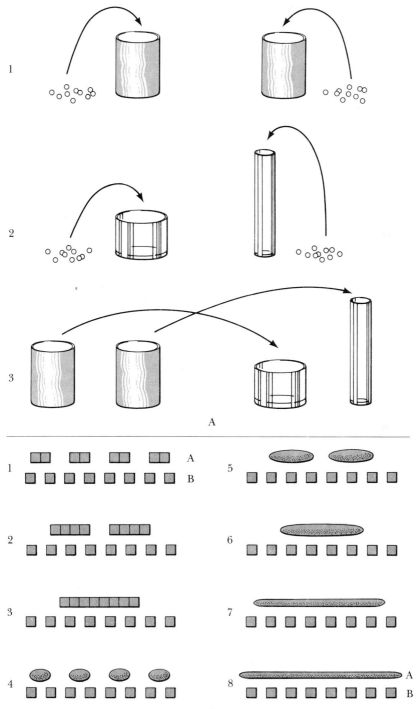

A

B

has been successfully used to accelerate the development of continuous conservations (Inhelder, Sinclair, and Bovet, 1974). Without the possibility of using units that allow one-to-one correspondence, the child will use the obvious and generally useful dimensions of length, height, or width for comparison and almost certainly come to an incorrect conclusion. Not even an adult can make correct judgements of equality with such information. Only by taking an algebraic identity as a unit can the child cope with the problem. Since the essence of continuous conservation is to give up precise measurement (see pp. 195–196), it should come as no surprise that recognizing the identity of two volumes of different shape in the conservation of liquid problem does not signify an ability to *construct* two equal volumes of different shape. The latter requires countable units. Furthermore, the counting must take place in three dimensions. The increasing number of dimensions is almost certainly responsible for the increasing difficulty of the three discontinuous conservation problems shown in Figure 8–9, involving as they do one, two, then three dimensions of comparison, with consequent increases in the amount of information that must be processed simultaneously. Growth in information-processing capacity could thus account for the eventual successful solution of the most difficult conservation tasks.

THE ROLE OF REPRESENTATION
IN THE DEVELOPMENT
OF CONCRETE OPERATIONS

We have not so far discussed the problem of representation, the problem of how the child thinks about problems, or rather *what* he thinks with when he thinks about problems. This is an area where there is some controversy. Some have argued that the preoperational child thinks exclusively in terms of pictures and cannot represent actions or events symbolically in any way (Bruner, Olver, and Greenfield, 1966). Piaget has carried out a number of experiments that would seem to point to the opposite conclusion, that preoperational children think in terms of words or symbols and that the restrictions of these, e.g., their limited information content, are responsible for at least some of their difficulties (Piaget, 1967b; Piaget and Inhelder, 1968). The experiments were extremely simple. Children of various ages were shown various displays and asked to reproduce the displays after a variety of time intervals, ranging from a few hours to a few months. For example, a picture of a tilted glass with water in it was reproduced by preoperational children in ways that suggested verbal storage of the form "a tilted glass with water in it." But not "knowing" how water behaves, preoperational children produced the displays shown in Figure 8–11. Paradoxically, when the same preopera-

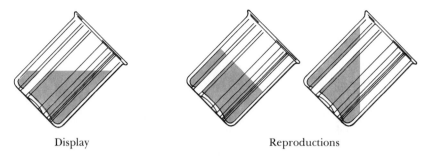

Display   Reproductions

FIGURE *8–11*
Reproductions of the display on the left by preoperational children show a lack of understanding of how water behaves in a glass.

tional children became operational, their "memory" improved and their reproductions became accurate. This could hardly represent an improvement in a memory image since they never saw the display again after the original presentation. Rather, it must have been a change in their interpretation of their symbolically encoded memory. This and many similar experiments seem to suggest that preoperational children are not able to form images of displays, but rather rely on symbolic descriptions for memory.

DEVELOPMENT IN
THE BLIND AND DEAF

The most interesting studies of representation are studies of children who lack one or other sensory modality, and so cannot represent events in that modality. As discussed earlier, blind children cannot represent spatial events in the same way as normal children do, since they never perceive the three-dimensional world that we do. The deaf, by contrast, are not exposed to language as we are. They do communicate, of course, but the auditory modality is not available to them for representation. O'Connor and Hermelin (1972) have called attention to another subtle difference that stems from the sensory handicaps of the blind and deaf, namely the way in which the two groups order incoming information. Events that occur at different times and different places may be ordered in terms of either their spatial or their temporal order. The ordering chosen will affect the answer to such questions as, "What came before X?" Will the word "before" be given a spatial or a temporal reference? In one of the studies by O'Connor and Hermelin it was found that deaf subjects never used a temporal ordering system but rather a purely spatial one. The blind, by contrast, used a purely temporal order and virtually never relied upon a spatial one (Figure 8–12). Normal subjects could use either. How would such ordering affect cognitive development?

Consider the conservation tasks that we have been discussing. We argued that some of these (the discontinuous problems) could be solved on the basis of immediately available information, by relying on the one-to-one correspondence rule applied to temporally simultaneous but spatially separate arrays, whereas as others (the continuous problems) were more difficult because they could be solved only by comparing two temporally separate items. The blind, who cannot and do not order events spatially, should find the two types of conservation equally difficult, since for them both will involve temporally separate comparisons. Compared with sighted children, whether hearing or deaf, they should be relatively disadvantaged on conservation problems normally solved by simultaneous comparisons. They should not be so disadvantaged on those conservation problems that

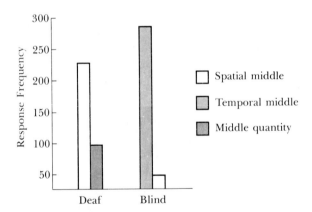

FIGURE *8–12*

Three digits were presented successively, either visually (for deaf subjects) from a display box with three apertures or auditorily (for blind subjects) from three loudspeakers arranged around the subject, to the left, in front, and to the right. The second digit was always presented on the left or right positions and never in the middle. The subject was then asked which of the three digits was the "middle" one. The graph shows that most deaf subjects chose the number presented in the spatial middle (the middle aperture), while blind subjects overwhelmingly chose the temporally middle number (the second number presented). A few deaf subjects chose the middle *quantity*, e.g., the number 10 in the series 10, 8, 15, while a very small number of blind subjects chose the spatial middle, i.e., the number heard from the loudspeaker in the middle location. (O'Connor and Hermelin, 1972.)

require comparisons in time. Available data supports both of these predictions.

What of the deaf? Any problem that requires temporal ordering should be more difficult for them since they do not spontaneously set events in a temporal frame. The conservations that require this, such as conservation of continuous quantity, should thus be more difficult for them, although they should have no more difficulty than normal children with the other conservations. Available data again support this prediction. Numerous authors have found delays in acquisition of conservation of continuous quantity of up to five years in deaf children. The delay was quite specific to that task and did not show up in other conservation tasks (Oléron, 1953; Oléron and Herren, 1961; Furth, 1964, 1971).

The fact that both blind and deaf children go through the same developmental progression as normal children, from preoperational to operational stages, would argue that images and words are not involved either in the errors of the preoperational period or in the successes of the operational period. Instead, as Piaget has argued, and as we concluded for the sensorimotor period, the units of thought would seem to be something quite abstract, i.e., both nonverbal and nonpictorial (Bower, 1977c). The ordering effects described above presumably reflect the lack of opportunity to use one or the other of the possible ordering principles. The ordering principles themselves are not sensory inputs; they are supramodal rules for ordering inputs through any of the senses. Audition demands a temporal order. Vision permits a spatial ordering, although temporal ordering is equally possible. The deaf are never required to express temporal ordering principles in speech and so presumably use them less than do hearing children. The blind can never use the spatial ordering possible with vision. Both thus face difficulties with some specific cognitive tasks.

SENSORIMOTOR CONCEPTS AND CONCRETE CONCEPTS

In Chapter 3 we defined development as an irreversible change in structure producing irreversible changes in functioning. Chapter 7 was devoted to an outline of the cognitive attainments of the sensorimotor stage. At the beginning of this chapter we described how these attainments disintegrate under the onslaught of language, i.e., with the need to communicate with others. If these attainments vanish so readily, are they indeed developmental? Are they even important in the overall context of development? Can we ignore infancy in our account of cognition? There is evidence that these attainments are important. The evidence comes from studies of children born blind (see pp. 140–142).

It seems that attainment of the sensorimotor concepts of space is necessary for attainment of the operational concepts. It is tempting to generalize and say that every sensorimotor concept is equally critical for its corresponding operational concept. However, the way that some sensorimotor concepts disappear under the impact of language makes this conclusion difficult to maintain. How could something that disappears be critical for subsequent development? How can something that no longer exists exert any kind of influence? This is the most difficult problem in constructing a theory linking sensorimotor and operational concepts. However, it is only a part of the larger problem of linking sensorimotor and operational development. Piaget has long maintained that sensorimotor development is critical for development of operational structures, yet the precise link between the two has never been specified. Earlier we noted that sensorimotor concepts can transfer perfectly well to a verbal response if the testing is done early enough. Transfer is thus one possible model for the relation between sensorimotor and operational responses. However, early transfer between sensorimotor and operational concepts is not the most common paradigm; conflict or transfer so delayed as to seem like reacquisition is in fact more common.

How does the conflict come about? By the end of infancy the child has developed concepts that enable him to deal with practical problems in the world around him. We have argued that many of these concepts are stored, their behavioral results having been schematized. When the child starts to talk he learns to use words that refer to the same aspects of the world he has learned to control behaviorally. The words are used for communication, to control the behavior of others and to control the behavior of the child himself. The learning necessary to use the critical words of the concrete-operational period ("more," "less," and so on) does not utilize the same type of information as is embedded in the sensorimotor concepts. A child can learn to use the word "more" very successfully just by concentrating on one dimension. "More to drink" equals a higher level in the glass; "more to eat" equals a larger number of things, regardless of size; "more to play with" equals a larger visible area, and so on.

This is not at all the kind of thing the baby learns during the sensorimotor period. Consider weight conservation. The child probably learns that the muscular force necessary to transport an object is not affected by changes in the shape of the object. This kind of information can happily coexist with the idea that "more" and "less" refer only to one dimension of an object, until the idea of "heavier" meaning "requiring more muscular force for transport" enters the child's lexicon. At this point there will be a conflict between the sensorimotor control of behavior and the verbal control of behavior. As we saw, the verbal control wins. This is quite reasonable. The sensorimotor concept is in store. The behaviors generated by it require no "thought." The verbal concept, by contrast, is still in play as the child struggles to use words like "more" and "heavier." In the beginning of language acquisition the verbal control is bound to lead to erroneous behavior while the sensorimotor solution will lead to correct behavior. What is the child to do? He knows two kinds of things:

SENSORIMOTOR	LINGUISTIC
The same object requires the same force for transport regardless of changes in its shape.	"longer" = "heavier" ("heavier" means requiring more force for transport)

The only solution is the operational solution, which comprises all of the information in the above two preexisting structures along with an algebraic idea of unit.

Similar processes operate in the development of conservation of liquid. Quite young children know that the quantity of a liquid is unaffected when it is poured from one container into another of a different shape. At the same time they have learned that "more" equals "higher." The two ideas come into conflict, and the only way out is again use of an algebraic unit. It is this combination of sensorimotor concepts with ideas of measure that can only be expressed in language that constitutes the major advances of the operational period. The sensorimotor concepts are the internal reality test for the ideas of measure expressed in language. The key word here is "internal." We have been emphasizing the role of conflict in generating cognitive advances. The conflict we are talking about is internal. What is internal as opposed to external conflict? An internal conflict can only arise within an organism when the organism has two incompatible ways of handling the same problem. An external conflict arises whenever the organism has one way of coping with a situation that does not accord with reality. The latter kind of conflict is easy to arrange. However, it does not typically lead to cognitive advances. Rather, it leads to retreat from the situation. One experimental situation that produced retreat was described in the last chapter (pp. 163–164). Others have been reported as the result of attempts to accelerate the development of concrete operations.* For the clearest examples of what happens when only external conflicts are imposed upon an organism, we must look again at the congenitally blind child. It seems clear that the blind child does not develop the spatial concepts of the seeing child, either in infancy or later. The blind child, we have argued, copes with the world in a one-dimensional way, organizing events in time rather than space. What happens then if such a one-dimensional mind is given three-dimensional problems? The answer is a general and progressive retreat from such problem situations.

---

*See for example Smedslund, 1961; Strauss, 1972; Brainerd, 1973; Inhelder, Sinclair, and Bovet, 1974.

Performance on quite simple spatial tasks actually declines with age among congenitally blind children.* Such children have no internal options when faced with these situations, no way to go but out of the situation—and out of the situation they assuredly do go. In other words, continually telling any child that he is wrong will only drive him from the problem situation unless he has the internal resources to look at the problem in a different way. The normal child is not likely to be harmed by external conflict because he does have alternative internal resources. Only with pathological individuals like the blind is it possible to do irremedial damage by introducing external conflicts.

CONCRETE OPERATIONS
IN PERSPECTIVE

The concrete-operational period is a busy period in development. We have discussed various ways in which concrete operations can become possible. The child must have a sensorimotor substructure plus a set of communicational demands before anything can happen. At the beginning of the chapter, I briefly described cross-cultural studies that indicated that not all concrete operations are attained in all cultures. It seems clear, however, that children in all cultures *can* attain all of them, although if this is not done in childhood it may become impossible. This problem will be discussed in Chapter 9.

Although the concepts acquired in the concrete-operational period are of obvious functional value, they contain within themselves the seeds of their own destruction. During the concrete-operational period the child learns to distrust his senses and to rely on schemas of measurement. This distrust is responsible for the final flowering of cognitive development, the attainment of formal operations, the subject of our next chapter.

From the point of view of cognitive development, the infant is alone in the world, i.e., he cannot ask questions or get answers from others. By the end of the concrete-operational period this is no longer so. The operational child can cooperate with others and can exchange information that he picks up from direct inspection of the world. But the operational child is still restricted to the world as it can be directly experienced. His basic world is not different from that of the infant—it is the world as it can be seen, heard, or touched. It is with the next great intellectual step, to the formal-operations stage, that the child begins to adventure beyond this world to unseen worlds, including the world of science.

---

* The percentage of *unsuccessful* responses from blind children to the task shown in Figure 8–2 was 8.3 at 8–9 years, 13.9 at 10 years, and 20·8 at 11 years.

9

Cognitive Development in Adolescence

The formal-operations period, when propositional thought develops, is the last advance in intellectual functioning that has thus far been described by developmental psychologists. But like the advance into language, its first symptom is a retreat. On entering the formal period, the child again makes errors that are more characteristic of much younger children. Consider the familiar problem of conservation of weight. Babies of 18 months or so can demonstrate a behavioral form of weight conservation. By eight years or so the child can express a verbal form of conservation of weight. The latter disappears about the age of 12, after the threshold of the formal period has been crossed (Dasen and Christie, 1972). It seems that the other conservation concepts suffer the same decline (see the review by Brainerd, 1973).

In Chapter 6 we argued that this decline is the result of an attempt to make the concepts more precise, an attempt to free them from their partial correlation with the real world, partial correlations that can lead to errors. For example, "bigger" usually equals "heavier," but not necessarily. Weight is an independent dimension but it is *not* one that is given directly through the senses. We can only experience the weight of an object of a given volume, and it is very hard for us to dissociate weight and volume so long as we only have the information coming through our senses. Small objects feel heavier than large objects of the same weight, presumably because they exert more pressure on the skin surface we use to gauge weight.

The child is given a great deal of evidence that experienced weight does change when shape is changed. At the same time, as in the popcorn example mentioned before, size can change drastically without affecting weight. Bread and cakes, as they rise, provide similar, though less dramatic instances. In not one of these cases is there any way that direct sensory information can be used to resolve the paradoxes.

Soluble substances provide a similar challenge to the senses. A lump of sugar is dropped into a glass of water; the level of the water rises; eventually the sugar disappears, but the level of the water remains elevated. Why? How? The sugar is no longer there, as far as the eye can see, and yet it is still producing an effect, as the eye can very well see. Again resolution of this contradiction cannot be given by the senses.

Both of these problems require the child to invent invisible events to explain what can be seen. The following protocols give an indication of how long this takes and how difficult the step is (Piaget and Inhelder, 1941). The children are discussing the popping of popcorn.

NOS (8; 0) Will the seed keep its size? — *No, it's going to get bigger, it'll swell.* — Why? — *It's the heat. It'll burn a bit, and then it'll swell up, just like when you burn your finger.* — How do you explain that? — *There are grains inside, the heat makes them come out.* — (The seed bursts) Is it still the same weight? — *It's got heavier.* — Why? — *Because it's bigger.* — If you look at this one (an unpopped kernal) under a microscope what do you think you will see? — *Small grains.* — And this one? (A popped kernel.) — *This one has more grains.* — How can you tell? — *Oh, no they have the same number but they have grown bigger.* — Is there more flour in this one (popped) than in that one (unpopped) or are they the same? — *There is more.*

MAT (10; 0) *The heat has blown them up. These seeds breathe the heat in.* — How so? — *The heat gets inside them and takes up room.* — But how? — *The grain has pores through which the heat can pass.* — Has it stayed the same weight? — *This one* (unpopped) *is heavier, and that one* (popped) *is lighter.* — Why? — *The air weighs less than the seed; it takes away part of the weight.* — Why? — *That one* (unpopped) *has not been opened up by the heat; when it opens, it loses part of its force.* — But how is it that this one (popped) is bigger and lighter? — *The heat takes up space, the stuff inside has been blown up.* — What stuff? — *Skins packed tight against one another.* — And what does the heat do? — *It pulls them apart.* — And if we could count them, would there be as many in here (unpopped) as in there (popped)? — *Yes, it's the same number because it's the same grains. One has been blown up and the other is closed, but it's the same.*

SORO (11; 0) *The heat has opened it up and then it burst.* — Why? — *The heat made it bigger.* — How? — *I don't know, I've never been told. There is some air inside.* — Are there more things in the seed than before? — *No, it's the same; it's just that the skin is liable to burst. It's grown bigger.* — How? — *It's opened out.* — What does that mean? — *It's collapsed, it's filled with air, by the heat I think.* — But how has it grown bigger? — *Here* (unpopped kernel) *it was all tight, that is squashed into a piece, but with the heat it's burst open.* — Does it weigh more? — *It weighs the same, because this one* (popped) *is exactly the same as that one* (unpopped). — How do you know? — *Because that one* (unpopped) *is in a piece, it's squashed together, but this one* (popped) *has burst with the heat.* — Draw the two seeds as you might see them under the microscope. — (He draws a large circle for the unpopped kernel, and a much larger one for the popped one with a set of intersecting lines representing the division of the grain. — *You can see that this one* (unpopped) *is quite full, full of white matter. If we put that one* (popped) *into this one* (unpopped) *we would fill it completely.* — Are you sure they weigh the same? — *Yes.* — How do you explain that? — *In here* (the gaps between the lines in the popped one) *there's nothing but air.* — How did it get in? — *It's got small holes, it's not all closed up like the first one.* — And what if we looked at them under the microscope? — *We should see a large ball with little holes.*

The step to the formal stage is essentially a step forward in the ability to imagine and construct hypothetical events to explain observable events. This ability to deal with the hypothetical is very much the characteristic of formal thought, particularly in its first adolescent flush.

CULTURAL INFLUENCE
ON FORMAL THOUGHT

Not every member of every culture attains the full flowering of formal thought. Indeed, one study suggested that only 25 percent of American college students have fully developed the formal system (McKinnon and Renner, 1971). There has been no research on why some individuals never make the step. Moreover, the advance into formal thought does not always take the same form. Whole cultures have never expressed the particular formal advances that Piaget has observed to be made by most Swiss teenagers. The step to speculation has more frequently led to magic and religion than it has to science. The general cultural factors that produce the scientific expression that Piaget has described have not been elucidated. There is no reason to believe that individuals in any culture are from the beginning incapable of making these discoveries. The making of the discoveries, though, seems to depend on cultural factors that are beyond our compass at the moment. It is salutary to recall that the law of floating bodies, routinely discovered by teenagers in Europe and America, was such a novel discovery to the philosopher Archimedes that he allegedly leapt from his bath and ran shrieking through the streets of Athens. In more recent times the concept of probability, again a routine adolescent discovery in Western European culture, was considered shocking and heretical, because it conflicted with the speculative religious ideas that predominated at that time (Hacking, 1975).

Dasen has pointed out that the factors we generally use to explain intellectual advance, namely conflict or contradiction, may produce consequences that are deleterious in Western eyes (Berry and Dasen, 1975). It is likely that the experiential conflicts described above will occur in all cultures. Unless the culture offers the substructure for what we in Western European culture consider normal development, then formal, or speculative, development will take a non-Western, magical path, which may well result in greater differences between the adults of different cultures than between the children. Unfortunately, there have been too few studies of these differences. None that I know of have attempted to shift adults from one pattern of explanation to another. A study of this kind would be of great theoretical and practical significance. At present, the closest we can come to studying such shifts is to look at past scientific revolutions within Western European culture. Innovative discoveries that have simplified our view of the world were generally resisted at the time they were put forward. Many eminent physicists went to their deathbeds convinced that Einstein was wrong; similar resistance was offered to Darwin. Max Planck wrote sadly that "a new scientific truth does not triumph by convincing its opponents and making them see the light, but rather because its opponents die and a new generation grows up that is familiar with it." It seems that adults become wedded to their own speculations and find it very difficult to shift to another system, even though that other system may simplify the world considerably.

THE SPECIFICITY
OF FORMAL THOUGHT

Some Piagetian-oriented anthropologists and historians of science have described as primitive or preformal those cultures that did not arrive at the specific concepts of our present-day Western culture. This is a strangely egocentric position. As we said above, the average Western teenager seems to solve problems that the most eminent men of bygone ages could not solve at all. Consider one of Piaget's classic studies, in which the subject's task is to discover what controls the rate of swing of a pendulum (Figure 9–1). The obvious possible variables are the weight of the bob, the length of the string, the height of the initial release, and the force imparted by the observers. Only the length of the string is important. The following protocols, presented from youngest to oldest, illustrate the way that discovery of the relevance of the single variable becomes possible (Inhelder and Piaget, 1955). The youngest children tend to think the initial push they give the object is what is important.

HEN (6; 0) (Gives some pushes of varying force.) *This time it goes fast . . ., this time it's going to go faster.* — That's true? — *Oh! Yes.* (No objective account of the experiment.) — (Next he tries a large weight with a short string.) *It's going faster.* — (He pushes it.) *It's going even faster.* — And to make it go very fast? — *You have to take off all the weights and let the string go all by itself* (he makes it work but by pushing). *I'm putting them all back, it goes fast this time* (new pushes). — (He remarks on the elevation.) *If you put it very high, it goes fast* (he gives a strong push). — (Then he returns to the weight explanation.) *If you put on a little weight, it might go faster.* — (Finally we ask him if he really thinks that he has changed the rate.) *No, you can't; yes, you can change the speed.*

Older children get beyond this but cannot separate the variables involved.

BEA (10; 2) (Varies the length of the string, according to the units two, four, three, etc., taken in random order, but reaches the correct conclusion that there is an inverse correspondence.) *It goes slower when it's longer.* — (For the weight, he compares 100 grams with a length of two or five with 50 grams with a length of one and again concludes that there is an inverse correspondence between weight and frequency.) — (Then he varies the height of the drop without changing the weight or the length—without intending to hold them constant, but by simplification of his own movements—and he concludes) *The two heights go at the same speed.* — (Finally he varies the force of his push without modifying any other factor and again concludes) *It's exactly the same.*

PER (10; 7) (This is a remarkable case of a failure to separate variables: he varies simultaneously the weight and the impetus; then the weight, the

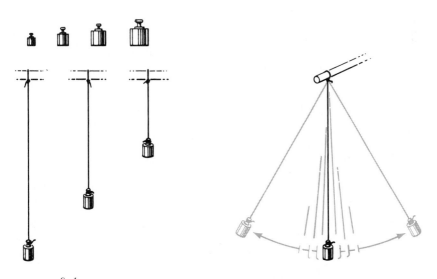

FIGURE *9–1*

The subject is presented with strings of various lengths and bobs of various weights. His problem is to discover what variable controls the rate of movement of the pendulum.

impetus, and the length; then the impetus, the weight, and the elevation, etc., and first concludes) *It's by changing the weight and the push, certainly not the string.* — How do you know that the string has nothing to do with it? — *Because it's the same string.* (He has not varied its length in the last several trials; previously he had varied it simultaneously with the impetus, thus complicating the account of the experiment.) — But does the rate of speed change? —. *That depends, sometimes it's the same. . . . Yes, not much. . . . It also depends on the height that you put it at* (the string). *When you let go low down, there isn't much speed.* — (He then draws the conclusion that all four factors operate.) *It's in changing the weight, the push, etc. With the short string, it goes faster,* (but also) *by changing the weight, by giving a stronger push,* (and) *for height, you can put it higher or lower.* — How can you prove that? — *You have to try to give it a push, to lower or raise the string, to change the height and the weight.* (He wants to vary all factors simultaneously.)

Eventually an empirical rule can be arrived at.

LOU (13; 4) (Also compares 20 grams on a short string to 50 grams on a long string and concludes) *It goes faster with the little weight.* — (Next, rather curiously, he performs the same experiment but reverses the weights: 50 grams with a long string and 100 grams with a short one. However, this time he concludes) *When it's short it goes faster* (and) *I found out that the big weight goes faster.* — (However, he has not concluded that the weight plays no role.) Does the weight have something to do with it? — *Yes.* (He takes a long string with 100 grams and a short one with 20 grams.) *Oh, I forgot to change the string.* (He shortens it, but without holding the weight constantly.) *Ah, no it shouldn't be changed.* — Why? — *Because I was looking at* (the effect of) *the string.* — But what did you see? — *When the string is long, it goes more slowly.* (Lou has thus verified the role of the length in spite of himself but has understood neither the need for holding the nonanalyzed factors constant nor the necessity for varying those which are analyzed.)

Finally, systematic experiments become possible.

EGG (15; 9) (At first believes that each of the four factors is influential. She studies different weights with the same string length (medium) and does not notice any appreciable change.) *That doesn't change the rhythm.* — (Then she varies the length of the string with the same 200 gram weight and finds that) *When the string is small, the swing is faster.* — (Finally, she varies the dropping point and the impetus, successively, with the same medium length string and the same 200 gram weight, concluding for each one of these two factors) *Nothing has changed.*

This is all very well and good. But there is nothing inevitable about the solution these children arrive at. Kuhn (1962) has pointed out how much these solutions owe to Galileo. He has pointed out that Aristotle could never have come to the result that Piaget's subjects so routinely did. For

Aristotle a pendulum was simply an instance of constrained falling. Aristotle believed that a heavy body is moved by its own nature from a higher position to a state of natural rest at a lower one. The pendulum was simply falling with difficulty, constrained by string, which was responsible for the time it took the body to achieve a state of rest. For Aristotle the only relevant variables were the weight of the stone, the vertical height to which it had been raised, and the time required for it to attain rest. The string was not critical; it was merely a constraint. Aristotle could never have come to the solution that today's teenagers do. Are we to say that Aristotle had a primitive, nonformal mind? The idea is obviously absurd. The specific forces he hypothesized were different from those common in our culture, but the two basics of formal thought, hypothetical processes and a system for manipulating them, were undoubtedly present. The essence of formal reasoning lies in two things: speculation about unseen events and causes, and fitting together propositions about these unseen events according to certain logical formulas, specifically the INRC group described in Chapter 6 (p. 139).

The attainment that best marks the emergence and establishment of formal thought is the ability to think in terms of *probabilities*. The essence of thought as we have portrayed it thus far is the attempt to find consistency in the data that confront us. In probability theory the data are not consistent in the precise way that most facts about the world are. Thinking in probabilistic terms gives us a way of dealing with chance events, events that do not have a direct causal relationship with anything. If the essence of formal thought is that it comprehends the possible as opposed to the actual, then the emergence of probabilistic reasoning is indeed the flowering of the formal period. It is also an attainment that shows more clearly than any other the all-pervasive influence of the general cultural milieu. Throughout infancy and thereafter the child has been searching for (and finding) order and consistency in the world around him. Probabilistic situations can only come as anathema to a mind prepared to find consistency in the world. Piaget and Inhelder (1951) presented children of various ages with the situation shown in Figure 9–2. The children were asked to predict what would happen when the box was tipped up and then back. For the youngest children something lawful and predictable in detail must always happen (Figure 9–2A). They predicted that the balls would return to their original positions or that there would be an ordered change of position for each set of balls.

> FER (5; 3) What if I tip the box? — *The balls will get all mixed up.* — How? — *The white will go there and the red there* (crossing of reds to one side and white to the other; he makes a drawing of four reds on the right and four white ones on the left.) — Where will that ball go if I tip the box? — *There* (return to the same place). — You had said that the white balls would go there and the red ones here? — *No, they will return to their places.*

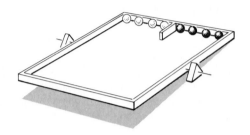

Predictions

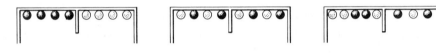

Trajectory Drawings

Return

Start

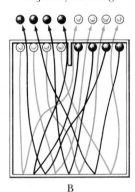
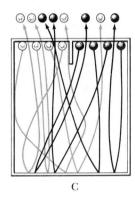

A   B   C

FIGURE *9–2*

Children of various ages are presented with the display shown at the top and asked what will happen when it is tipped up and back. According to the youngest children, the balls will always return to their starting points or all the red balls will cross to the opposite side while all the white balls will take their place (A). Older children realize there will be some mixture but do not fully understand its random nature (B). Eventually, the child comes to understand the interaction of the paths; he appreciates the random process of the mixing and that the outcome will be lawful but not predictable (C).

If asked to draw the paths the balls would take, the youngest children drew them without showing any interaction among the balls. Older children predicted that the return positions of the balls would be mixed but did not realize the random nature of this mixture (Figure 9–2B). Their drawings showed an awareness that the paths of the balls would cross but no allowance was made for the effects of these collisions; their drawings did not therefore coincide with their original predictions and showed an orderly arrangement of the balls.

The oldest subjects recognized that the outcome would be lawful but not predictable. They understood that the paths interact and their drawings of the paths and the final positions of the balls corresponded (Figure 9–2C).

ROS (12; 0) *I'm sure that it is going to get mixed up.* — And if I keep it up? — *Still more.* — Can they come back to their places? — *Oh, not to the same places.* — The red ones here and the white ones there? — *Oh, no, they're going to hit each other.* — And what if we keep it up until evening? — *They'll just get more mixed up.*

Such a child understands that the outcome is probabilistically determined.

Probabilistic knowledge rapidly reaches heights that are quite remarkable, at least in the light of history. Consider this problem posed by Piaget to a group of children from 10 years of age up. Twenty red and 20 blue marbles are put into a bag and successive pairs of marbles are drawn out. What will be the most probable distribution of the possible pairs, red-red, blue-blue, and mixed? As we might expect, the younger children simply could not cope. Children in the formal operations stage, however, knew just what was going on (Piaget and Inhelder, 1951).

MAR (12; 6) (Before drawing any.) *We will get two blues, or two reds, or a red one and a blue one.* — Which most often? — *Blue and red, I believe because it is mixed.* — Why? — *Because it is chance that mixes them. We will have mostly mixed ones.* — With 20 pairs? — *Maybe 10 mixed ones.* — And the others? — *Five for each one.* — Are you sure? — *We could get something slightly different, but less often.*

About 300 years ago the German philosopher and mathematician Leibniz, one of the greatest intellects the world has ever seen, the inventor of the calculus, failed to solve an exactly homologous problem. Hacking (1975) records the problem as one concerning dice. Given three dice to throw, what are the relative probabilities of obtaining a total of three versus a total of four? Leibniz said the probabilities were equal. Piaget's subjects, none of them geniuses, none of them more than 13 years old, would have skinned Leibniz in a game of craps. The problem they confronted was identical to the one facing Leibniz. The correct solution in both cases depends on differentiating partitions from permutations. In Piaget's situation there are three partitions: red-red, blue-blue, and mixed. Associated with the first partition is one permutation, red-red; likewise with the second. The third partition, by contrast, can be reached via two possible permutations, red-blue and blue-red. It is this latter fact, well appreciated by Piaget's subjects, that implies that the mixed partition will have twice as many entries as the others. In the problem faced by Leibniz, one can only throw a three using three dice with the partition, 1, 1, 1. One can only throw a four with the partition 1, 1, 2. The 1, 1, 1 partition can only be reached via one permutation. The 1, 1, 2 partition can be made via three permutations: 1, 1, 2, or 1, 2, 1, or 2, 1, 1. A four is thus three times as likely as a three, something Leibniz, one of the greatest minds of all time, could not comprehend, but something that today's teenagers comprehend without difficulty.

We don't know what it is in our present cultural milieu that makes probability such an accessible concept. We do have some ideas about why it was so inaccessible 300 years ago. Hacking points out that the very word "probable" had a totally different meaning 300 years ago; then it meant "approved." The idea of "chance" was not present much before that time. In Aquinian philosophy, the dominant view in Western Europe at the time, everything moved with a purpose. There was thus no room for chance in our modern sense. It took a whole intellectual revolution, beautifully described by Hacking, to bring about the changes in world view that today's teenagers find so easy to reconstruct. Since the best brains of the Renaissance world, faced with urgent demands from rich gamblers, simply could not come to probabilistic concepts, I can only argue that it is the change in world view, operating in some mysterious way, that makes the whole problem so easy today. Surely, no one would dare to say that Leibniz had a primitive mind in the sense that it was preformal. The "primitive" mind, as we said above, is nothing other than a mind that has taken an explanatory route different from that considered correct in our culture. Currently acceptable explanatory routes are in no way more absolutely correct than alternative routes that have been rejected.

THE GENERALITY
OF FORMAL THOUGHT

I hope this digression into the history of science has prepared you for the topic I wish to introduce: the generality of the specific formal attainments that Piaget has described. Piaget implies that everyone, at least in Western society, will get to these specific skills. I mentioned at the beginning of the chapter that only about 25 percent of entering American college freshmen can solve the standard Piagetian reasoning tasks. The complete data are shown in Table 9-1. American college freshmen are not "primitive" in

TABLE *9–1*

Differing levels of attainment on Piagetian tests achieved by a group
of college students (N = 131). (McKinnon and Renner, 1971.)

	MALE	FEMALE	TOTAL	PERCENT
Formal	25	8	33	25
Transitional	12	20	32	25
Concrete	16	50	66	50

any sense of the word. They are highly selected for intelligence. Nonetheless, many of them do not demonstrate the kind of formal intelligence that we should expect. Why is this?

The only answer we have comes from workers who have succeeded in producing formal skills in students who did not have them. They argue that the standard American education is authoritarian. Students are not encouraged to think formally about the information that is given them. Indeed, they are not encouraged to think at all in many courses. The appropriate frame of mind in this kind of situation is one of passive acceptance, not one of deductive reasoning. Passive acceptance will not help in the face of a scientific problem one is supposed to solve oneself. Exposing students to courses in which they are expected to actively involve themselves with the material of the course and with the theories used to explain that material can produce a flowering of formal thought in students who seemed far from it before the course (Table 9–2). This is not to say that the students in question were not formal thinkers before the course. They may have thought formally about everything in the world *except* the sort of material they were accustomed to seeing in school.

The specific attainments of the formal operations period are thus culturally specified. Within that cultural specification, can we use the ideas we have used before to explain the changes? Is conflict involved? Unfortunately, there have been no experiments at all that I know of on specific factors influencing attainment of formal skills. It seems perfectly possible that conflict is involved in the genesis of formal concepts. The essence of the formal period is the step away from what is to what is possible. At all times this step is forced by the impossibility of explaining what we see by what we see. However, by this stage it is surely clear that the groundplan for the solution to any of these conflicts must come from outside, from the social-cultural milieu of the developing mind. The individual mind may detect the conflicts, but only in a few rare cases does the individual mind resolve them. The rest of us take whatever solution may be floating in the air about us. We are ultimately creatures of our culture, save for those few geniuses who change cultures.

There has been no human cultural group that has not invoked un-

TABLE *9–2*

Comparison of growth in formal thought processes in two groups of students. The experimental group took courses in which they were expected to be actively involved in the course; the control group took courses in which they had only a passive role. (McKinnon and Renner, 1971.)

STAGE	FEMALES			MALES			TOTAL GAIN
	PRE-TEST	POST-TEST	NET GAIN	PRE-TEST	POST-TEST	NET GAIN	
Experimental							
Formal	4	14	23.8%	11	16	18.5%	21.7%
Transitional	14	17	7.2	6	8	7.4	7.3
Concrete	24	11	− 31.0	10	3	− 25.9	− 30.0
Control							
Formal	4	7	8.3	14	17	11.5	9.7
Transitional	6	11	13.9	6	7	3.9	9.7
Concrete	26	18	− 22.2	6	2	− 15.4	− 19.4

Experimental N = 69 (42 females, 27 males).
Control N = 62 (36 females, 26 males).

experienced, hypothetical entities to explain events in the world. There is no human cultural group that has not used the INRC group to derive predictions about the world. At the same time, no culture, not even our own, has as yet arrived at a set of hypotheses about the world that is completely satisfactory. The INRC group is implicit in the way we move in the world. Preoperational and operational children alike use it to justify their concepts of the world (pp. 193–194). Its use in manipulating propositions about unseen events is no more mysterious than its initial appearance in infancy to regulate the way we move (p. 172). The real mystery of the formal period, both phylogenetically and ontogenetically, is why humans take the step from a mind that is limited to coping with the perceptible properties of the world to one that invents entities and conjures up explanations for those perceptible properties. That step, to angels or atoms, is the most mysterious evolutionary step mankind has taken. Man the scientist is also man the myth-maker.

AN OVERVIEW OF COGNITIVE DEVELOPMENT

In the last three chapters we have described the outlines of a model of intellectual development. Intelligence in this model is a set of specific skills that can be used to generate knowledge. These skills are made possible by the genetic makeup common to all humans, and thus can be made to occur in all racial groups. When they develop and what particular form they take depends on the general cultural milieu (pp. 182–184), on specific sensory experiences (pp. 201–203), and on specific environmental events (pp. 191–192).

What of the relative roles of genes and the environment in cognitive development? The Piagetian account of the development of intelligence emphasizes the attainment of general concepts that can be applied in very different situations. Teaching a correct response in one situation will not necessarily help in other situations. There is no way in which one can teach "correct" responses to a Piagetian intelligence test in the same way one can train correct responses to a conventional intelligence test. A Piagetian test looks for the presence of certain concepts that will generate correct solutions to a variety of related problems. These concepts are specific and unique enough that they could be taken as "mental characters" of the human being, in the same way as eye color is a character. No racial group, no matter how reproductively isolated, has been shown to lack any of the concepts described by Piaget. Yet the specific concepts normally viewed as correct in Western culture will remain completely absent in the absence of the requisite environmental information. Thus, on a genetic model of development like that described on page 8, the occurrence or nonoccurrence of these concepts is entirely accounted for on environmental grounds, with no role left for specific genetic effects. But of course this is an overstatement of the case. The environment can only actualize what the genotype is capable of expressing. The development of intelligence is not an addition of genetic and environmental effects. It is an epigenetic process, wherein a biologically unique system, a baby, is transformed into a biologically unique organism, an adult, by an environment that is itself influenced by that individual as he or she develops.

What of rates of development? The age of attainment of the various Piagetian concepts in a normal population correlates very highly with IQ score, so highly that one devotee of tests has claimed that the Piagetian scale is the best measure of general intelligence that we have (Eysenck, 1971). But that scale is very plastic. There are hundreds of studies indicating that children can be accelerated along the scale by the various factors we have discussed before. The attainment of the various concepts is no rigid, maturational unfolding; it is a most plastic process, with not only age but even order of attainment subject to environmental influences. Furthermore, we know that there are cultures that *can* attain certain concepts but that routinely do *not*, unless critical environmental factors not normally a part of the culture are imposed. Given that, there can be only one answer to the question, "What is the relevance of genetic factors to the rate of development of intelligence?" That answer is none.

Rate of development within an age span does seem to be plastic. Of greater theoretical importance is the question of the eventual plasticity of development after completion of the formal, propositional stage. To what extent can someone who has adopted a magical view of the world transfer to a scientific view of the world? Indeed, to what extent can someone who has adopted one scientific view of the world transfer to another? The data that we have indicates that the process is very difficult indeed. Each new scientific revolution catches a whole generation of scientists unprepared. If they accept the new concepts, they have great difficulty comprehending them and using them. The classic case of this is the conflict between those physicists who compared light to a shower of pebbles and those who compared it to a series of waves. The two conceptions seemed completely opposed, and it was only a retreat to the symbolic ideas from which both metaphors were derived that permitted resolution of the two positions. The enemy here is schematization, casting abstract solutions in specific terms, the same enemy we blamed for transfer difficulties in the sensori-motor and operational periods (pp. 168–170 and 186–189).

It is schematization that prevents the transfer of sensorimotor knowledge to the concrete-operational level, and that limits our focus as scientists and prevents us from accepting new paradigms of knowledge (Kuhn, 1962). Schematization is an environment-dependent process, since our environment determines whether or not we use a solution often enough for it to be schematized, i.e., made specific. The nonlinear relation between frequency of use of a concept and its utility in the overall course of development makes the design of optimal environments for development a rather difficult problem—one that is a major current preoccupation of developmental psychologists. Since schematizations in the formal period are at a greater remove from reality than those of the earlier periods, they may be correspondingly harder to correct. This characteristic may set a limit on the cognitive development of any individual.

What of representation, the elements of thought? The availability of certain classes of sensory input is critical for the development of certain concepts. The blind and the deaf both suffer certain severe limitations compared to sighted-hearing children. The blind lack a whole class of experience, and so cannot develop concepts to cope with the problems normally posed by these experiences. The deaf are required to cope with events laid out in time less often than are the hearing, and so are less likely to use temporal ordering, even when it is required.

Finally, what is the role of the social world of the child during intellectual development? During the concrete-operational stage the communication requirements of the cultural milieu seem to be the most important single factor in the development of appropriate concepts. Children in diverse cultures learn to talk about what their specific culture requires them to talk about. By the time they reach adulthood they will probably be unable to acquire any other system of communication, and thus unable to acquire an alternative cognitive system.

What then are the determinants of intellectual development within the system we have been presenting? The most important determinant is the complex, motivational one we have been calling conflict or contradiction. Whenever our developing child becomes aware of a contradiction between two ideas about the world, particularly two equally valid ideas, processes are set in motion that resolve the contradiction, producing advances in comprehension and conceptualization. This is true at all stages of development. Environmental experiences that can induce conflict or contradiction are obviously of critical importance to cognitive development, yet we are woefully ignorant of the nature of the processes by which such conflict is resolved. Hopefully, the situation will change soon.

The factors described above may seem hopelessly inadequate to account for the complexities of cognitive development. We undoubtedly require more information about the operation of them all. Nonetheless, these few notions seem to help us on the way to a quantitative description of cognitive development, a description precise enough to replace the weak *post hoc* accounts we currently give. But perhaps I am a victim of my own schematizations.

CONTINUITY IN
COGNITIVE DEVELOPMENT

The account of cognitive development I have given here has emphasized the continuity of the process. Infants attain skills that foreshadow the attainments of a later age. They develop ideas of conservation. They work out concepts of space. They work out ways of formulating and testing hypotheses about the causal structure of the world. These attainments, obscure and unlikely as they are, are half of what is needed if human cognitive skills are to attain their fullest flowering. The other half, of course, comes from the social world of the developing child. Concrete operations develop as a result of communication needs interacting with sensorimotor skills. Formal operations are the final developmental attempt to comprehend the world, an attempt that is nonetheless shaped by the cultural milieu we live in. Behind all of this are the attainments of the wordless infant, in some fashion pushing and probing the developing mind to resolve the demands of the world of objects and the world of people.

While this emphasis on continuity has certain merits, it also has certain deficiencies. For example, it does not make clear where the essential difference is between a teenager and a baby. Obviously, the teenager has far more empirical knowledge about the world. He has been around much longer and has had far more time to gather information. In addition, the baby cannot handle the amount of information the teenager can. This is in part because he is smaller, in part because all the world is new, and so demands more information space. It is somewhere in this latter change that I think the most essential developmental changes reside. As we have seen, having found something out, the baby is apt to forget how he did it (in the sense that he no longer has the solution in the forefront of his thinking), and this limits the possibilities of transfer. The concrete-operational child can also find things out, can communicate and share his discoveries with others, but he still remains unaware of *how* he makes the advances he is making. Only at the formal level are the *methods* as well as the results of discovery fully available to the enquiring mind. With this awareness the possibilities of transfer become quite different. Acceptance of others' discoveries proceeds not from deference to authority but from an understanding of how the discoveries were made. The possibilities for teaching are thus very different. Ignoring these possibilities can have deleterious effects on intellectual performances. The existence of agreed methods of proof makes the imparting of information a quite different process, a process that far transcends the concreteness of the preformal child, limited as he is to believing what he can see.

The chief merit of the account of cognitive development given here is that it becomes easy to understand how development can go wrong, to go off on such a path that it resists the best intentioned attempts to set it back on normal paths. I think the account offered here makes it clear why remedial education can fail. Certain aspects of development in infancy are critical for subsequent development. There are several such aspects, which are of logically different types. Consider a baby faced with one of the simpler object-permanence problems, like the one in Figure 6–2 (p. 122). Once successful, that baby may be said to have learned three things.

Level 1. When the object is placed in the right-hand cup, it can be found in the right-hand cup.

Level 2. Objects remain where they are put.

Level 3. The world is a consistent and orderly place.

Each of these three statements could be verified in the object-permanence situation. However, the statements are very different in *type*. The first is specific to the object-permanence situation and has no wider application. The second is a general truth about inanimate objects in the world; its range of application is the whole world of inanimate objects. The third is even wider in application, constituting an hypothesis about the basic orderliness of the whole world.

Consider a child coping with a more difficult object-permanence problem, like the one shown in Figure 6–3 (p. 124). The successful child has again learned at least three things.

Level 1. The object straight ahead of me becomes the object on my right when I move 120° to the right around this table.

Level 2. The positions of objects relative to one another change with changes in my position relative to them.

Level 3. The world is a consistent and orderly place.

Again the hypotheses are all verified in the specific object-permanence situation, and again the range of applicability increases with increasing abstraction.

Consider a baby in a simple conditioning situation. The child is again learning at least three things.

Level 1. When I kick my foot the mobile goes round.

Level 2. I can control events in the world.

Level 3. The world is a consistent and orderly place.

I could go on multiplying examples of the multiple levels of learning that go on in any learning situation. I could easily increase the number of levels to five or so. In Chapter 7, on cognitive development in infancy, we saw evidence indicating, I think, that all of these levels of learning do occur. Success in any task is evidence of first-level learning. Transfer from one task to another conceptually similar task is evidence for second-level learning. What would constitute evidence for third-level learning? In a broad, perhaps too poetic, sense it might be the attempts of infants to find order in the world, attempts that ignore more immediate sources of reinforcement (pp. 174–175). More satisfactory would be evidence of "far transfer," transfer from one type of skill to other, totally different skills. Thus far we have only anecdotal evidence on this (Watson, 1966).

What is the relation between these levels? In Chapter 7 we argued that level two *precedes* level one in the solution to any given problem. We argued, indeed, that too much practice on any one problem could result in the loss of second-level solutions. What then is the temporal relation between level three and level two? By the time our baby is a few months old, I would argue, level three has become the motive that impels attempts to find level two and then level one solutions. The most compelling evidence to this point is that provided by Papousek (pp. 128ff), Monnier (pp. 129ff), and Bruner (p. 175). The baby has learned that the world is a consistent and orderly place. Faced with a new problem he tries to find consistency and order in it. The more he succeeds, the more he is convinced of the validity of level three, and so the more strongly he is impelled to find order in every problem situation.

It is surely clear that experience in infancy is critical for learning at all three of these levels. Furthermore, it should be obvious that perfectly commonplace experiences could produce quite different learning, particularly at the more abstract levels (levels two and three). For example, consider a baby faced with a mobile that moved every 30 seconds, regardless of whether or not the baby was doing anything. That baby would learn:

Level 1. The mobile moves by itself every 30 seconds.

Level 2. I cannot control events in the world.

Level 3. The world is a consistent and orderly place.

We would not need an experimental situation to produce such effects. In Chapter 5 we argued that the blind baby is in such a situation. Surely a baby whose parents keep it on a rigid schedule of feeding, washing, etc., regardless of its desires, is in a similar situation. Frequent enough exposure to this kind of experience could lead to extended passivity in the face of problem-solving situations. This child could be taught correct answers but would not go out and find them. Consider the baby whose world is sometimes contingent and sometimes noncontingent on his actions, e.g., a baby who is allowed to control mobiles sometimes and sometimes not. That baby will learn:

Level 1. Sometimes the mobile moves by itself; sometimes it moves when I kick my foot.

Level 2. Sometimes I control events in the world.

Level 3. The world is an inconsistent and disorderly place.

The long-term consequences of such learning must surely be very harmful, at least from the Western point of view. This child will never strive to find order in the world, for he basically believes in disorder. Similarly, he is unlikely to accept order when shown it. The only "order" he may admit is disorder, produced by unpredictable outer forces. Mead (1937) and Bateson (1972) have described the culture of Bali as one that believes in disorder and does not believe in personal efficacy, with child-rearing practices aimed, seemingly, at instilling this belief. Bateson described the effects of certain aspects of Balinese life that mainly affect social behavior but also have cognitive consequences.

> Typically, the mother will start a small flirtation with the child, pulling its penis or otherwise stimulating it to interpersonal activity. This will excite the child, and for a few moments cumulative interaction will occur. Then

just as the child, approaching some small climax, flings its arms around the mother's neck, her attention wanders. At this point the child will typically start an alternative cumulative interaction, building up toward temper tantrum. The mother will either play a spectator's role, enjoying the child's tantrum, or, if the child actually attacks her, will brush off his attack with no show of anger on her part. These sequences can be seen either as an expression of the mother's distaste for this type of personal involvement or as context in which the child acquires a deep distrust of such involvement. The perhaps basically human tendency towards cumulative personal interaction is thus muted. It is possible that some sort of continuing plateau of intensity is substituted for climax as the child becomes more fully adjusted to Balinese life. This cannot at present be clearly documented for sexual relations, but there are indications that a plateau type of sequence is characteristic for trance and for quarrels. . . .

Similar sequences have the effect of diminishing the child's tendencies toward competitive and rivalrous behavior. The mother will, for example, tease the child by suckling the baby of some other woman and will enjoy her own child's efforts to push the intruder from the breast.

In general the lack of climax is characteristic for Balinese music, drama, and other art forms. The music typically has a progression, derived from the logic of its formal structure, and modifications of intensity determined by the duration and progress of the working out of these formal relations. It does not have the sort of rising intensity and climax structure characteristic of modern Occidental music, but rather a formal progression. . . .

The formal techniques of social influence—oratory and the like—are almost totally lacking in Balinese culture. To demand the continued attention of an individual or to exert emotional influence upon a group are alike distasteful and virtually impossible; because in such circumstances the attention of the victim rapidly wanders. Even such continued speech as would, in most cultures, be used for the telling of stories does not occur in Bali. The narrator will, typically, pause after a sentence or two, and wait for some member of the audience to ask him a concrete question about some detail of the plot. He will then answer the question and so resume his narration. This procedure apparently breaks the cumulative tension by irrelevant interaction.

Closer to home, Watson (1966) has described how particular child-rearing practices could produce such level-three learning ("the world is an inconsistent and disorderly place") in early infancy. A child established in such beliefs would have possibilities for learning in later life that were totally different from those of a normal child. Furthermore, if, as we have argued throughout, the more abstract accomplishments of infancy are truly developmental, i.e., they produce structural modifications in the brain that are irreversible, it should be clear that the future learning that does occur will be determined by these accomplishments in infancy. Any future *education*, any future attempt to control learning, must take account of what has already been determined if it is to have any hope of success at all. This, it seems to me, may explain the seemingly paradoxical success of authoritarian regimes of compensatory education (Bereiter, 1972). These schemes, emphasizing obedient rote learning, would not be successful with middle-class children but are successful with less advantaged children. Is it too fanciful to suppose that the latter have a level 2 rule of the form: "I can't find things out; I do what I'm told"?* It seems that such children can succeed in learning the cognitive skills demanded by Western culture if their education is tailored to the level 2 rules they bring to the classroom.

COGNITIVE DEVELOPMENT
AND INTELLECTUAL ATTAINMENT

Bruner has rightly complained that Piaget has no way of distinguishing between Einstein and the average adolescent (Bruner, Olver, and Greenfield, 1966). Geniuses who profoundly change the world we live in are surely different from the rest of us who merely adjust to the world as we find it. However, Bruner's implicit assumption that the difference lies within the intellectual or cognitive realm is open to serious questions. Some of the problems Piaget asked Swiss teenagers to solve would have required the genius of Galileo in prior times. Was Galileo equivalent to the modern teenager? In a sense yes. Both use the same "laws of thought," both rely on unobservables to explain the observed, both are willing to forget some of the observed to account for the rest. But Galileo was an innovator whereas the teenagers in Piaget's studies are not. What produces innovation? It is surely something different from intellectual development per se. The motivation of innovators is different from that of the rest. Their social world is different (Hudson, 1975). Creativity can be nurtured in certain environments and suppressed in others. Nevertheless, the intellects of innovators are hardly different from those of conservatives. So mysterious is the difference that astrological influences have been seriously invoked to account for them (Figure 9–3). It seems highly likely then that personal motives and social evaluations are more important than simple intellectual competence. For example, scientific innovation requires social choices that cut one off from other modes of life, and protect one from some of the hardships of life, too. It seems unlikely that intellectual factors alone are

---

*The characteristics of an upbringing that would produce such a rule have been clearly demonstrated in the Horizon film *If at First You Don't Succeed — You Don't Succeed* (British Broadcasting Corporation).

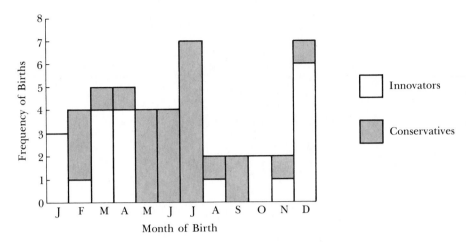

FIGURE 9–3
Innovators tend to be born in the winter months and conservatives in the summer months. (Holmes, 1974.)

responsible for these choices. Jencks (1972) found rather poor relationships between intelligence (as measured by tests) and attainment, professional status, or salary level. It seems more likely that the uses to which we put our intellectual competences is a matter of our own motivational structure and personality—a matter of the social world we live in.

10

Development of Language

The importance of language in cognitive development must be obvious by this time. Language is the bridge between development in the world of things and development in the world of people. Language is our specifically human mode of communication. While it may build on other ways of communicating, to be described in later chapters, the flexibility and range of human language is beyond compare as a means of communication. We can be certain in one sense that language is a genetically determined human accomplishment. It is genetically determined in that it is species specific. Humans and only humans can use language, and all humans do use language.

There is some controversy over whether language is a completely separate, genetically specified human capacity, or whether our use of language is a by-product of our other cognitive and motor skills. That we do have some biological predisposition towards speech is obvious, even at birth. Neonates are more attentive to speech than to any other stimulus. Studies of this kind will be described more fully in Chapter 14. By the age of six weeks or so, babies can discriminate very subtle speech sounds. Habituation techniques have been used to demonstrate that babies of this age can discriminate between *pa* and *ba* (Eimas *et al.*, 1971). If one of these stimuli is played repetitively to a baby, his attention to the sound source will wane. But as soon as a new sound is substituted there is a sudden recovery of attention, even though the physical difference between the consonants *p* and *b* is very slight (Figure 10–1). Similar results have been obtained with operant conditioning studies in which reinforcement is paired both with a response to one sound and with a different response to another different sound, e.g., a right turn of the head to *ba* and a left to *pa*. One of the most fascinating findings in this area is that babies can discriminate the sounds of languages they have never heard. For example, North American babies can discriminate the sounds of Chinese (Condon and Sander, 1974). Indeed, North American babies can discriminate these sounds better than North American adults can! This recalls the finding, mentioned in Chapter 5, that babies can produce the sounds of languages they have never heard. It thus seems that babies arrive in the world ready to listen to and produce the sounds of any of the world's languages. This broad ability does not last forever. By the age of seven or eight months babies may react with surprise and even fear to the sounds of a foreign language (Noirot, 1978).

At what point does this analytic and productive capacity become converted to actual language use? There are many ways of defining the onset of language use. In large part the definition depends on one's definition of language itself. This is an area of linguistic controversy that

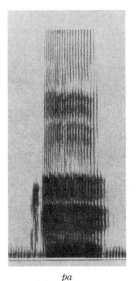
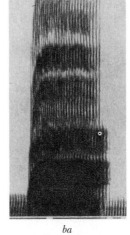

pa   *ba*

FIGURE *10–1*

Spectographic recordings of the sounds *pa* and *ba*. There is little discernable difference between the *p* and *b* sounds. (Courtesy of Speech and Communication Laboratory, University of Edinburgh.)

psychologists would do well to stay clear of. From my own point of view, the descriptions and definitions of language offered by Halliday (1975) are the most interesting. Halliday assigns seven functions to language.

The *instrumental* function—the "I want" or "gimme" function. It operates so that the language user can obtain the things or services of others that he wants.

The *regulatory* function is similar but has a different focus. The focus here is the control of the behavior of another. The function would include utterances like "do," "don't do," "let's do," and so on.

The *interactional* function—the "I and thou" or "me and you" function of language. It includes greetings as well as other kinds of verbal interchange with no other function than the communication of mutual awareness.

The *personal* function. For Halliday this includes all expressions of self-awareness or self-expression, including expressions of interest, pleasure, disgust, and the like. Halliday describes it as the "here *I* come" function of language.

The *heuristic* function—the "tell me" function. "What" and "why" are its key expressions. We use these expressions to get information about the world.

The *imaginative* function. This includes song, story, myth, fable, and science. It is the use of language to transcend the here-and-now of everyday reality.

The *informative* function. This is dominant in the adult's use of language. It is the communication of information to someone who does not already possess it. It is the response to another's heuristic use of language, although it need not be responsive; one can also initiate a verbal exchange with information that the other does not have.

Halliday (1975) has intensively studied the development of language in one child, his own son, Nigel. He places the beginning of language for Nigel at nine months, although he admits this is straining the definition of language. At this age the child made two sounds that had consistent meanings. One subserved the interactive function, the other the personal function. By $10\frac{1}{2}$ months his linguistic system had expanded dramatically to include four of the functions of language defined above.

> In the instrumental function he has one utterance which is a general demand, meaning something like "Give me that," and referring always to some object which is clearly specified in the environment. This contrasts with the specific demand for a favourite object, in this case a toy bird; and it is possible that this represents the one element in the system whose expression is in fact borrowed from the adult language: it may be an imitation of the sound *bird*. In the regulatory function he has a generalized request, which is always directed to a specific individual, requiring him or

her to do something that is again clearly specified in the context, usually by the fact of its having been done immediately before, so that it is equivalent to "Do that again;" this contrasts with an intensified form of the same meaning which carries with it the additional feature of urgency, which is conveyed by the form of the gloss "Do that right now."

In the interactional function, Nigel has a couple of initiating expressions and one response. Of the former, one is a form of greeting, used typically when another person comes newly to his attention, for example someone coming into the room as he wakes up; the utterance directs attention to a particular object, typically a picture, which is then used as the channel for interacting with this other person. The nearest one can get to this in a gloss is something like "How nice to see you, and shall we look at this picture together?," suggesting that the picture becomes the focus of what is in fact a form of interaction that is taking place through language. The other is again an intensified form, an impatient greeting which is not mediated by any joint action; it may be glossed by some such locution as "Nice to see you, and why weren't you here before?" In addition there is a response form, used by Nigel in response to a call or greeting when someone else begins to interact verbally with him. And finally there is a little set of meanings within the personal function, five in all, one of which expresses a state of withdrawal and the others the opposite, a state of participation, involving the expression of some form of pleasure or of interest.

The most interesting point about these sounds is that they had a recognizable meaning for the child's parents. Their function was readily identifiable. They were repeatable in repeated contexts. However, the sounds by and large were not imitations of sounds derived from the language of the adults around him. Halliday suggests that the child may utter sounds on a trial-and-error basis and repeat those that elicit the response desired of those to whom he is addressing the sounds. In effect, he is suggesting operant conditioning as the basis for the emergence of these early sound uses. Since, too, adults will tend to translate the baby's utterances into an acceptable adult form, there is a possibility of systematic modeling of the child's responses via the process of imitation, with reinforcement of an increasingly precise imitation (see pp. 25 and 304).

Be that as it may, by 16 months the child's meaningful utterances had expanded to around 50 (Table 10–1). At this point the sounds approximate standard English sounds more closely than the earlier sounds, to the extent that a stranger might be able to interpret the child's intent correctly. As Halliday points out, the small child "uses language to satisfy his own material needs, in terms of goods or services (instrumental); to exert control over the behaviour of others (regulatory); to establish and maintain contact with those that matter to him (interactional); and to express his own individuality and self-awareness (personal)."

Quite suddenly, recognizable words were produced around 17 months of age. At that point, too, there was a sudden emergence of a "grammar,"

TABLE 10-1

Nigel's language repertory at 16 months. The sounds cannot be accurately described except by using phonetic notation, shown in the *Articulation* column. The entries under *Approximate sound* are very approximate indeed. (After Halliday, 1975.)

FUNCTION	CONTENT SYSTEMS			ARTICULATION	APPROXIMATE SOUND	MEANING
Instrumental →	demand general →	initiation		ʔ nâ - - -	gnyah (*repeat*)	Give me that.
		response →	object present	yi - -	yee (*repeat*)	Yes, I want that.
			service or non-visible object	a:	ahhh	Yes, I want what you just offered.
	demand specific →	powder		bʷ g̀a(-); bug̀(-)	biwigah (*repeat*); boog (*repeat*)	I want some powder.
		clock		t́ka(-); tkɔ(-)	tikah (*repeat*); tikoh (*repeat*)	I want (*to go and get*) the clock.
Regulatory →	command general →	initiation →	normal	a; ɜ; ɜ̃	ah; eh; nyeh	Do that (*again*).
			intensified	m̂n̂ŋ	mnying!	Do that right now!
		response →	positive	ɜ̃ - - -	nyeh (*repeat*)	Yes (*let's*) do that.
			negative	áa ' - - -	nyahnyah	No, don't (*let's*) do that. Let's go for a walk.
	command specific →	go for walk				
		play with cat		pʷi - - -; peʷ	pwee (*repeat*)	Let me play with the cat.

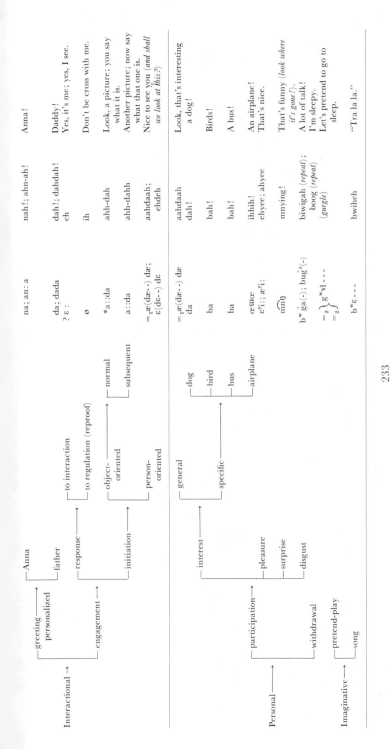

Interactional →

- greeting → personalized / father
- engagement → response → to interaction / to regulation (reproof)
- engagement → initiation → object-oriented → normal / subsequent
- engagement → initiation → person-oriented

Personal →

- participation → interest → general / specific → dog / bird / bus / airplane
- participation → pleasure / surprise / disgust
- withdrawal
- pretend-play

Imaginative →

- pretend-play
- song

feature	vocalization	gloss	meaning
personalized	na; an; a	nah!; ahn-ah!	Anna!
father	da; dada	dah!; dahdah!	Daddy!
to interaction	ʔɛ:	eh	Yes, it's me; yes, I see.
to regulation (reproof)	ø	ih	Don't be cross with me.
normal	*aː:da	ahh-dah	Look, a picture; you say what it is.
subsequent	aː:da	ahh-dahh	Another picture; now say what that one is.
person-oriented	=₁æ(dæ–) dæ; ɛ(dɛ–) dɛ	aahdaah; ehdeh	Nice to see you (*and shall we look at this?*)
general	=₂æ(dæ–) dæ	aahdaah	Look, that's interesting
dog	da	dah!	a dog!
bird	ba	bah!	Birds!
bus	ba	bah!	A bus!
airplane	œːɯɒ; ɛˀiː; aˀiː	ihhih!; ehyee; ahyee	An airplane! That's nice.
pleasure	m̂ñ	mnying!	That's funny (*look where it's gone!*).
surprise	bʷĝa(-); bug²(-)	biwigah (*repeat*); boog (*repeat*) (*gurgle*)	A lot of talk!
disgust	=₂gʷʌl---		I'm sleepy. Let's pretend to go to sleep.
song	bʷɛ---	bwiheh	"Tra la la."

233

i.e., an arrangement of at least two words according to rules. It was pointed out by Braine (1963) that such primitive utterances typically contain one of each of two classes of word. One of these, the *pivot class*, contains a small number of words, each used frequently. Pivot words always appear in a fixed location in an utterance. A particular pivot may be either first or second but is always in one of these positions and never in the other. The *open class* contains all the words not in the pivot class. It is typically much larger than the pivot class. Table 10–2 shows examples of pivot- and open-class words.

At this point the number of utterances the child can make expands drastically because the child can *create* them. The creative aspect is worth emphasizing. Children say things they have never heard, such as "allgone shoe," "allgone lettuce," "that doed" and so on, all of which are creations rather than imitations. The pivots are the parts of speech that communicate function in the child's language at this time. At this time, Halliday points out, grammar is still tied to function as specifically as the earlier one-word utterances were. "More," for example, as in "more milk," is used instrumentally and not informatively. The terminal step to a system that everyone would recognize as language comes when words become functionally derestricted, so that the whole vocabulary can be used to express all or most of the functions. This is the ultimate step into language, and it is still deeply mysterious.

Let us stop at this point and look back at what the child has accomplished and the processes that might account for his accomplishment. Early on in life the child has desires and must find means of satisfying these desires. Crying can obviously serve this function to a limited extent. Later in the first year other nonverbal methods of communication come in, such as pointing while pleading. The child will also discover that the sounds he can make can be effective in eliciting the care that he wants. Recall that these early sounds are functionally specific. The baby uses the same sound in repeated contexts to serve the same function. These sounds, no matter how wordlike, are not words in the adult sense, for an adult can use the same word in any functional context in which it is useful. What processes will lead the baby to this point? I believe the processes we have just been describing sound like nothing so much as the establishment of discriminated operants. The sound is the operant response, the context its stimulus control, and the satisfaction of the desired function the reinforcement. As far as I can see, the processes of operant conditioning could account for the sequence of development we have so far described. Indeed, the shift from "free" vocal production, with the precise meaning defined by gesture and situation, to productions that mimic adult sounds may also be explained on reinforcement terms. As Halliday points out, it is often very hard to interpret the free vocalizations that a baby makes, so that one must leave his desires unsatisfied. Any parent can verify this statement. If the child

TABLE *10–2*

Examples of pivot- and open-class words from three studies. (McNeill, 1966.)

BRAINE		BROWN		ERVIN	
PIVOT	OPEN	PIVOT	OPEN	PIVOT	OPEN
	boy		Adam		arm
	sock	my	Becky		baby
allgone	boat	that	boot		dolly's
byebye	fan	two	coat		pretty
big	milk	a	coffee	this	yellow
more	plane	the	knee	that	come
pretty	shoe	big	man		doed
my	vitamins	green	mommy		.
see	hot	poor	nut		.
night-	mommy	wet	sock		.
night	Daddy	dirty	stook		
hi	.	fresh	tinkertoy		other
	.	pretty	.		baby
	.		.		dolly's
			.	the	pretty
				a	yellow
					.
					.
					.
					arm
					baby
					dolly's
				here	pretty
				there	yellow
					.
					.

uses adult sounds, however, he is much more likely to get speedy satisfaction. Purely on the basis of reinforcement, reproduction should then triumph over free production.

What of the mysterious process of *derestriction*, the shift from using "words" to serve one function in one context to using them for many functions in any context? This is the essential step into language use that *is* language on anyone's criterion. Above we said that this last step is deeply mysterious. That is so, but the step is akin to other steps in development, even though they are equally mysterious. Consider the act of grasping. Grasping is initially the terminus of reaching, and such (nonreflexive) grasping never occurs without the prior occurrence of reaching. Furthermore, in its early stages grasping never leads to anything else. Later, of course, it can precede reaching and can serve as a link in a chain of behaviors—grasp a stick, reach out with the stick, and hit a bell, for example. The derestriction of words and the derestriction of acts may all be viewed as intances of *generalization*. Even so, this does not help us, for we do not understand generalization either. Yet I think these analogies emphasize the essential continuity between the initial processes of language acquisition and other aspects of behavioral development.

The later steps in language development can be viewed as a process of differentiation from this basic starting point. The process of expansion is shown in the samples of conversation from the same child at 28 months, 35 months, and 38 months in Table 10–3.

TABLE *10–3*

Samples of speech from a child at 28, 35, and 38 months of age. (Brown and Bellugi, 1964.)

CHILD (28 MONTHS)	ADULT
What dat . . . somebody pencil	Whose pencils are they?
Floor	Floor?
Where birdie go?	
Birdie	
Birdie up dere	
Birdie	
Read dat?	
Read dat?	Will you read it to me?
What inere?	Is that a hammer, Adam?
Hammer	
Hit hammer, mommy	
No Cromer ——, mommy?	
Hurt	Poor Adam. Did you hurt yourself?
	What happened, Adam?
Screw (did) happen	Screw happened. You didn't even have a screw.
have screw	
—— no down there . . .	
table . . . get broom	Does that one fit?
Yep, it fit	
Yep, it fit	Does it fit?
No . . . fit	
Put suitcase . . . for?	What did you put it in the suitcase for?
What dat?	That's tape. We'll use that one tomorrow.
All right 'morrow	Shall we use it tomorrow?
Yep	
Use morrow, yep	
Sure, use morrow	

TABLE *10–3* (*Continued*)

CHILD (35 MONTHS)	ADULT
What his name?	His name
His name, Ursla?	I know his name
No . . . I don't know his name	
I don't know	
Can't come up, fellah (to a yo-yo)	
Going pick pick up	
Lemme do again	
Don't . . . don't hold with me	
Turning round	Yes, it is turning around
It's stop	It stopped?
What dat . . . feeled . . . like?	
What dat feeled like?	It feels like rubber, I guess
I . . . going . . . drop my books	
(drops one book)	
An' what happens?	
I going drop it . . . inne dump truck	
No . . . please cry, cracker	What?
Cracker	Please what?
Please cry, cracker	Please cry?
Yes	How can a cracker cry?
	Crackers can't talk.
Why not . . . cracker can't talk?	
Romper domper tell me boo	
Romper domper tell me boo	
I got sompeing show you	
What's dat . . . you have?	
Why me go?	
Why me going?	
D'you want brush him?	
D'you want he walk?	
Where's it?	
Why you rolling up?	
Hey, why . . . why you waking me up?	
What you doing . . . taking out?	
Why you knocking me off?	I'm not knocking you off
Why not?	
I can't . . . couldn't . . . show it . . . to her	You're going to show it to her?
No	
I too big	
Those are mines	
Dat's mines	

CHILD (38 MONTHS)	ADULT
I like a racing car	
D'you like some?	
I broke my racing car	Oh, did you have one?
Yes	
Look at dat one	

(*Continued*)

238

TABLE *10–3* (*Continued*)

CHILD (38 MONTHS)	ADULT
Like dis part broke	What part broke?
Dis part broke, like that	
It's got a flat tire	
What is dat?	
It's a what?	
He . . . his mouth is open	
What shall we shall have?	
Why he going to have some seeds?	
Why it's not working?	
You got some beads?	Yes
Just like me?	
I got bead 'round myself	
Hit my knee	Hit *my* knee
Hit your knee	
What dat teacher will do?	
Why you pull out?	Dust in your hair
Who put my dust on my hair?	Can you tell Ursula what the lesson is . . .
	on the blackboard?
On the black which board?	
We going see another one	
We can read 'bout dis	
You wanto read?	
What is dat?	
What is dat got?	
It's got a flat tire	
When it's got flat tire, it's needs to go to	
the . . . to the station.	
The station will fix it.	
Tank come out through what?	
Really . . . tank come out through . . . here	
Mommy don't let me buy some	
What is dis?	That's a marble bag
A marble bag for what?	For marbles
	It would be good to carry tiny cars.
What id dat?	
Can I keep dem?	
Why I can keep dem?	
Now can I keep dem?	
We don' do some games	
It's broked?	

The expansion of vocabulary is striking. More interesting, however, is the expansion of grammar. The child's grammar now includes the use of certain words and word orders to communicate meanings that earlier were carried by context, intonation, facial expression, or some other nonverbal means. Halliday's subject Nigel initially expressed negation only in a regulative context ("Don't do") and the negation was expressed by a characteristic intonation pattern. Later the words "no" and "not" emerged. Typical negations at various stages are shown in Table 10–4. As can be seen in that table, constructions are at first perfectly standard; the negative begins or ends an utterance and appears nowhere else. At later stages children demonstrate an increasingly sophisticated ability to negate. The last set is especially interesting since it shows the creativeness of children's grammar. Consider the sentence "I think I don't better cut it." Adults would say "I don't think I'd better cut it." The children use a correct but rare negative form. Later of course their utterances will match the adult form.

What factors account for this progression? The actual expression of negation, particularly as a regulatory function, occurs in the form of screams of rage right after birth. Feeding, bathing, and diaper-changing can all elicit attempts at prohibitive regulation right away. Later in life the child becomes subject to prohibitive regulation. While most of this regulation is undoubtedly accomplished by nonverbal means, English-speaking parents will typically say "No!" or "Don't . . ." while physically restraining

TABLE *10–4*

Development of negation in children's language between approximately 18 and 48 months of age. (McNeill, 1970.)

FIRST STAGE	THIRD STAGE
No . . . wipe finger.	Paul can't have one.
More . . . no.	This can't stick.
No a boy bed.	I didn't did it.
No singing song.	You don't want some supper.
No the sun shining.	Donna won't let go.
No play that.	No, it isn't.
Wear mitten no.	I am not a doctor.
Not a teddy bear.	This not ice cream.
No fall.	They not hot.
	I not crying.
	He not taking the walls down.
SECOND STAGE	Don't kick my box.
I can't catch you	Don't touch the fish.
We can't talk.	Ask me if I not make mistake.
I don't sit on cromer coffee.	I not hurt him.
I don't like him.	
No pinch me.	
No . . . rusty hat.	FOURTH STAGE
Touch the snow no.	He thinks he doesn't have nothing.
This a radiator no.	I think it's not fulled up to the top.
Don't bite me yet.	He thinks he doesn't have to finish it.
Don't leave me.	I think we don't have a top.
That not "O," that blue.	I think he don't like us no more.
There no squirrels.	I think I can't find white.
He no bite you.	I think I don't better cut it.
I no want envelope.	I think I don't know what it is.
	I think I don't.

the child or otherwise exercising prohibitive regulation of his behavior. "No" and "don't" could thus be associated with negative regulation, by classical conditioning, and could become operants if the child succeeds in uttering them or approximating them in an appropriate functional context. Once the mysterious step of derestriction is taken, these negatives are available to change the meaning of any utterance the child can make. Which brings us up to the first stage in Table 10–4. What about development after that point?

An obvious source of information about grammar for the developing child is the language of the adults around him. Children can certainly hear words with a purely grammatical meaning in the speech of adults and can try them out in their own speech. If reinforced, the strategic use of a word or word order might then stay in the child's repertory. Evidence that this sort of process may operate is provided by a study by Cazden (1965). Cazden performed an acceleration experiment with $2\frac{1}{2}$-year-olds from working-class homes. Children were given one of two treatments, *expansion* or *modeling*. In the expansion condition the child spent half an hour, five days a week, for three months looking at picture books with an adult. Every utterance the child made was systematically expanded into an acceptable adult form. For example, if a child said "Doggie bite," the adult might say "The dog is biting." In the modeling condition the child also looked at picture books with an adult for the same amount of time. However, the adult was restricted to commenting on the child's utterance. If the child said "Doggie bite," the adult might say "Yes, he's mad." A control group was given no special experience. Before and after the training conditions the children were given a specially designed test of linguistic competence. The results were very clear. Relative to the control group the expansion group showed modest gains, while the modeling group showed enormous gains. This is about what we would expect if language development is a learning process in which the child picks up strategies from the utterances of adults around him, tries them out, and retains those that are reinforced. Since expansion, it seems to me, is effectively negative reinforcement, the only surprising result is that expansion provided any gains at all. Presumably, reinforcement outside the experimental situation could account for the gains.

At this point you may be wondering what innate processes are involved in language acquisition. The beginnings of sound discrimination and speech production appear to be genetically programmed, but thereafter language acquisition seems to be entirely a learning process, admittedly complex learning, but learning nonetheless, and therefore susceptible to reinforcement. Yet the derestriction of reinforced sounds appears to be a transition that cannot be explained on the basis of reinforcement. Also, the creative role of the child in language development cannot be over-emphasized. Children often say things in a way that do not appear in the language of the adults around them. Such utterances are commonly interpreted as primitive or poorly articulated versions of "correct" adult speech. This is not always the case. Children may produce utterances that are richer than those of their parents (Sankoff and Laberge, 1973). In other words, children may produce a construction that is novel but nevertheless comprehensible to those around them. In that case they will retain it and others will begin to use it. Adults no longer make these easy incorporations, so that it is they who remain linguistically primitive compared to their children. No one has, and no one probably ever will, collect all the utterances of any child, so our estimates of their creativity in the process of language acquisition will forever remain underestimates.

Similarly, we can have no real idea of the extent to which reinforcement processes are important in molding language behavior. The whole point of language is communication; failure of communication amounts to negative reinforcement. By the same token, successful communication is positive reinforcement for the rules that produced it. Some linguists seem to assume that only specific utterances can be reinforced. I do not see why. A rule of the sort "To negate an utterance, say 'no' plus the utterance" is as general a rule as that used by infants in search tasks, conservation tasks, and so on. In coping with such tasks the child is not tied to specific sets of responses or specific stimulus inputs. It seems obvious that general rules could perfectly well be reinforced in language as elsewhere.

I am arguing, in fact, that the processes and limitations of language acquisition are the processes and limitations of cognitive development in general, and that there is nothing very special about language acquisition. As in other aspects of cognitive development, the child seems to progress from abstract rules to specific schematizations in language. Some flesh has recently been put on this speculation by two series of fascinating experiments by Greenfield (1975) and her associates. Greenfield has tried, in essence, to show that the same structural principles that predict difficulty in a variety of cognitive tasks will also serve to predict difficulty in speech and in language comprehension.

A very simple example of such a principle is *hierarchical complexity*. Language by its very nature is hierarchically organized. As the following example illustrates, sounds are combined to produce a word, words are combined to produce a simple sentence, and simple sentences are combined to produce complex sentences.

Sounds	dæfodɪlz
Word	daffodils
Sentence	Daffodils are beautiful.
Complex sentence	Daffodils are beautiful, but I like bluebells better.

TABLE *10–5*

The acquisition of language, like language itself, is hierarchically organized. The production of sounds is followed by the production of words, and so on.

ITEM	AGE AT WHICH FIRST PRODUCED
Single sound, e.g., *ma, da*	6 months
Repetition of single sound, e.g., *ba ba ba*	8 months
First word, e.g., "mama"	12 months
Vocabulary of up to 50 words, including some two-word phrases, e.g., "blue car"	24 months
Sentences produced, e.g., "Mama, give me the blue car"	30 months

A speaker starts off with the idea of a complex sentence in his head and must then produce an output that consists of a string of sounds. Language development mirrors this sequential organization: the production of sounds precedes the production of words, the production of single words precedes the production of sentences, and so on (Table 10–5). At any one time the child is restricted to functioning at one level in the hierarchy, which of course includes all the levels below it in complexity. Exactly similar limits operate in constructive play, for example. Greenfield asked children between three and seven years of age to duplicate the constructions shown in Figure 10–2. The simplest was made up of three blocks. The second was more complex, involving as it did the combination of three instances of the first model. The third construction was the most complex, being made up of two instances of the second model and one of the first. The three- and four-year-olds were at best able to copy the simplest model. Five-year-olds could copy the first and second but not the third, while the six-year-olds could copy all three. Figure 10–2 shows the constructions produced by two children, both of whom were unable to cope with the *relations* involved in copying the models.

This study suggests that the child's gradually increasing ability to produce hierarchically organized strings of sounds is paralleled by an increasing ability to produce hierarchically organized sequences in areas of motor activity. If so, some underlying developmental change may be responsible for both.

In a second study Greenfield studied a more complex parallelism. The study had to do with the effects of *role change* in language and action

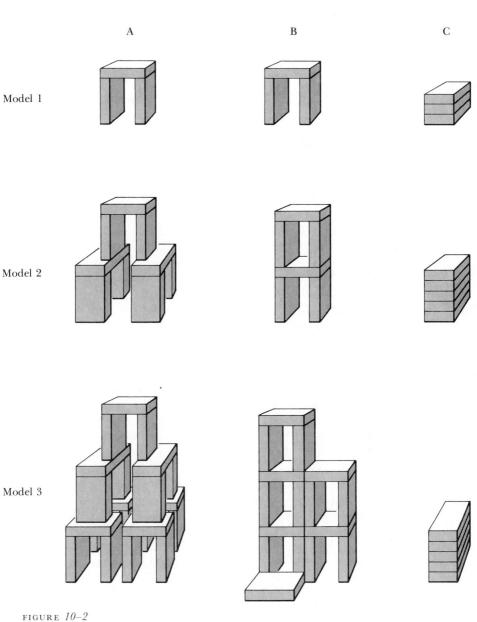

A   B   C

Model 1

Model 2

Model 3

FIGURE *10–2*
The motor skill required to copy the constructions on the left (A) has a structure similar to that involved in the production of words and sentences. The constructions on the right (B and C) are what two children produced. Most three- or four-year-olds can complete only model 1 accurately; most five-year-olds are able to complete models 1 and 2, but not 3; and most $6\frac{1}{2}$-year-olds can complete all three models perfectly. (Greenfield, 1975.)

(Goodson and Greenfield, 1975). The meaning of role change is illustrated in the following four sentences.

1. The dog bit the <u>cat</u> that chased the rabbit.
2. The <u>dog</u> that chased the rabbit bit the cat.
3. The <u>dog</u> that the rabbit chased bit the cat.
4. The dog bit the <u>cat</u> that the rabbit chased.

In each of these sentences the underlined word performs a function in two clauses of the sentence. In sentences 1 and 3 the underlined word serves a double function. For example, in sentence 1 "cat" is the object of the first clause and the subject of the second clause; within the sentence "cat" performs two functions that are different, i.e., a role change is involved. Sentences involving role change are harder to understand than sentences where no role change is involved (2 and 4 above), and are comprehended later in development. We know from Greenfield's study described above that manipulation is more difficult if a single element in a construction must serve two functions.* In this second study Greenfield studied the effect of role change in the construction of a more complex structure. The children, having successfully constructed a propeller in a way that did not involve a role change for any of the components, were then asked to assemble the propeller in the manner shown in Figure 10–3. This involves a change in role from "object" to "instrument" for one of the blades. The results indicated that requiring role change made the task much more difficult for subjects. From these studies it would appear that a difficulty thought to be specific to language is in fact found in other cognitive tasks; that is, the processes of language acquisition reflect general processes of cognitive development.

This point has been reinforced in studies of how children come to acquire the meaning of words. The process seems to be very much a process of learning, i.e., the child formulates hypotheses about the correct way to use words. The hypothesis formation and testing shows up when the child makes mistakes. Consider the problem of working out what the pronouns "I" and "you" mean. As the child hears them, he could formulate the hypothesis

I   = the speaker
You = the person spoken to.

---

* This point was also made in the study of children's ability to construct a tower from three cups of different sizes (p. 172). If a tower is to be built, one cup, the middle one, must be both "big" and "small"—"big" in relation to the smallest cup and "small" in relation to the biggest.

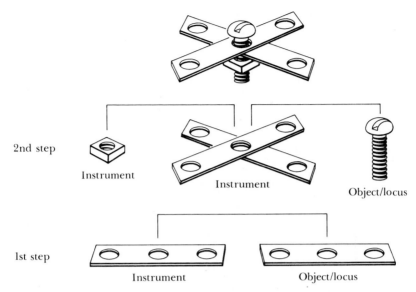

FIGURE *10–3*

The objects used in the task of constructing a propeller can be assigned roles
on the basis of their interrelationships in the construction process. When two
elements are combined in an asymmetrical way, one "acts" while the other,
the stationary element, is acted on, i.e., it serves as the locus of the action. Thus
the active element functions as "instrument" and the stationary element as
simultaneously "object" and "locus." Role change occurs if the child follows the
strategy shown here for constructing the propeller, since one of the blades changes
roles from a stationary element in one step to an active, instrumental element in
the subsequent step. (Goodson and Greenfield, 1975.)

He could equally well formulate the hypothesis

$$I \quad = \text{a grown up}$$
$$You = \text{himself (the child)}.$$

Some children certainly do develop the latter hypothesis (Clark, 1978).
For example, one child broke a toy, then offered it to his father saying,
"You broke it, I'll fix it." The rate of acquisition of conventional word
meanings is no faster than the rate of acquisition of artificial meanings,
e.g., learning to call a triangle with a red dot in it a "boff," or a circle
with a blue square in it a "klug" (Bruner, 1956). It is certainly no faster
than the acquisition of the natural concepts we discussed in Chapters 6, 7,
and 8. Consider the simple experiment shown in Figure 10–4. Children

FIGURE *10–4*

The child is shown a display like the one here. He is then asked who said the following to whom: "Come in," "Come out," "Go in," "Go out." The fact that only the mannikin can say "Come in" and only the rabbits can say "Come out" is learned slowly. That only a rabbit can say "Go in," and only to another rabbit, is even more difficult to understand.

will be six years old before they solve this kind of problem. Although the problem is in part one of spatial relations, this aspect of it is no more difficult than some of the spatial relations tasks solved by infants (pp. 158–159).

The acquisition of vocabulary and grammar proceeds at a very rapid rate after the initial steps are taken (Table 10–2). Along with this, language changes its role in the life of the child. From the beginning, the regulatory function of language is preeminent—the child uses language to regulate the behavior of others and others use language to regulate the behavior of the child. At some point, however, the child becomes able to use language, indeed cannot help using language, in a self-regulatory way. Halliday has suggested that the process of self-regulation through language may begin with the use of words as mnemonics (devices for assisting memory) to facilitate the child's compliance with the regulatory utterances of another. His son Nigel, before the age of two years, when told to "give the toothpaste to daddy and then fetch your bib," went off saying to himself "toothpaste . . . daddy . . . bib . . . toothpaste . . . daddy . . . bib." Here the child is "regulating" his own behavior with his own words (in response to the wishes of another, to be sure). The self-regulation seen in this example would seem to lie intermediate between external regulation and true self-initiated self-regulation. The cognitive sequence seems to lead from "I do what Mummy says!" to "I do what I say Mummy says" to "I do what I say." Obedience to the words of another is transposed into obedience to *words*, no matter what their source. The process again would appear to be one with a reinforcement history, albeit one that we cannot specify at this time.

An alternative route to verbal control of behavior lies in the transfer or *mediating* possibilities that it opens up. An experiment by Dunkeld (1972) may explicate this point. Children were first presented with a photograph showing a spotted cup tilted to reveal a piece of candy and a plain cup tilted to reveal nothing. They were then shown the real cups, both flat down with no candy in view. Their task, of course, was to retrieve the candy from the spotted cup. Children were unable to do this successfully until they could speak well enough to say of the picture, "The candy is under the spotty cup." Apparently, without verbal mediation the picture could not be related to the real-life situation. The critical step seemed to come when the juxtaposition of the picture of a cup and a real cup elicited the same word, permitting transfer. Paradoxically, it seems that words are necessary if pictures are to function as representations.

Last, of course, language is the medium for the transmission of information about the world from one person to another. If that information is to be used, language must come to control behavior. There is a payoff for the child in allowing words to control his behavior, since by so doing he is freed from the need to acquire from personal experience the rules needed to control behavior. Thus, the capture of cognition by language, which so perplexed us in previous chapters, seems to be an inevitable outcome of reinforcement in the physical and, more important, the social world.

Language probably also plays a crucial role in the third stage of cognitive development, the formal-operations stage, when we begin to think about things we cannot experience. The fundamental mode of thought at this level is *metaphorical*. The development of the use of metaphor is a topic that has hardly been studied at all. We know that the process begins very early. Halliday's son Nigel constructed metaphors before he was two years old, as did Piaget's subjects (Figure 10–5). However, the subsequent elaboration of the use of metaphor has hardly been looked at.

Language use is a capacity that does seem to have developmental limits on it. The later language learning begins, the less likely it is that language

Display   Child's Metaphor

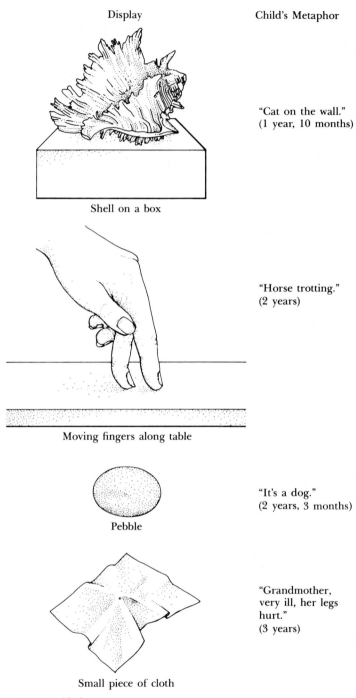

"Cat on the wall."
(1 year, 10 months)

Shell on a box

"Horse trotting."
(2 years)

Moving fingers along table

"It's a dog."
(2 years, 3 months)

Pebble

"Grandmother,
very ill, her legs
hurt."
(3 years)

Small piece of cloth

FIGURE *10–5*
Four metaphors produced by very young children. (Piaget, 1962.)

learning will occur at all. A possible basis for this, the takeover of the brain by nonlinguistic functions, was discussed in Chapter 5. This characteristic of language development, along with the very specificity of language, makes language the best example of an epigenetic process in human behavioral development. We shall return to the consideration of language as an example of epigenesis in Chapter 21.

IV

In this section we are going to consider the origins of individual differences in cognitive skill. As we saw in the last section the greatest variations in cognitive skill are cross-cultural. Within-culture variations are usually equated with differences in intelligence test performance. These differences are conventionally seen as the result of gene expression. However, tests of predictions derived from this hypothesis do not confirm it. Instead, differences in intelligence test performance seem to result from all three developmental factors, with gene expression playing no outstanding role.

11

Development of Intelligence Test Performance: I

The construction of intelligence tests has been a very successful enterprise for psychology. Few of us get through life without facing an intelligence test, usually with dread. What then is an intelligence test? What, indeed, is intelligence?

The word "intelligence" is used in two quite different ways. One, as defined by the Oxford English Dictionary, refers to the faculty of understanding. Intelligence in this sense is an all-or-none quality—humans have it, stones do not. This is the sense we have in mind when we ask if there is intelligent life on Mars. The second meaning refers to an attribute that varies among individuals. For example, we might describe someone as the "most intelligent" member of a class, or the "least intelligent," or of "average intelligence." This is the sense in which "intelligence" is understood in intelligence testing—as an attribute that varies in a quantifiable way.

It is fair to say that those responsible for the construction of intelligence tests over the last 70 years have not been interested in what differentiates intelligent from nonintelligent life. Rather, their concern has been differences between intelligent beings, with the question of the nature of intelligence in the first dictionary meaning put aside. Thus, from the point of view of intelligence testers, "intelligence" is what intelligence tests test. This notion, as we shall shortly see, has led to some difficulties for intelligence testers as they have tried to refine our common-sense uses of the words "intelligence" and "intelligent."

BINET'S TEST

The first intelligence test was constructed by Alfred Binet in the early years of this century. No intelligence test since has been more influential. A history of intelligence testing is largely the history of Binet's test and its immediate descendants. Binet constructed his test in response to a request for help from the officials of the Paris school system. The nature of that request and Binet's willingness to answer it have been critically important in the subsequent development of intelligence testing. Paris at that time had universal education up to high-school level. However, not all of those who entered the Paris school system profited from it, as judged by performance at the end of schooling. There was a wastage of resources, particularly teacher time and pupil time. Binet was therefore asked to devise a test that would pick out the less able students, who could then be sent to special schools to be taught a simplified curriculum. An objective test was required that would be independent of teachers' opinions. Among other things, it would have to separate the intelligent child who was making no effort from the genuinely unintelligent child. Note an important assumption in this request, that an individual's intelligence is a *constant* attribute, one that does not fundamentally change. At a given age, when the tests are conducted, the unintelligent are to be sent off to special schools where they will be taught in ways appropriate to their lack of intelligence. There is no possibility, on this assumption, that relative intelligence can change over time or through environmental manipulation. The unintelligent will always be unintelligent relative to the intelligent. Thus an implicit genetic theory of intelligence was the basis for the request that produced the first intelligence test.

Binet accepted the Paris school board's request as reasonable, and set about constructing the intelligence test (with T. Simon). He made one key assumption in constructing that test, the seemingly reasonable assumption that children grow in absolute intelligence, i.e., ten-year-olds are more intelligent than nine-year-olds, nine-year-olds more intelligent than eight-year-olds, and so on. He also believed that the intelligence test should not cover the same ground as school proficiency examinations, but that any other item could be used. Thus Binet constructed his famous hodgepodge of test items, some of which are shown in Table 11–1.

MENTAL AND CHRONOLOGICAL AGES AND IQ

The Binet-Simon tests attracted great interest and were soon translated into many languages. Louis Terman revised and standardized the test in 1916 using large numbers of American school children. Terman and his associates introduced the notion of intelligence quotient into their test,

TABLE *11–1*

Some items from the Stanford–Binet IQ test appropriate to different age groups. (From *Manual of the Third Revision, Form L–M*, by L. M. Terman and M. A. Merrill, Houghton-Mifflin, 1960.)

AGE

5	Copying a square
	Tying a knot
7	In what way are wood and coal alike?
	What makes a sailing boat move?
9	"One day we saw several icebergs that had been entirely melted by the warmth of the Gulf Stream." What is foolish about that?
	Tell me the name of a color that rhymes with "head."
11	In what way are a rose, a potato, and a tree alike?
13	Rearrange the sentence: "A defends dog good his bravely master."
	What do we mean by "obedience?"

known as the Stanford-Binet. Further revisions were made in 1937 and 1960.

The items in the Binet test are selected to fit the theory that intelligence grows with *chronological age* (CA). Test items are grouped into sets of six, appropriate to a specific age. The appropriate age level of an item is determined by the average age of children on first passing it. Thus about half of a group of eight-year-olds will pass all six items appropriate to eight-year-olds and half will not. Some of the eight-year-olds will pass some of the items in a set appropriate to nine-year-olds; some will pass some ten-year-old items, and a few will go even higher. Some eight-year-olds who cannot pass all of the items appropriate to their age may also not be able to pass all of the seven-year-old items but may pass all of the six-year-old items. Some may have to go down to the five-year-old level to pass all six items and some may have to go even lower. For this reason, the test performance of a child is converted into a *mental age* (MA) by taking as a base the highest age level at which the child can pass all six items and adding two months for each additional item passed from other, higher-level sets. For example, the mental age of an eight-year-old who passed all of the items from the nine-year-old level, four from the 10-year-old level, and two from the 11-year-old level would be 10 years. Another child who passed all of the five-year-old items, four of the six-year-old items, and two of the seven-year-old items would have a mental age of six years.

The determination of mental age is the first step in determining the *intelligence quotient* or IQ, which is computed as MA/CA × 100. The IQ of

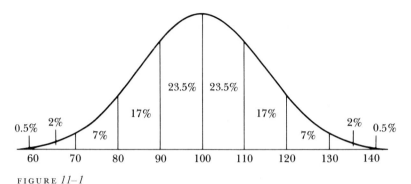

FIGURE *11–1*

Typical distribution of IQ scores in a Western European population. Intelligence is normally distributed like height (see Figure 1–5, p. 9).

the "average child" is defined as 100, i.e., mental age equals chronological age. An average eight-year-old would thus have an $IQ = \frac{8}{8} \times 100 = 100$. Children are regarded as "above average" or "below average" in intelligence if their IQ is above or below 100, respectively. The typical distribution of IQs in a Western European population is shown in Figure 11–1. Computation of IQ from mental and chronological ages works quite well for children. However, this method rapidly becomes useless after the age of 15 or 16. After that point mental age no longer seems to increase, whereas chronological age of course continues to increase. Thus, if we calculated IQ on the basis of mental and chronological ages, we would have the bizarre situation of IQ declining drastically with increasing age. To deal with this problem, the IQ of an adult is determined by first comparing the score of the individual's test with the scores of a population of age-group peers. The individual's score could be "average," i.e., better than 50 percent of the peer group, significantly above average, e.g., better than 95 percent of the peer group, or below average, e.g., better than only 15 percent of the peer group. This result can then be converted to IQ by determining the position of the individual in the distribution of IQs shown in Figure 11–1. The IQ of an adult thus refers only to his relative status in a population. It does not represent a mental age. A 40-year-old with an IQ of 125 does better on intelligence tests than 95 percent of the adult population, but he does not have a "mental age" of 50.

VALIDITY OF IQ TESTS

The Binet test has always been administered by one tester to one subject. It also relies heavily on verbal skills, thus discriminating against cultural groups whose verbal ability and literacy may not be high. Because of these limitations a number of tests suitable for administration to groups or designed to minimize verbal requirements have been developed. The best known of the latter is the Raven Progressive Matrices Test, an example of which is shown in Figure 11–2. While this test involves minimal verbal interaction between tester and testees, it may not necessarily be *nonverbal*. It would be impossible to solve some of the advanced problems in the test without casting them in verbal form.

Because of these differences between the Binet test and later tests, the question naturally arises whether all these tests measure the same thing, and if they do how valid any given test is. Roughly, the *validity* of any measuring instrument is the extent to which it measures what it is supposed to measure. Since it has been widely accepted that the Binet test measures intelligence, we can find out if any new test measures intelligence by giving both that test and the Binet to a large group. One can then compare the performance on the two tests. If the ranking of individuals is the same on both tests, we can conclude that both tests measure the same capacity.

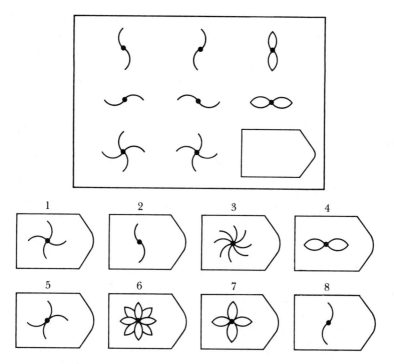

FIGURE *11–2*

A sample test item from the Raven Progressive Matrices Test. The task is to select which of the eight numbered drawings below would complete the matrix. The correct answer is number seven.

Psychologists use the *correlation coefficient* (r) to assess the amount of agreement between two measures. The correlation coefficient can vary from +1.0, indicating perfect agreement, to 0.0, indicating no correspondence at all, to −1.0, indicating complete disagreement. Five sample distributions are given in Figure 11–3, which may give you some indication of the meaning of particular correlation coefficients. Most intelligence tests used today correlate very highly with the Binet test, so it can be said that all of these tests measure the same capacity.

Nevertheless, the use of the Binet test as a measure of the validity of intelligence tests has led to the situation where the only answer we can give to the question "What is intelligence?" is that it is what the tests measure. Yet we still want to know if test intelligence is the same as what we mean by "intelligence" in ordinary language. In other words, is test intelligence a valid measure of the intelligence we see in everyday situations? The difficulty with this question is that it is very hard to get quantified estimates of intelligence in everyday situations. If it were possible to show that tests could predict which children would do well in school and college and which would do poorly, then it could be concluded that the tests do measure at least the sort of intelligence needed to do well at school. That was certainly the assumption of the Paris school board that commissioned Binet. Indeed, in many European school systems that assumption was to become a self-fulfilling prophecy, because low-scoring children at age seven or 11 were sent off to special schools from which they were not *allowed*, in general, to proceed to high school or college. By definition, high IQ score came to predict success in high school and college because *only those with high IQ scores could enter high school and college*. This kind of "validation" has never been allowed in the United States, where low IQ scores at a particular age have never been formally used to exclude individuals from access to higher education. It has thus been possible there to establish the predictive validity of IQ tests.

IQ does correlate with eventual educational attainment, but not very well. The actual correlation is between .50 and .60, which is significant but not very significant. The correlation between IQ and eventual work performance is even lower (Jencks, 1972).* These correlations might indicate that IQ tests do not completely measure intelligence, only some aspects of it. On the other hand, they might equally well indicate that IQ tests do measure intelligence but that variables other than intelligence are involved in educational attainment and job success. At the moment no one can honestly say which of these alternatives is correct. What intelligence tests measure is certainly related to performance in the real world, but it does not seem to completely determine it. Individuals who are below

---

*For white non-farm workers the correlation between IQ and income is .31, and between IQ and occupational status .45.

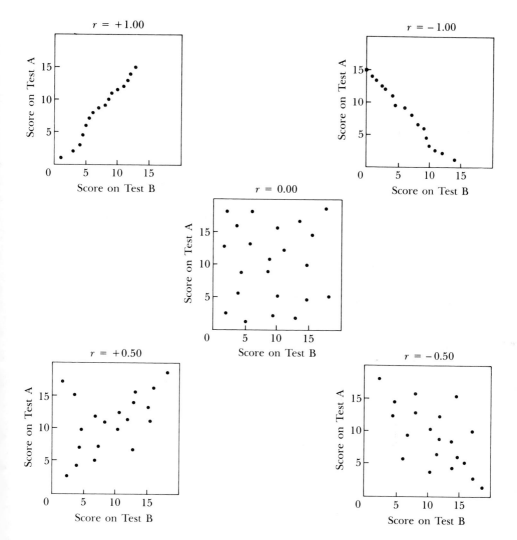

FIGURE *11–3*

Five examples of the distributions of individuals' scores on two tests illustrating different degrees of correlation. The correlation between the scores on two tests is perfect and positive ($r = +1.00$) when the individual with the highest score on test A also has the highest score on test B, the individual with the second highest score on test A has the second highest score on test B, and so on. The correlation is perfect and negative ($r = -1.00$) when the individual scoring highest on test A has the lowest score on test B, the individual scoring lowest on test A has the highest score on test B, and so on. When there is no relation between the individuals' scores on the two tests, a correlation of 0.00 obtains. Intermediate between positive and zero correlations is a slight positive correlation ($r = +0.50$), and intermediate between negative and zero correlations is a slight negative correlation ($r = -0.50$).

average in IQ may do better in school and in their careers than those who are well above average in IQ; however, they are not very likely to do so. An understanding of why this is so must await research on the factors other than intelligence that determine life success; we will be looking at some of these later. We will also need a better definition of "intelligence" in the first sense described earlier. But first we must review the data on the development of intelligence test performance, data that exemplify very clearly the relative merits of different types of theories of development. The remainder of this chapter is therefore concerned with the determinants of performance on intelligence tests.

Performance on intelligence tests is a very salient and very well studied developmental variable. We now know that as children grow older their performance on intelligence tests improves in absolute terms. But when the Paris school board commissioned Binet to devise an intelligence test, they wanted a test that would discriminate intelligent and unintelligent pupils as soon as possible so that they could be segregated into schools with instruction suitable to their respective abilities. On the face of it, such a request assumes that IQ is a constant attribute of an individual. Since an individual's environment can be changed, this assumption implies that the main determinant of intelligence test performance is the individual's genetic composition. (Indeed, many prominent names in the field of intelligence testing have argued that IQ scores would be meaningless if they were not genetically determined.) This scientific hypothesis was originally the basis for a set of noble social aims, among which was the attempt to discover those children from poor backgrounds whose initial school performance and manners did not reflect their "true," i.e., innate, potential. The question of the degree of innateness of IQ has thus been an important issue since the very beginnings of intelligence measurement.

RESEARCH IN IQ

The psychologist assessing the relative importance of genetic and environmental effects on intelligence test performance faces a variety of problems. The most difficult problem is that test intelligence is not a unit character that an individual either does or does not have in the same way as an individual does or does not have blue eyes. Since test intelligence has not been broken down into a number of yes/no characters, analogous to having or not having blue eyes, psychologists studying the inheritance factor in intelligence are forced to work with the sum total, the IQ. Having or not having blue eyes depends on one gene. If, however, IQ were genetically determined, it would be determined by so many genes that standard methods of genetic analysis simply would not be possible.

Psychologists have thus been forced to rely on less than ideal methods for the analysis of intelligence, methods which have nonetheless yielded extremely interesting data.

Kinship studies

One standard method of studying genetic factors in IQ is to correlate the IQs of genetically related individuals. Parents and their children have a 50 percent genetic overlap, since each child receives half of his genes from each parent. Siblings likewise have a 50 percent overlap, on the average, and are therefore good subjects for comparison. Grandparents and grandchildren can also be compared, although the genetic overlap is of course less. Perfect genetic overlap is found in monozygotic (identical) twins, whose genetic constitutions or *genotypes* are identical. Typical correlations between IQs of a variety of kin are shown in Table 11–2. As can be seen there, the greater the genetic overlap the greater is the correlation between IQ scores. The correlation between monozygotic twins approaches the correlation between IQs obtained from testing a single individual twice.

Unfortunately, such studies do not tell us what the relative roles of heredity and environment are, since environmental overlap is likely to be highly correlated with genetic overlap. Consider identical twins. They are born roughly at the same time. Growing up in the same family, they are exposed to the same influences at the same time. Because they look so much alike, their parents may even have difficulty in distinguishing between them sufficiently well enough to be *able* to treat them differently (although, in truth, very few parents of twins wish to do that anyway). To all intents and purposes, identical twins growing up in the same family have the same environment, as well as the same genotype. The high

TABLE *11–2*

Correlations between IQ scores of individuals with different genetic overlap. The theoretical values are those that would be found if intelligence was exclusively genetic. (Jensen, 1969.)

RELATIONSHIP	NUMBER OF STUDIES	CORRELATION	THEORETICAL VALUE
Monozygotic twins	14	+0.87	+1.00
Siblings	36	+0.55	+0.50
Parent and child	13	+0.50	+0.50
Grandparent and grandchild	3	+0.27	+0.25
First cousins	3	+0.26	+0.125

correlation between their scores could thus reflect *either* genotypic *or* environmental overlap, or some combination of the two. Although siblings raised in the same family have overlapping environments too, the overlap for them is less since they are born at different times. Since they do not look identical, and are of different ages, it is much less likely that they will be treated identically; in addition, parents' ideas on child-rearing may change between children. One could argue that there is environmental overlap between parents and their children as well, since parents do treat their children to some extent as they were treated in childhood—buying their children the same books they had, imposing the same patterns of discipline, and, in some countries, often sending them to the same schools. However, since the gross features of the environment change between generations, it is less likely that there will be environmental overlap for individuals of different generations. The correlations between grandparent and grandchild and between first cousins may exemplify this. IQ correlations between grandparents and grandchildren are lower than would be expected from the degree of genetic overlap between them, whereas IQ correlations between first cousins are higher than would be expected on this basis (Table 11–2). Since cousins grow up at about the same time, they probably have a more similar environment than grandparents and grandchildren do. This difference in environmental overlap might explain the fact that IQ correlations diverge so greatly from the theoretical genetic correlations.

It is in principle possible to separate genetic and environmental effects on IQ by comparing the effects of diverse and homogeneous environments on populations with known genetic overlap. The greatest effort in this area has gone into studying the IQs of monozygotic twins who were separated at birth and brought up separately. Since these twins were thus not raised in the same family, their environments could not be identical in the same way as the environments of monozygotic twins raised together. There have been thus far four major studies of monozygotic twins raised apart. The results of the studies are shown in Table 11–3. As can be seen there, separation of monozygotic twins does in fact reduce the correlation between their IQs, although the correlation is still typically higher than that of dizygotic twins, even when the latter are reared together. Some researchers have argued that the correlation between the IQs of monozygotic twins reared apart is itself an estimate of the effect of genotype on IQ. This argument seems plausible but suffers from one major flaw. It is perfectly possible that adoption agencies will put separated identical twins into environments that are similar in some respects important for the development of IQ. There is no way that we can find out whether this is the case. However, we do know that the more different the environments of two separated monozygotic twins, the more different their IQs will be. Figure 11–4 shows the relationships between environmental and IQ

TABLE *11–3*

The correlation between IQ scores of identical twins that have been separated is lower than the correlation between identical twins raised together. For comparison, data on nonidentical twins are given. (1: Burt, 1958; 2: Newman, Freeman, and Holzinger, 1937.)

	GROUP TESTS		INDIVIDUAL TESTS	
	1	2	1	2
Monozygotic (identical) twins				
Raised together	.94	.92	.92	.97
Raised apart	.77	.73	.84	.67
Dizygotic (nonidentical) twins				
Raised together	.54	.62	.53	.64

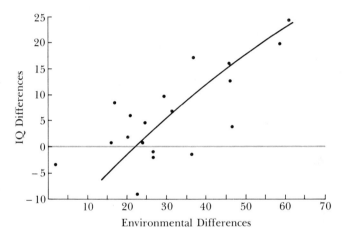

FIGURE *11–4*

Differences between the IQ scores of identical twins reared apart are plotted against differences between their respective environments (assessed on a scale of 70 points). IQ difference was calculated by subtracting the IQ of the twin from the environment assessed as least socially and educationally advantageous from the IQ of the twin in the better environment. From the graph we can see that where the environments are only 30 or fewer points apart differences in IQ are less than where environments differ by more than 30 points. (Data from Anastasi, 1958.)

differences found in one study of monozygotic twins. The correlation between these differences is .79. The largest difference is 24 points. However, we cannot conclude from this that the maximum effect of environment on IQ performance is 24 points, for the obvious reason that the environments in this study were not the most different environments conceivable. As with the height experiment discussed in Chapter 1, we could not possibly bring up one twin in the worst possible environment and the other in the best possible. Without such an attempt, however, we could not measure the maximal effects of environment on IQ. What the data on monozygotic twins reared apart do tell us is that IQ performance is not purely determined by heredity. The fact that IQ correlations are slightly higher between monozygotic twins reared apart than between dizygotic twins reared together implies that both genetic and environmental effects determine these correlations, but these data do not themselves tell us what the relative contributions are. This may seem surprising to those readers familiar with the many popular and technical articles in which data like the above are used to obtain very precise estimates of the genetic contribution to IQ scores. Estimates ranging between 80 and 40 percent (even as low as zero!) have been bandied about with great confidence but without justification (see the review by Loehlin, Lindzey, and Spuhler, 1975).

Statistical problems

These estimates have stirred passions in the United States and elsewhere. Those who claim to have calculated the genetic factor in IQ have been accused of racism; their opponents have been accused of wanting to suppress freedom of inquiry. In fact, much of the controversy is scientifically pointless, or more accurately baseless. The statistical methods upon which the whole controversy is founded simply cannot support the weight of inference that has been attached to them (Watson, 1972). Those interested in estimating the relative roles of genes and environment using these methods claim that $IQ = G + E$, where G is genetic influence and E environmental influence. It is further argued (e.g., Jensen, 1972) that the ratio of G to E is 80 : 20, i.e., that genetic influences are four times as important as environmental influences. Watson (1972) generated some artificial IQ values from different possible combinations of G and E. He then applied standard statistical techniques to these IQ scores to see if he could rediscover the combination law he had started with. One set was generated on the assumption that $IQ = G + E$, with G being four times the value of E. Applying standard techniques to these scores, Watson found that the analysis gave 80 percent to G and 20 percent to E and that the relation was additive. In other words, the statistical techniques did rediscover the law originally used to generate the data. He then generated IQs using the law IQ = G × E, with E being twice the value of G. His analysis of these IQs showed that G was responsible for 86 percent of the variance and E for 14 percent, and that the relation was IQ = G + E in a ratio 22 : 9, a complete reversal of the combination law that had been used to generate the scores.

Watson found that whether he generated his artificial IQs with the law IQ = G + E, or IQ = G × E, or IQ = $\sqrt{G \times E}$, and no matter which ratio of G to E he used, G "proved" to be far more important than E. What Watson has shown is that existing statistical techniques simply should not be applied to IQ scores in order to find out which combinations of genetic and environmental effects are responsible for the scores. If we really want to find these things out we must turn to quite different techniques.

Constancy of the individual IQ

One source of data on the determination of IQ that has been largely ignored is data on the stability of individual IQs. The use of IQs in practical situations depends on the assumption that IQ is constant and cannot be altered. One would not segregate children into specialized schools on the basis of intelligence if one thought that their IQs were likely to change, or could be changed. The use of IQ in educational selection depends strictly on the belief that IQ is constant, which in turn assumes that IQ is largely genetically determined. For the educational use of IQ tests to be justifiable, the IQ must prove to be very stable indeed. A number of studies have tried to test this hypothesis (Bayley, 1955; Hilden, 1949; Honzik, Macfarlane, and Allen, 1948). Figure 11–5 shows the correlation between IQ at maturity (age 18) and various earlier ages. Test intelligence at age one bears no relationship to test intelligence at maturity, but the correlation does increase after age one quite rapidly, reaching a plateau around age 11. Nevertheless, even at age 11 the correlation with IQ at maturity is still far from perfect, and at younger ages the correlation is a long way short of the value we would want for selection purposes. In fact, the low correlations between early and later IQ strike a death blow to any largely genetic theory of IQ, at least if taken at their face value.

If IQ were genetically fixed, either entirely or in part, we should theoretically be able to predict adult IQ scores at the moment of conception. If IQ were entirely genetic, the correlation between early and late IQs would have to be +1 between any two ages. If IQ were 80 percent genetic, the correlation between scores at any two points in time would have to be +.9. Neither of these values has been found. Indeed, no model based on a high *fixed* genetic contribution to IQ fits the data on IQ development,

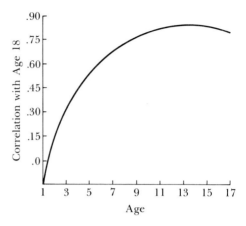

FIGURE *11–5*

Correlation between IQ at
maturity (age 18) and various
earlier ages. (Composite data
from a number of studies;
Bloom, 1964.)

for any fixed model would predict much higher correlations between early
and late intelligence than in fact we find. One could compute the genetic
contribution to IQ scores only on the basis of certain assumptions about
the effects of environment on IQ scores, e.g., that the effects of environment
are cumulative over time. Suppose that our criterion age for intelligence
testing is 18 years. At age 15 the individual will thus have been exposed to
15/18 of the total environmental effects that will determine his IQ at
age 18. At age 12 he will have been exposed to 12/18 of the total environmental effects that will determine his IQ at 18; at age nine, 9/18; at
age six, 6/18; and so on. These are the proportions of IQ variability at
age 18 (our criterion age) accounted for at younger ages, on the hypothesis
that the environment determines IQ score by way of cumulative effects.
They can be converted into theoretical correlations between IQ at the
criterion age and any given younger age by the formula

$$ r = \sqrt{\frac{\text{younger age}}{\text{criterion age}}}. $$

Plotting these theoretical correlations against age produces the curve
shown in Figure 11–6, which represents the correlation we would expect
between IQ score at one age and at a later criterion age if the criterion IQ
score is entirely determined by environmental variables operating in a
simple cumulative fashion during the life of developing individuals. The
theoretical curve is similar to the curve that is actually obtained
(Figure 11–5), with the obtained curve showing slightly lower correlations.
The difference between the two is presumed to reflect the genetic contribution to IQ. On this analysis the contribution would be rather small,
about 10 percent.

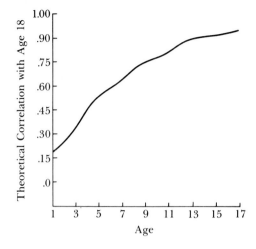

FIGURE *11–6*

Theoretical correlations between IQ at age 18 and various earlier ages, based on the cumulative environmental effects theory.

Analyses of this sort have been challenged on a number of grounds, which we must consider before giving any credence to the very low figure for genetic determination obtained above. The simplest objection is that the low correlations obtained between IQ scores for individuals at younger and older ages arises from the fact that IQ tests for young children do not measure the same kind of test intelligence that tests for older children do, and that correlating scores on the two kinds of tests seriously under-estimates the "true" correlation of intelligence in younger and older children. This is quite possible. However, if it is the case, then much of the justification for intelligence testing at any age disappears, since there is no age at which an IQ score predicts perfectly an IQ score at a later age. Figure 11–7 shows correlations between IQ scores at a variety of ages and the correlations expected on the basis of cumulative environmental effects. Only one of the observed correlations is as high as those expected. There is thus no evidence that at some age we can begin testing "true" intelligence.

An alternative hypothesis to explain the poor correspondence between individual IQ scores at younger and older ages has been offered by Jensen (1972) and by Jencks (1972). They propose the *polygenic* hypothesis, that the genes determining IQ come into operation sequentially. Accordingly, when we give an IQ test to a young child we are testing the effect of only a few of the genes that will determine his adult IQ. The older the child, the greater the amount of relevant genetic information that will have been expressed in the form of brain growth, and so the better will the correlation of IQ be with adult scores. Although this hypothesis is perfectly plausible, it is somewhat unlikely. On the polygenic model, the correlation between IQ scores of siblings should increase with age as more of their common

268

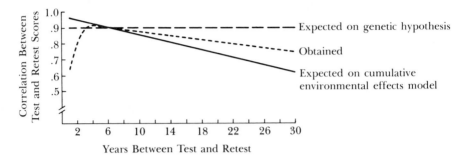

FIGURE *11–7*

Test-retest correlations in the same adult individuals as a function of interval
between tests. All individuals were over 18 and hence on a genetic model the
correlations should be virtually perfect and should not change with age. On a
cumulative environmental effects model the correlations should decline with age.
The data fit neither extreme hypothesis.

genes express themselves in structure. But one study found a correlation
of .75 between the IQ scores of dizygotic (nonidentical) twins as early as
age two (Wilson, 1972). This is a higher correlation than one would expect
on a fixed genetic model, and a much higher correlation than one would
expect on the polygenic model. In fact, it is much higher than the
correlation obtained for older dizygotic twins (Table 11–3)—a puzzle for
a genetic theory of IQ.

One final objection to the type of analysis given above applies equally
well to environmentalist models of IQ. That is, the *group* correlations these
analyses are based on seriously underestimate the kind of individual swings
in IQ that can occur. Figure 11–8 shows the enormous swings in IQ of
three individuals over the course of their development. These swings are
far too large to be explained on the basis of either genetics or the cumulative
effects of environment. Nor are they open to more obvious environmentalist
explanations, such as health, since the child with the worst health record
(case 2) was the one who showed the most stable IQ of the three. We have
seen nothing so far that would allow us to explain swings of this magnitude.
Such data should caution us against the simple combinatorial theories we
have discussed in this chapter. While we must eventually account for such
changes, we obviously cannot do so with this type of theory.

Lastly, there is the fact that as far as we know the growth of the brain—
the structural expression of the genes most relevant to the question of
intelligence—is over by age 20 at the latest. On a strictly genetic model,
the correlations between an individual's scores on the same test given at
different times should stabilize at a high level. In fact they do not. They

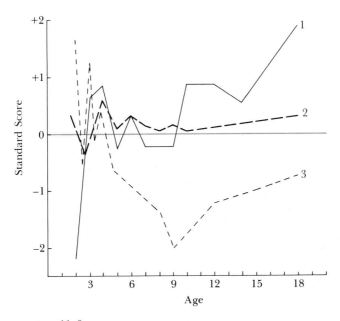

FIGURE *11–8*

IQ scores attained over a 16-year period by three children.
The scores are expressed as standard scores, i.e., zero
represents the mean score obtained for all the children in
this study, while positive and negative numbers represent
units of standard deviations above and below the mean. It
is clear that an individual's score can change drastically
over time. (Honzik, 1948.)

are better predicted by a cumulative environmental effects model than a
fixed genetic contribution model.

An experimental scientist faced with the problem of determining the
relative roles of genes and environment in the determination of IQ scores
would directly manipulate genes or environment to determine their effects.
The data reviewed thus far are not experimental; they are descriptive.
Descriptive studies are a necessary prerequisite for experimental studies,
and it is to these we turn in our next chapter.

12

Development of Intelligence Test Performance: II

As we saw in the previous chapter, the central issue in the study of IQ scores is what proportion of the score is determined by genes and what proportion by environment. The two obvious experimental possibilities are to manipulate the genes, by selective breeding, or to manipulate the environment. In the latter case, only enriching manipulations are ethically feasible.

SELECTIVE BREEDING AND IQ

Selective breeding experiments are of course not feasible for human populations, and so we cannot study genetic effects directly. Nevertheless, we can study the "selective breeding" that occurs naturally, without external intervention. Such studies are very far from ideal from the point of view of experimental genetics. None of the studies described below meets the criteria for a selective-breeding experiment that a geneticist would require. However, data from such studies are the only data we are likely to get about direct genetic effects on IQ scores, and must therefore be taken into account in any discussion of those effects. Such studies are made possible by the fact that definable groups of humans score differently on the same intelligence tests. American blacks, for example, score an average 15 points below American whites on IQ tests (Figure 12–1). This difference, given the present state of our knowledge, could result from either genetic or environmental differences. If it results from genetic differences, we can make certain predictions about the IQ scores of the progeny of interracial matings. The progeny, of course, are likely to be black, and so studies of such children in the United States are not likely to be informative, since any environmental effects that might have produced the IQ difference in the parent may operate equally on the child. The occupation of Germany by U.S. troops after World War II created a population in which genetic effects on IQ scores can possibly be separated. I refer to the illegitimate children of white German women and U.S. soldiers, both black and white. All the children grew up in Germany.

One investigator collected IQ data on a sample with black fathers and a sample with white fathers (Eyferth, 1961). The two groups were matched for age, maternal income, living conditions, and as far as possible school and neighborhood. If we accept that the matching was quite precise, we can make some quite precise predictions about the IQs these children should have if IQ is largely genetically determined. There are some complexities to the analysis, however. First of all, we do not know what the actual IQ scores of the fathers were. But we can assume that both sets of fathers were representative of blacks and whites in the U.S. army. Since the average black serviceman scored 15 points below the average white serviceman, on that basis alone the half-black progeny should score 7.5 points below the white progeny, if IQ is primarily determined by genetic factors.

However, there is another effect which complicates the picture: the phenomenon of *regression to the mean*. Children of parents who score above or below a population mean tend to have scores intermediate between their parents' scores and the population mean. This has quite drastic effects on predictions of scores when the mean values are different in two

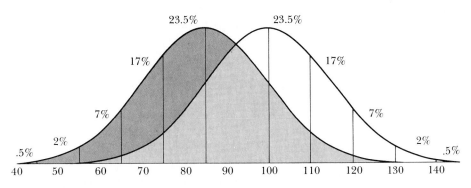

FIGURE *12–1*

Distribution of IQ scores for white and black populations in the United States. Most studies find a 15-point difference between the groups. As the graph shows, approximately 44 percent of blacks but only 9.5 percent of whites have an IQ less than 80, while 9.5 percent of whites but only 1.5 percent of blacks have an IQ higher than 120.

populations. Consider the offspring of white U.S. parents with an IQ of 90. The mean in the U.S. white population is 100, so regression to the mean dictates that the average score of the offspring should be 95, midway between the parents' values and the mean value. Consider now the offspring of black U.S. parents whose IQ is 90. Since the U.S. black population mean is 85, the score of offspring of black parents with IQs of 90 should drop to 87.5. Thus, even if the black serviceman had the same IQ scores as their white counterparts, their progeny would score on average 3.75 less. If we take the more conservative assumption that the two groups were representative, then the predicted difference between the two groups grows to 11.25 points $(7.5 + 3.75)$, if IQ differences are primarily genetic in origin. In fact, there was no difference between the two groups at all. The mean IQ of children with white fathers was 97, while that of children with black fathers was 96.5. These results suggest that the differences in IQ of the parent populations were primarily *environmental* in origin. Note that this does not imply that *all* IQ differences are environmental in origin, merely that differences as big as those between the U.S. black and white populations, a 15 point difference, probably are environmental in origin.

This conclusion has been substantiated by a number of sophisticated genetic analyses of blacks within the United States. For example, if the average difference between blacks and whites in the United States is to be accounted for by genetic differences, we would expect that within the black population those who had a higher proportion of "white" genes would score higher on IQ tests than those who had a lower or zero proportion of "white" genes. In the absence of direct information about ancestry, estimates of these proportions can be made by analysis of blood groups, since black and white people do differ in this respect. Two studies have used this information to compute white/black genetic proportions and correlated the results with IQ scores (Osborne and Suddick, 1971; Loehlin, Vandenberg, and Osborne, 1973). The correlations were zero or insignificantly negative, again indicating that the differences between IQ scores of the U.S. black and white populations are probably environmental in origin. Less sophisticated studies relying on reports of ancestry have come to similar conclusions (Tanser, 1939).

MANIPULATION OF ENVIRONMENT

None of the data reviewed above could be called experimental by any stretch of the imagination. Since it is humans that we are dealing with, the only experimental manipulations that are at all possible are those that involve manipulation of the environment. There have been a very large number of studies of this kind. I think it is fair to say that the majority of these studies have been able to produce only very slight gains in intelligence test performance, as Jensen (1969) has shown. If we accept the environmentalist viewpoint outlined in Chapter 11, it is obvious that the majority of feasible experimental manipulations will produce only very slight gains. If we assume that environmental effects are cumulative and that a "good" environment will subtract from the effects of a "bad" environment, how much improvement could we expect from, say, giving children from a "bad" environment three hours per day in a "good" environment during their fifth year of life? If we make the assumption that children are awake about 15 hours per day, it is obvious that the "good" environment would only operate during four percent of their lives. The remaining 96 percent would be spent in the "bad" environment. If we assume that a "very bad" environment drops IQ by 30 points and a "very good" environment boosts IQ by 30 points, it can be seen that children given the enriching experience of a very good environment for two percent of their life should be 1.2 points better off than controls left in the very bad environment all the time $((30+30)/50 = 1.2)$. This is slightly lower than the values reported by Jensen (1969) for studies of that sort, but not much lower. Obviously, there is no way to assess the full possible effects of environments on this basis. The only way we could hope to do so would be to take much greater control over environment, something that is difficult to do in an experimental study.

There have been some studies in which natural variations in environment were exploited. One study investigated the changes in IQ performance of children growing up in isolated American mountain communities that were low in many of the amenities available to the average American child (Wheeler, 1932). Between 6 and 16 years of age their IQ scores dropped by over 20 points. Other researchers studied changes in the IQ scores of children in homes where school achievement was emphasized and as many instructional aids as possible were offered (Sontag, Baker, and Nelson, 1958). Gains of 20 points between ages 3 and 12 were found. The only experimental study which has reported gains of this magnitude is the preschool project for black children under Heber's direction in Milwaukee, Wisconsin (Heber, Dever, and Conry, 1968; Heber and Garber, 1970). This program truly does attempt massive control over the environment of its 20 subjects:

At the Infant Education Center, the infants receive a customized, precisely structured program of stimulation. The infants are picked up in their homes early each morning by their infant teachers and are transported to the Center where they remain until late afternoon. Infant stimulation teachers follow an intensive program which has been prescribed in detail. Essentially, it includes every aspect of sensory and language stimulation which we believe may have relevance for the development of intellectual abilities. Its major emphases are efforts designed to facilitate achievement motivation, problem-solving skills, and language development.

When given IQ tests at $5\frac{1}{2}$ years of age, children in this program scored 125 points, compared to a score of 95 for a control group, a difference of 30 points. It is interesting to note that the control group evidently showed some improvement in their IQ scores merely through being tested for IQ. The control group's parents had an average IQ of 75 (10 points less than the mean black adult IQ), so we would expect the children's IQs to be 80, when in fact they were 95. Other researchers using similarly massive control have reported similarly large gains (Robinson and Robinson, 1971; Ramey, Campbell, and Nicholson, 1973).

What then are we to conclude about the effects of heredity and environment on IQ scores? The answer, I am afraid, is not very much. Environmental influences can seemingly shift IQ scores through a range of about 50 points, if we look at the maximum gains and losses that have been reported. If we control for heredity, by using separated identical twins, the largest difference reported is 24 points. Whether 24 points or 50 points represents the true effect of environment is something we cannot say, simply *because we have no way of measuring environmental similarity.* We can say that two individuals are genetically identical but we simply cannot say that two environments are identical. That is our first problem. With no measure of environmental overlap or difference, the equation $IQ = f(G, E)$* becomes insoluble. We cannot measure E and we cannot therefore determine the function rule relating G and E. Our equation contains four variables, two of which are unknowns, and so we simply cannot solve it. In fact, our equation may contain three unknowns. If there is one thing that all of the foregoing should have brought out it is the problems of IQ scores themselves. This problem is most sharply focused in the many critiques of the Milwaukee project. Heber himself writes:

> Our experimental infants have obviously been trained in skills sampled by the tests and the repeated measurements have made them test-wise. They have been provided with intensive training to which no comparable group of infants has ever been exposed, to the best of our knowledge. Have we, thereby, simply given them an opportunity to learn and practice certain intellectual skills at an earlier age than is generally true? And if so, will their apparent acceleration in development diminish as they grow older?

Others have been yet more critical of the fact that some of the training given the Milwaukee children consisted of material that was in the tests themselves (e.g., Page, 1972). These criticisms seem to betray a gross confusion about the relationship between intelligence and IQ tests. In Britain IQ tests were formerly administered at age 11 to determine the whole subsequent pattern of a child's education. A small industry sprang

---

*IQ = some function of the relation between genes and environment.

up devoted to teaching children how to do well on tests. The largest gains claimed were of the order of 15 points. Suppose that it were true—which it obviously is not— that all of the gains registered in the Milwaukee project could have been due to teaching the children how to do IQ tests. We could then make the following statements.

1. Intelligence is what intelligence tests test.
2. Practice on intelligence tests improves intelligence test performance.
3. Therefore practice on intelligence tests improves intelligence.

Anyone who dissents from the conclusion (3) can only do so by disagreeing with the first premise. Disagreeing with this premise leaves us in the peculiar position of trying, via environmental manipulations that we cannot identify, to manipulate a variable that we cannot identify—a completely hopeless situation from an experimental or social point of view. There is obviously some genetic determination of intelligence. There is obviously some environmental determination of intelligence. To go beyond these truisms, to say what determines what, will require much more precise definitions of intelligence than intelligence tests have given us. Such definitions are not impossible in principle, but they have eluded us in practice.

THE NECESSITY OF DEVELOPMENTAL RESEARCH

Meanwhile, what can we say about development? Psychologists who adopt extreme hereditarian positions are in fact saying that development is exclusively the ordered expression of information coded in the genes. The data used to support this position have not in the past been derived from studies of development but rather from patterns of correlation between adults, individuals whose development is complete. The possibilities for testing the genetic hypothesis on adults have been exhausted, and no conclusive answers have been obtained. Surely it is obvious that the only sensible thing to do is examine the process of development directly. That way we may be able to define what does develop and what does not, so that we can begin to establish just what factors determine what segments of development. While the study of IQ development exemplifies many of the problems and techniques of developmental psychology, the IQ measure is a remote abstraction from the day-to-day ways by which we come to cope with the world around us. Development is too rich a process to be encapsulated in a single number. If we are ever to understand development, we must look at the real thing, real children in the real world.

V

It is now time to turn our attention to social development. The newborn, as we shall see, enters the world with some social skills, which in the course of development will be refined and increased but may also be suppressed or redirected, often irreversibly. Although the need for social contact is all-pervasive in human society, a person's environment can radically alter the expression of that need. Social development and cognitive development seem to proceed together, as each new intellectual advance increases the possibilities of social awareness. This is most obvious among young adults, whose social perceptions are affected by their ability to think logically about moral issues, with the result that they often come into conflict with the ideas of the parents on whom they have been dependent for so long. Sexual roles and choice of occupation are both affected by the young person's social milieu and both help determine the eventual place of the individual in adult society.

277

13

Problems
of Social
Development

Human beings are the most social of animals. No individual human could grow and survive without the active help of other humans. No single human could bring about the conditions that have allowed our species to spread to every corner of the globe, forcing the environment to give shelter and sustenance, whether in the snows of the Arctic or the dry waste of the desert. The massive artifacts that characterize human civilizations—cities, power plants, sewage works—all depend for their conception and construction on the cooperative interaction of large numbers of humans. The development of human knowledge, although very much an individual process, nonetheless depends on processes of education that are essentially social. The pupil-teacher relation is social; science is an activity carried out by a community of coworkers; the dissemination of knowledge is a social process. The idea of humans existing as individuals, coming together only for purposes of reproduction, as some other animals do, is ludicrous. That single humans are less likely to survive the hazards of the world should be obvious enough. Less obvious, perhaps, is the probability that they would be unable to survive the sheer loneliness that would result from isolation. It is surely not without importance that solitary confinement is one of the ultimate punishments used in repressive penal institutions. The anguish of the lone individual has been well expressed by many writers.

Among psychologists, William James (1890) wrote that "the original source of terror . . . is solitude." In his study of man's need to associate with others, Schachter (1959) quotes a prisoner who had been put in solitary confinement: "Gradually the loneliness closed in. Later on I was to experience situations which amounted almost to physical torture; even that seemed preferable to absolute isolation." Schachter also quotes a religious solitary who wrote that "solitude is full of strife and pain." The fact that even loneliness of a less severe sort is an unpleasant state is attested by the success of organizations whose sole function is to allow people to meet with other people, to overcome the solitary state that many of us live in in our modern impersonal cities.

Human adults do congregate, they do form social groups, and there seems to be something intrinsically rewarding in these activities, beyond whatever other functions they may serve. Schachter described an experiment in which volunteer subjects were locked alone in a windowless room. After two hours isolation, one subject felt as if he were going to pieces; he nearly kicked down the door of his cell to get out, to reestablish human contact. Other subjects reported tension, anxiety, nervousness, apparently simply as a result of their isolation. It would seem, from Schachter's experiments, that this anxiety state may be assuaged by the opportunity to congregate with anybody else at all—although human social relations are not normally so promiscuous. Human relationships may be characterized in very many ways—there are probably as many types of relationships as there are pairs of people. However, there are two important types of relationship, both in the day-to-day life of adults and from the standpoint of development. These are (1) authority relations, which can be looked at as either leader→follower or follower→leader relations, and (2) democratic peer relations.

AUTHORITY RELATIONS

Authority relations are those that occupy the greater part of the waking hours of most of us. Unless both are very lucky, the relationship between student and teacher is an authority relation, as is the relationship of a teacher to his head of department. Most companies are organized around authority relations. Armies are organized in this way, as are some churches. Even some supposedly "fun" organizations, such as the Boy Scouts, are, if my hazy recollections are correct, organized in an authoritarian way. Some people might protest the inclusion of authority relations in a chapter that purports to describe social relations. Although authority relations are between people, it is the threat of external sanctions that keeps authority relations intact. Powerful negative sanctions can be explicit in authority relations. When an employee disobeys his boss, thereby breaking the authority relation, he risks losing his job. When a soldier disobeys a commanding officer in wartime, he risks being executed. Surely it must be the brutal reality of these sanctions that produces the behaviors that typify authority relations, and not any kind of social motive. Tempting as this reduction is, however, I am sure it is incorrect. Authority relations between human adults do exemplify social motives, motives that cannot be reduced to fear of consequences that are themselves non-social.

Consider the famous experiments of Stanley Milgram (1963). Milgram advertised for subjects to participate in an experiment on the effects of punishment on learning. The volunteers who came in were told that their role was that of teacher in the learning situation. They were introduced to their pupil, who was then taken into an adjoining room and strapped into a chair wired for electric shock. The "teacher's" task was to present his pupil with a series of stimuli, each of which had one and only one correct response. Each time the pupil gave an incorrect response, the "teacher" was required to give the pupil an electric shock. If incorrect responses continued, the shock level was to be increased. Failure to respond counted as an incorrect response and was to be punished with an increased level of shock.

In fact, the experiment was not an experiment on the effects of shock on learning and the pupil was not really the subject. The experiment was a study of the limits of obedience to authority—in this case represented by the scientist who had recruited the "teacher." The pupil was actually an accomplice in the experiment; he deliberately made mistakes for which there was no real electric shock. However, there was no way the "teacher," the real subject of the experiment, could have known this. The "voltage generator" in the experiment had a calibrated dial ranging from 15 to 450 volts. In addition, the upper range of the dial was marked "Extreme Shock" and then "Danger: Severe Shock." As the experiment went on, the pupil continued to make errors deliberately and the teacher duly increased the shock. By prearrangement the pupil would begin to moan when the setting on the shock generator reached 75 volts. He would continue to moan until the setting reached 150 volts, at which point he would ask to be let out of the experiment. At the 180 volt setting the pupil would cry out that the pain was too much, that he just couldn't take it anymore. As the voltage generator moved up through "Extreme Shock" towards "Danger," the pupil would begin to pound on the wall and beg to be released from the experiment. Of course, this behavior counted as "failure to respond," according to the experimenter's instructions, so the "teacher" was required to continue administering shock. Finally, at the highest voltage reading the pupil stopped responding in any way; even the moans and cries ceased. Even at this point, according to the experimenter's instructions, the teacher was to increase and continue the shock treatment.

The subjects in this experiment, the "teachers," were a random sample of ordinary Americans. They did not appear to be disturbed in any way prior to the experiment. They were in no way beholden to the authority figure, who had no sanctions to impose upon them, no punishments for disobedience, and no rewards for obedience. To what extent then would the subjects obey the scientist's commands? Milgram asked some 40 psychiatrists to guess the outcome of the experiment. The predictions were that the bulk of the subject population would stop at 150 volts, when the pupil asks to be let out. They predicted that fewer than one percent would go all the way and administer the highest shock on the dial. In fact, about 65 percent of subjects went to that limit, administering electric shocks to a fellow human being who was, as far as they could tell, almost certainly unconscious, maybe even dead. And why did they do this? Why did they do something they, along with the rest of us, must have felt to be wrong and immoral? The only answer that Milgram has come up with is that they were obedient to authority because human beings *are* obedient to authority. Even many of the subjects who ultimately rejected the authority of the scientist-experimenter did so out of obedience to a yet higher authority. For example, a professor of Old Testament Liturgy stopped at 150 volts as soon as the pupil asked to be freed from the experiment. When asked, indirectly, why he had opposed the authority of the experimenter, he answered, "If one has as one's ultimate authority God, then it trivializes human authority." As Milgram points out, this subject did not repudiate authority but rather maintained obedience to what he saw as a higher authority.

Milgram argues that obedience to authority is an inevitable outcome of the processes of development in society. From the beginning, he says, the child is exposed to parental regulation. Parents train their children to be obedient even as they are training them to be "good." Even while a parent is teaching that it is wrong to inflict pain, while he is saying "Do not inflict pain," he is also, implicitly, saying "Obey me." Thus, Milgram argues, parental inculcation of morals is simultaneously an inculcation of obedience. When the child takes his first steps away from the family, he typically enters a school where obedience is rewarded and disobedience punished. Eventually, says Milgram, the child learns as a social axiom, "Obey the man in charge." On this hypothesis, obedience to authority is a developmental process and as such should be of prime concern for developmental psychologists.

PEER RELATIONS

Peer relations are quite different from authority relations. The essence of a peer group is that all of the members of the group are equal in one another's eyes. Certainly, a peer group may at any time have a leader, but leadership may change from time to time and the leader has no way of forcing the rest of the group to obey him. The only sanction on the behavior of an individual in a peer group is fear of expulsion from the group, and that sanction applies as much to a leader as to anyone else. In that case, can we expect peer relations to exert as strong an influence on individual behavior as authority relations do?

There is a great deal of research on this point and the results would seem to indicate that peer-group influences are just as strong as authority influences. One would hesitate to call a temporary assembly of strangers, called together for one reason or another, a peer group. One would expect the individuals in the group not to care particularly about isolation (expulsion) from the group, for after all the group is going to dissolve in a fairly short time. The individuals in it thus would have no particular need to keep the others happy and would hardly fear any specific consequences of disagreement with the others. Nevertheless, in a classic series of experiments Solomon Asch (1958) found that such temporary peer groups powerfully affected the behavior of individuals in the group. In one of the basic experiments a group of seven students were assembled and given the following instructions.

> This is a task which involves the discrimination of length of lines. You see the pair of white cards in front. On the left is a single line; on the right are three lines differing in length. They are numbered 1, 2, and 3 in order. One of the three lines at the right is equal to the standard line at the left—you will decide in each case which is the equal line. You will state your judgment in terms of the corresponding number. There will be 12 such comparisons. As the number of lines is few and the group small, I shall call upon each of you in turn to announce your judgment, which I shall record here on a prepared form. Please be as accurate as possible. Suppose we start at the right and proceed to the left.

In actual fact, all save one member of the group were accomplices of the experimenter—there was only one subject in the experiment. The accomplices had been instructed to give unanimous incorrect responses on some trials. The purpose of the experiment was to assess the effect of group judgment on individual judgment. The actual inequalities in line length that the subject was required to ignore in order to agree with the majority varied between .25 and 1.75 inches. However, in none of the trials was the discrepancy so small that any subject could really have been in doubt about the correct answer. Nonetheless, nearly 40 percent of the subjects denied the evidence of their own senses and agreed with the group. Those who did not were obviously under some stress as judged by their expressions and behavior as well as by their own reports. One reported that every time he disagreed he "felt disturbed . . ., like an outcast." It is noteworthy that in this experiment the "authority" of the group was to some extent pitted against the experimenter's authority, for the instructions did after all stipulate that the responses were to be as accurate as possible. The experience of being a subject in this type of experiment is vividly described by Lisa Alther in *Kinflicks*.*

---

* *Kinflicks*, Lisa Alther, Harmondsworth, England: Penguin, 1976, pp. 254–256.

"We're all here now," said a tall, dark hunched senior who had a painting exhibit in the arts center at that very moment. The psychology project was apparently hers. Eddie and I and two others sat side by side; the senior and another girl stood in front of us. A third girl sat in the corner taking notes.

The senior explained the rules. She herself would hold up a constant control card made of cardboard. The other girl up front would hold up a succession of cards of different lengths. One at a time, we four subjects were to say whether the second card was longer than, shorter than, or the same length as the control card. It seemed simple enough. In fact, it seemed downright simple-minded. I couldn't believe that these hypercreative upper-classmen couldn't come up with more intriguing ways to spend their time.

After several practice runs, the experiment began in earnest. I was sitting on the far end and was always the last to express my judgment, but it really didn't matter because we all agreed anyway. Yes, yes, that card was shorter than the control. And that one was longer. And so on. I was becoming very impatient and irritable. After all, I *did* have a paper to write.

During the sixth round the atmosphere of bored agreement suddenly shifted, and I found the three others blandly agreeing that a card was shorter, which to me was obviously longer.

And again. "Longer," said the first girl.

"Longer," agreed the second.

"Longer," said Eddie with a yawn.

"The *same*," I insisted staunchly.

And yet again. I kept glancing around furtively as the others perjured with indifference the testimony of their senses. Or at least of *my* senses.

"The same," said the first girl.

"The same."

"The same," agreed Eddie.

"*Longer*," I mumbled belligerently. Damn! How could they call it the same, when it was so obviously longer?

"Shorter," said the first girl.

"Shorter," said the second.

"Shorter," said Eddie, stretching luxuriously.

"The same?" I suggested uncertainly. It *couldn't* be shorter. Could it? The others glanced at me with surprise.

"Longer," said the first girl, about a card that to me was clearly shorter.

"Longer," confirmed the second girl.

"Longer," agreed Eddie.

Unable to endure the social isolation any longer, I intentionally belied the verdict of my eyes and said casually, "Longer." It felt marvelous to be in step with the others. I breathed a deep sigh of relief.

"The same," said the first girl.

"The same."

"The same."

"Shorter," I wailed pitifully. Was something wrong with my eyes? I squinted and then opened them as wide as possible, trying to rectify my apparently faulty vision. Then I stared so intently at the control card that my vision blanked out altogether and I couldn't see anything for a few seconds. Eddie and the first girl looked at me, then glanced at each other and shrugged.

After two dozen of these runs, in which they agreed and I differed, or in which they agreed and I pretended to agree, interspersed with runs in which we all genuinely *did* agree, I could no longer tell what was shorter or longer than what. I would see a card as shorter. The others would call it longer, and before my very eyes the card would quiver and expand until it did in fact look longer. Or it would waver playfully back and forth between long and short.

Soon I was feeling nauseated, and my eyes were burning.

Similar strong effects were obtained in a "group" situation in which the face-to-face pressures of the Asch situation were quite absent. Crutchfield (1955) put subjects into separate booths. Each subject had to signal his response by pressing a lever. Any group pressure would be mediated by a row of lights indicating how the other subjects responded to the same question. These signal lights were completely under the control of the experimenter, who thus could make up a fake consensus on any incorrect response he chose. Here again the groups are completely temporary and ad hoc, as in Asch's experiment, but here the subjects are relatively isolated from whatever face-to-face pressures might occur in Asch's situation. Nevertheless, the pressures were powerful enough to produce markedly absurd responses from a large proportion of subjects (Table 13–1).

That such ad hoc groups can exert such a strong influence on human adult behavior is powerful testimony to the effect of social motivations in a peer-group setting. The desire to be at one with the group, even a group of strangers, led subjects to deny the evidence of their own senses, even to deny their own worth in some cases. How much more powerful is the sort of peer group most of us belong to—a long-standing group with mutual interests, a shared past history, shared norms of behavior, and shared

TABLE *13–1*

The experimental subjects in this study were under group pressure to agree with statements with which they might otherwise not have agreed. (Crutchfield, 1955.)

STATEMENT	AGREEMENT	
	CONTROL	EXPERIMENTAL
"I doubt whether I would make a good leader."	0	37%
"The star is the greater area." ● ★	0	46%

attitudes towards the rest of the world. The desire to be part of a group is thus a strong motive in the human adult. Whatever the role of grouping behavior in the long-term survival of mankind, it is because they satisfy our desire to affiliate, to be with other humans, that we value our peer groups.

I have argued thus far that human adults are basically social animals. The desires to affiliate and conform are very strong in most adults. Someone who has no desire to affiliate is commonly called a psychopath; such individuals are truly deviant, truly abnormal. Leaving aside that small category, however, there are still wide individual differences in strength of social motivation. The strength of an individual's social motives is commonly used as an index to personality. Some people have a very low tolerance of authority relations, a characteristic that can be valuable for society at large. A lack of respect for authority combined with sufficient respect for a peer group, such that the individual will try to convince the peer group of the rightness of his case, can lead to revolution. Any other combination of conformity or nonconformity to authority or the peer group is possible. A diagrammatic representation of this, along with the labels we might attach to certain personalities on this measure, is shown in Figure 13–1. The point is that since it is society that defines normal personality, it is by our attitudes to socialization and the variety of our social motives that we will be categorized as normal or abnormal. It is in this sense that a description of an individual's social motives is a description

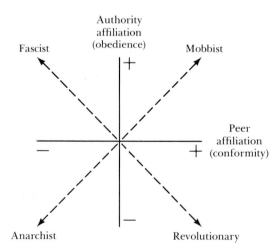

FIGURE 13–1

Authority affiliation and peer affiliation can be represented as independent dimensions of personality.

of his personality. The study of the development of social behavior and social motives is thus also to a large extent the study of the development of personality.

DEVELOPMENT OF SOCIAL BEHAVIOR

The development of social behavior has been a popular research area for many years. Like every other area of developmental psychology, the study of social development has been polarized between extreme nativism and environmentalism. Often these labels are not used but their basic concepts are. The most basic issue that a theory of social development must confront is the issue of whether or not humans are inherently social—whether or not they are born with a need to affiliate with others. It is fair, I think, to say that the most popular theory has held that social motives are not inherent but are derived from more basic motives. There are many variants of this "cupboard-love" theory of social motivation.

Social learning theory

Social learning theorists, such as Sears (1951) and Miller and Dollard (1941), have proposed the most explicit version of the cupboard-love theory. Basically, social learning theory begins with the observable fact that babies from birth do have basic physiological needs, such as hunger and thirst, and that some adult, usually the mother, supplies the baby with food and liquid, thereby reducing the painful feelings of hunger and thirst. In the terminology of social learning theory food and liquid would be referred to as *primary positive reinforcers* and as such are supposed to be intrinsically rewarding. Since the mother is always there when these intrinsic rewards are given, the mother comes to be associated with the primary positive reinforcers and thereby becomes a *secondary reinforcer*. The process is directly analogous to the processes of classical conditioning described in Chapter 2. The presence of the mother will thus become rewarding in itself.

Since the young infant has limited information-processing abilities, i.e., cannot register all of the information present to his senses at any one time (Chapter 4), only some of the aspects of the mother will become rewarding, such as the sounds she makes, the sight of her face or, more likely, some salient features of it, perhaps the way she touches the baby, kisses it, and so on. All of these aspects of a mother, according to social learning theory, can become secondary reinforcers. Since, initially at least, the mother can and does attempt to reduce any and every discomfort that the child suffers, she, or rather some aspects of her, will come to signal pleasurable relief from all of the pains and irritations that beset the newborn baby. Thus, by association she will become the most rewarding of stimuli. Any behaviors of the baby that bring the mother into his close proximity will thus be rewarded by the fact of her presence, as will any behaviors that keep her in close proximity to him.

So far as other humans resemble the mother they will elicit the same kinds of proximity-seeking behaviors, by processes of *stimulus generalization* (see pp. 27–28). Broader social responses, with peers, will begin as soon as the child can perceive similarities between peers and his mother. The more peer behavior resembles his mother's behavior, the more peer behavior overlaps with that of the mother, the more reinforcing the child will find peer contact to be. Since the mother, and other humans, will tend to reinforce with their presence behavior that they find rewarding, the developing child's behavior will be shaped in a socially acceptable direction. These are, according to the theory, the beginnings of social obedience and compliance. On this account there is nothing intrinsically social about social motives and social behavior. The motives are derived from other, more basic motives, and the behavior is selected by reinforcement. Other behaviors could equally well be selected.

What should be the consequences of abnormal mothering conditions? Suppose a child were nurtured by machines. According to the theory, the child should not develop any desire to maintain proximity to humans nor any behaviors that would have that as their effect. This lack of social motivation and social behavior would be dependent upon continued nurturance by machines. If humans at any time became essential for the child's preservation, then they would gain secondary reinforcement value and social motives and social behavior could begin at once. Thus a completely unsocialized child could become socialized at any point in his life span. As we shall see, this prediction sets social learning theory apart from other theories of social development.

Psychoanalytic theories

Psychoanalytic theories of social attachment are also versions of the cupboard-love theory. Sigmund Freud, the founding father of psychoanalysis, asserted that human beings have basic biological predispositions not only to satisfy their need for self-preservation but also to relate to other human beings. These he called the ego or self-preservative instincts and the sexual instincts. The term "sexual" in psychoanalytic terminology can be equated with "social" as we have been using it here. However, as Freud (1949) himself wrote: "The sexual instincts are at the outset supported upon the ego instincts; only later do they become independent of these, and even then we have an indication of that original dependency in the fact that those persons who have to do with the feeding, care and protection of the child become his earliest sexual objects: that is to say, in the first instance the mother or her substitute."

The Freudian account of peer relations is somewhat more complex. Psychoanalysts assume an initial lack of differentiation between the self and the outside world. Thus, at least part of the social instinct will be directed by the child upon himself purely as a result of his failure to differentiate between self and other. As differentiation proceeds, some residue of this primitive self-love will remain and will guide the choice of objects (persons) on whom to direct the social instincts. The most important adult social objects chosen throughout development are those chosen because they share the characteristics of the primary caretaker, usually the mother. Peers will be chosen and will be satisfying social objects insofar as they share the characteristics of the child himself. Freudian theory thus offers an account of the origins of both authority and peer relations.

The subtleties of the Freudian account of social development need not detain us here. We should note, however, that Freudian theory differs considerably from social learning theory in its analysis of the consequences of abnormal mothering. For psychoanalytic theorists the normal pattern of childcare, where the child is looked after continuously by a single mother figure, is absolutely essential if development is to proceed at all. To understand why, we must comprehend two other Freudian terms, *ego* and *superego*. Ego refers to the whole system of strategies and behaviors that an individual develops to attain satisfaction of his needs in the world. The superego is that part of the ego that is responsible for maintaining friendly and cooperative relations with others by keeping their needs and requirements firmly in mind. According to the theory, the newborn child has neither ego nor superego. His mother functions as his ego, satisfying his needs, and as his superego, restricting some of his impulses. Gradually, as the child develops, the mother transfers more of these functions to the child. As the child develops he is expected more and more to satisfy his own needs and control his own desires. The ego and superego as they develop become an internalized mirror of the system of rules and constraints that were imposed by the mother during the process of development. Obviously, if the child does not have a sexual (social) bond to his mother or a mother figure, there is no effective ego or superego to guide and control the child and therefore no model for the internalized ego and superego that must subsequently develop. Further, psychoanalytic theory assumes that a primary sexual bond *will* be formed, whether or not there is a mother figure present to serve as its object. In the absence of a mother figure there could be excessive self-love along with love of nurturant objects, such as feeding bottles, a combination that could hardly lead to satisfactory ego and superego development. The late introduction of a mother figure could well be fruitless, according to Freudian theory, if primary sexual bonds have already been established. Only if these are undone and replaced with a sexual bond to a mother figure can development be redirected to a normal path. The later this is attempted, the less likely it is to succeed, according to the theory.

Despite these differences, psychoanalytic theory is in agreement with social learning theory that human beings are not social by nature. Even in psychoanalytic theory the sexual (social) instincts are originally part of the self-preservative instincts.

Cognitive theories

The above two classic versions of cupboard-love theory have each given rise to theories that reject their conclusions about the origins of social behavior. A number of so-called cognitive theories of social development have descended from social learning theories. These theories postulate that there are a range of stimuli inherently attractive to human infants. These include stimuli that move, make noises, have areas of high contrast (such as eyes), and irregular outlines. Since human beings have all of these attributes, they are naturally attractive stimuli to infants. However, according to the theory, they are in no way *uniquely* attractive and do not elicit behaviors that could not be elicited by some other animate or inanimate object. The desire to maintain contact with these attractive objects gives them the role of reinforcers that thus shape behavior by their presence or absence. Since adults will only reinforce infant behavior that is reinforcing to themselves—an adult will smile at an infant who smiles at him but may ignore the same infant if he cries—acceptable social behavior will be shaped according to the same principles as in social learning theory.

Cognitive theorists rely on changes within the perceptual-conceptual structures of the child to explain other aspects of social development. These explanations are usually *a posteriori*. They will be considered in the next chapter along with the data on which they are based. Let us note for the moment that cognitive theories of social development assume no specific innate social motivation and no specific innate social behaviors. Like social learning theory, they postulate no difference between social and other forms of development. In principle, according to cognitive theories, the absence of a mother need have no consequences for development at all. The shaping that is normally reinforced by the mother might be more effectively reinforced by objects with the right stimulus properties.

Bowlby's ethological theory

The social development theory that has descended from psychoanalytic theory is the ethological theory of Bowlby, described and massively documented in his landmark work, *Attachment and Loss* (1969; 1973). The phenomenon that we have been calling social behavior Bowlby would call "attachment behavior," at least in the stages of infancy and early childhood. Attachment behaviors are those that result in proximity or contact between mother and child. The nature of attachment behaviors and the stimuli that elicit them will naturally vary with the age of the child.

Nonetheless, at all ages the behaviors have a common terminus; they are switched off by the presence of the mother. Thus a crying baby who is not hungry, thirsty, or in pain will most probably be quieted if he is picked up. Crying here is the attachment behavior; being picked up produces the proximity that terminates the behavior. Bowlby is very careful not to say that the baby cries because he wants to be picked up. He views such foresight as most unlikely in young infants. Nor of course does he argue that the biological mother must do the picking up. He does point out that in most cultures it is the biological mother who will respond to the baby's attachment behaviors; even if it is not the biological mother who responds to these behaviors, some other particular individual will do so. Bowlby claims that that individual will become the baby's effective mother, i.e., the only focus for his attachment behaviors. Many, indeed most, early attachment behaviors are unlearned. Others, such as calling for "Mummy," are obviously learned. Corresponding to the early unlearned behaviors are a set of unlearned stimuli that can specify proximity. These include the human voice or voice-like stimuli.

Bowlby argues that normal processes of perceptual development allow the child to come to identify his mother figure and differentiate her from strangers. Also, the child develops fear of strange things, including strange people, which will eventually restrict his attachment behaviors to the familiar, nonfearful mother. Bowlby also gives fear or anxiety a primary role in the elicitation of attachment behaviors; even though the behaviors will occur as naturally as breathing, they will be more likely to occur if the child is anxious or fearful. Inasmuch as attachment behaviors result in the appearance of a human figure who removes the source of anxiety or fear, that figure will come to be associated with reduction of anxiety or fear. However, in terms of Bowlby's theory, anxiety reduction is a secondary consequence of attachment behavior, not its cause. This is the major difference between Bowlby's theory and the psychoanalytic and social learning theories. Bowlby does not think of attachment behavior as something derived from relief of discomfort. To this extent Bowlby views attachment behavior or social behavior as a system existing in its own right, and not derived from more primitive systems of need.

Bowlby views attachment behavior as something that rapidly becomes specific to the individual. Relations with peers are of a different order; they are not associated with relief of anxiety and cannot substitute for adult attachment figures. Nor, indeed, in Bowlby's theory, can one adult successfully substitute for another. A child's relations with other adults has more to do with the way his primary attachment figure behaves toward other adults than with any resemblance the latter may have to the primary attachment figure. Bowlby thus denies the validity of the generalization process assumed by social learning theorists. In this respect Bowlby's theory repeats the Freudian emphasis on the superego functions of the mother figure. It is the mother figure who provides the child with a model of how he should behave towards other humans.

The differences between the theories outlined here will become more comprehensible when they are applied to real-life social development. The next chapter will thus describe some of the basic steps in social development that these theories are intended to account for.

14

The Social
World of
the Newborn

The primary question that must concern any student of social development is whether or not infants come into the world with any basic or primary social motivation. Are infants social animals or must they be socialized? As we saw in the last chapter the theoretical consensus is that infants are not inherently social. Most theories begin with the assumption that there is initially nothing special about people in the world of the infant. Any special status that people come to have, according to these theories, is derived from something that is fundamental, such as people's ability to give the infant freedom from hunger. Such an analysis would surprise many mothers. Many mothers betray in their conversation a belief that their baby is a social organism. "She cries because she wants to be picked up." "He likes company." "She prefers men to women." "He knows how to get around his mother." "She knows how to get her own way." Mothers will spontaneously make such remarks about very young babies, babies scarcely out of the neonate period. Such testimony is typically not taken seriously by behavioral scientists, whose attitude towards babies is much more cynical than that of the average parent. This can cause some conflict when the behavioral scientist becomes a parent. It is hard to tell oneself that it is only cupboard love as one's child snuggles comfortably in one's arms, cooing and smiling contentedly.

Leaving aside such difficulties, what does it mean when the parent says his or her child is "sociable?" What does the behavioral scientist mean when he says the child is "nonsocial?" What is the essence of a "social" behavior? While we know as adults what it is to be social, what we have in mind is largely a set of behaviors that we could not possibly expect infants to display. Few, if any, psychologists have gone beyond the obvious manifestations of social behavior to enquire after the essence of sociability. Indeed, the best discussion of the meaning of the term "social," as well as the most useful to psychologists, was written by the theologian Martin Buber. Buber (1923) argues that in our own experience we can discriminate between I-thou relations and I-it relations. I-it relations characterize the way we relate to things in the physical world. The most typical of these involve use, abuse, manipulation, fabrication, consumption, and so on. I-thou relations, by contrast, involve assumptions of equality, empathy, likeness, communion, feelings of interaction between beings with shared responses to the world and events in it. In our own minds we know whether we are dealing with I-thou or I-it relations. We can also tell whether another human is dealing with us as an "it" or "thou." We know when we are being manipulated and when we are in a state of communion with another. Further, we can tell with some precision whether two other human beings are in an I-thou or I-it relation.

Buber's account of the essence of the social world is more complex than this; it seems to be phenomenologically true without further investigation, to some of us at least. However, its main interest for us here is that it suggests several distinctive features of social activity that could be used to identify social behavior, if it occurs, in young infants. The broadest distinction is that behavior towards people should be different from behavior towards objects. If an infant has a set of behaviors that is specific to people, one that does not overlap with a set of behaviors elicited by objects, then we might suspect that these are social behaviors. If, on the other hand, the infant's responses to people are no different from his responses to objects, then we would be forced to conclude that the infant had no differentiated social behavior or social awareness. Even if we did find a class of behavior that was specifically directed toward people, we could not, on Buber's criteria, conclude that the behavior was necessarily social; the behavior would have to be, to some extent, interactive and communicative as well—it would have to change in some way with the behavior of the other person. This immediately raises problems of how to define interaction and communication. These terms are easy enough to comprehend when we think of our own relations with other adults, but there are difficulties in defining them in relation to a nonverbal organism such as an infant. For the moment let us leave the problem of definition aside; we will come back to it when we have looked at evidence bearing on the first decisions we must make. One of these is whether or not the infant has a set of behaviors that are specific to people.

SMILING

If one asks parents of six-week-old babies whether their babies are at all sociable, they will almost unanimously answer in the affirmative, basing their reply on the fact that the baby smiles at them. A baby's smile is a wonderful thing (Figure 14–1). Its effects on parents are immediate; suddenly they feel that the sleepless nights and continuous fatigue are all worthwhile. The amount of time the parents *want* to spend with their baby as opposed to the amount of time they have to spend with him goes up quite significantly, once smiling has begun (Newson and Newson, 1963). It is no wonder that the smiling response has attracted so much empirical investigation, with literally hundreds of research papers addressing themselves to the problem of its genesis and control. Taken together, these studies show that the smile is not the straightforward social signal to other humans that it appears to be.

FIGURE *14–1* A full-scale smile.

Smiling of sorts can be observed in the first few hours after birth.* However, these early "smiles" strike observers as being incomplete; unlike real smiles, they do not involve crinkling of the eyes. These facial expressions are not regarded as social behavior simply because the average adult does not register them as smiles. Parents often explain them as grimaces of slight pain due to passing gas. This explanation is probably incorrect. These early smiles are in fact less likely to occur when the baby is flatulent, which is usual after feeding, than at other times. During the first two weeks of life these primitive smiles can be elicited only when the baby is not fully awake but not completely asleep either. During the first week of life the response can be elicited by gentle stroking of the baby's skin, by a not too intense change in visual stimulation, or by presentation of low-intensity sounds. None of these stimuli seem particularly effective and none of them, we should note, are specific to humans. In the second week of life the "smile" retains its incomplete quality but it is more specific to humans in that the human voice becomes a more effective stimulus than other sounds, e.g., a bell, whistle, or rattle.

During the third week of life we see real smiles (Figure 14–2). They are shorter in duration than the smiles that will come later, but they do involve the whole face. By far the most effective stimulus for this smile is the human voice, particularly a female voice. Wolff found that a female voice could elicit smiles even from a baby who was crying or feeding. The visual aspects of humans are not in themselves effective at this age, although they do increase the effectiveness of the vocal stimulus. In the course of the fifth week of life there is a dramatic shift in the control of smiling; the voice loses its authority almost completely, and the effective stimuli are primarily visual. In Wolff's study it was the face, and particularly the eyes, that seemed to be most effective in eliciting smiling.

Everything we have mentioned so far would seem to indicate that smiling is a behavior that is quite specific to people. The response would thus fit the first of the criteria for sociability that we outlined above. There is also some evidence that the behavior is interactive, the second of the criteria for sociability that we asked for. It seems certain that the behavior is not just an automatic reflex triggered by perception of a particular set of stimuli. Ambrose (1961) found that smiling can be terminated by picking up the baby, even though this results in all of the person-specific stimuli coming even closer to him than before he was picked up. More direct evidence on interaction comes from a study by Brackbill (1958). Her procedure was basically an operant conditioning procedure. Every time the baby smiled the experimenter smiled back, talked to the infant, and picked him up. Not surprisingly, the rate of smiling increased. However,

---

*The following account of the development of smiling is based on the work of Wolff (1963).

FIGURE *14–2* A smile in the third week of life.

it increased in a specific way; putting down the baby became a signal for smiling, since smiling led to being picked up again. The baby and the experimenter had linked their behaviors in a quite precise way, which is one feature of interaction. Whether we should call this an *interaction pattern* or merely a consequence of a reinforcement schedule is an open question. Nevertheless, it would seem from these results that the young infant may have at least one social behavior. Unfortunately for the argument, more careful investigation of smiling has undermined both of the foundations for the claim that smiling in early infancy is a truly social act.

Why do infants smile at faces? Many investigators have tried to find out what is special about the human face. The consensus is that its special characteristics have little to do with "humanness" per se. It was discovered many years ago that there was no need to present an entire, real face to elicit smiling. A crude mask like that shown in Figure 14–3 will do. From that it was but a short step to the discovery that a plain piece of cardboard with two eyelike blobs on it would also elicit smiling. Now such results do not mean that the infant is not smiling at a "face" when he is smiling at a card with two dots on it. There is evidence that infants are even more likely than adults to fill in the missing parts of a stimulus and "see" the

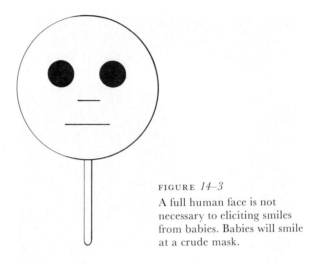

FIGURE *14–3*
A full human face is not
necessary to eliciting smiles
from babies. Babies will smile
at a crude mask.

whole thing when only a part is actually present (Bower, 1966). It is possible that, just as adults "see" a few lines as a face (Figure 14–4), infants will see a plain card with two dots on it as a face. However, such explanations become increasingly untenable when one considers other data on early smiling. For example, it has been found that a card with six dots on it is more effective in releasing smiles than one with two dots on it, and that it is even more effective than an entire, real human face (Ahrens, 1954). "Completion" will not explain away this kind of result. Indeed, it seems that the infant will smile at any pair of high-contrast stimulus objects, and the more pairs the better. It seems that it is not the "faceness" of a face that elicits smiling from a baby but its "contrastiness," the fact that it contains two dark shiny areas, each surrounded by a white shiny area.

The strongest evidence that smiling is not a social response in our sense comes from John Watson (1973), an investigator who has focused on the interaction aspect of sociability. Watson did not set out to investigate the nature of social stimuli in infancy. His initial concerns were the processes of and constraints on learning in early infancy. Learning, you will remember, consists in the detection of a contingent relationship between a response of the organism and an event in the organism's environment. Watson has argued that in the Western world the infant is most likely to be presented with contingencies that he can detect when an adult plays with him. Watson argues that the games adults play with babies are all variants of a prototypical "game" whose main feature is presentation of clear and simple response-event contingencies. For example, each time the baby opens his eyes wide the adult will touch him on the nose, or perhaps each time the baby waves his arms the adult will poke his tummy or blow on it. The actual responses and events are not critical. What is critical is that every time the baby emits a particular behavior he elicits a specific behavior from the adult. The baby thus can detect a contingency relationship in the context of the "game." Watson argues that this experience releases vigorous smiling in infants, and, further, that it is the detection of contingencies that is the primary cause of smiling.

The bulk of the evidence for the hypothesis comes from observations of smiling in the context of contingency detection. Recall the experiments of Papousek described in Chapter 6 (pp. 128–129). Papousek found that successful contingency detection was accompanied by clear smiling and cooing that was certainly not elicited by the stimulus he had presented, since the babies barely even glanced at it, and did not smile when the event occurred on a noncontingent basis. Papousek's experiments were the main reason why we decided that contingency detection is its own reward in learning situations, that it is an inherently pleasurable event. Other investigators have also noticed smiling in the course of learning experiments. Hunt and Uzgiris (1964) observed that infants who were given mobiles that they could control showed clear smiling and cooing while controlling the mobiles. Other infants who were not able to control the mobiles showed no particular smiling in the experiment at all. Watson himself has carried out the most systematic experiments on the role of contingency detection in the genesis of smiling. In two experiments he gave eight-week-old infants an unambiguous contingency to detect. By moving their heads they could move a mobile suspended over their cribs. Control groups saw a mobile that moved independently of their own movements. The infants were put in the experimental situation for 10 minutes each day for 14 days. The infants with control over the mobile all began to show clear, vigorous smiling in the experimental situation on the third or fourth day, just about the point at which their patterning of head movements began to differ significantly from that shown by the group with

FIGURE 14–4
These few lines are sufficient for adults to regard the drawing as a face.

no control over the mobile. That is, they began vigorous smiling at about the time their behavior showed that they had detected the contingency (Figure 14–5).

In an additional study Watson worked with an eight-month-old infant who had been characterized as a developmental failure. This baby had never shown any appreciable movement of any kind and had never really smiled at anyone or anything. Within two hours of being given control over a mobile this baby showed not only increased activity but also vigorous and prolonged smiling in the experimental situation, virtually the first smiling the child had ever shown.

The above results, particularly the study of the retarded infant, strongly reinforce the hypothesis that the primitive cause of smiling in infancy is the infant's awareness of contingencies, that it is the "contingency game" that elicits smiling, and that the reason why people come to elicit smiling is because only people play the "game" with babies and so become associated with the pleasure derived from learning. As Watson succinctly puts it, "The game is *not* important to the infant because people play it, but rather people become important to the infant because they play the game." Strange as this hypothesis may sound at first, it is not only consistent with

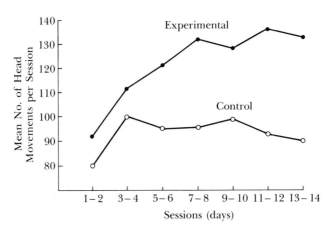

FIGURE *14–5*

Infants in this experiment were shown a mobile for 10 minutes every day for 14 days. The experimental group could control the movements of the mobile by moving their heads against a pillow. Infants in the control group saw the same mobile moving but had no control over its movement. The graph shows the mean number of head movements made by the infants over each 10-minute session (the results are given for two-day periods). It is clear that sometime on the third or fourth day the experimental group learned that they could control the mobile, since it is after that point that their rate of response begins to diverge from that of the control group. (Watson, 1973.)

FIGURE *14–6*
The orientation of the face most effective for eliciting smiles from babies is the one on the left. (Watson, 1973.)

Watson's data but also explains some rather puzzling data about the effectiveness of faces as stimuli for smiling. Some years ago Watson found that the orientation of a face was important in determining its effectiveness in eliciting smiles. He presented babies with the same face in three different orientations, 0, 90, and 180 degrees (Figure 14–6). Now the average Western baby sees his mother's face mostly in the 90-degree orientation. That is how she will be seen when she is feeding or changing him, and these activities do fill the greater part of the time that mothers spend with their babies. If smiling were associated with faces as a result of faces being associated with food, the average baby should associate food most with the 90-degree orientation, and so should smile most when the face is at 90 degrees. If on the other hand smiling were simply elicited by high-contrast blobs, as the studies discussed earlier would suggest, then there should be no difference between the three orientations of the face. What in fact happens is that infants from about eight weeks of age on smile about twice as much at the face in the zero-degree orientation as at the other two, a result that neither of the above hypotheses could have predicted. Why does it happen? Because, says Watson, when an adult begins playing a contingency game with an infant, the adult will typically make sure his face is at a zero-degree orientation relative to the baby, and the baby will thus come to associate the pleasures of contingency detection with faces at that orientation.

What are we to make of the smile then? On the one hand we have data indicating that the smile is a response, if not to people, at least to stimuli that are specific to people, such as voices and faces (Wolff, 1963). Not so, say the opposition. The smile is simply a response to high-contrast stimuli, stimuli of a sort common to all human faces but in no way specific to them (Bowlby, 1969). Not even that, says Watson. The smile reflects contingency detection and is not specific to any stimulus at all, save by association with the experience of contingency detection. Some theorists (e.g., Piaget, 1936; Kagan, 1967) have attempted to bring order to these diverse results by proposing that the smile is really a response to anything familiar. This hypothesis would seem to cover all of the instances of smiling that we have reviewed thus far. However, it is not consistent with cases where smiling does *not* occur. Why, for instance, should infants stop smiling in response to their mother's voice, as Wolff found they did at about six weeks of age? If the familiarity hypothesis were correct, they should surely smile more as the voice becomes more familiar. Why did the infants in Watson's control group (those with no control over the movements of a mobile) not smile at their mobile, which became just as familiar to them as the mobiles presented to those infants who had control over them (and who did smile)? On the familiarity hypothesis there should have been no difference. Why indeed should a face in a zero-degree orientation elicit more smiling than the same face in the more familiar 90-degree orientation? Why have infants never been observed to smile at their feeding bottles or their cribs? (Bowlby, 1969) The list could go on. But enough has been said, surely, to rule out familiarity as a general explanation of smiling.

What then are we to make of the smile? I think that most of our problems with the smile stem from our use of the term "*the* smile." The use of the definite article here is obviously nonsensical. There are smiles and then there are smiles—smiles of laughter, amazement, contempt, flirtation, and all the rest (Figure 14–7). We can identify all of these smiles when emitted by adults (Eibl-Eibesfeld, 1971). Washburn (1929) described some differences between the smiles of infants. But child psychologists have not even tried to find out if infants have different smiles in different situations. I would not presume to generalize beyond the results of Washburn's original study. However, I think it is clear that one way, possibly the only way, left open to us to clarify the muddle over smiling is to refine what we mean by "smiling," to look more closely at the actual behavior to find out if babies show different specific smiles in different specific situations. Perhaps there is a specific social smile, a specific smile of amusement, and a specific smile of satisfaction, corresponding to the three types of stimuli that have been claimed to elicit smiles. Until we look to see, we will not be able to make any sense of the response.*

This long discussion of smiling has not left us much the wiser about the question that we began with: Are infants inherently sociable or must they be socialized? Fortunately, although smiling has been the most popular behavior investigated in this context, there are other behaviors that are in

---

*Recent research indicates that there may well be different sorts of smiles in infancy (Dunkeld and Bower, 1979).

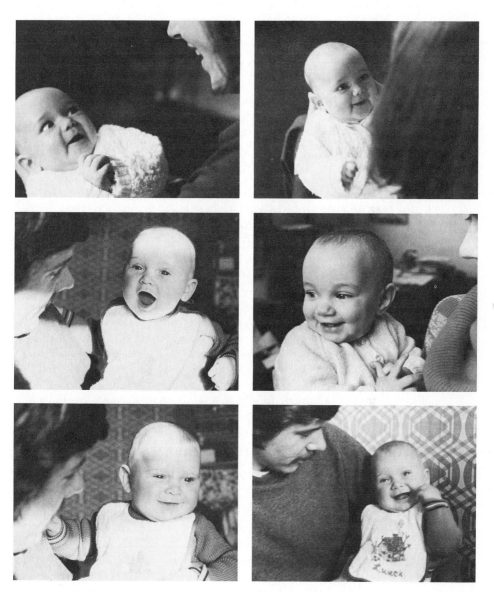

FIGURE *14–7*

It is apparent that all these smiles are not the same. Does it make sense then to assume a single cause for all of them?

fact more satisfactory indicators of sociability and that indicate, I would maintain, that infants are born as social animals and do not require socialization. The first such behavior I shall discuss is imitation.

IMITATION

Imitation has traditionally been thought of as something that develops late in infancy and requires an elaborate cognitive structure before it can be manifested (Piaget, 1962). However, a number of recent investigations have shown that the capacity for imitation is present in the very first weeks of life (Dunkeld, 1972b; Maratsos, 1973; Melzoff and Moore, 1977). Infants have been observed to imitate adults in opening the mouth, puckering the lips, widening the eyes, opening the hand, moving the fingers, and protruding the tongue (Figure 14–8).

Is this behavior specific to humans? None of the studies so far conducted have addressed themselves to this question. However, the answer must definitely be in the affirmative for the imitative behaviors that have been seen are quite specific to *parts* of humans. That may seem a pointless thing to say but consider that infants are observed to imitate *eye* opening, *mouth* opening, and *hand* opening. In each case the infants open and close one part of their own bodies. When the model opens and closes her eyes, the baby does the same; when the model opens and closes her mouth, the baby does the same. There are no confusions—the baby does not open his mouth when the model opens her hand. In other words, what the baby picks up from the behavior of the model is not just "opening" but opening of a particular body part. Surely, therefore, we could hardly expect to see any imitation if we presented a baby with, say, an opening and closing matchbox. The baby, from what we have seen, knows very well that no part of him corresponds to a matchbox. He would not map the opening-closing matchbox onto any part of his own body and so would hardly imitate it. Imitation, then, is specific to people. The behavior can only be elicited by people. It thus meets our first criterion of sociability.

It also meets in almost too direct a way the requirement of mutuality. To imitate another we have to be aware of some identity with the other. By imitating, the baby is showing us that he knows he has eyes, mouth, tongue, hands, and that these parts of him correspond to parts of us. I would argue that imitation is an affirmation of identity, evidence that at some, however primitive, level the baby knows he is one of us. The behavior is also interactive in some sense. The baby will imitate the adult, but he will also show a rapt attention if the adult imitates him and the frequency of the imitated behavior will increase. At the most basic level, two persons are interacting if the behavior of each influences the behavior of the other. This is certainly true in mutual imitation sessions.

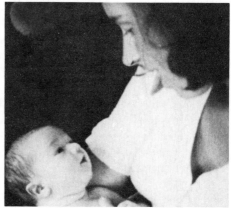

FIGURE *14–8*
A six-day-old baby will imitate her mother sticking out her tongue.

The behavior does not seem to be communicative, however. Rather, it appears to be communional, satisfying in itself to both participants as an affirmation of their mutual awareness of one another. That is not a tough-minded way to put it but seems to me to distill the delight in imitation that many mothers express when they discover that their baby can and will imitate them. Finally, the behavior is in no sense manipulative. Babies do not imitate in order to satisfy basic needs, such as hunger.

Imitative behavior thus meets, at however simple or primitive a level, all of our criteria for a social behavior. The behavior is present very early in life, early enough that we can use it, I think, as evidence of inherent sociability, sociability not derived from anything supposedly simpler or more basic.

INTERACTIONAL SYNCHRONY

The second behavior that demonstrates inherent sociability appears even earlier than imitation, within hours of birth in fact. The behavior in question is called interactional or communicational synchrony. This imposing term refers to a type of motor behavior seen whenever one human being speaks to another. Both speaker and listener move together in a very subtle dancelike fashion, in quite precise synchrony with the speaker's speech. The movements are usually very small and the participants may be quite unaware of them. The most important point about interactional synchrony is that infants have been shown to engage in it within hours of birth (Figure 14–9). What is the significance of this behavior? In adults it is communicational but not communicative; interactional synchrony transmits no precise messages, but rather a degree of togetherness, rapport, participation, nonisolation, which is exactly the base required for an I-thou relation. The behavior is specifically human; in infants it can be elicited only by human speech and no other auditory stimulus. By virtue of interactional synchrony "the neonate *participates* immediately and deeply in communication and is not at birth a social isolate" (Condon and Sander, 1974).

It thus appears that we have another behavioral index of inherent sociability. The infant from birth divides the world into people and objects and has behaviors that are specific to people and specifically for people. No one could argue that either behavior is shaped with a view to obtaining any reward or reinforcement other than that deriving immediately from the exercise of the behavior. Neither behavior has any instrumental validity—they are I-thou behaviors and not in any way I-it behaviors.

BABBLING

While imitation and interactional synchrony are striking for their very precocity, one other behavior that is surely social is babbling. Babbling begins about four weeks of age and is primarily elicited by the human voice. However, the behavior is not simply an elicited response. Wolff (1963) reports that by six weeks of age one can engage a baby in an *exchange* of 10–15 vocalizations, particularly if one imitates the baby's sounds. Some weeks later the baby begins imitating the adult with whom he is interacting, evidence of the baby's sensitivity to the mutuality possible in this situation and therefore evidence of true interaction rather than a simple reflex response to a stimulus.

Each of the three behaviors described above has been said to be self-perpetuating; their very occurrence makes them more likely to recur. They are also self-terminating. They are thus quite unlike instrumental behaviors—I-it behaviors—such as crying. A baby may cry when he is

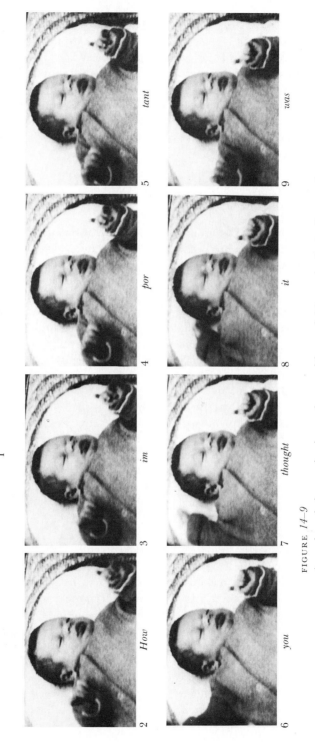

FIGURE *14–9*

A newborn baby moving in synchrony with an adult's words. At the first word the left hand goes up (2). The index finger then moves across with each syllable (3, 4, 5). The right hand is raised (6), moves to the left (7, 8), and moves down again.

hungry, thirsty, or in some other state of discomfort. Crying terminates when the baby is fed, or given something to drink, or changed, or whatever. It is interesting to note, however, that crying can be terminated by social interaction. The opportunity to interact with an adult seems to have the same motivational status as food or water. Indeed, one pediatrician has gone so far as to write: "A most important cause of crying in this period is loneliness or a desire to be picked up. . . . It is remarkable how many mothers fail to realize that babies want and need cuddling . . ." (Illingworth, 1955).

REACTION-SPECIFIC ENERGY

There is an important distinction to be made between the viewpoint outlined here and the viewpoint of Bowlby, which was briefly described in the last chapter. Bowlby would group the social behaviors described here with crying and view them all as instrumental behaviors, with the function of keeping the baby's caretakers in close proximity to him. This view ignores the difference between self-terminated and externally terminated behaviors. It also implies that the sight of an adult, or some other cue to adult proximity, is somehow intrinsically rewarding. On the viewpoint advanced here it is the opportunity to engage in social behavior that is rewarding, and adult proximity is only rewarding inasmuch as it permits social interaction.

The appeal of Bowlby's position is that it relies on nothing more complex to explain "social" behavior than a developed perceptual system. That plus the "attractive" stimuli emitted by humans is all that is required to account for behaviors that Bowlby views as essentially instrumental. This view, I feel, does violence to the differences between self-terminated and externally terminated behaviors. Also, although Bowlby's theory is ethologically based, it ignores some of the important discoveries of ethology concerning the motivational basis of behaviors, particularly unlearned behaviors.

It was ethologists who introduced the concept of *reaction-specific energy*, a concept that is most important in the present context. This concept maintains that reactions or behaviors can be self-generating and require no cause beyond themselves. There are classic descriptions of hunting birds fed by hand who will go through the motions of "hunting" and "pouncing on" prey that are not there. Domestic cats do the same, pouncing on imaginary mice. Such animals are not hungry nor is there real prey to excite them, and yet they go through all the motions of hunting and killing. These behaviors are instances of reaction-specific energy; they are self-generated and the exercise of them is itself reinforcing. If animals and birds are not permitted to exercise such behaviors, they find the lack of opportunity inherently unpleasant (Thorpe, 1956). Such behaviors are normally released in the presence of functionally appropriate stimuli. However, they can occur in the absence of any stimuli. They may also be released by some functionally irrelevant stimulus, in which case the behavior is said to be *redirected*. Such inappropriate objects may come to be preferred to the appropriate stimulus because the occurrence of the behavior is in itself reinforcing. Again, the ethological literature is replete with examples. For instance, there is the case of the homosexual male mallard ducks described by Schutz (1965). None of these birds ever show female behavior, so that copulation is never possible. Nonetheless, they continue to direct or redirect their courtship behavior toward males, even in the presence of available females.

I would argue that humans are born with specific social behaviors that have the characteristics of reaction-specific energy. The behaviors are self-generated and self-terminated; their occurrence is self-reinforcing and human adults can become associated with that reinforcement. Lack of opportunity to exercise the behaviors should be unpleasant. Finally, since the behaviors are specifically human and require a specific pattern of interaction, the opportunities for redirection are necessarily very restricted. I will close this chapter by reasserting that, on the evidence reviewed thus far, humans are born social animals, ready to interact socially with other humans; they find their fellow humans in themselves reinforcing, and not simply valuable aids to food and physical comfort.

15

The Rise
of Primary
Attachments

In the last chapter we looked at the very beginnings of social behavior. In this chapter we shall look at the continuation of the process through infancy. The main feature of this period is the development of attachment to a few specific individuals, or perhaps only one. Generally speaking, the neonate will display social behavior towards any human. This becomes less true with each passing month. Eventually he will become fearful of adult strangers. At that point the baby's desire for social interaction will only be satisfied by perhaps one individual, usually the mother. Separation from that individual may result in distress for the baby, who may cry, scream, or throw himself to the floor. These two phenomena, fear of strangers and separation anxiety, appear in very obvious form at about the same time, around eight months of age, and are generally thought to be linked. They are persistent features of children's behavior until well into the third year. After this time they are apparent only in special circumstances.

STRANGER FEAR AND
SEPARATION ANXIETY

Early forms

It must be emphasized at the outset that stranger fear and separation anxiety do not themselves emerge suddenly at around eight months of age. What does appear at this age are the behaviors normally used to index these two classes of behavior. However, forms of stranger fear and separation anxiety can be found in the first weeks of life, if one is willing to accept different behavioral indexes for them. Genevieve Carpenter (1975) was able to show that two-week-old infants were capable of remarkably refined discrimination between their mother and a female stranger. In her experiments she used a viewing box like that shown in Figure 15–1. The window was big enough that the entire face of a human adult could be presented in it. In one study the baby was presented with six different stimuli: (1) the mother's face presented silently; (2) a female stranger's face; (3) the mother's face talking to the baby; (4) the female stranger's face talking to the baby; (5) the mother's face "talking" to the baby, but with the stranger's voice presented; and (6) the female stranger talking, but with the mother's voice. The babies looked longest at their mother talking to them in her own voice. The next most attractive stimulus for them to look at was their mother's face, presented in silence. Both of these were significantly more attractive than the stranger's face presented with

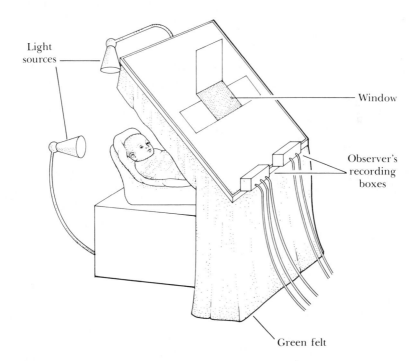

FIGURE *15–1*

The apparatus used by Carpenter for studying infants' responses to the faces and voices of mothers and strangers. Infants viewed the adult through the window.

the stranger's voice. Thus even by two weeks of age there is identification of the mother and preference for her. Perhaps the most interesting result came from the two mismatch conditions, the mother's face with the stranger's voice and the mother's voice with the stranger's face. The babies found both of these presentations aversive, as shown by the way they tried as hard as possible not to look at the faces in this condition, sneaking occasional furtive glances at the face, and occasionally bursting into tears. This mixture of familiar and unfamiliar seemed to elicit, if not outright fear, at least something that was well on the way to it.

Other studies have also demonstrated early forms of stranger fear using a variety of situations and behavioral indexes. Ambrose (1961) found what he called prolonged nonsmiling to strangers in infants of about 14 weeks of age. Other investigators (e.g., Bronson, 1972) have noted signs of uneasiness, gaze aversion, and freezing (abrupt cessation of movement) by babies of 16–20 weeks of age when approached by a stranger. Such behavior is commonly taken as an index of fear in humans and other animals.

A similarly precocious form of separation anxiety has been found by Sander (1969). Sander studied the behavior of babies awaiting adoption and their "mothers" over the course of the first two weeks of life in a hospital. Each infant was assigned a "mother," an experienced caretaker whose sole task was to look after the infant 24 hours a day. After 10 days of living with these mothers, the infants were assigned a new caretaker. Even on the first day without their original mother the infants showed signs of upset. They cried more often and for longer periods, although they were being cared for perfectly adequately. This is separation anxiety in embryonic form.

Classic forms

None of the early forms of stranger fear or separation anxiety are as dramatic as the classic forms. The term "stranger fear" as classically used refers to a complex of behaviors, central to which is prolonged loud crying on approach by a stranger, with turning away or movement away if the baby is mobile. This severe type of behavior is rarely seen before eight months of age; thereafter it gradually increases in intensity, reaching a peak in the second year of life and then gradually diminishing (Figure 15–2). However, the behavior is not as unambiguous and simple as Figure 15–2 might indicate; in the life of any individual baby there is some variation from month to month in the intensity of his responding, even if the testing situation is kept constant. There is also considerable variability in the type of response. Babies left in a strange environment with a strange adult may approach and cling to the adult, showing more fear of the place than the person (Ainsworth and Wittig, 1965). The "strangeness" of the person also

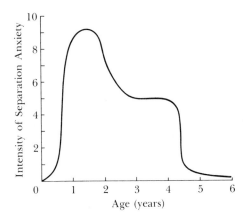

FIGURE *15–2*

Changes in separation anxiety
with age. Because this is a
composite of several studies,
the scale represents only
relative intensity and direction
of change.

plays a role; an adult wearing a mask elicits more fear than a stranger
without a mask (Morgan and Ricciuti, 1969). Whether the mother is
present or not also affects the child's behavior on meeting a stranger.
Paradoxically, a stranger is more terrifying when the mother is present and
only four feet away than when she is absent or the child is on her knee
(Bowlby, 1969; Morgan and Ricciuti, 1969).

Separation anxiety is classically used to describe the child's response to
prolonged separation from the mother.* The classic form of the behavior
consists of protest at separation—screaming or sobbing continuously for
hours or days. Initially the infant will reject attempts at comfort offered by
strangers, but if the separation is prolonged, he will eventually interact
somewhat with these new caretakers. When the mother returns the infant
will cling strongly to her, although he may intermix this with some
negative behavior toward her. The child suffering from separation anxiety
is a pathetic sight, made all the more pathetic by the fact that attempts to
reduce the anxiety seem only to increase it. Separation anxiety in this
intense form seems to appear around seven months of age; thereafter it
increases in severity and then declines over a period of years (Schaffer,
1971). The separation must be prolonged if the child is to run the full
sorrowful course of separation anxiety. However, the beginnings of the
state can be seen whenever the mother leaves the child. Her disappearance
provokes a syndrome of behaviors: attempts to follow her that will not be
diverted by other adults, crying that only terminates when the mother
returns, and other behaviors that indicate a degree of attachment to a
single, unique figure.

---

* As used here, the term "mother" should not be taken to mean the biological mother or even
the principal caretaker, but rather that figure whose absence induces separation anxiety. This
person is usually, but need not be, the biological mother.

The developmental course of separation anxiety has been studied by a number of investigators. Schaffer and Emerson (1964) studied the responses of infants between five and 52 weeks of age to a variety of very short separations from their mother or some other adult. These included having the adult put the child down while remaining visible, leaving the child in a room with others, leaving the child alone in a room, or leaving the child alone outside. The percentages of infants who showed protest in each of these situations at different ages are plotted in Figure 15–3. Young babies particularly disliked being put down after having been held, and they tended to protest when any adult left them. The protest was not specific to any particular adult and could be terminated by the appearance of any adult. From the age of seven months, however, specific individuals became more and more important. Nearly one-third of Schaffer and Emerson's sample showed separation anxiety toward two or more people right away. Of those children showing anxiety on separation from a single individual, the majority showed it toward their mother; a few showed it for their father or a grandparent only. While in the early stages anxiety only on separation from a single individual was the rule, it became very much the exception by 18 months of age, when a mere 13 percent of the sample protested only on the departure of a single individual. Nearly one-third of the group protested on departure of as many as five different individuals.

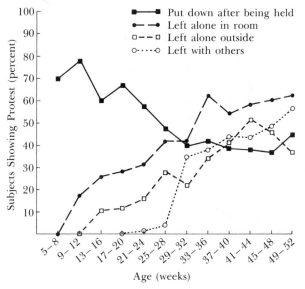

FIGURE 15–3

Protest responses of babies of various ages to four types of separation. (Schaffer and Emerson, 1964.)

This is still, of course, quite limited anxiety compared to the virtually indiscriminate protest shown by these same infants at the beginning of the study.

Later development

Separation anxiety remains high for some time after infancy. One study examined the behavior of children from two to seven years of age on parting from their mother to go to a day care center. It was found that there was little decline in protest until about four years of age, after which there was a precipitous drop (Shirley and Poyntz, 1941).

The degree to which the child seeks the proximity of the mother is related to the degree of anxiety he feels about possible separation from her. This observation has led some investigators (e.g., Spitz, 1950) to regard separation anxiety as the corollary of stranger fear. In one case the child seeks the proximity of an adult, in the other he avoids proximity. There is ample evidence that proximity-seeking in normal situations declines to a rather low level by five years of age and that even when it is elicited by, say, a stressful situation, it is no longer directed towards a single or small number of people. Rosenthal (1965) placed children from three to five years old in an observation room alone with either their mother or a female stranger. When the children entered the room they saw a slow burning alcohol lamp on a stainless steel tray. Next to it was a pair of scissors, a white facial tissue, and a pencil. A sound track produced loud banging, a child crying, or a high-pitched shriek for 20 seconds every three minutes; the sounds were heard through a red door leading to another room. After about 12 minutes, at a time when the child was looking at the door, it opened slowly and a hand in a black, arm-length glove reached in slowly and put out the lamp, after which the arm withdrew and the door was closed. In this horrifying environment proximity-seeking behavior toward the mother did not change with age. However, proximity-seeking behavior directed toward the stranger did increase with age. Indeed, for the oldest children it was insignificantly different from the behavior directed toward the mother.

These studies indicate that stranger fear and separation anxiety are more or less over by the age of five years. This is in accord with the observations of pediatricians who have commented on the fact that children over this age are unlikely to be upset on entry to hospital, although this separates them from their mother and introduces them to a large number of strangers at the same time. It also accords with the almost universal practice of educational systems the world over of beginning schooling—thus separating the child from his mother and introducing him to strangers—somewhere between five and seven years of age.

Theories of development of stranger fear and separation anxiety

Stranger fear and separation anxiety thus occur over a long segment of development, permeating a great deal of the life of the child during that time. The lives of the child's parents, too, are largely shaped by these states; preventing or minimizing them are a major preoccupation of many parents. A very large number of psychologists and psychiatrists would trace a host of adult personality disorders to experiences of separation anxiety in this five-year period of childhood. What are the causes of separation anxiety and stranger fear? Why do they develop suddenly, or seemingly suddenly, in the second half of the first year and persist for the next four to five years? The theories of social development outlined in Chapter 13 have given a variety of answers to these questions.

Social Learning Theory   Social learning theorists have not, so far as I know, attempted to give an account of stranger fear within the context of learning theory. This is not surprising, for a strict learning theory account could not explain the behavior. Social learning theory claims that infants learn to make social responses towards adults because adults become associated with satisfaction of food or comfort needs. These social responses are elicited by the child's caretakers (see pp. 287ff). In so far as strangers resemble the caretakers, they should elicit the same social responses; the more different they are, the fewer responses they should elicit. This is simply an example of the principles of stimulus generalization discussed in Chapter 2. Nevertheless, even though social learning theory might predict very weak social responses to adults who are very different from the primary caretakers, there is no way it can account for responses to strangers that are totally opposite to those elicited by the primary care-takers. On strict learning theory grounds, the appearance of stranger fear is a mystery.

However, learning theories can account for separation anxiety in the following ingenious way. The presence of the mother becomes associated with the relief of discomfort; her absence is associated with discomfort. By a process of classical conditioning, therefore, the absence of the mother will come to evoke feelings of discomfort. Apart from the slight oddity of absence of an object serving as a stimulus, this hypothesis fits perfectly well into a learning theory framework and could certainly account for the appearance of separation anxiety.

Bowlby's Theory   Bowlby would accept that such a process could occur and could account for separation anxiety. He also speculates that fear at separation could develop autonomously as a result of processes of matura-tion (Bowlby, 1973). He points out, however, that it would be impossible to separate a learning theory account from a maturational account, since, as far as he knows, in every culture mothers leave their babies long enough on occasion for the babies to experience some discomfort during the mother's absence. Stranger fear in Bowlby's model is the result of maturation of a fear of strange objects of all sorts coupled with an increasing perceptual ability to detect that an object actually is strange or novel. This account fits in with a great deal that is known about fear in animals. In many species of animals fear of strange objects increases during ontogeny, and it seems quite plausible that young humans would show the same developmental pattern.

Psychoanalytic Theories Psychoanalytic theories have elaborated an approach to separation anxiety and stranger fear that links the two as reflections of a single process. The single process is itself fear of separation, stemming from the physical discomfort associated with absence of the mother. In this respect psychoanalytic theory is no different from learning theory or Bowlby's ethological theory. However, a number of psychoanalytic theorists (e.g., Spitz, 1950) have gone on to propose that once the child has come to fear separation, the sight of a strange adult (a "not-mother" figure) will elicit fear by reminding the child of his absent mother. On this theory stranger fear should thus be absent or at least less intense in the presence of the mother, since by simple inspection the child should be able to reassure himself that he has not suffered separation from his mother. As we saw above, the relationship between presence of the mother and stranger fear is not quite as simple as this theory would require. The most paradoxical phenomenon is that with the mother only a few feet away a stranger elicits more fear than he would if the mother were not there at all, or than he would if the child were on her lap. However, with some adjustments the theory might be made to fit the data. It is quite in accord with what we know about perception that if both mother and stranger are presented simultaneously it would be easier for the child to detect the "not-mother" attributes of the stranger. It is also surely possible that the child could associate the situation with the experience of having been left with a babysitter. The simultaneous presence of mother and "not-mother," with mother not coming to him, might well come to signal to the baby that his mother is about to leave. The psychoanalytic theory, the most parsimonious of those we have looked at so far, is thus not completely ruled out.

These theories are all basically similar. All assume that absence of the mother is unpleasant because it signals unattended distress. All of the theories, even Bowlby's, assume that it is only by association with primary discomfort that separation from the mother can come to elicit anxiety. The only issue that differentiates the theories is whether stranger fear is intimately connected with separation anxiety or is explained otherwise.

Non-nurturant attachment

Despite this theoretical consensus on the cause of separation anxiety, there is evidence that calls this explanation into question. In their study of the development of separation anxiety Schaffer and Emerson (1964) found that for more than one-fifth of the infants they studied separation anxiety was directed toward an individual who took no part whatsoever in their physical care. Since this was someone whose presence had never signaled relief from physical discomfort, their absence could hardly signal incipient discomfort; yet the separation anxiety was just as intense as that shown by infants with more conventional targets. Schaffer has suggested that the characteristic of an adult that determines whether or not he becomes a "target" for separation anxiety is the adult's readiness to interact with the infant. It is thus *social* attentiveness that is critical, rather than attentiveness to simple physical needs. Schaffer has not gone beyond this highly interesting observation to elaborate a theory of how social attentiveness could elicit separation anxiety. Nonetheless, his observations on the antecedents of separation anxiety offer a strong challenge to the conventional theoretical wisdom.

There are other data that also challenge the theoretical consensus. None of the theories mentioned could predict that a child would show anxiety at separation from anyone other than an adult, or on separation from a child at least old enough to assume the nurturant functions of an adult. Nor could they predict that separation anxiety could be mitigated by someone incapable of assuming a nurturant role. Heinicke and Westheimer (1966) report, however, that separation anxiety is greatly diminished if a child is in the company of one of his siblings, *even if that sibling is younger than he is.* The two children serve to allay each other's anxieties. While we might assume that a one-year-old might have received some nurturant attention from a two-year-old, the converse could obviously never have happened, and yet anxiety on separation from the mother is as effectively reduced for the one as for the other.

There are also ample data that twins suffer acute separation anxiety when separated from each other; even with his mother present a twin will show intense anxiety in the absence of the other twin (Burlingham, 1952). I observed twin girls who were first separated when they were just one year old. An infection in one twin had resulted in a high fever during the night. The children's pediatrician, called late at night, advised that the twins be separated. Accordingly, before the healthy twin woke up her sister had been taken to a separate bedroom. (The twins normally shared a bedroom but not a bed.) Next morning, during the changing, dressing, and feeding routine of the healthy twin, the ill sister was asked for several times. After breakfast the healthy twin crawled back to her bedroom and stood beside her sister's empty bed. When she was retrieved she began to cry in earnest, and neither her mother nor her father could console her. When her ill sister was brought out of bed for medicine and some food, she quieted instantly. However, she grabbed her sister tightly and protested vigorously when they were separated again. She refused to eat her lunch. When put down for her afternoon nap she climbed out of her crib, opened the door and was discovered sleeping on the floor at the door of the room her sister was in. The anxiety could not be mitigated by her parents; only the presence of her sister would do. Eventually the parents gave up the separation idea and the anxious behavior ceased. There is simply no way that anticipation of discomfort can account for this behavior. Two infants as young as a year old have certainly never been in a nurturing relationship to one another, and yet their separation anxiety can be just as intense as that of a single child for his mother.

Perhaps the most striking instance of child-child attachments ever described is that observed in a group of six refugee children by Freud and Dann (1951). Shortly after the birth of these children, their parents were deported and killed. The six children arrived at the Tereszin concentration camp when they were about six months old. There they were looked after by a continually changing and overworked group of adults, themselves inmates of the camp. Apparently, these six were the only babies in the camp among a large number of older children. At the end of the war the six children went together first to Czechoslovakia and then to England. When they arrived there, at between three and four years of age, their attachments were to one another. They showed intense anxiety if separated from one another but no attachment to any adult nor any signs of anxiety over separation from adults. This extraordinary case study again points to the fact that we cannot derive separation anxiety from fear of lack of nurture. These children had never fed one another. While together they had experienced unimaginable stresses and horrors, which, on any of the theoretical accounts we have looked at, should have led them to associate one another with stress. Instead, it was separation that produced the stress, a result quite beyond the compass of any of the theories we have looked at.

COMMUNICATIONAL ANALYSIS

What is it that one child can do for another that will so attach them to one another that they show severe separation anxiety when parted? Nurture certainly has nothing to do with it. What is offered, I would propose, is communication.

Child–child interaction

There have been very few studies of child–child interaction in the first year of life. Bridges (1931) studied the development of social relations between babies in an institution. She observed the babies' interaction from the age of one month to two years. She reports that by the age of seven or eight months babies would smile at one another and reach out to one another. By 11 months of age the babies were imitating one another's movements and babbling sounds. Bridges describes these sounds as social. "From this age on children were observed to be jabbering nonsensically and laughing at [with?] each other." Remarkably, the children did not try to incorporate the real words they knew into this exclusive interchange. Bridges interpreted the interchanges between the children as expressions of general sociability. Thus, these institutionalized infants began to interact socially with their peers between seven and 11 months of age. Apparently, twins brought up at home, where opportunities for interaction are more frequent than in an institution, begin to interact socially with one another at an even earlier age. Numerous parental reports give four to five months as the first date of mutual smiling and mutual imitation, from which date on the interchanges become more and more common.

If it is social behavior that leads one child to become attached to another, to the extent that they will show quite severe anxiety on separation from one another, surely it is not stretching the bounds of plausibility to suggest that the anxiety of single children on separation from a parent has the same antecedents. Identification of antecedents, of course, does not explain in the least the immediate causes of anxiety in the separation situation itself. What is it about prolonged interaction with one individual that renders separation from that individual so traumatic and makes other individuals objects of fear?

To answer that question I think we must recall what we said in the last chapter about the origins of sociability. Sociability begins with a kind of interactive behavior called interactional synchrony. A great deal is known about nonverbal communication in adults (Birdwhistell, 1971; Bateson, 1972). It is known that the patterning and significance of body movements differs between cultures and even between social groups living in the same city. Two adults who "speak" different body languages can quickly come to deep misunderstanding and mutual hostility simply as a result of misreading one another's body signals (Heider, unpubl.). It is a fairly safe assumption that babies are not born knowing any specific nonverbal "language." However, it is a fairly safe bet that they start to learn the "languages" of those with whom they interact from the very moment that interaction begins. That is, they learn how to time reciprocal behaviors to permit smooth interaction, learn what behaviors will elicit what other behaviors, how best to prolong social interchanges, what movements signify termination of interchange, and so on.

Adult–child interaction

Mother–infant communication is a busy research area at the moment, and there is little doubt that we shall soon know a great deal about the

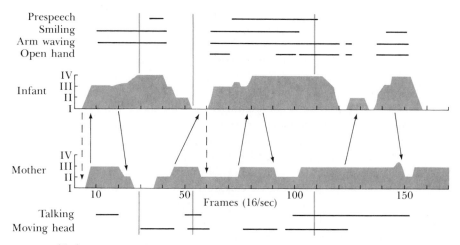

FIGURE 15-4

Analysis from motion pictures of a short sequence (10 seconds) in a "conversation" between a mother and her eight-week-old baby. The roman numerals indicate intensity of animation; the arrows indicate points in the interchange where the behavior of one influences the behavior of the other. The baby twice becomes animated and "talks" to his attentive mother, who closely supports and tries to control his mood. The mother becomes quiet and attentive during prespeech, but she almost always accompanies more excited signals, such as arm-waving, head-tossing, smiling, and calling out, with similar movements of her own. The baby, not the mother, terminates the episode by abruptly turning away. (Trevarthen, 1975.)

development of nonverbal language. However, there is already the data of Sander, referred to above, which indicates that caretaker substitution produces upset in the second week of life. Sander pinned the disruption to the inability of the new caretaker to reproduce the interaction patterns used by the original caretaker. In the feeding situation, for example, he found that adult–infant pairs soon established rhythms of sucking and ways of filling the gaps between bursts of sucking, with social activities which were initiated and terminated according to quite precise "clocks." Similar rhythms permeated the changing situation and the routine of putting the child to bed. The substitute caretaker did not know this interaction pattern and thus did not respond on schedule to the baby's signals, nor did the baby respond to hers. They were thus in the situation of two adults missing and conflicting with one another's signals, and some upset was thus an inevitable consequence.

These early interaction patterns are soon refined. Trevarthen (1975) has described how two-month-olds hold "conversations" with their mothers using an elaborate mixture of babbling and body movements. These interchanges have a conversational structure in which each partner waits for the other to finish before beginning again, with each statement having a duration that is specific to the pair (Figure 15–4). Not only are the rhythms of these conversations specific to a pair, but so also are the contents. Some pairs focus on vocalization, others on body movement, others on body contact, and others on a characteristic sequence of all three. Even each of these activities has a wide variation. For example, a mother's vocalization has a characteristic rhythm, e.g., iambic, trochaic, dactylic, or spondaic, in interacting with her child. A stranger *cannot* enter into one of these pair-specific languages. It is this inevitable failure of communication that eventually produces the behavior we call stranger fear, and not simply "strangeness."

There is some evidence for this hypothesis in Carpenter's observations, reviewed above. Even more striking evidence comes from a study of the effectiveness of social reinforcement in increasing the frequency of smiling in babies (Wahler, 1967). The subjects were three-month-old infants. Wahler compared the effectiveness of the mother versus a stranger in giving social reinforcement. After a five-minute baseline period, during which the reinforcing adult stood motionless, reinforcement began. Reinforcement consisted of calling the baby's name, smiling, and patting him on the chest everytime the baby smiled. These activities must surely have been part of the baby's daily interaction routine with his mother. That strangers could not master this routine is shown by the fact that they produced a decrease in smiling during the reinforcement period (Figure 15–5).

The baby here is in a situation similar to that of an adult approached by a stranger speaking a foreign tongue and conveying the impression that he expects to be understood. Particularly if there is no ready means of escape and if the stranger is bigger than I am, I find such situations quite anxiety provoking, and a baby could hardly find them less so. For the baby, the degree of distress will depend on just how well articulated are the communication routines he shares with his mother. The less articulated they are, the more easily a stranger should fit into them. Minimal interaction on the stranger's part can be handled by minimal interaction on the baby's part. A very active stranger, though, would demand more of the baby and by his own ignorance of the baby's body language would frustrate the baby's attempts to cope with these demands—breaking in on the baby's "utterances," remaining silent when the baby expects him to "talk," and so on. This is roughly in accord with the findings of Schaffer (1966) that the more socially engaging a stranger is, the greater the fear he will elicit. Indeed "fear" may be the wrong word here. The finding that a baby in a strange environment will cling tightly to a stranger who would normally elicit stranger fear should remind us of the complexity of stranger fear (Ainsworth and Wittig, 1965). If a strange adult can mitigate the anxiety-producing qualities of a strange environment instead of adding to them, the two types of strangeness can hardly be equated. The communication needs of adults in strange environments are adequately served by nonverbal signals of togetherness; actual verbal interchange need not

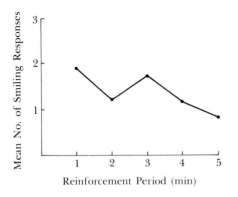

FIGURE *15–5*

Three-month-old infants were reinforced for smiling during a five-minute period by their mothers or by strangers. The graph shows that the infants' responses to strangers declined during the period of reinforcement.

occur (Schachter, 1959). It seems likely that a baby's communication needs in anxiety-provoking situations are similarly satisfied. It has been observed that mobile babies exploring a strange environment show more communicational activity, particularly vocalization (Rheingold, 1969). This presumably serves to reinforce the feeling of "togetherness" during physical separation.

One can thus make a case for communication breakdown as the source of stranger anxiety. Conversely, increasing skill in communication can, I think, account for the decline of stranger fear. In particular, as a child becomes verbally fluent, he can be expected to communicate and be communicated with in ways that are more specific than those afforded by nonverbal communication. As we saw in Chapter 10, the child does not reach this stage much before the age of four, about the age at which stranger fear is disappearing.

Can a communicational analysis illuminate the problem of separation anxiety? I think it can. Recall Schaffer's assertion that the most likely target for separation anxiety is the person with whom the baby is accustomed to interacting and with whom he therefore has a communicational routine. The departure of that individual thus means that the baby is effectively alone, since his growing communicational intimacy with that person puts a certain distance between himself and others who do not understand him as well. We can surely accept that such a situation could cause anxiety in a young child (remember that in Chapter 13 adults described long periods of solitude as extremely distressing). Communication difficulties can also account for the negative behavior shown toward individuals who attempt a surrogate role. Such an analysis could also explicate the problems that may arise between mother and child after a prolonged separation. Some of their communication skills with each other may have slipped with time, or been altered by attempts to communicate with others. If attachments result from the formation of communication routines, it is no wonder that the average child develops an initial attachment to one person only; it is surely easier to learn one language than several. At the same time, it should come as no surprise that children gradually increase the number of their attachments as they increase their communication skills. The need for communication may explain why the presence of a younger sibling can mitigate the anxiety of separation from the parents. Although the younger sibling cannot satisfy physical needs, he can communicate effectively and therefore prevent feelings of solitude. Finally, a child exposed to a number of communication figures would be expected to develop more generalized communication skills than a child who experienced only one communication partner and should therefore suffer less on separation. This is in fact the case (Schaffer and Emerson, 1964). If one reviews the literature for the characteristics of attachment figures, the only common factor found seems to be communication. Some attachment figures nurture, some do not; some cuddle, some do not; some are occasionally violent, others never. All, however, do communicate, and it seems to be this characteristic that defines them as attachment figures.

MATERNAL DEPRIVATION AND THE FORMATION OF ATTACHMENTS

An important segment of scientific opinion holds that attachment to a single mother figure, and maintenance of that attachment, is essential for normal personality growth. This view is most associated with Bowlby, who was among the first to call attention to the problem of maternal deprivation.

The affectionless character

Bowlby (1951) has argued that lack of opportunity to attach oneself to a single figure can lead to development of what he calls an affectionless character, a more or less psychopathic personality characterized by an inability to form relationships with anyone, accompanied often by an extreme charm of manner that enables the individual to manipulate others with ease. It must be emphasized that there is no evidence that an affectionless character is an inevitable outcome of growing up in an environment where the growing child has little or no opportunity to form attachments to a single adult figure. In some cases, for example the six refugee children studied by Freud and Dann, attachments formed by children for another are sufficient for personality growth to proceed. However, in the extreme case where there is no one, not even another child, who is a constant enough companion for attachment to develop, it seems that there is a tendency toward development of an affectionless character. There have been numerous studies of the development of children raised in impermanent institutions with a constantly changing population and staff. It has been found that residence in such an institution past the age of three years tends to produce affectionless characters.

Can a communicational analysis explicate this phenomenon? It is certainly easily dealt with by the various theories of social development outlined in Chapter 13. Psychoanalytic theorists would describe these individuals as narcissistic, with themselves as their own love objects, and as lacking the superego that is given by an adult attachment figure. Social learning theory would argue that such individuals are simply generalizing the behaviors that were reinforced in the institutional environment; since nothing "deeper" than superficial contact was ever reinforced in the institution, why should any "deeper" behavior emerge unless demanded by the environment? Such a theory is therefore more optimistic in that it would hold that the affectionless personality could be changed by appropriate reinforcement. By contrast, Bowlby argues that there is a critical period for attachment formation, much like the critical period for language development described in Chapter 10. If a bond is not formed in the first three years of life it never can be formed, with the inevitable consequence of development of an affectionless character. According to Bowlby, the primary bond is the model that specifies all later bonds, and if it is very superficial, later relationships can only be superficial.

If the analysis of attachment behavior presented here is correct—that it is a crucial stage in the development of communication skills—what does this imply for children raised in an environment with no constant communication figures? First, such children should not be able to develop the communication skills typical of their chronological age since they are never given the opportunity to do so. Second, since we view communication as an acquired skill, it follows that the more practice such children have in communication, the more readily they will catch up to display the skills typical of their age. This seems to be true at least during infancy. Schaffer (1963) studied the consequences of moderately prolonged institutional care in infancy. His subjects were children who had entered one of two institutions prior to the onset of such manifestations of attachment as separation anxiety. In neither institution was it possible for the infants to form specific attachments, for there were no constant figures in their environment. However, one group was in an institution where there was a high ratio of staff per baby, so that there was a good deal of social interaction, even if with different individuals. The others were in a more overworked institution where interaction was at the minimum level necessary for physical care. Schaffer studied these babies after their return home to discover how long it took them to begin showing the attachment behaviors typical of their age. As a communicational analysis would predict, the babies from the second institution took twice as long as those from the first. However, all of the babies did normalize their social behaviors.

In general, it seems that the longer deprivation of an attachment figure continues, the harder it is to develop attachment to an individual. Ultimately, it may become impossible (Rutter, 1972). The evidence seems to point to a genuine developmental effect, quite like the effects of congenital blindness discussed in earlier chapters. If a child is raised in an impersonal institution until the age of three, with no opportunity to form deep and exclusive communication routines with anyone, subsequent transfer to an environment where this is possible will not typically produce these deep communicational possibilities. The child will tend to remain shallow, perhaps charming, but basically affectionless. On the other hand, if a child is raised in a normal home environment until the age of three, with every opportunity to develop deep and exclusive communication, the transfer to an impersonal institution will not inhibit his ability to form profound relations. The opportunity to engage in the profound forms of communication we have been describing thus seems to produce genuine, developmental effects, effects that are irreversible.

The deviant personality

Bowlby has also argued that loss of an attachment figure during the developmental period in which separation anxiety occurs makes it probable that a deviant personality will develop. There is some evidence that at first sight seems to support this point, but which disappears on closer analysis. In the Western world at least, separation from an attachment figure usually occurs as a consequence of death or divorce. On Bowlby's hypothesis there should be no difference in the effect on children, since in both cases an attachment figure is lost. However, it turns out that the nature of the separation does matter. Death of a parent is not correlated with development of deviant personality. Divorce is correlated, but only divorce that is preceded by disharmony. Even then the correlation is less than that for homes in which parental discord continued rather than terminating in divorce (Rutter, 1972). There is thus no evidence to support Bowlby's hypothesis that separation from an attachment figure in itself produces a deviant personality. Indeed, as we shall see in Chapter 20, there is more reason to believe that a deviant personality may develop if communication with an attachment figure is deviant, even though, or perhaps especially if, there is no separation from that attachment figure.

16

The Rise
of Peer
Attachments

The previous chapter was concerned with the development of attachments in early childhood. But just as the child will predictably pass from a stage of social promiscuity in early infancy to a desire for the company of a single person—usually an adult, and usually in fact his mother—so it is also normal for the child to wean himself of that attachment and spontaneously spend less and less time in the company of his original attachment figure. What we have been calling attachment is commonly called dependence, and what we call detachment is commonly labeled independence. In fact, the terms "dependence" and "independence" are both misleading. They reflect a mother-centered view of the child's development. While the average child does come to spend less and less time with his mother, he does not spend the rest of the time in a solitary state pursuing independent aims. Rather, he spends more and more of his time with peers of his own age.

Even within the nursery school age range there is a clear decline in all forms of social interaction with adults and a corresponding increase in social interaction with peers. This trend continues right through adolescence, as far as we can judge (Table 16–1). In rare cases it may even continue thereafter, resulting in the child forsaking his parents completely. It must be emphasized, though, that the increasing independence of the growing child is not a reflection of an increasing desire for solitude, but rather of the increasing attractiveness and availability of age peers.

TABLE *16–1*

Preferred association of fourth–tenth graders.
(Bowerman and Kinch, 1959, based on data from several studies.)

	4TH	5TH	6TH	7TH	8TH	9TH	10TH
Family	75.2%	65.9%	62.1%	51.9%	20.9%	21.2%	15.2%
Neutral*	15.8	24.4	25.0	22.2	39.1	37.6	29.1
Peer	8.9	9.8	12.9	25.9	40.0	41.2	55.0

*Preferred some other group (e.g., much older or younger friends) or showed no preference for family versus peers.

This trend is a problem for theories of social development, although more of a problem for some than for others. Those theories that emphasize the role of the mother in development have the greatest problem, particularly if her nurturant role is seen as fundamental. It is difficult to see how responses to a mother figure could generalize to a child, or indeed, generalize to the extent that an age peer is preferred to the mother. Even Bowlby, who does not accept nurturance as the source of the mother-child bond, can find no way to explain child-child bonding save by invoking a "magical transformation" at about age two and a half that suddenly makes other children attractive companions (Bowlby, 1972). Psychoanalytic theories explain peer attraction as a reflection of the child's narcissism. The child loves himself, and since other children are like him, processes of generalization will ensure some love for them. None of these theories is really satisfactory. Magic is not a desirable invocation in a scientific theory. The psychoanalytic theory, while ingenious, does not explain the trend, with age, away from adults toward peers. There is no doubt that this trend is due in part to an increase in the availability of other children and the increasing mobility of the growing child. Nonetheless, even if increased mobility were to account for the whole of the trend we would still be left with the question of why peers are so much more attractive than parents, and excessive narcissism somehow does not seem satisfactory as an explanation.

The shift of attachment to peers is somewhat less mysterious if looked at in terms of a communicational analysis. We have argued that from birth human beings seek communional relations with others. We also claimed that at the root of this kind of relation there must be some sense of mutuality. We have also argued that development of communication skills can cut a child off from others who do not have the same skills. We have already seen that the world of the child is not the same as the world of the adult, and indeed goes through several revolutions in the course of development. This difference in world view is sufficient, I would argue, to explain the preference for peers that is shown by children at all ages. It is only the child's cognitive equals who can share his world view and with whom he can communicate satisfactorily anything in the way of shared experiences. Further, inasmuch as the child finds his view of the world spurned by adults, he finds himself in a sense isolated from them and rejected by them. The more "educative" the parent the worse the situation, since the more the parent rejects the child's view the more rejected the child must feel. The parent's refusal to accept the child's different view of the world constitutes a refusal to accept the child as he is, a stranger in the adult's world.

ADULT REJECTION OF "CHILDISH" THOUGHT

The best evidence that adults cannot accept children as they are comes, I fear, from the comments that many of the best child psychologists have made about children. The process of rejection begins, I think, well before the child is actually capable of communicating much of anything about his view of the world. Recall the description in the last chapter by Bridges of conversations between infants of 15 months. The children were often observed "jabbering nonsensically at one another." "Jabbering nonsensically" is an extremely pejorative way of describing what these babies are doing. Babies of this age utter long "sentences" that do not contain "words" of any known language but still have the prosodic features of adult utterances, the combinations of stress and intonation that signify statements, questions, answers, commands, and so on. There can be little doubt that many babies enjoy shaping and exchanging these prosodic strings of "nonsense." There can be little doubt that adults find it difficult to enter such exchanges. The most patient of mothers is soon reduced to saying, "Is that so?" or "Is that a fact?" when it comes her turn to speak. More conscientious mothers may seize some segment of the utterance that bears a resemblance to a real word and try to make the child say that. So a child may come up and say interrogatively, "Wah doo chee ka pu nup gogo?" and his mother may reply "Cup! Say cup!" Whatever the child's real desire in this situation, it is probably not to say "cup." Charlotte Bühler (1930) suggested that these utterances are purely social. I would agree and add only that the exchange of them obviously delights children, a delight that few adults can share.

Egocentrism

The situation becomes all the more complex and difficult when the child begins to try to communicate items of information about the world. The difficulty is severe enough that the world's most famous child watcher,

Jean Piaget, went so far as to assert that children below the age of eight or so are basically egocentric and do not really communicate at all (Piaget, 1926). This claim, if correct, would vitiate the whole basis for the theory of social development that has been advanced here. I do not think the claim is correct and feel that it shows the tendency, uncharacteristic of Piaget, to impose adult norms on children's communication. Piaget and his co-workers came to this conclusion after analyzing and classifying over 1,500 utterances made by two children in the course of their play at the famous Maison des Petits, a nursery school in Geneva. Piaget (1926) established eight classes of utterance, three of which were said by Piaget to be purely egocentric. These were:

1. *Repetition*, where the child repeats an utterance he has just heard.
2. *Monolog*, where the child talks to himself.
3. *Collective monolog*, where two or more children talk to themselves but take turns doing so, as if engaged in a dialog or conversation.

In the sample of utterances collected, repetition constituted about four percent, monolog about 10 percent, and collective monolog about 30 percent of the children's utterances, so that nearly half of everything these children said was, on Piaget's criteria, egocentric, not directed at anyone else in any truly social way. Since the proportion is said to decrease with age, such a finding would be fatal for the present theory of social development. Fortunately, a variety of other studies, while validating the utility of Piaget's classifications, have indicated that they do not imply any genuine egocentricity. For example, Vygotsky (1962) took one implication of Piaget's use of the world "egocentric," that the presence or absence of respondents should not make any difference to the frequency of verbal utterances, and tested it by checking the verbalizations of various children left, each in turn, with other children who were deaf mutes, or left with other hearing children in a room in which the noise of an orchestra made it impossible for them to hear one another. He found that in all cases the frequency of these supposedly egocentric utterances declined drastically, indicating that the presence of a respondent, with the possibility of a response, was a key element in their production. In other words, "egocentric" utterances have a social function, no matter how unlikely this may look to an adult.

While this hypothesis may be true for many of these utterances, and is in accord with my own theoretical position, I feel sure that utterances that appear to be egocentric appear so only because of our adult inability to understand the child's logic, the child's motivations, and even the child's sense of humor. Consider the following example of what Piaget calls repetition. J says to E "Look E, your underpants are showing." P, who is in another part of the room, says "Look, my underpants are showing, and my shirttail, too." Piaget remarks that "there is not a word of truth in this." He characterizes P's statement as an instance of repetition, completely nonsocial, said purely for the pleasure of hearing the words. It seems to me more likely that P spoke as an attention-getting device, with humorous intent, first because P actually topped E's claim to attention by claiming an exposed shirttail as well, and second simply because the statement is not true. Calling people's attention to a state of affairs that is nonexistent is something that children do find humorous, or at least they laugh at those they have fooled. Most adults do not find this kind of thing funny. Nonetheless, it is a state of affairs that children do find amusing. A great deal of the repetition Piaget observed was probably in fact competitive boasting with humorous intent.

According to Piaget, the most common form of egocentric speech, indeed the most common type of speech among children, is "collective monolog." Here again I feel the classification betrays a misunderstanding of children's logic. Also, it ignores the fact that children who know one another well sometimes speak in a code that is not meaningful to outsiders. While I feel I could interpret Piaget's own examples, I shall instead explain the dialog behind what appears to be a "collective monolog" between my own twin daughters. The following conversation took place just short of their fifth birthday, while we were temporarily living in the United States (C and P = twins, F = father, E = older sister).

(1) C: I weigh 3½ years.
(2) P : Well, I weigh 4 and so do you.
(3) C: I'm getting a radio on Sunday.
(4) P : There's a ghost in our cellar, isn't there?
(5) C: America's very nice, though.
(6) C: John's in Edinburgh.
(7) P : What's the baby twins' mummy?
(8) F : Brigitté.
(9) P : Brigitté . . . Brigitté . . . Brigitté.
(10) C: Shut up, Penny.
(11) C: You're stupid, Penny.
(12) F : (To C) You can say Brijeet, too.
(13) C: See, I told you.
(14) P : Well, tomorrow *I'm* climbing in the window.
(15) C: You give me a sore head with your crying.
(16) C: (To her elder sister) Will you give me a nut? E: No.
(17) C: You gave Penny a sweater.
(18) P : When are we going to Switzerland again?

(19) C: Daddy, will you take us to Switzerland and me to that shop?

(20) P : Yes, you have a sweater and me have a kite.

(21) C: Hee, hee, hee, and scare the big jumbo jet. Hee, hee, hee.

Statement 1 reflects a confusion between age and weight. C in fact weighs three and a half stone (1 stone = 14 lbs) and P partially corrects her sister about their age. This correction brings to C's mind their birthday on Sunday and the various presents they have been promised. Mention of the birthday reminds P of the fact that at birthday parties in their home in Britain they are allowed to explore the cellar, which they believe to be haunted. Being away from home, they have no haunted cellar to provide them with a birthday treat. C responds by acknowledging (5) that the United States has its drawbacks but that it is nonetheless very nice; she continues thinking of home and particularly of a friend who had recently visited with his wife and twin infants (6). Mention of the friend elicits a question from P about the friend's wife (7). F tells C and P the name (8) and P repeats it (9). Everyone in the family knows that C cannot pronounce the name, hence statements 10 and 11. F attempts to keep the peace with statement 12, and C then asserts her dominance (13). Statement 14 is elicited by C's assertion of dominance; the most recent competitive clash between the sisters was over who should climb in a window and unlock the doors when their father forgot his keys. Statement 15 is a response to the implied threat in 14; P's most frequent tactic in quarrels is to scream very loudly. The context of statements 16 and 17 is obvious. Statement 18 reflects the fact that the coveted sweater was bought in Switzerland at a particularly wonderful shop, whose name neither child can pronounce. The shop sells wonderful kites, one of which went up so high that it allegedly interfered with the landing of a 747 jet.

However much the sisters' speech looks like collective monolog it most certainly is not. The meanings underlying it are associational, the simple association of ideas, but there is nonetheless a conversational logic underpinning the exchange and the logic is clear to both children, so that what seems like two independent monologs is really a genuine conversation. Because adults by and large do not converse on the basis of leaping associations, which are quite natural to children, they find such conversations hard to follow and hard to engage in.

There are even more private levels of children's thought that are far more impenetrable to the adult mind. Piaget has confessed that he was more or less forced to rely on adults' recollections of childhood to gain some insight into children's magical view of the world (Piaget, 1926).

Being as restricted, then, and yet as active, my mind took refuge in an infantile species of natural magic. This contended with the definite ideas of religion which my parents were continuing, with too mechanical a persistency, to force into my nature, and it ran parallel with them. I formed strange superstitions, which I can only render intelligible by naming some concrete examples. I persuaded myself that if I could only discover the proper words to say or the proper passes to make, I could induce the gorgeous birds and butterflies in my Father's illustrated manuals to come to life and fly out of the book, leaving holes behind them. I believed that when at the Chapel we sang, drearily and slowly, loud hymns of experience and humiliation, I could boom forth with a sound equal to that of dozens of singers, if I could only hit upon the formula. During morning and evening prayers, which were extremely lengthy and fatiguing, I fancied that one of my two selves could flit up and sit clinging to the cornice, and look down on my other self and the rest of us, if I could only find the key. I laboured for hours in search of these formulas, thinking to compass my ends by means absolutely irrational. For example, I was convinced that if I could only count consecutive numbers long enough, without losing one, I should suddenly, on reaching some far distant figure, find myself in possession of the great secret. I feel quite sure that nothing external suggested these ideas of magic. . . .

All this ferment of mind was entirely unobserved by my parents. But when I formed the belief that it was necessary for the success of my practical magic that I should hurt myself, and when, as a matter of fact, I began, in extreme secrecy, to run pins into my flesh and bang my joints with books, no one will be surprised to hear that my Mother's attention was drawn to the fact that I was looking "delicate."

All children at some stage believe in magic, but it is something they keep very much to themselves.

Children's humor

Although more accessible than the child's magical view, children's humor is also frequently incomprehensible to adults. Why do children find the following rhyme so clever and repeat it so often?

> Mrs. White had a fright
> In the middle of the night,
> She saw a ghost eating toast
> Half-way up the lamp post.

Why do they like this one even more?

> Do you want a sweet?
> Suck your feet!

Why do children enjoy the seemingly disconnected tales that adults describe as "utter nonsense"?

> I went to the pictures tomorrow
> I took a front seat at the back,
> I fell from the pit to the gallery
> And broke a front bone in my back.
> A lady she gave me some chocolate,
> I ate it and gave it her back.
> I phoned for a taxi and walked it,
> And that's why I never came back.

Or the following.

> One fine day in the middle of the night,
> Two dead men got up to fight,
> Back to back they faced each other,
> Drew their swords and shot each other.
> A paralyzed donkey passing by
> Kicked a blind man in the eye,
> Knocked him through a nine inch wall
> Into a dry ditch and drowned them all.

Even the more "meritorious" (in some adult eyes) can pall after a while.

> Ma wee man's a miner,
> He works at Abbeyhill,
> He gets his pey on Setterday
> And buys a half a gill.
> He goes to church on Sunday
> A half an hoor late,
> He pulls the buttons aff his shirt
> And puts them in the plate.

Even less amusing to an adult are tales without an end. "It was a dark and stormy night and the Captain said to the Bosun, 'Bosun tell us a story,' so the Bosun began, 'It was a dark and stormy night and the Captain said to the Bosun. . . .'"

The point about children's humor is that it is *children's* humor. Adults do not enjoy it or share in it, but children most certainly do. It is something children enjoy only with one another.

ADULT REJECTION
OF ADOLESCENT THOUGHT

Similar conflicts can arise between adolescents and their parents, even though they share a more similar view of the world than do young children and adults. As we saw in Chapter 9, adolescents are relentlessly logical.

Their parents are less likely to be so consistently logical and may even find themselves rejecting logic. This point is brought out in an experiment by Allan (cited in Welford, 1958). Allan presented adult subjects with four sets of statements. Two examples are:

Set B
1. A right action is an action that will bring about at least as much good, or, failing that, will avoid at least as much evil as any other action open to the agent at the moment of acting.
2. A good man is a man who always does what seems to him, after due consideration, to be right.
3. It is always wrong to tell a lie or break a promise.
4. Suffering in itself is undoubtedly evil.
5. In some cases it seems obvious that the only consequence of telling the truth or of keeping a promise will be to cause more suffering than would result from the opposite behavior.

Instructions
Read carefully the statements printed on the sheet and answer the following questions.

Questions
1. Are these statements compatible one with another?
2. If not, what is the least number that must be rejected to yield a completely consistent set?
3. Write out such a list, containing the fewest possible rejections, and state briefly wherein lies the incompatibility between those you reject and those you retain.

Set C
1. The diversion of labour to the production of machinery and other forms of capital goods is an essential step in the industrialization of a nonindustrial country and must cause a temporary fall in the standard of living of the laboring classes of the country concerned.
2. People who are not familiar with an industrial economic system will never voluntarily submit to a reduction in their standard of living simply on the promise of better things to come.
3. There are only two ways of surmounting this obstacle in the path of industrialization: (i) by borrowing from abroad in order to keep up the standard of living at home; (ii) by making illegal the forming of trade unions and strikes and so making the workers wholly subject to the heads of industry.
4. Only after industrialization had advanced to a high level of efficiency in various parts of the world was it possible to adopt the expedient of borrowing.
5. No Communistic government wishing to industrialize can hope to obtain such loans.

Instructions

Using the facts stated on the sheet, state any conclusion or conclusions you think are justified by them and explain briefly how your conclusion or conclusions follow from the facts.

Two types of responses to these statements were given: either logical deductions or comments based on experience. Here are two examples of the former.

Schoolteacher, age 32, in answer to question 3 of set B:

According to statement 5 a lie would in given circumstances cause less suffering, therefore (statement 4) would be less evil than the truth, and would (statement 1) be a right action. Under these circumstances a good man in doing right would tell a lie. As statement 3 states it is always wrong to tell a lie, it must be rejected.

Clerk, age 34, in answer to set C:

The first conclusion justified from the facts stated is that, while a non-Communist state would meet no insuperable obstacle in the path of industrialization, it would be impossible for a Communist state to become industrialized. The fact that people unaccustomed to an industrial economic system would not accept a reduction in their standard of living, necessary to achieve industrialization, can only be surmounted in two ways. These are both open to a non-Communistic state, provided a sufficient amount of industrialization has occurred in other parts of the world to permit of a loan. A Communistic state would be unable to effect such a loan, however, and is thus faced with the alternative of suppressing trade unions and strikes and making the workers subservient to the heads of industry, which is incompatible with Communistic doctrines. If it adopted this course it would cease to be a Communist state.

A second conclusion is that the first states to become industrialized must have done so by a policy of repression as, with no other states industrialized, loans were impossible.

Here are two examples of responses based on experience rather than logic.

Extra-mural lecturer, age 46, in answer to question 3 of set B (the subject rejected statements 1, 2, and 4 in answer to question 2):

The rightness or wrongness of an action must, as I think, be determined by its end-result. Thus a good man is the one who does what is right according to the light he possesses. Experience has taught me that to adhere absolutely to the truth or even to a promise may lead to suffering—personal suffering, and moreover suffering to other people. This is contained in statement 5. Regarding 4, I might add that suffering is evil, though in some cases it may be a form of discipline which can result in some kind of good. Even so, I find it difficult to justify it. I am forced to regard it as an evil which ought to be eradicated.

Industrial welfare officer, age 49, in answer to set C:

Regarding paras. 1 and 2: people will not cooperate unless they are educated to appreciate (1) the actual position as it applies to the individual and the nation as a whole; (2) unless the leaders are quite frank and can be trusted to give them a square deal, before, during, and after a national crisis.

There must be an incentive to work, to regard work not as a painful necessity but as a pleasure, or a means of obtaining satisfaction unobtainable in any other way.

Regarding para. 3: (1) Borrowing from abroad is a short-term expedient which tends to confuse the issue, creates a wrong impression among the workers, and makes the borrower subject to the financial dictatorship of the country lending the money, restricts the market and leads to a state of distrust, &c. (2) The making illegal of trade unions and strikes is the best way to foment unrest, workers suffering from frustration will find an alternative outlet for their emotions, will not cooperate with the heads of industry, and will listen to the worst if it offers some redress for their suppressed opinions.

Regarding para. 4: "Borrowing" as we now understand it only becomes possible when the majority of the major countries have adopted a monetary standard. "Bartering" has been in universal practice ever since history has been recorded, and no doubt existed before.

Regarding para. 5: Communistic governments had and do obtain loans.

Among subjects over 35 the vast majority of responses were comments rather than logical deductions.* Thus parents and their teenage children may disagree about the very rules of discussion, with neither appreciating the virtues of the other's position.

Basically, I am arguing that the growth of independence from parents is a function of a growing dependence on peers for social satisfaction. Only peers can provide the social interaction the child wants because they are his cognitive equals. I am proposing that the shift can be accounted for by the same social motive that creates attachment to parents. The barriers to communication between adults and children (and adolescents) created by different world views do not exist between children of the same age, who share the same world view. The discovery that there are people with whom such total communication is possible is surely enough to explain the child's growing preference for peers over parents.

---

*Only 28.4 percent of the answers given by subjects over 35 were deductive, compared to 70.7 percent for those subjects under 35.

OVERATTACHMENT
OF PARENT AND CHILD

While the shift from parent to peers is normal, it can be disrupted. Some children develop anxious attachments to their parents that prevent them from venturing into the world of their peers. The so-called school phobia results in children not attending school and so deprives them of the company of peers who are at school. School phobia is to be distinguished from truancy. The phobic child typically advances some anxiety about school as the reason for staying at home and not attending school. The truant, by contrast, does not stay at home; he simply does not go to school, often in the company of a fellow truant. The truant is not anxious about school—he merely prefers other things. Bowlby (1973) has reviewed the literature on school phobia and claims that the true reasons for what appears to be a phobia with regard to school fall into four classes, none of which are concerned with school per se.

1. An anxious parent actually keeps the child at home for company.
2. The child stays at home because he is afraid that something will happen to his parent while he is away at school.
3. The child is afraid something will happen to him while he is at school and so stays at home to avoid that.
4. The parent thinks something will happen to the child at school and so keeps him at home to prevent that.

The first reason is the commonest and may occur in conjunction with any of the other three. The last reason is the least common basis for refusal to attend school, and, it would seem from Bowlby's review, is in many cases a response to or a memory of some tragic event in the parent's past, such as the death of a sibling of school age. Such behavior, while not rational, is easily comprehensible. Of greater interest are the other three reasons, all of which represent a distortion of the normal pattern of parent-child attachment. This seems to be so even for the third reason listed, that the child stays at home because he is afraid something dreadful will happen to him while he is at school. The dreaded event in many cases is abandonment by the parent. In the cases Bowlby cites it is clear that there were threats made by the parent to abandon the child, to walk out and leave him, or to leave him at school and not collect him, or something else of the same sort. The child's behavior is thus a perfectly rational way of preventing this occurrence. If he does not leave home, his parent will have no opportunity to leave behind his back.

The second reason is tragically similar to the third, with the added burden for the child of a realistic fear that his parent will die or commit suicide. In these cases the parent has actually threatened to desert the child, as a disciplinary measure, but with the added threat of death. In some of the cases of alleged school phobia described by Bowlby the children were in fact showing an admirably rational way of coping with such threats. In one case a 13-year-old girl and her 11-year-old brother evolved a shift system to keep an eye on their widowed mother. The girl stayed at home during the day, while her brother went to school; in the evenings she went out while her brother stayed at home. This pattern only became obvious when the brother fell ill and so was constrained to be at home during the day. His sister seized this opportunity to go to school. In this case the children's father had recently died. The mother blamed the children for this, habitually saying that she would die, too, if they didn't behave, and threatening to desert them. Her daughter, far from avoiding school, was in actual fact standing guard over her mother, and sharing the task with her brother. However, the guardian role played by these children was not attractive to them. They did quarrel about whose turn it was to watch mother. When she could, the daughter did go to school. Furthermore, once the mother's threats had been talked out in the course of family therapy, both children showed normally independent behavior for their age.

What this indicates, I think, is that attachments to peers and attachments to parents are different systems that can come into conflict. The two children described above were able to apportion their time between the two attachment systems. This outlet is not available to those children kept at home for the first reason, that their parent wants them there for company. Eisenberg (1958) has described how the mother's possessiveness may be manifested quite nonverbally. The mother may *say* that she wants the child to go to school but communicate very well, in a nonverbal way, that that is the last thing she wants. He describes the typical behavior of some mothers with nursery school age children exhibiting school phobia. Accompanying their child to nursery, they sit in close proximity to him. When the child moves out to join the other children these mothers will typically follow the child, periodically interrupting whatever he is doing to wipe his nose, check his toilet needs, etc, each such interruption being followed by the child's withdrawal from the group, much to the mother's verbally expressed dismay.

One mother described by Eisenberg was prevailed upon to leave her twins in the nursery. "She bade them good-bye with many reassurances of her early return. They played on unconcerned. She stopped again at the door to assure them they had nothing to fear. They glanced up but played on. Having gotten her coat, she made a third curtain speech in a tremulous voice, 'Don't be afraid. Mommy will be back. Please don't cry.' This time one of the twins actually did cry until the mother left." Describing the mother of an older child, Eisenberg recounts how she told the psychiatrist "You won't be able to get him to leave me," while clutching tightly at her child's hand, saying nonverbally to the child, "Please don't leave me." The situation in which a mother says to her child, "You must go to school," but says it in a quavering voice with tremulous gestures, is guaranteed to make any normally affectionate child stay at home. Mothers who do this typically over-indulge their children, catering to their every whim. But, as Bowlby says, the child prevented "from taking part in school or play activities with his peers . . . is chronically frustrated, and, because allegedly given everything, is not even free to expostulate." Such a child typically resents the situation and yet can do nothing about it. This resentment again points up the separate nature of peer and parental attachments. On many theories of attachment there is no reason why spoiled children should yearn for age peers, when in fact they do. Peer attachments can thus hardly be mirror images of parental attachment; peers are not mere surrogates for the primary attachment figure.

ATTACHMENT TO PARENTS AND PEERS

Many articles have been written about the kinds of parental behavior that will make it easier for a child to detach himself from his parents. The pathological cases described above make it clear, I think, that the social need for peers will itself ensure detachment. In any case, the term "detachment" is inappropriate. Although a child spends less and less time with his parents as he grows, he is still attached to them. The attachment simply becomes covert. It will remain covert unless the parents threaten it, in which case attachment-preserving behavior, of which school phobia is an extreme variant, will emerge.

These same factors—the social need for peers and continuing covert attachment to parents—can explain the apparent paradox that children of the most attentive and available parents are most independent (Longer, 1973). They know where their parents are most of the time and so feel free to wander on their own, secure in the knowledge that they can find their parents whenever they want them. This is not to say these first attachments are permanent. Parental attachment can wither away if parents do not adjust their interaction styles with their children as they grow. For example, authoritarian parents who do not discuss their dictates with their children may ultimately snap the attachment bond, particularly in adolescence. The same is true of very permissive parents, who do not communicate with their children even at the level of discipline. A host of studies testify that it is those parents who continue to communicate with their children who best maintain the attachment relation in adolescence. Thus, just as communication is responsible for the formation of primary attachments, so it seems to be responsible for the continuing existence of these attachments parallel with the later developing system of peer attachments.

17

Social Conformity: Parents Versus Peers

Although parents obviously have considerable control over the child's behavior, the rise of peer attachments, described in the last chapter, clearly introduces another source of social control into the life of the child. But while parental control usually recedes and eventually terminates at some point in an individual's life, peer constraints continue to be effective throughout life. How soon do these constraints begin to operate? Numerous experiments have tried to answer this question, using group-pressure situations similar to those described in Chapter 13. The subject is put with a group of his peers; by prearrangement, the peers make a judgment that is more or less clearly wrong, or at least different from one that the child would have made by himself. The measure of peer influence or *compliance* is the extent to which the child shifts from his own (correct) judgment to that of the peer group. The results of such studies present a fascinating developmental picture.

It appears that children between three and six years old are quite impervious to peer-group influence. A number of studies have found no evidence whatsoever of peer pressure on the child's judgment at this age (Hunt and Synnerdale, 1959; Starkweather, 1964). Not one child in these studies shifted consistently in the direction of the group's judgment. By contrast, a similar study found that children between seven and 10 years of age were highly compliant; they shifted consistently in the direction of the peer group consensus (Berenda, 1950). Even more interesting was the finding that children 11 to 13 years old were somewhat *less* compliant than the next youngest age group. This decline in compliance (from the peak reached between seven and 10 years) was not an artifact. Other studies have found a decline throughout the teenage years from a peak reached somewhere between six and 13 years of age (Iscoe, Williams, and Harvey, 1963). It thus seems clear that peer influence is *curvilinearly* related to age; nursery school age children are the least compliant and children 7–10 years old are the most compliant, while older children and adolescents are intermediate.

CONFLICT BETWEEN PEER-GROUP AND PARENTAL PRESSURES

A great deal has been written about the *possible* dilemmas a child could find himself in as a result of conflicting pressures from his peer group and parents. In reality, as a number of authors have pointed out (e.g., Conger, 1971), in the course of normal development such *cross pressures* are most uncommon. In fact, peer-group and parental pressures are likely to push in the same direction throughout the child's life. This still leaves open the question of the relative importance of the two types of pressure. Even if both sources are pushing in the same direction, it is of interest to know which pressure is the more effective.

A few studies of this problem have used artificial dilemmas to assess the relative importance of parents and peers in decision-making at different ages. For example, Utech and Hoving (1969) presented children between the third and eleventh grades with a set of 11 dilemmas. One of them was the following.

> Susan likes music and is trying to decide whether to join the band or the choir. *Her mother and father think* that being in the band would be more fun because the band plays at all the basketball and football games. Susan's *friends think* she would have more fun in the choir because the choir goes to many different towns to sing. What do you think Susan will decide to do? (1) Do as her parents say and join the *band*? (2) Do as her friends say and join the *choir*?

In an alternate form of each dilemma the advice of friends and parents was reversed; in the above case, for example, friends advised the band and parents the choir. The children were administered one set of dilemmas and then 10 days later the other set, on the pretext that the first set of answers had been lost. The measure of peer compliance was the number of dilemmas that were resolved by following the advice of friends in both tests. Note that this meant reversing the actual choice of activity in the two tests, joining the band one time and the choir the next. A parental compliance measure was computed in the same way. If the same *activity* were recommended in both tests (e.g., join the band) the responses were scored as noncompliant. The results showed that parental compliance declines steadily with age, almost in step with an increase in peer compliance, so that the oldest subjects in the study, the eleventh-graders, were significantly more peer compliant than parent compliant. While other authors have found parental compliance higher than peer compliance at one or another of the ages studied by Utech and Hoving, the conclusion that the trend is away from parents and toward peers has not been challenged in any developmental study. Thus, even though the advice of peers and parents is normally consonant, it would appear that peer advice is more salient at the later stages of development.

Several features of these data are extremely interesting. Why, for example, are nursery school children so unaffected by peer pressures? Why does the effectiveness of peer pressure rise then eventually decline with age? Why do peers tend to replace parents as the more potent force in decision-making? None of these questions has an obvious answer, at least in terms of the implicit or explicit theories of development that psychologists have formulated. For example, Milgram (1974) has argued that obedience, particularly obedience to authority figures such as parents, is continually reinforced in society. On this view, compliance should increase continuously with age rather than showing the decline that it does. The fact that there is a decline in all forms of compliance is also, I think, a rebuttal of the idea that a person's actions are more a function of the situation he finds himself in than of who he is. If this idea were correct, an individual would generally behave the same in similar situations, regardless of his stage of development. The course of development is toward individual freedom from pressure. This is true even of individuals in Milgram's obedience situation, as we shall see below.

All theories of attachment have problems with the pattern of data described above. Generalization of obedience to parents into compliance with peers is certainly conceivable, but even granting the superior attraction of peers it is hard to see how such a hypothesis could account for the decline in obedience that has been observed.

PIAGET'S ARGUMENT: OBEDIENCE
TO PARENTS IS SECONDARY

It is very widely assumed that the model processes that establish social compliance are begun in the home, that it is parental demands for obedience that produce the generalized habit of compliance. This assumption has been regarded as common sense based on common observation. Nonetheless, it has been challenged by Piaget, whose views on this aspect of social development can be interpreted as an argument that it is peers who produce compliance and parents who benefit from it. This is a far from orthodox position and yet a case can be made for it. Moreover, Piaget's hypothesis can account for the anomalies of the development of compliance. A crucial part of the case hinges on a question of terms, on the exact meanings of the words "obedience" and "compliance" at different stages in development. Is the compliance of a three-year-old the same as that of a seven-year-old, a teenager, or an adult? Most discussions of obedience or compliance seem to assume that the words refer to the same process at all ages. While this may suit theoretical preconceptions, it does not fit with common sense or observation. The young child complies because he sees no alternative. Indeed, in Western societies the young child is given no alternative. Refusal to comply is met with sanctions (often physical) and disobedience is usually not tolerated. Reynolds (1928) found that negativism (the refusal to comply) declined to a very low level before the age of four. I doubt whether more households permit noncompliance in young children today than in 1928. The survival of the children would be at risk if they did. Not only does the child have no real alternative to obeying the parent, but also he has no way of making the parent obey him. The parent can reward or punish the child but the child has no way of rewarding or punishing the parent. The relationship between parent and child is not reciprocal; it is *heteronomous*.

What happens when a young child is thrust into a peer group? Suddenly, enforced compliance is gone. Every child can do as he wishes vis-à-vis every other child, with perhaps certain constraints imposed by any adults present. One child cannot make another comply with his wishes. Young children, accustomed to the pain-pleasure payoffs associated with parents, see little reason why they should comply with the wishes of another child. It is a commonplace observation that the first few sessions of any nursery school or play group are taken up with solitary play, with little interaction between the children. Soon, however, the children begin to play together. They begin to utter and receive requests for cooperation. The essence of communication is that it is reciprocal. Communication only occurs if there is a sharing of time and some sympathy between those trying to communicate. Group play requires the same interchange. There is no way that two or more children can play together without a sharing of time, facilities, and roles. The basic groundplan for cooperation is the same as that for communication. Unlike communication, though, group play requires compliance from *every* member of the group. While two children might form a leader-follower pair, mimicking the parent-child relationship, there is evidence that children, particularly those cast as followers, will resent and avoid this level of relationship. Turner (1957) quotes the following conversation between two six-year-olds discussing a mutual friend George, who always seems to know what the other children should be doing.

> George is so bossy. He thinks everyone has to do as he says.

> I don't see why we have to mind George. He isn't any mother or teacher or anything.

Even though "mature," competent George was good at assigning roles, his habit of domination was resented. The children in fact preferred "immature," undirected Gifford, who pushed no one anymore than he was willing to be pushed himself. While children's play groups do have leaders, the leaders must be willing to be led, if they are not to be forsaken completely. In fact, it would seem that in these cooperating groups *all* children comply one with another, the other's compliance reinforcing each individual's own compliance. The give-and-take of communication is the model for the sharing that we see in play. Play can also reveal to the child for the first time the reinforcing effects of his own compliance. By complying with the group, the child can unite himself more tightly with the group.

Turner (1957) has written a beautiful description of the process of group formation and group decision-making in young children. Her group of five- to seven-year-olds were encouraged to use parliamentary procedure, strictly according to Robert's rules. They were even asked to draw up a written constitution. It is amazing that this document was largely arrived at by the children themselves. As Turner's description makes clear, the most self-willed of children will come to accept and use group rules. Although rules govern the behavior of all self-regulated groups of children, they are far less explicit or formal in most groups.

Discovery of reciprocal compliance

I am suggesting that peer-group compliance is something that children discover when they begin to interact with other children. Children discover with other children that social relationships can be reciprocal. The groundplan for social reciprocity already exists in the reciprocity of communication. As soon as a child can hold a conversation he knows all that is basically required for social cooperation.

I would further argue that this discovery changes the nature of the child's obedience to his parents. Parent-child relationships can hardly appear reciprocal to the young child. Since reciprocal compliance in a peer group is rewarded, the experience of reciprocal relations in a peer group will lead the child to seek a similar relationship with his parents. If such a relationship proves possible, it will replace the earlier obedient relationship. If it proves impossible, the knowledge of its possibility, gained with peers, may disrupt the obedient relationship. How could the child discover whether or not he and his parents had a reciprocal relationship? Not when his parents yield to his requests, since that has always occurred to some extent. What would be important, I would suggest, is evidence that parents view the child's compliance as something he is doing for them. Young children know very well what their parents do for them. What is not obvious is what the child does for his parents. If parents signal that they feel rewarded when their children comply, they are signaling to them that their relationship is reciprocal. On the other hand, if they merely punish them for noncompliance, they are not signaling reciprocity but rather continued autocracy. This is pretty much the pattern that Crandall and his colleagues (1958) found in their study of compliance in a group of six- to eight-year-olds. The degree of the child's compliance towards parents and other adults was significantly correlated with the degree to which compliance elicited positive reactions from the parents. Punishment for noncompliance was unrelated to compliance.

I have been asserting that the virtues of compliance are only discovered in interaction with peers, and that the autocratic parent-child relationship cannot generate the same kind of compliance. This is, I would argue, not *necessarily* true: it seems that children *do not* discover reciprocal compliance in interaction with adults, although it is possible that they *could*. Crandall and co-workers (1958) found that the compliance of nursery school children, children who were just beginning to interact with peers, could not be predicted from parental behavior; prior to peer experience, parental behavior is unimportant, presumably because it is seen as autocratic. Turner (1957) cites the difficulties experienced by a child transferred from a school where discipline had been strictly enforced: "Henry had been looking upon his classmates, not as a *source* of opinion, but as a *conveyor* of it!" Conforming to group norms was slowed for this child by his prior experience in an adult-run, autocratic system. Not only is peer group compliance slowed by lack of exposure to peers, it is also greatly facilitated by early experience with peers. Faigin (1958) studied children in a *kibbutz*, an Israeli farm community in which children are separated from their parents each day and raised in large groups. These children showed peer compliance at a much younger age than children without such early peer experience.

The idea that reciprocal compliance is discovered in peer groups also explains the decline in compliance with parental wishes. The more difficult parents make reciprocal compliance, by continuing to be autocratic, the less attractive compliance to their wishes will be. At the same time, the more permissive parents are, the less they care whether or not the child is compliant, the less attractive will compliance to their wishes become. Parents who have a reciprocal interaction with their children probably will retain their compliance overall. Those who do not have such a reciprocal relationship will in all probability lose that compliance (Conger, 1971).

MORAL DEVELOPMENT
IN CHILDHOOD

None of the above says anything about the decline in all forms of compliance observed during the later stages of development. To comprehend this change, I think we have to look at an aspect of social development that has not been mentioned so far here. I am referring to moral development, a field of study in itself and one that provides the best possible paradigm for the later stages of social development. Piaget's study, *The Moral Judgment of the Child* (1932), is still the single most significant publication in this field. Piaget distinguished two types of morality in children, which he arrived at by observing children's games and by presenting the children with a variety of moral problems. The first, *heteronomous morality*, is built on constraint and punishment, reflecting the sanctions imposed by adults. It is an absolute morality in which intentions are not considered. Punishment —vengeful, expiatory, and retributive—is accepted as just. The second type is *cooperative* morality, in which the social bond is the most important source of moral behavior and reciprocity is its most desirable manifestation. It is a more relative moral system; intentions are important; punishment is evaluated in terms of the overall social system. In development, heteronomous morality precedes reciprocal morality.

Morality in games

In the games that children play there is evidence of these two types of morality succeeding one another. In the game of hide-and-seek, for example, young children are firmly attached to the rules of the game and cannot really understand that the rules could be changed. The rules are seen as having a divine or at least parental origin, that has nothing to do with the convenience of the players.

> MOL (6; 6) Are there things you must do and things you mustn't do in this game? — *Yes. The things you must do are the rules of the game.* — Could you invent a new rule? . . . Supposing you said that the third who plunged was "he"? — *Yes.* — Would it be all right to play that way or not? — *It'd be all right.* — Is it a fair rule like the others? — *Less fair* — Why? — *Because the last one has to be "he."* — And if everyone played that way, would it become a fair rule? — *No.* — Why? — *Because the game isn't like that.* — How did the

rules begin? . . . How do you know how to play? — *I learned the first time. I didn't know how. We played with a little girl who told us.* — And how did the little girl know? — *She learned.* — And did your Mummy play when she was little? — *Yes. The school teacher taught her.* — But how did it begin? — *People learned with the school teacher.* — Who made up the rules, grown-ups or children? — *Grown-ups.* — And if a child invents a new rule, is that all right? — *No, it isn't.* — Why not? — *Because they don't know how to.*

AGE (7) (Admits that the third child to be caught could be regarded as "he," but she refuses to recognize this new rule as fair.) Is it a real rule? — *Yes.* — Is it fair? — *No. Because that is not the way you play.* — (The conversation is resumed after break.) Would that new rule be all right? — *No, because the first one who is caught has to be "he."* — Why? — *Because otherwise it wouldn't be fair.* — But if everyone played like that? — *It wouldn't do because the third mustn't be "he."*

BON (7) (Admits that her companions would be pleased with such an innovation, but this would be not fair.) Why? — *Because it upsets the whole game, because it's wrong.*

ROS (8; 6) (Invents a new rule.) *You might say that only one goes and hides and then the others would go and look for her.* — Would that be all right for playing? — *Yes.* — Is this new way fairer than the other way or less fair? — *Less fair.* — Why? — *Because you don't play with that one.* — But if everyone played that way? — *Then it would be just a little bit fair.* — Why a little bit? — *Because, after all, it is a little the same way.* — But it isn't quite fair? — *No.* — Why? . . . And if everyone agreed to play that way would it be the same, or would it not? — *It would be all right* (reluctantly). — Which is best, always to play the same way or to change? — *To change* (still reluctantly). — Why? — *Because that game is truer.* — Which one? — *Not the one I made up.* — Then is it best to change it or to leave it as it is? — *Best to leave it.* — (The game of "ilet cachant" has been invented by "a Gentleman.") Has it been changed since then, or is it the same as when it was invented? — *Yes, it hasn't been changed.* — But if people want to, they can change it? — *Yes.* — Can children? — *Yes.* — If they invent something will it be more fair or less fair? — *Less fair.* — Why? — *Because it isn't the real game.* — What is the real game? — *The one the gentleman invented.* — Why? — *Because that is the one you always play.*

LIL (8; 10) How did the game begin the very first time of all? — *I think a lady invented it.* — Do you think the game has changed since then? — *People may have changed it.* — Who changed it, grown-ups or children? — *Grown-ups.* — But do you think children can change it? — *Yes, they can.* — Could you, for instance, if you wanted to? — *Oh, if I wanted to, yes.* — Would it do or would it not do? — *It would do just as well.* — Would your friends be pleased? — *They'd be just as pleased.* — Would it be as fair or less fair? — *Less fair.* — Fair in what way? — *I think the lady who invented it invented it better.* — Why? — *Because grown-ups are cleverer, because they have been at school longer than children.*

Despite this, as Piaget observes, young children are quite ready to cheat in a hide-and-seek game by looking when the others are hiding, and so on. The situation is quite different with older children, as the following answers will make clear.

> BAG (10; 4) (She is asked to judge a new rule suggested by one of her companions and which consists in not "struggling" when you are caught.) Is it just as fair or less fair? — *Just as fair.* — Is it a real rule or not? — *A real rule.* — What is a real rule? — *It's something you play at really and truly.* — But no one has played yet with the rule invented by your friend; is it real all the same, or not? — *It is real.* — Would it work? — *Yes.* — Would your friends be pleased or not? — *Not pleased, because they'd never want to be "he"* (in that way). — And if they agreed about it, would it be fair or not? — *Yes.*

> CHO (9) Is this rule as real as the others? — *No.* — Why? — *Because you never play that way.* — Would it be all right to play that way? — *Yes.* — Would your friends like it? — *Yes.* — Is this new rule more fair or less fair than the other? — *Both the same.* — Which is the most real? — *Both the same.* — How did rules begin? — *Somebody invented them.* — Who? — *A child . . . There were some kids who were playing and the others did the same thing.* — Were the rules those children made fair? — *Yes.* — When is a rule fair? — *When it's all right for playing.* — When is it real? — *When it's all right for playing.*

The rules of the game are now cooperatively worked out. Any rule that preserves the game is as good as any other rule, and the better the game the better the rule. Also, since the rules are something that the children see as devised by themselves to permit cooperative play, is it not surprising that they are better observed at the (later) cooperative stage than at the (earlier) heteronomous stage.

Lying

The odd effects of a morality shaped by adult constraint are expressed even more clearly in children's views on lying. These views were studied by means of little stories containing various types of deceit. Consider the following two stories.

> A little boy [or a little girl] goes for a walk in the street and meets a big dog who frightens him very much. So then he goes home and tells his mother he has seen a dog that was as big as a cow.

> A child comes home from school and tells his mother that the teacher had given him good marks, but it was not true; the teacher had given him no marks at all, either good or bad. Then his mother was very pleased and rewarded him.

The first contains a palpable inaccuracy (even the biggest Swiss dog is not as big as a cow), but one that obviously is not intended to deceive. By contrast, the second contains a lie that is not obvious and does exemplify intention to deceive. Which is the worse lie in the eye of the child?

> FEL (6) (Repeats the two stories correctly.) Which of these two children is naughtiest? — *The little girl who said she saw a dog as big as a cow.* — Why is she the naughtiest? — *Because it could never happen.* — Did her mother believe her? — *No, because they never are* [dogs as big as cows]. — Why did she say that? — *To exaggerate.* — And why did the other one tell a lie? — *Because she wanted to make people believe that she had a good report.* — Did her mother believe her? — *Yes.* — Which would you punish most if you were the mother? — *The one with the dog because she told the worst lies and was the naughtiest.*

> BUG (6) Which is naughtiest? — *The one with the cow.* — Why is he the naughtiest? — *Because it isn't true.* — And the one of the good marks? — *He is less naughty.* — Why? — *Because his mother would have believed, because she believed the lie.* (This is not a slip. We have met with many cases of children of 6–7 who, like FEL and BUG, measure the naughtiness of a lie by the degree of its incredibility to adults. Consequently the lie about the good marks is not so bad because the mother will be easily taken in by it!) — And why did the other child tell the lie about the cow? — *Because he was telling his mother a lie.* — Which would you punish most? — *The one who said he saw a dog as big as a cow.*

These answers make it quite clear that for the child who is still at the stage of heteronomous morality deeds are good or bad depending on their consequences or probable consequences with adults. A bad lie is one that will not be believed, and so will probably be punished. A lie that is believed and even rewarded by an adult is not really naughty at all. In view of the average child's experience with the average adult, this bizarre morality is perhaps hardly surprising. The answers of older children were dramatically different.

> LOUR (8) Which is the naughtiest? — *The one who told about the teacher.* — Why is he the naughtiest? — *Because a dog like that doesn't exist and because it is naughtier to tell a lie.* (Thus, LOUR reverses the argumentation used by the previous subjects, and from the fact that a dog is never as big as a cow he concludes that to exaggerate in this way is not to lie.) — Why did the one with the teacher tell a lie? — *So that his mother should reward him.* — And the other one? — *For a joke* (Fr: *blague*). — Which would you punish most? — *The one who said what the teacher hadn't said.*

> PIT (9; 3) (The naughtiest is the one of the teacher) *because he said he had been very good so that his mother should give him some pennies or some chocolate.* — And why did the other one say he had seen a dog as big as a cow? — *Because he thought a cow was a dog and because his brain wasn't working properly.*

Here the very improbability of the "dog as big as a cow" story makes it forgiveable, since it is not likely to deceive. The other lie, deliberately deceitful and successful in its effect, is viewed as worse. The role of intent in the evaluation of action is brought out yet more clearly by the following pair of stories.

> A child who didn't know the names of streets very well was not quite sure where the Rue de Carouge was (a street near the school where we were working). One day a gentleman stopped him in the street and asked him where the Rue de Carouge was, so the boy answered, "I think it is there." But it was not there. The gentleman completely lost his way and could not find the house he was looking for.

> A boy knows the names of the streets quite well. One day a gentleman asks him where the Rue de Carouge is. But the boy wanted to play him a trick and said, it is there, and showed him the wrong street. But the gentleman didn't get lost, and managed to find his way again.

Young children view the innocent boy in the first story as the naughty one because his act resulted in the man getting lost. The malicious intent of the child in the second story was completely ignored. The older children completely reversed these evaluations, even though they thought adults might not agree with them. A child seven and a half years old makes this point when asked what would happen if the two men were to meet their respective guides again.

> . . . *One of the gentlemen would scold the boy* (more than the other). — Which gentleman? — *The one who didn't find his way.* — Would he be right? — *No, he wouldn't be right, because the boy didn't know the way.*

Among younger children behaviors are only good or bad in so far as they are likely to be punished by adults. Piaget asked his subjects why people should not tell lies. For the younger subjects the only reason was that lying resulted in punishment.

> ZAMB (6) Why must we not tell lies? — *Because God punishes them.* — And if God didn't punish them? — *Then we could tell them.*

> ROC (7) What happens when you tell lies? — *You get punished.* — And if you didn't get punished, would it be naughty to tell them? — *No.* — I'm going to tell you two stories. There were two kiddies and they broke a cup each. The first one says it wasn't him. His mother believes him and doesn't punish him. The second one also says that it wasn't him. But his mother doesn't believe him and punishes him. Are both lies that they told equally naughty? — *No.* — Which is the naughtiest? — *The one who was punished.*

BURD (7) (He tells us, in connection with the stories of the dog and the school teacher, as we saw in the preceding paragraph, that the lie which the mother knows is untrue is the worst. Then he adds spontaneously the following curious explanation.) *What she knows is the worst.* — Why? — *Because when she knows then she can scold at once. When she doesn't know she can't scold at once. The child doesn't know why he is being scolded. He doesn't remember any more.* — But when is a child naughtiest, when he is scolded at once or when he is not scolded at once? — *He is naughtier when he is scolded at once.*

If a lie is not punished then it is not a lie at all. By contrast, for the older children a lie is wrong because it violates the social bond and the principles of reciprocity.

DIN (8, but precocious) Why must we not lie? — *Because if everyone lied no one would know where they were.*

AUF (9) Why is it naughty to tell a lie? — *Because mother believes it.* (Exactly the opposite criterion from that used by the little ones.)

LOC (10) Why is it naughty to tell a lie? — *Because you can't trust people any more.*

KEI (10) (The lie about the school teacher is worse than the lie about the dog because) *the one about the teacher you couldn't know* (that it was a lie).

Young as they are, the older children are aware that social life and social order are based on mutual respect and trust, and that lying strikes at the very foundations of this reciprocity.

Ideas of fairness and justice show a similar transformation; adult commands are always seen as fair by young children, whereas they may be seen as unfair by older children. The following stories were presented to children of various ages.

I. Once there was a camp of Boy Scouts (or Girl Guides). Each one had to do his bit to help with the work and leave things tidy. One had to do the shopping, another washed up, another brought in wood or swept the floor. One day there was no bread and the one who did the shopping had already gone. So the Scoutmaster asked one of the Scouts who had already done his job to go and fetch the bread. What did he do?

II. One Thursday afternoon, a mother asked her little girl and boy to help her about the house, because she was tired. The girl was to dry the plates and the boy was to fetch in some wood. But the little boy (or girl) went and played in the street. So the mother asked the other one to do all the work. What did he say?

III. Once there was a family with three brothers, one older one and two who were twins. They all used to black their boots every morning. One day the big one was ill. So the mother asked one of the others to black his boots as well as his own. What do you think of that?

IV. A father had two boys. One of them always grumbled when he was sent messages. The other one didn't like being sent either, but he always went without saying a word. So the father used to send the boy who didn't grumble on messages oftener than the other one. What do you think of that?

The youngest children all agreed that the child in the story should obey the adult request, as these answers show.

BAR (6; 6) Story I: *She ought to have gone to get the bread.* — Why? — *Because she had been told to.* — Was it fair or not fair to have told her to go? — *Yes, it was fair, because she had been told to.*

ZUR (6; 6) Story I: *He ought to have gone.* — Why? — *To obey.* — Was it fair, what he had been asked to do? — *Yes. It was his boss, his chief.* Story II: *He should have gone.* — Why? — *Because his sister was disobedient. He ought to be kind.*

HEP (7) Story I: Was it fair what she was asked to do? — *It was fair because she had to go.* — Even though it was not her job? — *Yes, she had been told to go.* Story II: *It was fair because her mother had told her to.*

ZIG (8) Story II: *He ought to have done both things because his brother wouldn't.* — Is it fair? — *It is very fair. He is doing a good deed.* (Zig seems not to know the meaning of the word "fair". But he has given us elsewhere an unequal division as an example of unfairness. In this Story II, therefore, what is just is identified with what is in conformity with obedience.)

Older children, by contrast, do not see an adult command as necessarily legitimate. Fairness is no longer *inherent* in adult commands, as these answers show.

DOL (8) Story III: *It wasn't fair. They should each have been given one boot.* — But the mother had said they must. — *The other one should have been given a boot.* — Ought they to do as they were told, or divide things equally? — *They should have asked their mother.* Story IV: *It's not fair. The father should have asked the other one too.* — But that is what the father had said. — *It's not fair.* — What should the boy have done? Gone the messages, or not gone, or told the father to send the other boy? — *He should have done nothing. Not gone.*

CLA (9; 8) Story II: *She ought to have done her own work and not the other one's.* — Why not? — *It wasn't fair.* Story I: *She oughtn't to have done it. It was not her job to do it.* — Was it fair to do it? — *No, it was not fair.*

SCHN (12) Story II: *She shouldn't have done it. It's not fair that she should work twice as hard and not the other.* — What was to be done? — *She should have said to her mother, "It's not fair. I ought not to do double the work."*

The oldest children showed an even more complex understanding, an awareness that even unfairness must sometimes be accepted in the interest of the common good.

PER (11; 9) Story I: *He went to fetch some.* — Was it fair? — *It wasn't fair, but it was obliging.*

BALT (11; 9) Story II: *She did it.* — What did she think? — *That her brother was not very nice.* — Was it fair that she should do this? — *It wasn't fair, but she did it to help her mother.*

CHAP (12; 8) (Answers with regard to Story I that "he thought his chief was a nuisance," but in connection with Story II he says) *It depends on whether he's a good boy. If he is fond of his mother, he will do it; otherwise he'll do the same as his sister so as not to have to work any harder than her.*

PED (12; 5) (Makes the distinction which seems to us to characterize the present type most clearly, and this in connection with Story I.) *He must go and fetch the bread.* — What did he think? — *My master orders me to; I must help him.* — Was it fair? — *Yes, it was fair because it was from obedience. It wasn't quite fair if he was made to go, but if he accepted to, it was fair.* (One could not formulate better the principle of autonomy which characterizes the attitude we are speaking of: if you are forced to do something against equality, it is unjust, but if you accept to do a service, you are doing something superior to strict justice, and you are behaving with equity towards your chief.)

GIL (12) Story II: *He wasn't pleased.* — Did he do it? — *Oh, yes.* — Was it fair? — *No.* — Why did he do it? — *To please his mother.*

FRI (12, female) Story II: *She might have refused. She thought that her brother would go and have a good time and that she would have to work.* — Was it fair or not to do it? — *Not fair.* — Would you have done it or not? — *I would have done it to please my mother.*

The proportions of children of various ages who found the adult requests in these stories acceptable are as follows:

Age	6	7	8	9	10	11	12
Percent	95	55	33.3	16.6	10	5	0

This decline clearly parallels the decline in compliance with adults described earlier (pp. 343ff). At the same time, ideas of reciprocity, cooperation, and equity between peers are gaining strength. As Piaget says, "equalitarian justice develops with age at the expense of submission to adult authority and in correlation with solidarity between children."

MORAL DEVELOPMENT
AFTER CHILDHOOD

Piaget's investigation of moral judgment stopped with children of about 12 years of age. As we saw earlier, the oldest children in Piaget's sample were well aware of the fact that game rules are established simply by convention. They were quite able to envision changing the rules of the game. The rules were there only to allow the game to be played, and were justified on the basis of equality and reciprocity. The next stage of moral development extends this to all societal rules. All laws and social conventions are acceptable only in so far as they are accepted by a majority in the society and attain the greatest good for the greatest numbers. Their force comes from this acceptance. At the same time, laws are seen as having only a relative validity. This relativism can become extreme in some cases, so extreme as to make all laws seem arbitrary. Kohlberg (1963) found some examples of extreme relativism, given in response to the following dilemma.

> In Europe, a woman was near death from a very bad disease, a special kind of cancer. There was one drug that the doctors thought might save her. It was a form of radium that a druggist in the same town had recently discovered. The drug was expensive to make, but the druggist was charging ten times what the drug cost him to make. He paid $200 for the radium and charged $2,000 for a small dose of the drug. The sick woman's husband, Heinz, went to everyone he knew to borrow the money, but he could only get together about $1,000 which was half of what it cost. He told the druggist that his wife was dying, and asked him to sell it cheaper or let him pay later. But the druggist said, "No, I discovered the drug and I'm going to make money from it." Heinz got desperate and broke into the man's store to steal the drug for his wife.
>
> Should the husband have done that? Was it right or wrong? Bob, a junior in a liberal, private high school, says:

>> There's a million ways to look at it. Heinz had a moral decision to make. Was it worse to steal or let his wife die? In my mind I can either condemn him or condone him. In this case I think it was fine. But possibly the druggist was working on a capitalist morality of supply and demand.

> I went on to ask Bob, "Would it be wrong if he did not steal it?"

>> It depends on how he is oriented morally. If he thinks it's worse to steal than to let his wife die, then it would be wrong what he did. It's

all relative, what I would do is steal the drug. I can't say that's right or wrong or that it's what everyone should do.

Bob started the interview by wondering if he could answer because he "questioned the whole terminology, the whole moral bag." He goes on:

> But then I'm also an incredible moralist, a real puritan in some sense and moods. My moral judgment and the way I perceive things morally changes very much when my mood changes. When I'm in a cynical mood, I take a cynical view of morals, but still whether I like it or not, I'm terribly moral in the way I look at things. But I'm not too comfortable with it.

Here are some other juniors from an upper-middle-class public high school:

> Dan: Immoral is strictly a relative term which can be applied to almost any thought on a particular subject . . . if you have a man and a woman in bed, that is immoral as opposed to if you were a Roman a few thousand years ago and you were used to orgies all the time, that would not be immoral. Things vary so when you call something immoral, it's relative to that society at that time and it varies frequently. [Are there any circumstances in which wrong in some abstract moral sense would be applicable?] Well, in that sense, the only thing I could find wrong would be when you were hurting somebody against their will.

> Elliot: I think one individual's set of moral values is as good as the next individual's . . . I think you have a right to believe in what you believe in, but I don't thing you have a right to enforce it on other people.

> John: I don't think anybody should be swayed by the dictates of society. It's probably very much up to the individual all the time and there's no general principle except when the views of society seem to conflict with your views and your opportunities at the moment and it seems that the views of society don't really have any basis as being right and in that case, most people, I think, would tend to say forget it and I'll do what I want.

Such relativism, as Kohlberg points out, does not and cannot persist, since it removes any effective guide for action, leaving the individual paralyzed in a social void. What can (but does not always) take its place is a new set of rules that are no longer concrete and specific, as social contract or legalistic rules must be. Rather, they are abstract rules from which concrete rules can be derived. These rules embody ideas of reciprocity (Do unto others . . .), equality, and mutual respect for the rights of all. The discovery of such rules solves the behavioral indecisiveness of relativism and restores an absolute necessity to moral judgment. Note that these rules, the highest expression of moral thought, are but formulations of the principles that children discover earlier and use in the course of interacting with their peers in the playground.

What does the discovery of these abstract rules have to do with compliance? A great deal it would seem. Kohlberg (1965) repeated Milgram's experiment on obedience to authority (pp. 281–282) using a group of subjects that included individuals who had attained this higher level of moral development. Over 75 percent of these individuals refused to obey the experimenter and give the shocks, a stark contrast to the vast majority of the subjects who had not attained the higher level of moral development and who did obey. Milgram's situation presented a dilemma to the subjects with the higher level of moral development. The pursuit of human knowledge is a laudable end. However, it does not have the same importance as the principle that human suffering should be prevented and so did not control the subjects' behavior.

I am arguing that the development of moral and social autonomy, a relative freedom from automatic compliance with peers and obedience to superiors, is essentially development of a set of principles that can be used to judge group norms and group and individual pressures. These principles thus provide a solution to the problem of relativism, one that permits the individual to become autonomous within his social group. This high-level autonomy is a late development. Indeed, it seems that it is not always reached (Figure 17–1). However, even the 12-year-olds in Piaget's study (p. 355) showed an awareness that compliance is a matter of individual choice and not an absolute duty. I would argue that the decline in peer compliance described above and its replacement by a relative autonomy are results of this awareness.

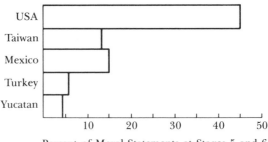

Percent of Moral Statements at Stages 5 and 6

FIGURE 17–1

Sixteen-year-old boys from various cultures were asked a number of moral questions. For example: "Should a doctor put to death a fatally ill woman who requests death because of her pain?" This graph shows the percentage of replies (in each culture) that reflected attainment of the highest levels (stages V and VI) of moral development. (Kohlberg and Gilligan, 1971.)

SOCIAL DEVELOPMENT—AN OVERVIEW

The attainment of relative autonomy within the social order marks the terminus of social development. The individual who is aware of his relations with his fellow man, the nature of the social order and the social contract, and the deeper principles that justify them, has reached a plateau or peak beyond which there seems to be no possible advance, either in theory or in fact (Kohlberg, 1964). This therefore seems an appropriate point to stop and look back upon social development as it has been outlined here.

The basic postulate of the theory that has been proposed here is that humans are basically social animals, that from birth we have a need for social interaction with others, a need that is quite independent of physiological needs. In Chapter 14 evidence was presented showing that the child enters the world with some readiness to communicate with others. Communication is the prototype of all possible social interaction—it is necessarily reciprocal, necessarily mutual, and involves at least the sharing of time. Communication is also a learned skill. In the beginning the infant's communication is largely specific to interaction with a single adult and this shuts him off from those people who do not speak his "language"; increasing skill remedies that problem, however.

In Chapter 16 we pointed out that even at the level of verbal communication it is hard for an adult to fully enter the world of the child. If more than simple communication is desired the difficulties are even greater. While not impossible, it is surely clear that it is difficult for a parent-child relation to be reciprocal. Parental commands are absolute and disobedience is not tolerated. The parent is the source of all good, and the child in his own eyes cannot reciprocate. It is only when the child enters a peer group that he can discover the possibilities of reciprocal interaction. It is only with a peer group that the child can find that rules and laws have a function in promoting group activity. The discovery of democratic consensus is really only possible in a peer group. With entry into a peer group, the child can use the reciprocity inherent in his communication skills as a model for reciprocal social activity. With the experience of reciprocal social activity the child can evaluate his relationship with his parents. To the extent that the parent-child relationship has the reciprocity that child-child relations have, the relationship will be strengthened, and vice versa. As far as compliance is concerned, we can say that the child moves from obedience to consent.

As the child's group experiences increase, he has the opportunity to learn that group rules are conventional and can be changed, that some rules are better than others, that some are just pointless and should be changed. Along with this there seems to develop an awareness of what the group does for the individual as well as the limits that must be placed on what the group may expect from the individual.

The development described thus far is necessarily social. Communication skills and the discovery of reciprocity and conventions can only occur in social groups. They require social experience. In all probability, progress beyond this point to the state of relative autonomy does not require more social experience. It seems that the individual who has reached a state of awareness of the relativism of social norms and the arbitrary nature of any specific set of rules cannot but also be aware of the utility of these norms. At this stage, which few individuals reach, progress can only be made by deduction or discovery of the root principles from which all conventions are derived. This is an intellectual discovery, which can be made alone or communicated by another. While it requires the earlier phases of development, unlike them it does not seem to require social experience.

I am proposing that social development has three phases.

1. The development of communication skills.
2. The discovery of reciprocity and the functional values of conventions.
3. The discovery of the principles from which all conventions can be derived.

Development must be ordered through this sequence. Without communication skills social interaction could not begin, and so social reciprocity could not be discovered. Until some conventions have been accepted, the idea of a deep structure for conventions can hardly occur. The first two of these phases require specific kinds of experience. Obviously, communication skills can only be developed in concert with other humans. But is it as obvious that the second phase requires peer-group experience? It cannot be so obvious since none of the major theories of social development assign peer-group experience a major role in social development in general or moral development in particular. Instead, they emphasize the role of the parents, an emphasis that is surely mistaken, given the data reviewed in this chapter. The issue is a difficult one, since we do not have access to children growing up without peers. However, we do have some data on the opposite condition: children given earlier than usual exposure to peers. Faigin (1958) found that children raised in a *kibbutz* were precocious in moral development, arriving at concepts of reciprocal justice years before Swiss or American children. By the age of three the *kibbutz* children had well-developed rules of social interaction, rules that were put to use and that all of the children were aware of. Compliance with such rules and awareness of the rules is a much later development in American children, who do not have the early peer experience of *kibbutz* children. Similar results have been reported by MacNaughton (1974). It thus appears that enhanced opportunities for peer interaction produce accelerated development, at least through the second phase of social development.

Peer-group experience would thus seem to be important for social development, in particular for the advance through the second phase to the attainment of relative autonomy. As I said above, it seems that the requirements for the last stage of social development are not social but are more probably intellectual. We will consider this issue in detail at the end of the book.

18

Adolescence
and Role Choice

Adolescence, in the Western world at least, is probably the second busiest period of development, second only to infancy in the number of critical events that can occur. Perhaps the most important event during adolescence is the choice of a role by which the individual can enter society as an independent figure, contributing to as well as taking from the larger social group. Choosing a role very much defines one's status in society. Since role choice is very much a process of self-definition, adolescence may be described as a time of self-discovery or self-creation.

SEXUAL DEVELOPMENT

The period we call adolescence is marked by a significant biological event, the onset of sexual maturity, accompanied by the appearance of secondary sexual characteristics, facial hair, pubic hair, breasts, and the dramatic changes in height, weight and body proportions that were mentioned in Chapter 1. The most significant of these changes is the sexual change. The views of some psychologists on this aspect of development are exemplified by the following statement: "With a changing body reverberating with a dramatic onslaught of the glandular system and its products, the maturing adolescent is throbbing with impulses and desires hard to contain, including sexual urges continually sensitizing the individual for consummation" (Sherif and Sherif, 1964). The same authors write, "It is well known, of course, that the social setting does set limits or bounds within which biological impulses can be carried out, heaping sanctions on the individual who transgresses these bounds. But less seldom is the positive aspect emphasized, using here the term 'positive' in a directional sense." In some contrast to this viewpoint, another pair of authors write that the increase in male sex drive is "imperious and biologically specific. The adolescent must find . . . the means of obtaining sexual discharge without excessive guilt and means of control without crippling inhibitions" (Byrne and Griffith, 1966). Girls of course are supposedly quite different: ". . . control of impulses is likely to constitute a considerably less urgent problem for girls." How such views can have survived several decades of cross-cultural research plus the dramatic changes seen in recent years within certain cultures is quite mysterious.

There is no evidence at all that the human sex drive is a biological imperative. The objects of the sex drive, the form and frequency of its expression, are all socially controlled. Cultural variations in homosexuality and heterosexuality are well known (e.g., Ford and Beach, 1951). Cultural variations in the expected or desired frequency of heterosexual activity vary from the once per five years of the Dani of New Guinea (Heider, 1974) to the once per day of young Americans. Indeed, even between geographically or linguistically much closer groups there are great variations (Table 18–1). Within any group there will be individual variation around a mean, with some individuals reducing the frequency of their sexual behavior to conform to the norm and others striving to attain it. However, individual intracultural variations are trivial beside the inter-cultural variation that has been observed. All cultures seem to assume that they are normal and that others are bizarre. The proportion of people in a culture who profess to be sexually content does not vary with the culture's norm for sexual activity, but rather with that culture's norm for complaining of sexual frustration, a variable that is independent of the culture's norm for activity (Heider, 1976). All of these results imply that the hormonal changes that introduce adolescence make sexual behavior possible but do not regulate its occurrence absolutely. Given the requisite hormones, sexual behavior seems to be as much a product of our social milieu as the language we speak.

If society determines the forms of sexual activity, how much more must it determine the secondary aspects of sexuality, namely sexual roles. Kagan (1964) described these for Western society: "In sum, females are supposed to inhibit aggression and open display of sexual urges, to be passive with men, to be nurturant to others, to cultivate attractiveness, and to maintain an affective, socially poised and friendly posture with others. Males are urged to be aggressive in face of attack, independent in problem situations, sexually aggressive, in control of regressive urges, and suppressive of strong emotion, especially anxiety." At the time this was written, girls were supposed to be domestic and their socially most acceptable role was that of wife and mother. Men, on the other hand, were supposed to work,

TABLE *18–1*

Percent of male and female college students in five countries reporting various sexual behaviors. (From Luckey and Nass, 1969. Copyright 1969 by the National Council on Family Relations. Reprinted by permission.)

	UNITED STATES		CANADA		ENGLAND		GERMANY		NORWAY	
	F	M	F	M	F	M	F	M	F	M
Light embrace or fond holding of hands	97.5%	98.6%	96.5%	98.9%	91.9%	93.5%	94.8%	93.8%	89.3%	93.7%
Casual goodnight kissing	96.8	96.7	91.8	97.7	93.0	93.5	74.0	78.6	75.0	86.1
Deep kissing	96.5	96.0	91.8	97.7	93.0	91.9	90.6	91.1	89.3	96.2
Horizontal embrace with some petting but not undressed	83.3	89.9	81.2	92.0	79.1	85.4	77.1	68.8	75.0	93.6
Petting of woman's breast area from outside her clothing	78.3	89.9	78.8	93.2	82.6	87.0	76.0	80.4	64.3	83.5
Petting of woman's breast area without clothes intervening	67.8	83.4	64.7	92.0	70.9	82.8	66.7	69.6	58.9	83.5
Petting below the waist of the woman under her clothing	61.2	81.1	64.7	85.2	70.9	84.6	63.5	70.5	53.6	83.5
Petting below the waist of both man and woman under clothing	57.8	62.9	50.6	64.8	61.6	68.3	56.3	52.7	42.9	55.1
Nude embrace	49.6	65.6	47.6	69.3	64.0	70.5	62.1	50.0	51.8	69.6
Coitus	43.2	58.2	35.3	56.8	62.8	74.8	59.4	54.5	53.6	66.7
One-night affair involving coitus; didn't date person again	7.2	29.9	5.9	21.6	33.7	43.1	4.2	17.0	12.5	32.9
Whipping or spanking before petting or other intimacy	4.5	8.2	5.9	5.7	17.4	17.1	1.0	.9	7.1	5.1
Sex on pay-as-you-go basis		4.2		4.5		13.8		9.8		2.5
Total responses	(688)	(644)	(85)	(88)	(86)	(123)	(96)	(112)	(56)	(79)

to do practical things, and to provide for a wife and children. These stereotyped roles have changed somewhat in the last 15 years, but stereotypes of male and female roles still exist and there is obvious pressure on the child well before adolescence to conform to the sex-typed roles appropriate to his or her age. At younger ages a "real" boy climbs trees, gets dirty, tears his clothes and plays war games with his friends; a "real" girl is neat and tidy, plays with dolls, and helps her mother around the house.

Dramatic evidence that these roles are learned very early in life comes from the research of Money and his associates (Money and Ehrhardt, 1972). Money worked with individuals who were assigned an incorrect biological sex at birth, because of embryological vicissitudes that affected their physical appearance at birth, without affecting their basic hormonal or chromosomal sex. Genetically male children who were raised as girls grew up to be women in the full social sense of the word. As girls they played with dolls; as they grew older they went out with boys and looked forward to marriage and full-time homemaking as their role in society. Genetically female children raised as boys grew up to be socially acceptable men. However, some of these individuals had their assigned sex changed during development, to make it consistent with the chromosomal and hormonal sex. The results were normally unfortunate unless the change was made prior to the age of three years. Children who were changed before three took the change without trauma and grew up in the appropriate gender. Those who were reassigned afterwards, by contrast, showed considerable difficulty in learning to adjust to the new role.

It would thus seem that by the age of three girls have learned the skills of being a girl and boys have learned the skills of being a boy, so that a switch of role to that of the opposite sex is difficult. If such early social specialization in fact occurs, it is hard to see how anyone other than the parents could be involved, although the mechanisms of the process are not at this time clear. There is evidence of different parental responses to babies of different sex even in the first half of the first year. For example, parents of both sexes spend far more time talking to and touching infant girls than boys (Moss, 1967; Rebelsky and Hanks, 1971). Goldberg and Lewis (1969) suggest that this produces more "girlish" behavior; talking and touching become a larger component of the social communication routine of baby girls than of baby boys. Many more studies are necessary before we will understand the details of the shaping process.

Parental influence seems to wane rapidly once the child gets to school and falls under the influence of peer groups. Mussen and Rutherford (1963) measured the masculinity of first-grade boys using the IT scale (Figure 18–1). They found it was quite unrelated to parental attempts to encourage what they considered appropriate sex-typed behavior. This is not terribly surprising. First, the choosing of social roles is as much subject

Toys

Clothes

Child figures

FIGURE 18–1

Masculinity-femininity is assessed by showing the child an IT card, a card with a sexless child figure on it. The child is then asked to choose from various other cards which toy IT would like to play with, which clothes IT wants to wear, which child it would like to play with, etc. (Brown, 1956.)

to reinforcement as any other behavior, and, following the patterns of social development in general, the peer group is a more potent source of reinforcement than parents. Second, it seems likely that the source of "male" or "female" behavior is the behavior of other boys and girls. By watching children of the same sex a child can learn by observation and imitation what the "appropriate" sex-typed behavior is. Although the mechanisms involved in such learning are mysterious at present, the process is familiar enough. Boys and girls can discover what boys and girls do by observation and imitation of others perceived as like them, far better than they ever could by heeding their parents, who have probably forgotten how six-year-olds behave, or who do not know how present-day teenagers behave. Learning by observation continues throughout life. It has been found that young adults pay more attention to the hero of a film if they are male and to the heroine if they are female (Maccoby, 1962). The idea that sex-role learning is mediated by observation could explain why it is that the correlation between parents' views of appropriate sex-typed behavior and their children's views becomes slightly significant when the children reach adulthood. Memories of parental behavior may serve as a model of adult behavior for the young adult, particularly the young parent. This may explain the observation that parents treat their children as they themselves were treated, even when they clearly remember resenting such treatment. This probably results from their following the only model for parental behavior that they have ever known, namely their own parents (Bowlby, 1951).

Sex-role learning is not a mysterious process, although it relies on mysterious mechanisms. Children at all stages of development are reinforced by approval and acceptance from parents, peers, and society at large for behaving in particular ways, ways that these various groups see as appropriate for the sex of the child. They can learn by observation of others on TV, in films, or magazines. Such learning is not necessarily permanent. Sex roles and sexually appropriate behavior can be changed. This will be discussed further in the section on role-changing below.

SOCIAL ROLE CHOICE

The most important role for adults is that associated with being a man or a woman, but the next most important is the social role, which is largely determined by occupation. The decision to take up a particular occupational role is crucial in many ways. It determines one's future life style and position in society. Society expects individuals in particular occupations to behave in particular ways, and most people do in fact follow this occupational role stereotype, at least in dress and manner (Argyle, 1969).

It is widely agreed that occupational choice is a developmental process.

The individual does not simply develop up to some age and then look around for an occupation that fits the way his or her development has gone. Rather, decisions about occupations interact with other choices in development so that by the time the occupational choice is made the individual has already to some extent fitted himself or herself for it. Ideas of occupations themselves change in parallel with the broader paths of social development. This point is brought out in a study of age-related changes in attitudes toward occupational prestige (Gunn, 1964). Gunn took 11 occupations from the North-Hatt ranking of occupations by prestige (the North-Hatt list is a very stable measure of the prestige that adults attach to various occupations):

	RANKING
Doctor	93%
Lawyer	86
Owner of a factory employing 7,100 people	82
Teacher	78
Electrician	73
Policeman	67
Garage mechanic	62
Clerk in a store	58
Filling station attendant	52
Janitor	44
Shoe shiner	33

This list was given to boys from grades one to twelve. The boys were asked to rank the occupations, their father's occupation, and their own intended occupation, and to justify their rankings. First- and second-graders did not show clear orderings of prestige; there was a number one job and the rest were often "about the same" for these children. The number one job was often their father's job and their own intended job. "Policeman" was given a very high ranking because it was seen as dangerous. One feature of these young boys' responses was that no job was denigrated.

In grades three through six there was an increasing tendency to evaluate jobs in terms of social utility, the good they do for the community at large. This fits well with what we saw of social development in the last chapter. The social service criterion was quite rigorously applied. One fourth-grader ranked his father's job, landscape architect, below filling station attendant. "It's not really needed," he said. "It just helps to make things look fancy."

Between grades seven and 10 other criteria began to emerge, in particular monetary rewards, educational requirements, and power over others, all of which became progressively more important through the twelfth grade. By the eleventh grade the boys' earlier positive attitude to all workers had disappeared. A janitor is "an old man who can't do anything else"; a service station attendant's job "is a way of making a small amount of money"; a bootblack "is fun for the feebleminded." Not unsurprisingly, boys whose fathers had these low-status jobs rated them higher than did boys whose fathers had high-status jobs, a reinjection of a personal element that was absent earlier. The attitudes characteristic of various age groups mirror social development, from the extreme of social compliance and exaltation of the group to relative autonomy. However, social utility remains a potent criterion of occupational prestige from grade three on.

The hierarchy arranged by the oldest boys in Gunn's study was virtually the same as the one arranged by adults. Prestige is obviously a potent variable in determining vocational aspirations, since, all other things being equal, most individuals would choose a high-prestige social role over one with low prestige. If we recall that high-prestige occupations are usually socially useful, this does not imply any ignoble motives.

Social constraints on role choice

Availability of a role is also important in role choice, and with increasing age there is increasing awareness that not all roles are equally available to all individuals. In particular, roles that require expensive college education are not available to those who will not have access to such education. Since parents usually have to foot the bill for preparing for a high-prestige role, it is not surprising that parental attitudes toward vocational choice are of primary importance. Vocational aspirations are one area where parent-compliance outweighs peer compliance, as Table 18–2 shows.

Many young people face a conflict between the desirability of a role and its availability, a conflict that seems to be resolved by reducing *cognitive dissonance*. The theory of cognitive dissonance holds that when humans simultaneously hold two contradictory (dissonant) beliefs, the more malleable belief will shift so as to reduce the dissonance (Festinger, 1957).

TABLE *18–2*
Percent of teenagers aspiring to high-status occupations as a function of peer and parental pressures. (Simpson, 1962.)

OCCUPATIONAL ADVICE OFFERED BY PARENTS/PEERS	SOCIAL CLASS OF RESPONDENTS	
	WORKING CLASS	MIDDLE CLASS
Parents high, peers high*	71.4%	81.9%
Parents high, peers low	55.6	78.0
Peers high, parents low	35.7	72.5
Peers low, parents low	25.6	30.1

* High = advise high-status occupations; low = advise low-status occupations.

When there is conflict between desirability and availability of occupational roles, the more available occupations gain in prestige while less available occupations lose prestige. In one study (Caro, 1966), middle-class and working-class boys in senior high school ranked two sets of occupations of different prestige. On a seven-point scale, in which one was the highest value, the mean rating of high-prestige occupations was 2.65 and low-prestige occupations 3.89. Taking each group of boys separately, however, it could be seen that a higher than average value had been placed on those occupations that would in fact be available to them. Middle-class boys, who could expect to attain high-prestige occupations, rated such occupations at 2.29 (i.e., higher than the overall mean) while working-class boys, who could expect only lower-prestige jobs, rated low-prestige jobs at 3.49 (again, higher than the mean of the group as a whole). Gunn's study (1964) indicates that these differences probably are a result of reduction of cognitive dissonance. In her study, tenth-graders of upper- and lower-class background approximated the average adult ranking of occupations. However, there were significant class-related deviations by the eleventh and twelfth grades. For example, upper-class boys ranked "teacher" above "factory owner," whereas lower-class boys ranked the same role below "electrician." Some growing awareness of the practical realities of role choice undoubtedly contributed to these shifts.

It is obvious enough that no one will choose an occupation that he does not know to exist. What is not so obvious is the way this ignorance perpetuates social class divisions, even in societies where education for example is available to all, with subsidy, if required (Hudson, Johnston, and Jacot, 1972; Hudson, Jacot, and Sheldrake, 1973). Perceived availability should, in an ideal world, encompass all available choices, and the steps necessary to attain them. This information should be made available to adolescents as they make critical decisions about future occupations. In England 14-year-olds make choices about school subjects that determine whether or not, some four years later, they will be able to enter university and, if they do, what subjects they will be able to study. These vital choices are often made in complete ignorance of their probable consequences. A similar situation occurs in the United States, where many high-school students make choices that divert them from a path that will lead to their desired occupation (Super and Overstreet, 1960).

Sexual constraints on role choice

The most obvious victims of social restriction of role choice are women. If society sees women primarily as wives and mothers, it would not be surprising that growing girls would make many critical decisions during development that would make them unsuitable for any occupation other than that of wife and mother. Academic competitiveness, for example, is viewed as unfeminine and seems to decline somewhat in girls between 6–10 years and adulthood (Kagan and Moss, 1962). The change in relative academic performance is even more striking, with girls outperforming boys up to fourth grade and dropping significantly behind by late adolescence. Kagan suggests that this reflects sex-typing pressures. Particularly intriguing is his hypothesis that early school activities—reading, writing, painting, singing—are seen as feminine, whereas high-school activities are seen as masculine. Milton (1957) found that in high school and college girls performed significantly less well on mathematical problems than did boys, unless the problems were put in a feminine way. Here are two sample problems with their "feminine" versions.

The problem presented below is how to arrange the position of the three small rectangles, A, B, and C, in the large rectangle, so that the large rectangle can be divided exactly in half. Each half of the large rectangle must contain one A, one B, and one C rectangle. What is the minimum of small rectangles which must be moved? Show how the large rectangle would be divided.

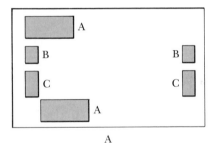

A

Two roommates want to rearrange their furniture so that each would have exactly one half of the room. The present furniture arrangement is given below. What is the minimum number of pieces of furniture they will have to move? Show how the room would be divided.

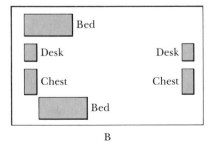

B

Suppose a simple organism, like an amoeba, divides into two once every three minutes. Every new organism divides into two every three minutes. A single amoeba is placed in a jar and in one hour the jar is filled with amoebae. How long will it take to fill the jar if we start with two amoebae instead of one?

Suppose that you are interested in how fast a rumor spreads through a girls' dormitory. One girl can tell another girl the news once in three minutes. Every new girl can tell another girl the news once in three minutes. If one girl gets a piece of information it takes one hour for the news to get all around the dorm. How long will it take for a rumor to cover the whole dorm if two girls hear it at the same time?

These slight changes were enough to improve the performance of the female subjects in Milton's study, indicating surely that schoolgirls do inhibit their intellectual performance, unless the exercise of it is seen as consonant with the "feminine" sex type. This inhibition can be manifested in self-imposed restrictions in the choice of subjects in high school, which would lead to less freedom of choice in college, and eventually to restricted possibilities of vocational choice. The conventionality of these choices is shown by their cultural relativity. American girls avoid physics and chemistry as "unfeminine." Oriental girls prefer them, even if they are being educated in American colleges (*The Guardian*, August 29, 1978).

The potency of sex-role constraints on women's academic performance is shown in an experiment by Horner (1970). She presented college women with the sentence, "After first-term finals, Ann finds herself at the top of her medical school class." They were asked to complete the stories. The stories produced showed a strong fear of success.

1. Fear of social rejection. This reaction appeared most frequently. The negative affect and consequences described were rooted mainly in affiliative concerns, including fear of being socially rejected and fear of losing one's friends or one's datability or marriageability. Fear of isolation or loneliness as a result of the success, as well as the desire to keep the success a secret and pretend that intelligence is not there, were also included. The following are examples of stories in this category.

Anne has a boyfriend, Carl, in the same class, and they are quite serious. Anne met Carl at college, and they started dating about their sophomore year in undergraduate school. Anne is rather upset and so is Carl. She wants him to be higher scholastically than she is. Anne will deliberately lower her academic standing the next term, while she does all she subtly can to help Carl. His grades come up and Anne soon drops out of med school. They marry and he goes on in school while she raises their family.

Anne doesn't want to be number one in her class. She feels she shouldn't rank so high because of social reasons. She drops down to ninth in the class and then marries the boy who graduates number one.

2. Concern about one's normality or femininity. This group comprises stories in which negative affect and consequences are free of any affiliative concern and independent of whether anyone finds out about the success. Typical reactions in this category include doubting one's femininity, feeling guilt or despair about the success, and wondering about one's normality.

> Anne is completely ecstatic but at the same time feels guilty. She wishes that she could stop studying so hard, but parental and personal pressures drive her. She will finally have a nervous breakdown and quit med school and marry a successful young doctor.

In another study the same sentence was given and the girls asked to describe Anne. She was described as:

1. Snotty, conniving, goody-goody, conceited, brainy, tall.
2. Hard-working, devoted. Wears long skirts. Not feminine; tall, straight. Doesn't go out.
3. Masculine looking. Has short hair. Straight—doesn't smoke dope. Very smart, very competitive with men, not unattractive. Dates, but not a steady boyfriend.
4. Quiet, until you get her going; meticulous—goes overboard in this way, not terribly concerned about her appearance. If she does go out, she probably goes out with older men or else she doesn't go out. Med students may be friends but only that. Not more intelligent than boys in her class but more willing to "grub" and do work. Driven person; maybe a liberal but not radical. Don't think she's examined whether it's all worthwhile.

Horner's conclusion that between junior high and college intelligent women acquire a motive to avoid academic success in order to remain feminine does not seem unreasonable.

The problems of women in choosing social roles are patently obvious and have received a great deal of study during the past decade. There are similar problems for men who wish to enter occupations classified as feminine, problems that have received less study than they deserve. Minority groups almost certainly are pressed in similar ways.

ROLE CHANGE

One of the most interesting characteristics of role selection is that it does not in fact seem to be totally irreversible. As Argyle (1969) has observed, fulfilling social expectations for a particular role is a process that is continually monitored by society. Deviations from behavior considered appropriate to a particular role are communicated, not always explicitly, so that the individual can correct his behavior; if he does not choose to correct his behavior, he can change his role. Discovering a new role for oneself is not so easy, but with skilled help can be accomplished.

One of the most fascinating approaches to role change was that developed by Kelly (1955). Kelly emphasized that a person is what he does. No matter how wonderful a person is inside, it is his deeds that define him in the eyes of others. By changing his behavior an individual can change the way other people see him and thus find a new and possibly more satisfying role. Kelly manipulated role changes in a very direct way. For example, one individual described himself (in the third person) in the following way.

CHESTER ULRATH

Chester is a very intelligent person and would possibly be capable of considerable and noteworthy achievement if it were not for his undisciplined personality and personality problems. His emotional life is rather retarded due to his unfortunate experiences in youth, and he tends to be somewhat childish emotionally. He is sometimes disturbed by little distractions, such as irritating noises, people talking loud in the library, etc. His main emotional difficulty seems to manifest itself as a paranoic outlook toward life. Nothing infuriates him more than being treated as if he wasn't worth much or doesn't count. When he is disturbed, his paranoid tendency can be quite pronounced, and, for example, he may interpret the negligence or inadequacy of another person, in a situation, as a personal "slap" at him—although the offender may really not intend this at all. In justice to him, however, it must be said that his paranoid tendencies do not appear too strongly unless he is provoked by a real incident or is in a disturbed or a depressed state. His other big emotional weakness is his tendency to become depressed for intervals of time. Something can depress him and he will remain depressed for a week or so. This interferes with his ability to concentrate and work well. Since marriage, however, this tendency to become depressed has not been as strong as it used to be. The depressive periods are not dangerous or especially involved, but they do interfere with his outlook and efficiency.

On the positive side of the picture, he has an excellent sense of humor much of the time; he has a sympathetic outlook toward others' problems, and he has very good insight into himself, which mitigates, somewhat, his emotional problems and undesirable tendencies.

He is shy in his social behavior, especially towards some types of girls. He therefore does not associate socially as much as he should, and so he has few personal friends. He mistrusts many people he does not know well, and has inhibited relations with them. However, in recent years, he has deliberately tried to improve his social participation and has had some success. His understanding and attitude toward people has improved and is improving.

His early life was somewhat unfortunate. His mother—was a very neurotic but loving person who was extremely overprotective, and who interfered with his social development in play groups. His father was a very kind man who showered him with everything within his means, but who did not understand him very well. He got along quite well with his parents, but due to his mother's shielding, he rebelled from her supervision during his last years of grade school.

His school and college records were better than average, but did not reflect his real intelligence, due to his emotional disturbances and the resulting inability to concentrate or work consistently. However, since his marriage, his ability has manifested itself in a high level of college work. He excels the majority of students in his classes when he works well. He is confused about his future career, and is a little scared to go out and compete for success as the supporter of a family. He has the capacity and background for an academic career, but does not like the seclusion, withdrawal, and lack of human interest that is involved in many academic fields. This vocation also might interfere with his attempt to achieve a more effective adjustment to society, and for these reasons he may reject this career. On the other hand, he feels that his social inhibitions would interfere with his effort to reach the top in a more applied field, such as the ministry. In any case, he will need independence in his work; he detests hierarchical systems with their petty rivalries and their petty tyrants.

His marriage is successful, and, for the most part, has been a source of increased security and happiness to him. There were many marriage problems at first, but the majority of them have been handled quite well. Although both he and his wife are somewhat neurotic, they are quite well matched in that they meet the vital personality needs of each other, and understand each other rather well. He is far from the ideal marriage partner, however, because he tends to be domineering, possessive, sometimes jealous, and overly sensitive. His possessiveness and jealousy, although he masters them fairly well now, may inhibit his capacity to be a good father. If he continues to become more secure, as he has been doing, he may be able to control these selfish tendencies more in the future.

Obviously, Chester was discontented with himself. Kelly invented a new role for him, that of Timothy Ellman.

TIMOTHY ELLMAN

At least once a day Timothy Ellman has to pinch himself to make sure that what has happened to him is real. So much of what has happened to him he had never believed could really come true. Many a time as a child he used to daydream about going to a great university and sharing the exciting company of scholars, but in his heart he never really believed it could come true. But for Timothy reality has outrun imagination!

One of the most surprising events in Tim's adventure has been the discovery of the fascinating person who consented to become his wife. Their marriage has provided a never ending source of new interests and new experience for both of them. He has come to see his wife as more fascinating than he had ever believed any woman could be, but even more surprising to him is his discovery that she appears to find him fascinating also.

Tim faces the future with wide-eyed and simple trust. It would never occur to him to deface it by trying to carve his own initials conspicuously upon it. If the future from this point on is only half as generous as she has been in the past, he will continue to count himself as the most fortunate of men. He finds himself impatient for the future to reveal what she has in store for him next, career, responsibilities, family, children, new friends he awaits with breathless anticipation.

In this setting Tim's response to friends and social situations is one of rapt and spontaneous interest. Each new revelation of a colleague's ideas causes him to pause and think. Thus his conversation has a deep undertone of unhurried thoughtfulness and empathy with the other person.

His inner life is not wholly without turmoil. One of the things, for example, which causes him concern is the possibility that people will be misled into thinking of him as being a more technically competent and sophisticated person than he really is. He is constitutionally opposed to taking on any "intellectual" front. For him "intellectualism" comes perilously close to destroying the rich vitality of life.

Chester was asked for the next two weeks to act the part of Timothy Ellman.

It is suggested that the role be played out as completely as circumstances will permit during a two-week period. The role player should read it three times a day, eat it, sleep it, think of himself by the new name, feel as the new character would feel, and generally commit himself wholly to the role. It is hoped that the role player will keep daily notes on his experiences.

This seems very artificial, and indeed that was Chester's first response, as this excerpt from his diary shows.

May 23 Wed. (first conference). My first look at Timothy. I felt like I was trying on a new suit that was the wrong color and size. I did not yet understand what kind of a person Timothy really is, and had some hostility to the role. The role seemed very incomplete. How does Timothy act in situations not covered by the role? Is Timothy a spineless, weak individual (has he character) or not? Is his wife really a "fascinating" type of person? I felt difficulty in playing the role. How can I be concerned about being thought more competent than I really am?

However by May 26, Chester was able to write the following:

While the aspects of Timothy's personality can be applied, it is difficult to think of myself as Timothy because of the interference of old habit patterns. I played the role rather well with some of my wife's friends who visited us for the week-end. I felt rather at ease doing this. The social situation was good in this case and I felt relatively successful in acting as Timothy.

May 27 Sun. Same situation as yesterday. After the guests left, my wife complimented me on getting along with the guests so well. I felt that I was accepted by these people.

Finally, he could write:

> The important things that I got out of this experience are: one, that a person can improve his adjustment to life by emotionally redefining his world and his role in it, and, two, several specific ways in which I can redefine my world and my role in it, and, three, the actual experiencing of the results of such a redefinition, demonstrating to me, to some extent, that continued effort in emotionally redefining my world would bring increased happiness and emotional maturity.

Of course, Chester was given a great deal of help in formulating his new behaviors. Perhaps Timothy was not so different from Chester. However, Kelly cites numerous examples of much greater role changes. One was a woman seen by her teacher-training supervisor as too stupid for anything save caretaking, but who within a year was urged by others to continue towards a Ph.D. degree. The effect of others' evaluations on intellectual performance is an important, if controversial, issue (Rosenthal and Jacobson, 1968; Jensen, 1969). What Kelly's research shows is that an individual can change his own behavior and thereby change both the way other people see him and his social role.

Changing roles can be as difficult as changing one's eye color. The successful lawyer who wishes to become a schoolteacher will probably manage it easily. But the high-school dropout who wishes to become a successful lawyer faces more difficulty. Nevertheless, role taking, a developmental process, permits us the luxury found nowhere else in development of retracing old paths and taking a new one. Thus, although the adolescent is pressed and pushed into particular roles, he retains some choice about the vocational and social roles he will play and is not locked into a permanent social role by the expectations of his immediate social group. Flexibility, however, depends on the availability of information about other roles and an awareness that one can change. Lacking either of these two, the individual can no more change his role than his eye color.

VI

In this section we shall be concerned with individual differences in social development, those characteristics of an individual we refer to when we speak of personality. These differences are often seen as the result of gene expression. On the evidence reviewed here this seems rather unlikely. Instead, differences in personality are seen as the result of individual differences in experience, a process akin to the one we described in the section on cognitive development, which leads to individual systems of belief about people.

19

Problems of Personality Theory

The study of personality and its development is the branch of psychology that has received the most popular attention. For many people psychology *is* the study of personality. It is by way of such famous students of personality as Freud that most laymen form their ideas about psychology. In previous chapters the word "personality" has been used in a commonsense way. In this chapter we will discuss the technical uses of the word.

What is it that a psychologist who studies personality tries to study? The belief that motivated personality studies, at least until recently, was that there are a few stable characteristics of persons that determine their behavior in diverse situations. By defining a person in terms of these few characteristics, it was hoped that one could predict the behavior of the person in any, or at least many, specific situations. A description of an individual in terms of such characteristics was a description of the individual's personality. In everyday life we use many words to describe the personalities of people we meet. There are more than 17,000 words in English that can be used to describe personality. If pressed we can usually specify some incident to justify a description. If we describe someone as bad tempered, for example, we can usually dredge up an instance of "bad-tempered behavior." The scientific study of personality has largely consisted of an attempt to find a few terms to serve for the enormous variety available in the language. It was hoped these few terms would describe enduring aspects of a person, perhaps even aspects of his brain structure or brain chemistry, that controlled the way the individual *could* behave in any specific situation. Some theorists have therefore happily assumed that they could describe innate unchanging characteristics. Others have assumed that what they call personality has a developmental origin. All have believed, however, that by some age, perhaps 20, personality is "set like concrete." Along with this there is a necessary pessimism about the possibility of change in personality, about the possibilities of psychotherapy, and about our ability to help those unhappy individuals who are classified as having an *abnormal* personality (Laing, 1959).

The net result of this approach has been a large number of personality tests. These tests have been reviewed in great detail by a number of authors. I feel it is fair to say that these tests have not been very useful. They have not predicted behavior significantly well outside of the test situations themselves. I mention them mainly because the tests are used, in theory at least, to determine personality attributes that the individual himself is supposed to be quite unaware of. A significant assumption of traditional personality theory is that the individual is unaware of the basic determinants of his own personality, which are presumed to lie in the *unconscious*. Thus, if some individual seems in need of help, or indeed comes asking for help, his own explanations of why he needs help are not likely to be heeded.

The concept of the unconscious has been of great significance in psychology. Indeed, this idea has been one of the most significant factors shaping the life of men in the twentieth century. However, it has not proved useful in studies of personality. The idea that the individual is driven by motives of which he is unaware, viewing the world so to speak through spectacles he does not know he has on, has not been as profitable as it should be, either for the explanation of individual behavior or for the cure of aberrant behavior. With respect to developmental psychology the idea has been worse than useless, since it has led to the study of development via adult recollections rather than direct observation of children. The significance of adult recollection is in the recovery of "unconscious memories"; such "memories" are regarded as realizations of desires that were themselves "unconscious," and not true memories of actual events. The multiple levels of "unconsciousness" involved in such reconstructions must, at the very least, make the validity of the reconstructions somewhat suspect.

SITUATIONAL DEFINITION
OF PERSONALITY

Recently an alternative approach to personality has gained strength, winning adherents from experimental psychologists and psychotherapists alike. At the core of this new approach is a rejection of the whole idea of personality as it was outlined above. The traditional study of personality is an attempt to find a few stable characteristics of a person that will predict the person's behavior in any, or at least many, situations. The alternative approach to personality is best characterized in William James's famous statement that "a man has as many selves as there are distinct groups of persons about whose opinion he cares" (1890). In other words, there are no stable characteristics of persons that produce predictable behavior from them in any situation. An individual's behavior is a function of the situation he is in.

At one level this seems to be common sense. A man may be aggressive and demanding with his subordinates, friendly and cooperative with his peers, respectful yet independent with his superiors, hostile yet pliant to his wife, submissive and affectionate with his children. A description of this sort might characterize thousands of men in any Western society. The important point, however, is that the description is not internally consistent. "Aggressive," "demanding," "friendly," "cooperative," "respectful," "independent," "pliant," "hostile," "submissive," "affectionate"—the adjectives all contradict one another. If we inspect our acquaintances, and ourselves, I think we will find that we are all contradictory in this way. Does this mean that we have multiple selves, or multiple personalities, in the traditional sense, or does it mean that we should avoid the use of words like "self" and "personality" and simply describe behavior in specific situations as a function of the situations and the individuals' past history? (Gergen, 1971).

The Hartshorne and May study

Before looking at that issue, a most significant one, we should look at some data indicating that personality, or the behaviors that index it, really does change from situation to situation. The classic study of this problem was carried out over 50 years ago by Hartshorne and May (1928). They were interested in such personality characteristics as honesty, self-restraint, self-control, and altruism. Their subjects were school children. Honesty was assessed with a variety of test situations in which there were opportunities to cheat, with a low or high risk of detection, a low versus a high payoff for cheating, and so on (Table 19–1). Other personality traits were assessed with similar tests.

The results were very clear indeed. Honesty was entirely situationally determined—honesty in one situation did not predict honesty in another. The correlations between performance in the various test situations were virtually zero. The same results were obtained for the other personality traits. Thus, looking at even such seemingly basic personality traits as honesty or self-control, these investigators were unable to find any

TABLE *19–1*

Sample deception tests used by Hartshorne and May (1928) to study such "personality characteristics" as honesty, self-restraint, self-control, and altruism.

---

1. Cheating

EXAMPLE: Information test

Children were required to circle in ink the correct answer to items such as "Bombay is a city in (China) (France) (Japan) (India)." After completing the test it was handed in and duplicated. Later the original test paper was returned to the child with a key showing the correct answers so that he could mark it himself. The corrected paper was then compared with the duplicate to ascertain whether or not the child had cheated by altering his original answers after seeing the key.

2. Stealing

EXAMPLE: Planted-dime test

A box containing several puzzles, including one puzzle that involved the use of a dime, was given to children. When each child returned his box, it was checked to see whether or not the dime had been stolen.

3. Lying

EXAMPLE: Pupil questionnaire

Some time after the previous tests the children were asked to fill in a questionnaire, mostly concerned with general questions, but including such questions as:

33. Did you ever cheat on any sort of test?

41. Did you actually do this test all alone without getting help on it?

Answers were compared with the results of previous tests to see whether cheaters lied or not about their cheating.

---

evidence for constant characteristics controlling behavior in all situations. Hartshorne and May conclude their study with the following summary.

> The results of these studies show that neither deceit nor its opposite, "honesty," are unified character traits, but rather specific functions of life situations. Most children will deceive in certain situations and not in others.
>
> Self-control was found to consist of still different sets of habits, each set fairly distinct from the others.
>
> Whatever behavior is studied, the general picture holds true. Conduct represents an association between a certain type of situation and a certain type of response. Such terms as "honesty" and "self-control" are names which the observer may . . . apply to this or that group of conducts, but there is no evidence that in grades 5 to 8 the children themselves have developed any great sensitiveness to such general terms, either as motives or as cues to action.

It seems evident that the general principle [is] specificity. In proportion as *situations* are alike, conduct is correlated. In proportion as *situations* are unlike, conduct is uncorrelated.

Related studies

One might object that the subjects in the Hartshorne and May study were not fully developed personalities (see pp. 381–382). As we noted above, most theories of personality allow some time before personality is presumed to be set. However, numerous studies of adults lead to the conclusion that their behavior, too, is situationally determined. One interesting study was in fact intended as a critique of traditional personality tests. The experimenter asked his subjects to take the same test under two conditions. In one condition they were to pretend they were applying for a job as a salesman; in the other they were to pretend they were applying for a job as a librarian in a small town (Wesman, 1952). The distribution of self-confidence ratings in the two conditions was remarkably different (Figure 19–1). This study is mainly cited as evidence that personality tests can be faked. This is to miss an important point. Performance on the *same test* differs, depending on whether the *same testee* is applying for a job as a salesman or for a job as a librarian. Performance in a personality test is a sample of behavior, and the nature of behavior changes, depending on the situation.

Similar implications can be drawn from studies of the same subjects taking different tests designed to measure the same personality attribute.

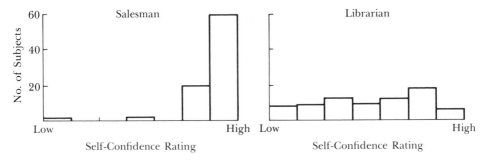

FIGURE *19–1*

Subjects were asked to complete a personality test, first as a salesman might and then as a librarian might. As the distribution of self-confidence ratings shows, the subjects obviously believed that the salesman would be much more self-confident than the librarian. (Wesman, 1952.)

TABLE *19–2*
Structure of a study of attitudes toward male authority figures,
both real and symbolic. The results are given in Table 19–3.
(Burwen and Campbell, 1957.)

OBJECT	MEASURES
Father	Interview; description of self and others; autobiographical inventory
Symbolic authority	Interview; Thematic Apperception Test (scored globally); TAT (scored objectively); judgments of photos of older persons; attitude survey
Boss	Interview; description of self and others; autobiographical inventory; socio-economic questionnaire
Real peers	Interview; description of self and others; autobiographical inventory
Symbolic peers	Same as above

In one study attitudes of adults towards male authority figures were studied (Burwen and Campbell, 1957). The immediate objects of study were the subject's father, his immediate superior, symbolic older men (presented in the Thematic Apperception Test), immediate peers, and symbolic peers. The structure of the study is shown in Table 19–2. Twenty measures were obtained from each subject. A summary of the obtained correlations is shown in Table 19–3. As can be seen there, measures of attitudes towards the same person derived from different tests showed very low correlations. For example, attitudes toward bosses derived from different tests correlated only .09; attitudes toward fathers correlated only .03 with attitudes toward bosses. The overall results of this study provide no support at all for the idea that there is any general attitude toward authority figures, or indeed for the idea that there is any such general attitude.

A number of studies have attempted to demonstrate a more direct situational determination of "personality." Many of these studies have used written self-descriptions as indexes of personality. These indexes can be changed by quite simple manipulations. Morse and Gergen (1970) carried out one study that is especially interesting because of its simplicity. The subjects in their experiment were under the impression that they were applying for a well-paid summer job. As part of the application process the subjects were asked to fill out a questionnaire on self-esteem. After this had been done, one of two "stooges," supposedly another applicant for the job, was brought in. The stooge did not communicate with the subjects at all. After some minutes in the presence of the stooge, the subjects were asked to complete a second questionnaire on self-esteem. The second questionnaire

TABLE *19–3*
Results of the study described in Table 19–2. The data represent correlations between different attitudes as well as correlations between different measures for the same attitude. For example, subjects' attitudes toward their bosses and symbolic authority figures correlated only 0.08. Subjects' attitudes toward their bosses intercorrelated only 0.09. All the correlations are consistently low, and thus provide no support for the idea that there is a general attitude toward authority figures. (Burwen and Campbell, 1957.)

ATTITUDE TOWARD		F	SA	B	P	SP
Father	F	.35	− 12	.03	.06	.08
Symbolic authority	SA		− 15	.08	.10	.06
Boss	B			.09	.13	.03
Peers	P				.22	.07
Symbolic peer	SP					.01

would normally show a high correlation with the first one. The experimental variable was the appearance of the stooge. One stooge, Mr. Clean, was a striking figure. He wore a dark business suit and shiny shoes and carried a neat attache case. When he opened this to remove several freshly sharpened pencils, he revealed a textbook on statistics and a book by Plato. The other stooge, Mr. Dirty, wore a torn, smelly sweat shirt, no socks, cut-off jeans. He had a day's growth of beard on his face. After he sat down, he tossed a worn and tattered copy of a popular paperback novel, *The Carpetbaggers*, onto the table. The experimenters describe Mr. Dirty as seeming to be generally dazed by the whole procedure. A comparison of self-esteem before and after exposure to the stooges showed that the self-esteem of those subjects exposed to Mr. Clean dropped significantly, while that of those exposed to Mr. Dirty increased considerably (Figure 19–2).

Gergen (1971) carried out another experiment that showed the same sort of plasticity in self-descriptions. The subjects were naval officer trainees. The trainees were told that they would be working in two-man teams on a particular task. Half of the trainees were told that the task involved plotting maneuvers for a ship in danger. The task was described as stressful, requiring great precision in the processing of a large amount of information. The other trainees were told that while they were going to discuss fleet maneuvers with their partners, the primary aim of the study was to find out how well the participants could get along with one another. Each trainee was then given an evaluation of himself that had supposedly been written by his partner. In fact, the evaluation had been filled out by the subject himself about a month previously. The subject was asked to evaluate himself using the same questionnaire so that the partner could

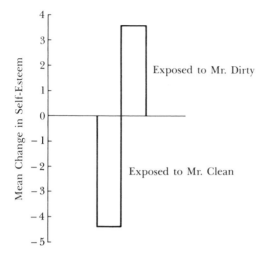

Exposed to Mr. Dirty

Exposed to Mr. Clean

FIGURE *19–2*

When subjects were exposed to Mr. Dirty between completing a first and second questionnaire on self-esteem, their self-esteem increased on the second questionnaire. The reverse was true for subjects exposed to Mr. Clean between questionnaires.

check the "validity" of his "predictions." Recall that the "partner's" evaluation was in fact the subject's own evaluation of himself, an evaluation that remains quite stable in real life. What happened in the experimental situations? In the first, subjects changed their self-evaluation in the direction of becoming logical, well-organized, efficient, hard workers. In the second, they became less logical, less organized, more free and easy, and friendlier than they had presented themselves as before. Furthermore, the vast majority of the subjects stated that these second self-descriptions had been perfectly accurate and honest. Only a minority of the subjects felt that they had presented a social mask that did not mirror their true selves.

Similar changes have been made to occur in situations that involve more than just pencil-and-paper responses. Hastorf (1965) describes an experiment in which timidity and dominance were manipulated. Four persons were put together into a discussion group. Each participant was allowed to speak only when a signal light, visible only to him, was lit. During the first 15 minutes all four subjects were allowed to speak (all lights were on). The subject who spoke least during this period was identified by the experimenters as the most timid. During the next 15 minutes only this individual was allowed to talk. During the last 15 minutes everyone was allowed to speak again. However, the timid subject was no longer timid. He was almost as dominant during the final 15-minute open discussion as he had been during his 15-minute monolog. His confidence in his own contributions had been decisively changed by the experience of having the others sit silent and attentive for 15 minutes while he spoke.

THE MULTIPLICITY
OF PERSONALITY

The above studies all attest to the pliability of "personality," the situational specificity of the behavior we label as indicative of an individual's personality. One could look at the results in another way. One could say that the situations in fact changed the individual's personality and thus retain the traditional idea of personality. For example, we behave one way with subordinates, another with peers, and still another with superiors; family behavior is switched on when we go home, conjugal behavior when we enter the bedroom. Our different personalities are manifested in different places, each segregated from the other. Many psychologists have argued that keeping the situations separate is essential for mental health, or happiness. On this view, putting an individual in a situation where two incompatible responses are required causes conflicts that can be harmful. This reasoning stands behind the conventional wisdom that one should neither employ nor teach a spouse, that the conflict between the behaviors elicited would severely try the relationship.

Although one could put the same individual in three different Hastorf situations—in one allowing him to be dominant, in another requiring him to be passive, and in the third to be in an intermediate state—no such experiment has been done as far as I know. All of the experiments that I know of are like those reviewed above. An individual's "personality" is measured in respect of some dimension; his situation is modified in some way; the effects on his behavior as an index of that dimension of personality are then assessed. Designs of this sort leave open the issue of whether one is changing "personality" or simply shaping behavior in a specific situation. There is some clinical evidence that the latter is the case. For example, Ayllon and Michael (1959) attempted to change the behavior of a psychotic patient by focusing on her verbal behavior. The verbal behavior of psychotics is indeed bizarre, as the following example of a conversation between two psychotics illustrates (Laing, 1967).

JONES: (*Laughs loudly, then pauses.*) I'm McDougal myself. (*This actually is not his name.*)

SMITH: What do you do for a living, little fellow? Work on a ranch or something?

JONES: No, I'm a civilian seaman. Supposed to be high muckamuck society.

SMITH: A singing recording machine, huh? I guess a recording machine sings sometimes. If they're adjusted right. Mm hm. I thought that was it. My towel, mm hm. We'll be going back to sea in about— eight or nine months though. Soon as we get our—destroyed parts repaired. (*Pause*)

JONES: I've got lovesickness, secret love.

SMITH: Secret love, huh? (*Laughs*)

JONES: Yeah.

SMITH: I ain't got any secret love.

JONES: I fell in love, but I don't feed any woo—that sits over—looks something like me—walking around over there.

SMITH: My, oh, my only one, my only love is the shark. Keep out of the way of him.

JONES: Don't they know I have a life to live? (*Long pause*)

SMITH: Do you work at the air base? Hm?

JONES: You know what I think of work. I'm 33 in June, do you mind?

The agents in the Ayllon and Michael experiment were the nurses in the ward, who were instructed to ignore the patient's psychotic talk and reinforce her "sensible" talk. Verbal behavior was sampled every 30 minutes. The change in frequency of psychotic talk is shown in Figure 19–3. The surprising increase after the tenth week is explained by the fact that three sources of reinforcement for psychotic talk came on the scene: a social worker, a volunteer visitor, and a hospital employee who was not part of the experiment. It seems that "psychotic talk" was reserved for these individuals—an instance of situational specificity. Also noteworthy is the authors' comment that the nurses were disappointed that the change in the patient's behavior was restricted to verbal behavior. The study may thus point to combined situational and behavioral specificity. The reinforcement given to psychotic talk after the tenth week was inadvertent; it was not part of the experimental design. Nevertheless, this one study does illustrate the kind of switching on and off of different personality-indexing behaviors that is lacking in the other studies reviewed above. The decline in psychotic talk to the nurses does not index a change in personality but a shaping of behavior appropriate to a situation.

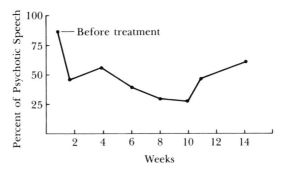

FIGURE *19–3*

About 85 percent of the speech of subjects in a mental institution was psychotic before treatment. After 10 weeks of treatment the percentage of psychotic speech fell to around 30 percent.

TABLE *19–4*

The three faces of Eve. (Thigpen and Cleckley, 1957.)

	EVE WHITE	EVE BLACK	JANE
Neurotic	×		
Sober	×		×
Well behaved	×		×
Controlled	×		×
Mature			×
Competent	×		×
Lively		×	×
Retiring	×		
Mischievous		×	

LABELS AND PERSONALITY

The three faces of Eve

We can now return to our major question: Does the situational specificity of behavior index "multiple personalities," multiple selves inside the same skin, or should we simply drop the use of words like "personality" and "self"? Although the latter course might seem the more sensible, many psychologists incline to the former (Pages, 1949; Zax and Stricker, 1963). Why is this so? One reason seems to be nothing more or less than practicality. Even when investigating those cases of extreme behavioral splitting that we label schizophrenic, it seems to be more useful to discuss the multiple selves of the schizophrenic rather than specific behavior in specific situations. The most famous multiple personality in recent times was Eve (Thigpen and Cleckley, 1957). The three faces of Eve were described very differently (Table 19–4). These descriptions allow one to identify virtually any behavior as originating from Eve 1, 2 or 3, simply by inspecting to see if it fits with the verbal descriptions of the three Eves. The verbal labels we use are thus useful, although they may have sinister effects, as we shall now see.

The Stanford Prison study

Human behavior is *generative*. Thus, if a person is given a particular label in a situation and accepts the label, fidelity to that label will generate behavior that is appropriate and original and not simply a repetition of previous behavior. The best example of the role of labels in generating behavior is the notorious Stanford Prison study (Zimbardo, 1972). Here is one account of what happened in this study (*Stanford Daily News*, October 12, 1971).

The research project was designed to help understand what goes into creating and maintaining a prison and what the prison experience does to the prisoners, guards, and power establishment. The study was in part to examine what are the effects of arbitrarily labeling one person "guard" and another "prisoner."

The study began with an ad in the city newspaper where applicants were offered $15 a day for a two week study. The first 70 applicants were screened so that the final 24 chosen were psychologically and medically well-adjusted college students. By the flip of the coin they were arbitrarily divided into guards and prisoners and the project was ready to begin.

Zimbardo described how the Palo Alto police got the study rolling. "On a quiet Sunday morning a Palo Alto Police car swept through various neighborhoods of the city, picked up each of the boys who were going to be prisoners individually. We had told them simply to wait at home and they'd be contacted. The police booked them, frisked them, fingerprinted them, blindfolded them, put them in detention, and the boys still in a state of surprise were picked up by our men and brought down to our prison in the basement of the Psychology Department.

Each had been arrested for suspicion of an alleged crime. The prisoners were stripped naked, deloused, and put into uniform by the "guards." A stocking cap covered his hair and made it look as if he had his head shaved. A locked chain was attached to one ankle which was to be worn at all times, and the prisoner put into a cell with two others and not allowed to talk."

What happened the ensuing week was crushing in its implications. The group labeled guards, dressed in uniforms and mirror sunglasses and put in charge under the supervision of Zimbardo and his three graduate student "wardens," became perverted by the sense of power they felt.

They taunted, upbraided, and humiliated the prisoners, often making them stand for long hours and count off their numbers. By the third day of the experiment the guards were controlling prisoners' lives, telling them when they could go to the toilet, if indeed they could at all, controlling their meals, and deciding who should get blankets or other "privileges."

The prisoners were equally affected by the experience. On the second day there was a prisoner rebellion where some prisoners barricaded themselves in, refused to eat, ripped off their numbers, and started screaming obscenities at the guards in an effort to assert their freedom and individuality.

This rebellion was put down by a reinforced group of guards using physical force and psychological tactics. After this the prisoners became increasingly servile, following the whimsy and arbitrary commands of the guards. On the fifth day one prisoner made a last futile attempt to assert his individuality and freedom by refusing to eat.

Although he had formerly been a hero for the other prisoners, he now became a source of trouble. The guards put this prisoner in the "hole," a small 2 × 4 closet, and told the other prisoners that if they wanted him out of the hole for the night they would have to give up their blankets. Although it wasn't cold, the prisoners voted to keep their blankets and let him rot in solitary.

This behavior of otherwise well-adjusted college students was elicited purely by the arbitrary labels "prisoner" and "guard." A great deal of human behavior seems to be elicited by fidelity to the label of the moment, overriding past history and reinforcement contingencies. The best known instances of this process come from fiction—*The Secret Life of Walter Mitty*, *The Seven-Year Itch*, or *Gumshoe*. The appeal of such works lies in the fact that they reflect processes we know go on in others and in ourselves, to some extent.

The argument that we are all multiple personalities within a single skin may seem strange. We are used to thinking that it is only the mentally ill who have several selves. The psychologist Kenneth Gergen (1971) described his feelings after reading over his correspondence one evening.

> I came across a completely different person in each letter: in one I was morose, pouring out a philosophy of existential sorrow; in another I was a lusty realist; in a third I was a lighthearted jokester; and so on.
>
> I had felt completely honest and authentic as I wrote each letter; at no time was I aware of putting on a particular style to please or impress a particular friend. And yet, a stranger reading those letters all together would have no idea who I am. This realization staggered me. Which letter, if any, portrayed the true me? Was there such an entity—or was I simply a chameleon, reflecting others' views of me?

Gergen concluded, of course, that he was quite normal and healthy and that we all share his multiplicity to some extent. The difference between normal individuals and those labeled "mentally ill" does not seem to be internal multiplicity per se but rather the way in which the individual experiences this multiplicity.

THE SCHIZOPHRENIC EXPERIENCE AND THE IDEA OF A "TRUE SELF"

The major characteristics of the schizophrenic experience, according to R. D. Laing (1959), the controversial British psychiatrist who has revolutionized the way we think of schizophrenia, is that the multiple selves of the schizophrenic have never been reconciled, either with one another or with a concept of a "true self" that can serve as a "deep structure" for the many faces that we present to the world. We could all write a description of our "true self." We normally feel that some part of our true self is engaged in interactions with others, so that although only aspects of it inform any one of our many social selves, we nonetheless have a feeling that we are being true to our real self, at least most of the time. A violation of that feeling produces shock, guilt, horror, and excuses ("I must have been drunk").

The schizophrenic, according to Laing, never has this feeling, or else loses it. He sees his physical self, his body, as an actor playing parts. His true Self observes this actor but is not invested in it. In some cases there may be no true Self, or only a vanishing fragment of one (Goffman, 1959). Consider the case of Julie (Laing, 1959). Laing writes that psychotherapy with Julie was more like group psychotherapy than individual therapy because of the number of selves that Julie presented.

These various partial systems [multiple personalities] could be identified, at least to some extent after getting to know her, by reason of the consistency of the role each played in what one might call the intrapersonal "group" they comprised.

For instance, there was the peremptory bully who was always ordering her about. The same peremptory voice would make endless complaints to me about "this child." "This is a wicked child. This child is wasted time. This child is just a cheap tart. You'll never do anything with this child. . . ." The "you" here might be referring directly to me, or to one of her systems, or I could be embodying this system.

It was evident that this bullying figure within her was for much of the time "the boss." "She" did not think much of Julie. "She" did not think Julie would get well, nor that she was worth getting better. She was neither on her side, nor on my side. It would be appropriate to call this quasi-autonomous partial system a "bad internal mother." She was basically an internal female persecutor who contained in concentrated form all the bad that Julie ascribed to her mother.

Two other partial systems could be readily identified. One fulfilled the role of an advocate on her behalf to me, and a protector or buffer against persecution. "She" frequently referred to Julie as her little sister. Phenomenologically, therefore, we may refer to this system as "her good sister."

The third partial system that I shall introduce was an entirely good, compliant, propitiating little girl. This seemed to be a derivative of what some years before was probably a system very similar to the false-self system I have described in schizoid cases. When this system spoke, she said, "I'm a good girl. I go to the lavatory regularly."

There were derivations also of what seemed to have been an "inner" self, which had become almost completely volatilized into pure possibility. Finally, as I remarked earlier, there were periods of precarious sanity in which she spoke in a pathetically scared, barely audible tone, but seemed to be more nearly speaking "in her own person" than at any other time.

Let us now consider these various systems operating together. The examples I give are of her more coherent utterances.

I was born under a black sun. I wasn't born, I was crushed out. It's not one of those things you get over like that. I wasn't mothered, I was smothered. She wasn't a mother. I'm choosey who I have for a mother. Stop it. Stop it. She's killing me. She's cutting out my tongue. I'm rotten, base. I'm wicked. I'm wasted time. . . .

This child doesn't want to come here, do you realize that? She's my little sister. This child does not know about things she shouldn't know about.

This child's mind is cracked. This child's mind is closed. You're trying to open this child's mind. I'll never forgive you for trying to open this child's mind. This child is dead and not dead.

You've got to want this child. You've got to make her welcome . . . you've got to take care of this girl. I'm a good girl. She's my little sister. You've got to take her to the lavatory. She's my little sister. She doesn't know about these things. That's not an impossible child.

Note how the "boss" enters after Julie has begun denouncing her mother, followed by the "good sister," who is interrupted by the "good-little-girl" ("I'm a good girl"). Only at the very beginning is there any evidence of a "true" Julie. It must be emphasized that it is not the multiplicity of Julie that is bizarre, nor is it the inconsistency of her multiple personalities. It is the fact that "she" is no part of any of her personalities. By contrast, consider the character Preedy in William Sansom's *Collected Stories* (1960):

But in any case he took care to avoid catching anyone's eye. First of all, he had to make it clear to those potential companions of his holiday that they were of no concern to him whatsoever. He stared through them, round them, over them—eyes lost in space. The beach might have been empty. If by chance a ball was thrown his way, he looked surprised; then let a smile of amusement lighten his face (Kindly Preedy), looked around dazed to see that there *were* people on the beach, tossed it back with a smile to himself and not a smile at the people, and then resumed carelessly his nonchalant survey of space.

But it was time to institute a little parade, the parade of the Ideal Preedy. By devious handlings he gave any who wanted a chance to see the title of his book—a Spanish translation of Homer, classic thus, but not daring, cosmopolitan too—and then gathered together his beach-wrap and bag into a neat sand-resistant pile (Methodical and Sensible Preedy), rose slowly to stretch his huge frame (Big-Cat Preedy), and tossed aside his sandals (Carefree Preedy, after all).

Preedy presents as many contradictory selves as does Julie, but he is *in* all of them, not merely observing them.

We began this chapter with an account of traditional personality theory, a theory that we found grounds to reject. We then presented an alternative approach to personality. The contrast between the two approaches is well put by Mischel (1968).

Global traits and states are excessively crude, gross units to encompass adequately the extraordinary complexity and subtlety of the discriminations that people constantly make. Traditional trait-state conceptions of man have depicted him as victimized by his infantile history, as possessed by unchanging rigid trait attributes, and as driven inexorably by unconscious irrational forces. This conceptualization of man, besides being philosophically un-appetizing, is contradicted by massive experimental data. The traditional trait-state conceptualizations of personality, while often paying lip service to man's complexity and to the uniqueness of each person, in fact lead to a grossly oversimplified view that misses both the richness and the uniqueness of individual lives. A more adequate conceptualization must take full account of man's extraordinary adaptiveness and capacities for discrimination, awareness, and self-regulation; it must also recognize that men can and do reconceptualize themselves and change, and that an understanding of how humans can constructively modify their behavior in systematic ways is the core of a truly dynamic personality psychology.

To that I would add that the same person on the same day can conceptualize—or label—himself in different ways without thereby being abnormal.

WHAT IS PERSONALITY?

We have reviewed some data indicating that the behaviors traditionally regarded as indexes of personality can be varied in the same individual by varying the situation of the individual. Are we then to believe that individual behavior is entirely determined by the situation? Surely not. We have seen enough data in this and preceding chapters to realize that this is not the case. Recall the data presented in Chapter 17 on the development of compliance to peer-group pressure. The developing human typically moves from a stage of noncompliance to extreme peer-group compliance to relative autonomy. Recall, too, the data presented in Chapter 17 on changes in response to Milgram's authority situation (p. 358). Those who had developed higher levels of morality behaved differently from those who had not. Recall, too, a major theme of this book, that the situation an individual finds himself in is not simply a function of the situation as it might be "objectively" described; it is also a function of the previous situations that individual has been in. The psychological environment of an individual at any time is as much a function of the individual's developmental history as it is of any "objective" features of that environment.

The best example of that was our discussion in Chapter 15 of the affectionless child (pp. 324–326). There we compared two types of children. One is raised in a happy loving home until two or three and then doomed to a large impersonal institution for the rest of childhood. The other is raised in an impersonal institution until two and then placed in a loving, warm, affectionate family for the rest of childhood. The prognosis for the former is very favorable; that child will probably grow up in all respects "normal," capable of deep, satisfying, intimate relations with others. The future of the other is less happy; some such children are "affectionless" when they leave the institution—they are "shallow," "facile," "charming," and incapable of any deep relationships. The first child has learned something of the form, "People are for loving." The other child has learned that people are not to be trusted, that commitment is dangerous. These second-order learning experiences (pp. 222–226) are very powerful. As we saw in Chapter 15, the malign effects (the affectionless character) are rarely reversible. The "same" situation is not the same for these two children. Their worlds, their *psychological* worlds, are completely different. They can never be in the same social situation, for the same "objective" situation will be seen by them in completely different ways. Events in the world are interpreted by different people in different ways. The precise interpretation given is dependent on the individual's past history. Since no two individuals have the same past history, no two individuals will interpret the same event in the same way. It is therefore nonsense to talk of two individuals being exposed to the same environmental event. Inasmuch as they interpret the event differently, there are two different events to be taken into account in evaluating the behavior of the individuals.

Behavior is situationally determined. But the situation that determines behavior is a function of the objective situation and the way the individual perceives it. The way the individual perceives a situation is a function of his developmental history. Indeed, it is worth recalling here that no *experiment*, certainly none of those described in this chapter, produces invariant effects. There are individual differences in the response to any situation. Personality theory should be a theory of what produces individual differences.

Does this mean we should resort to the simple personality labels mentioned at the beginning of this chapter? Not at all. Rather, we should look back at the chapters on cognitive development. There we looked at how individuals learn to interpret the physical world. We did point out that there are individual differences in these interpretations, but the differences are largely a function of the demand characteristics of the environment of the individual. These interpretations can be organized into systems or structures that merit the name "theories." Just as we form theories of the physical world, so, I would maintain, do we form "theories" of the self and the social world. Each of us has his or her own "theory" of the self and the social world; one's own "theory" *is* one's personality.

Thus, just as a scientific theory of cognition is concerned with the way that individuals arrive at an interpretation of the physical world, so should a scientific theory of personality be concerned with the way in which individuals arrive at an interpretation of themselves and the social world. I would maintain that the structures that determine individual differences in "personality" are in fact different "theories" about the self and the social world, with all of the complexity that is characteristic of theories of the physical world.

Unfortunately, there have been few attempts at describing a systematic structure for personality and certainly none that have attained the complexity of existing descriptions of the systematic structure of cognition. Nonetheless, we can, I think, outline some of the features a systematic description would have to cope with.

Individual theories about the self and others

A basic decision in formulating our individual theories of the social world must be the decision that "I" exist, with its corollaries that "I" am different from other people and that "I" am not as others see me. Along with this must come the awareness that different modes of interaction are required with different people, that "I" must present different faces to different people (pp. 389–391). Another basic decision about the self is "I am a boy" or "I am a girl." With this must go some idea about appropriate sex- and age-linked behavior (pp. 362–367). At some time the child must decide about the kinds of relations with others that are possible. As we pointed out above, the affectionless child formulates a theory about people that is different from that of the normal child. At some point in development the child must formulate an idea of his own competence. "I can do x but not y." Seligman (1975) has pointed out how "learned helplessness" characterizes the ghetto child. Such a child has formed the theory "I can do nothing."

Sometime in life we must formulate the idea "I am attractive/unattractive to the opposite sex." One must then decide what one is going to do about it. This leads into the ideas of responsibility and morality that we glanced at earlier (pp. 348–356). All of these statements about the self and others are "theoretical" statements; they are several stages removed from behavior but they can control behavior. We have already looked at the origins of some of these ideas. All of them pop up in the course of development at some time. Some of them seem to be irreversible; others are plastic in the extreme (see the review of Kelly's work, pp. 373–379). In the next chapter we will look in more detail at the developmental processes involved.

THE VALIDITY OF PERSONALITY THEORIES

Before closing I would like to draw a contrast between cognitive development and personality development. In Chapter 9 we pointed out that scientifically innovative ideas typically cause confusion when first introduced but rapidly become part of the cultural clothing we all wear.

In other words, we can incorporate scientific innovations into our own interpretations of the world. Is there any evidence that we similarly incorporate well-known theories of personality into our own interpretations of the self and the social world? It is fashionable to deny the very possibility. Pundits tend to bemoan the fact that the awesome technological power created by man's ingenuity is in the hands of a primitive Stone Age beast—human personality, they say, has not changed since the Stone Age. This is unutterable rubbish, of course. As contributions to our under-standing of social behavior and personality such notions rank well below the *Peanuts* cartoons. More seriously, it is clear that our conceptions of the social order have been drastically changed by major thinkers, many of whom have paid the ultimate price for their innovations. Jesus Christ changed our ideas of man and man's relation to man, as did St. Paul. These ideas were changed again by Luther, Knox, and Calvin, who had very explicit *psychological* ideas to peddle, ideas of predestination for example. Closer to our own time, Marx put forward new social conceptions that have become incorporated into individual theories of the social world.

At a somewhat less exalted level, the twentieth century has seen the promulgation of explicitly psychological theories of man, many of which have been incorporated into the personal theoretical systems through which we all view ourselves and the social world. Various psychologists have commented on this. Kelly wondered whether anyone had an inferiority complex before Adler formulated the idea. Similar speculations have been offered regarding the Oedipus complex and the Electra complex. I sometimes wonder if anyone had an identity crisis before Erikson brought the idea to our attention. Certainly William James never worried over the necessary multiplicity of personality. Nowadays most students seem to go through an identity crisis and know it. Casual observations of this sort can be bolstered by examination of literary sources. Literary sources are not scientific data, but they are to some extent a reflection of the personality theory of the writer, and the writer himself reflects the theories of his time. Consider the history of Oliver Twist, as explained by his creator, Charles Dickens.

> But we must start at the beginning, with the new-born babe being carried in the arms of a fuddled old workhouse servant. His mother died just after he was born. She was nameless and the father unknown. At the age of ten months, Oliver was taken from the workhouse to be brought up at Mrs. Mann's "baby farm." Mrs. Mann fed her charges so little that she made a profit out of the sevenpence ha'penny she was paid each week for each child. Oliver grew up pale and thin. On his ninth birthday, he and two other lads were thrashed and locked up for daring to say they were hungry.

What would be the fate of this child today in post-Freud, post-Bowlby days? Recall that Bowlby has argued that *any* disruption of one-to-one mother-child relations must have deleterious consequences for the child. An author beginning with this scenario, post-Bowlby, would produce a delinquent, a criminal, a monster possibly, at the least a violent revolutionary. He could not create the pious paragon that Dickens did. Consider the attitudes toward women outlined by Flaubert in *Madame Bovary*, Joyce in *Ulysses*, and Erica Jong in *Fear of Flying*; the views of women presented in these three books are totally different. The two later books are, I think, clear reflections of newer psychological theorizing. Indeed, *Fear of Flying* and *Portnoy's Complaint* are quite alarming indicators of the extent to which psychoanalytic ideas have become embedded in the popular culture. Pavlovian notions have even entered the paperback bookstalls by way of such books as *Gravity's Rainbow*, one of whose major "jokes" depends on comprehension of backward conditioning.

Changes in psychologists' conceptions of people are thus incorporated into everyone's view of the social world, just as changes in scientists' views of the world are eventually incorporated into everyone's view of the physical world. There is one possibly important difference between the two processes. While few informed people would maintain that theories of the world are "true," in any absolute sense, new theories are in general "better" in that they are simpler and handle more data with fewer variables. The experimentation generated by a new theory in general suffices eventually to disprove it and push up something yet newer. The status of personality theories is rather different. A personality theory is a theory about people. People can read the theory. People can label themselves in terms of that theory. As we saw above, people will act in accord with labels. Furthermore, an individual can be categorized by others in terms of one theory or another, and will then be expected to behave in ways consistent with the theory. Since people are by and large compliant (see above), the individual may begin to behave as expected. These two processes raise the strange possibility that a well-popularized psychological theory could become true, even if it were unutterable nonsense when propounded. Hopefully, the theory offered here escapes this burden of responsibility, since it intends to be nothing more than a theory about how people form "theories" of personality.

20

Personality Development

In the previous chapter we argued that the proper study of personality theorists should be the study of how people form their own "theories" about themselves and others. While this would align personality theory with cognitive theory, it is not a course that has recommended itself to many. Traditional theories of personality development have organized themselves around such issues as the controversy of nativism versus empiricism.

A GENETIC BASIS
FOR SCHIZOPHRENIA?

The most compelling case for nativism in personality development lies in the argument for a genetic basis for schizophrenia. On this view, schizophrenics are individuals with an abnormal genetic constitution—environment is irrelevant. Such a view contradicts everything that has been said in the preceding chapter. On our view, schizophrenia is an erroneous personal "theory" of the self. Nonetheless, nativism is a view that is widely held. It is quite widely believed that mental illnesses result from genetic defects. Defective genotypes are presumed to produce mentally ill phenotypes, no matter what the environment. Confirmation, denial, social reinforcement, are quite unimportant from this point of view. It should not surprise us to find again the comparison of monozygotic (identical) and dizygotic (fraternal) twins presenting its Janus face at this point. If a mentally ill phenotype results from a defective genotype, then identical twins, who have exactly the same genotype, should show perfect concordance for mental illness. If one twin is mentally ill, the other twin should be mentally ill in exactly the same way; if one twin is schizophrenic, the other twin should be schizophrenic; or if one twin is depressive, the other twin should be depressive, no matter what their environments are. Monozygotic twins thus play their usual critical role in personality theory as in theories of intelligence.

Existing data show quite clearly that mental illness is not an expression of a defective genotype. There have been three extensive studies of the incidence of mental illness in twins. Only the first and least adequate study found any evidence to support the genetic hypothesis of mental illness. That study by Kallman (1950) has been criticized for sampling errors (Kringlen, 1967). Kallman's psychiatric criteria have also been criticized; according to Kallman's criteria, if one twin were permanently psychotic and the other simply neurotic, they were regarded as concordant for mental illness. Lastly, his diagnosis of zygosity was very inexact, relying largely on external appearance. Tienari (1963) points out that hospitalization itself, and many methods of treatment, will change external appearance. Thus, twins who were discordant for mental illness would tend to be classified as dizygotic by Kallman, even if they were in actuality monozygotic.

These objections do not apply to the two other studies, those of Tienari (1963) and Kringlen (1967). Tienari collected from birth registers a list of all male twins born in Finland in a 10-year period (the restriction to males is the only flaw in the study). Zygosity was established by blood typing, a foolproof method. The concordance figures obtained in Tienari's study depend on the precision of the psychiatric criteria used. With very precise criteria the concordance rate for monozygotics was zero, for dizygotics five percent. With somewhat laxer criteria the concordance rate for monozygotics was 19 percent, for dizygotics 14 percent. Neither pair of figures supports a strong genetic hypothesis.

The most extensive study of the three is Kringlen's. Kringlen obtained from public records a list of twins born in a 30-year period in Norway. This list was compared with the publicly available list of all individuals who were ever admitted for psychiatric care in Norway. Kringlen thus obtained a list of every member of a twin pair who had been classified as mentally ill. Zygosity was then established by blood typing. On a precise definition of mental illness the concordance figures were 25 percent for monozygotics and eight percent for dizygotics; with a looser definition the figures were 38 and 12 percent. While the difference between monozygotics and dizygotics is significant, the concordance rate for monozygotics falls a long way short of that predicted by the genetic hypothesis.

The data can be comprehended from an environmentalist viewpoint, particularly if we note that illness in most cases became manifest after the twins had been forced into somewhat separate lives, by jobs or marriage or the like. The role of environment is quite clear in the case histories

Kringlen presents. Three of these are of particular interest since they concern monozygotic twins brought up apart. I will present these cases in Kringlen's own words (1967).

Case A (No. 22)   . . . Twin A developed a malign schizophrenia and is still in hospital, severely deteriorated. Twin B is still without nervous symptoms, well adjusted to work and family.

The twins grew up in approximately similar environments from a social and geographical point of view, but the primary family group was entirely different for the two twins. During infancy the mother seems to have been indifferent not to say resentful, toward the preschizophrenic twin and definitely favored twin B. When separated, at 20 months of age, twin B went to live with a normal family, had both a mother- and a father-figure, and was brought up, apparently rather strictly, although within normal limits. The later schizophrenic, twin A, had no father-figure during this period, and his foster-mother seems to have been anxious and overprotective. In childhood the later schizophrenic had slight neurotic symptoms and showed less aggression than his co-twin, who presented no such symptoms and was more quick-tempered.

On reunion at 16 years of age, the twins were much alike in body and mind, though the later schizophrenic was more introverted. This trait became gradually more marked, particularly after the age of 19, and at 29 he became manifestly psychotic.

One can point to marked differences in external milieu in this case, but one lacks exact information about methods of upbringing and the emotional atmosphere in the home, so that any definite conclusion about etiological environmental factors cannot be drawn. Many have been brought up without a father-figure and have been oversheltered and not developed schizophrenia.

Case C (No. 66)   Like the previous pair, these twins were not only discordant with respect to psychosis, but discordant to a considerable degree in personality traits. [Twin A was schizophrenic.] Twin B . . . was not particularly intro- or extroverted; he was rather parsimonious and meticulous, religiously inclined, and an abstainer. At times he experienced under stress some tenseness and dyspeptic troubles.

In other words, one is faced with two persons who are vastly different in terms of psychological control. One of them is "loose" and develops psychotic reactions under stress. The other is more controlled, but his control mechanisms do not impede his daily activities, and he is well adjusted.

Both twins clearly reflect their childhood milieus. Twin A was brought up in an unstable home partly disorganized, with weak social control. Mostly he could do as he pleased; there was no discipline or direction, and he roamed about and had abundant contact with other children.

Twin B was brought up in a strict, but apparently sympathetic, religious home, and he had less contact with other children. Except for a period from four to seven when he was cared for by a maid, he seems to have experienced a happy childhood.

Case D (No. 55)   Twin A developed a schizophreniform benign psychosis around 40. Twin B has never been psychotic. The more interesting aspect of these twins to me is the different personality developments. Twin A became an extroverted, gay and lively woman with less strict sexual morals. She has a "normal" association with alcohol and is not particularly religiously inclined. Twin B, on the other hand, became a reserved, quiet, rather controlled spinster with strict sexual morals, actively religious, and a teetotaller.

It seems to me that these women to a large extent are reflections of their later childhood and adolescent environments. One cannot, however, exclude the possibility of marked differences in personality before the age of separation. Both stayed with their "psychopathic" mother during their first years of life, in circumstances of economic hardship. Both seem to have been rather equal in personality traits at this time, and anxious and insecure toward their mother.

Twin B was sent to work as a shepherd girl at a somewhat lonely farm at the age of 8. Her sole company was the sheep and the elderly earnestly religious couple, who had no children of their own. Later on she came to another farm where she thrived better because there was a girl in the house. But here also she was strongly influenced by religion and became attached to a sect which maintained that one ought not to show one's emotional feelings.

Twin A was sent away from home for two years, somewhat later than B, at the age of 10. She was, however, happy to leave her cruel mother, and materially she was much better off on this larger farm. Here there were plenty of children to play with and life was more gay.

Since puberty both twins have worked on various farms and later on in smaller towns as housemaids.

These cases show quite clearly how the same genotypes can be transformed by different environments. Indeed, they show a quite remarkable long-term effect of childhood experiences, a point we shall return to below.

THE ROLE OF THE ENVIRONMENT IN PRODUCING SIMILAR PERSONALITIES IN IDENTICAL TWINS

Among investigators of identical twins, Kringlen alone has tried to examine the way that environmental influences can affect the behavioral similarities between monozygotic twins. In a recent paper he reported on the development of similarities and differences in temperament of monozygotic and dizygotic twins (Kringlen and Jorgenson, 1975). Temperament was defined in terms of nine variables, which could be related to what we have been calling "personality."

1. *Activity level.* This variable describes the level, tempo, and frequency with which a motoric component is present in the child's behavior, and the diurnal proportion of active and inactive periods. Does the child show a

high, moderate, or low activity during situations such as bathing, feeding, playing, and dressing?

2. *Regularity*. The predictability of such functions as hunger, feeding pattern, elimination, and sleep-wake cycle. Does the child behave regularly or irregularly with regard to sleeping, hunger, and stool?

3. *Approach withdrawal*. This variable measures the child's initial response to new stimuli, such as food, play, and people. Does the child show approaching attitudes or does it withdraw?

4. *Adaptability*. This variable measures the infant's ability to modify its initial negative reactions to new stimuli in a positive direction. In other words, with what speed and ease is the current behavior modified in response to altered environmental structuring?

5. *Intensity*. This variable measures the energy level of response irrespective of quality or direction. How energetic are the child's reactions? Does it cry intensely or does it fret?

6. *Threshold of responsiveness*. This variable measures the intensity level of stimulation required to evoke a discernible response to sensory stimuli, environmental objects, and social contacts. What degree of intensity of stimuli is necessary to elicit response?

7. *Quality of mood*. This variable measures the amount of pleasant, joyful, or friendly behavior contrasted with unpleasant, unfriendly behavior or crying. Does the child generally show kind and gentle behavior, or is it usually sour, aggressive, and crying?

8. *Distractability*. This variable measures the effectiveness of extraneous environmental stimuli in altering the direction of ongoing behavior. To what degree can one distract the child? To what degree can external disturbance stimuli change the [infant's] behavior?

9. *Attention span and persistence*. This variable measures two categories which are related. Attention span concerns the length of time a particular activity is pursued by a child. Persistence refers to the continuation of an activity in the face of obstacles to the maintenance of the activity direction. Attention span, in other words, refers to the ability to concentrate on a particular activity. Persistence means a child's ability to pursue its activity despite present hindrances.

Two extremely interesting results emerged from this study. First, between the ages of two and nine months monozygotic twins become more alike in temperament while dizygotic twins become less alike. That this is not due to genetic effects is shown by the second fascinating finding. The more alike monozygotic twins were in appearance, i.e., the more likely they were to be confused by their parents, the more alike in temperament they became by the age of nine months. That is, the harder it was for the parents to *treat* the babies differently, the more similar their temperaments became. Monozygotic twins who look unlike are as genetically identical as are monozygotic twins who look extremely alike. On genetic grounds, monozygotic twins who do not look identical should be as similar in temperament as those who do. They are not, however. This is a striking demonstration that a large part of the concordance between monozygotic twins is produced by the environment. Since monozygotic twins are generally alike in appearance, they are treated alike and develop alike. When they are treated differently, they can develop very different personalities.

ALTERNATIVES TO NATIVISM

If we are to argue that schizophrenia, and therefore other aspects of personality, are not inherited, we must make some effort to say what does determine them. The standard alternative to nativism is some kind of learning theory. Learning theory approaches have frequently been offered. Even psychoanalytically oriented theorists like Laing rely on a version of learning theory (Laing, 1959). Laing uses the word "confirmation" to denote what others would call reinforcement.

Confirmation may be conditional or unconditional, i.e., it may be given only in response to certain behaviors or it may be continuously given. Laing also distinguishes between positive confirmation, negative confirmation, and denial. Some examples of parent-child disciplinary encounters may clarify these ideas. Imagine a child who is angry because his parents will not fall in with his wishes. The parents could ignore the child, perhaps even shutting him away in his own room. This example of "love-withdrawal" would be an instance of denial. By isolating the child, the parents are denying his existence when he is angry—when he is angry he is not there for them. If these same parents warmly reinforced the child's behavior when he was good, thereby giving him positive confirmation, the child overall would be in receipt of conditional positive confirmation. Alternatively, parents could beat a child until he stopped being angry. This assertion of power would represent negative confirmation. If the same parents bestowed warm praise and affection whenever the child did things of which they approved, the child would at that time be in receipt of positive confirmation. The combination of negative and positive confirmation adds up to unconditional confirmation of the child's existence and significance to his parents. If a pair of parents denied the child by ignoring his good behaviors and confirming his existence only when he did something of which they disapproved, the child would be in receipt of conditional negative confirmation. Another pair of parents might resort to reasoning with the child, accepting that he has a right to be angry, giving him positive confirmation when he is angry. This along with praise for approved behaviors would represent unconditional positive confirmation.

Laing proposes that behavior that results in confirmation, whether positive or negative, will be retained and strengthened. Behavior that results in denial will be dropped. This is rather different from a conventional learning theory. Confirmation is thus *the* specific technique of reinforcement in personality development, more important by far than simple pleasure or pain. We can readily envisage a continuum of parent behaviors ranging from unconditional denial to unconditional positive confirmation. Laing (1959) also posits the importance in development of the *double bind*.

The double bind in development is described as the denial of behaviors originating in the child and confirmation only of those behaviors elicited or instigated by the parent. A mother who feeds her child on a rigid schedule is applying a double bind. The parent who prevents a baby crawling by encouraging him to walk puts him in a double bind; crawling originates with the child, but the parent will confirm only walking, a behavior the parent elicits from the child. The parent who gives the child an unwanted toy and rewards him for playing with it is putting him in a double bind. Laing cites the mother of a schizophrenic girl who gave her daughter an expensive sweater that could not conceivably have fitted her. The love and confirmation represented by the gift was accompanied by a straightforward and extreme denial of the daughter (the sweater's size). Laing, with Bateson and others, considers the double bind to be a prime cause of schizophrenia (Bateson, 1972; Bateson *et al.*, 1956).

Laing's theory, outlined above, is obviously open to observational and perhaps even experimental validation. However, recall the evidence cited in the last chapter that personality-indexing behavior is plastic in the extreme, at least in adults. As different sources of confirmation appear, we might expect to find changes in behavior, corresponding to the changing sources of confirmation. On Laing's model, we should find consistent developmental effects only where the environment is consistent. An exception might occur if the pattern of confirmation were such as to produce self-maintaining and self-perpetuating behavior patterns. Suppose only aggressive, hostile behavior was confirmed in a child. The generalization of this behavior to newly encountered individuals would surely restrict the possibility of ever receiving any other kind of confirmation.

Effects of feeding schedule on personality

So far as I know there are as yet no published studies of personality development from a Laingian point of view, although I believe such studies are underway. However, there are data in the literature that are interpretable within that theoretical system. One variable that has been quite well studied is the effects of feeding schedules during infancy on subsequent development. Mothers may feed their babies only when the baby evidences hunger. At the other extreme, a mother might feed her baby entirely on a predetermined schedule, say every four hours, even waking the baby for feeding. In terms of Laingian theory these two extremes should have quite different effects on personality development. Unfortunately for research in this area, few mothers fit either extreme.

In a survey carried out by Sears, Maccoby, and Levin (1957) the average mother tried to stick to some kind of schedule but was willing to modify the intervals by as much as 50 percent if the baby wanted it. Only eight percent of mothers adhered to a rigid feeding schedule. Following Laing's model, a rigid feeding schedule constitutes a frequent denial of the infant's internally generated desire for food. This should result in extinction of autonomous desires for food and perhaps, by generalization, extinction of other internally generated desires and behaviors. It should also result in reinforcement of behaviors imposed or elicited by adults. The conjunction of the extinction of internally generated behavior and the reinforcement of behaviors instigated by adults should lead to a loss of independent, expressive behavior and a gain in dependent behavior elicited by others. The actual data that are available do not contradict this prediction, although they hardly support it very strongly. Thus Sears and co-workers found that dependency in nursery school children was positively correlated with rigidity of feeding schedule in infancy. Dependency as defined in this study included asking adults what to do, asking adults for help, staying close to adults, and so on. The pattern at least fits in exactly with the Laingian hypothesis. Murphy (1962) found similar results. However, the bulk of the rest of the work on the relation between infant feeding schedules and later personality indexes shows no relationship at all. Since most of the other studies tested the effects of feeding in infancy on personality indicators measured much later in development than the preschool period used in these two studies, this lack of correlation is hardly surprising. As we pointed out above, many other sources of confirmation can enter the child's life, particularly after he goes to school. These new sources could readily change the relative frequency of dependent or independent behavior.

Effects of discipline on personality

The second area that has been of considerable interest to psychologists is the effects of disciplinary practices on behaviors used to measure personality. The main types of disciplinary style were described above. Their effects on aggressive behavior have been studied by a number of investigators. The most interesting effect, from a Laingian point of view, is that parents who practice love-withdrawal (or denial) in response to their child's aggression produce children who are very unlikely to manifest aggressive behavior. These children are very rarely hostile toward their parents, their peers, or other adults. By contrast, parents who rely on power assertion, using physical punishment or negative confirmation, tend to produce the most aggressive children of all. Those parents who use conditional negative confirmation, denying the child except when he does something of which they disapprove, tend to produce children who are aggressive enough to be antisocial, to the extent of being labeled delinquent. These disciplinary effects are somewhat stronger than the effects of rigid feeding schedules. This is not really surprising since discipline, unlike scheduled or unscheduled feeding, is continuous so long as the child lives with his parents (Becker, 1964).

Hoffman and Hoffman (1970) also studied the effects of various disciplinary patterns on personality. The children in the study were all in the seventh grade and classified as "normal" by their teachers. They were presented with the beginning of a story in which a child was given the opportunity to go into a closet and get at a box that his parents had told him he must never touch. The children were required to complete the story. One type of completion, which the authors refer to as "ego-alien completion," was particularly interesting. Here the child typically meets with disaster, such as falling and breaking his neck, shooting himself with a gun that is in the box, or poisoning himself with chemicals in the box. Such completions, while rare, were most characteristic of children whose parents' usual disciplinary technique was love-withdrawal. What could such a completion mirror or represent? Surely it is not too far fetched to suppose that this physical destruction is a representation of the loss of personality that the child feels when his parents withdraw their love from him. In Laingian terms, loss of love is loss of personal existence, the loss of "I."

The most interesting evidence of the long-term effects of denial comes from case studies of mentally ill patients. Recall Julie, the patient described in the last chapter (pp. 393–396). Her life history was a history of denial of her self-generated behaviors with confirmation of behaviors imposed by the other members of her family. It appears that throughout infancy Julie was rewarded or confirmed only for acts that originated with her mother. Her mother's account of Julie's feeding and weaning make it clear that her mother was in control, never Julie. Particularly striking is her mother's account of the object-permanence game. Julie was never allowed to throw objects for her mother to retrieve. Instead, as soon as she could crawl, her mother threw things for Julie to retrieve, an inversion of the normal game, again constituting a denial of Julie's self-generated behavior and a confirmation of those behaviors elicited by her mother. Throughout early childhood Julie seems to have been totally dependent on her mother, protesting at separation well past the normal age.

By the age of 10 Julie had reached a stage at which her mother had to direct her before Julie would do anything. This behavior was continually confirmed by her mother. A crisis began when Julie was a teenager; her mother began to insist that Julie go out by herself, have boyfriends, and so on. Here is a prime example of a double-bind. Julie's dependence is now denied. The autonomy that would bring her confirmation is not possible after 15 years of dependence. Reasonably enough, at this point Julie railed against her mother, accusing her mother of having smothered her, of not letting her be a person, and so on. The significant thing about these diatribes was that they were self-generated, and they did win confirmation, although negative. Her family called her mad and punished her both physically and verbally. This was seemingly the first time in Julie's whole life that anything she initiated received confirmation of any sort. From then on, labeled "mad," confirmed as "mad," she became mad. It is in this last stage, I think, that the power of confirmation is shown. Laing argues that the basic motive that shapes personal behavior is a search for confirmation of the "I" within us, whether confirmed negatively or positively. On this view it is to be expected that Julie's "I"-confirming behavior, her madness, would continue and flourish. On strict social reinforcement principles it is more difficult to understand why Julie did not remain dependent or start to show the mother-directed "autonomy" that her mother wanted. Only by accepting the power of confirmation, even negative confirmation, can we comprehend Julie's path of development.

The power of confirmation: a case study

While findings of this sort do fit in with a Laingian theory of personality, they would also fit with any learning theory that included adult attention as a powerful reinforcer. The only problem for a standard learning theory might be the extreme power of adult attention. Just how powerful attention can be is shown in a study of Lovaas and his associates (1965). The subject in that study was a girl of nine years. Her behavior problem was a tragic one: incipient self-destruction as a result of physically self-destructive behavior, which included battering her head and arms against sharp corners of furniture, doors, or whatever. The violence of these attacks was such that the child's skin was usually bruised, swollen, and discolored. She had once set her hair on fire by thrusting her head into an electric wall heater. As Lovaas points out, one would not initially think of this as a behavior nurtured and maintained by reinforcement. One would think that the pain consequent on the behavior would result in the suppression of the behavior. Nonetheless, Lovaas was able to show that even this extreme form of self-destructive behavior was a function of social reinforcement (in his terms) or confirmation (in Laing's terms).

Lovaas was able to reduce the frequency of self-destructive behavior to zero by manipulating the contingencies of confirmation. There is no way of overestimating the significance of such an accomplishment. Self-destructive children usually spend their lives in a straitjacket or deep in a drug-induced sleep, avoiding physical death at the price of death in life. Lovaas's study was quite complex. In one part of the study every instance of self-destructive behavior was followed by a remark addressed by the investigator to the patient: "I don't think you're so bad," delivered in a warm and reassuring manner. This particular remark was chosen because there are theories of self-destructive behavior that assume that it results

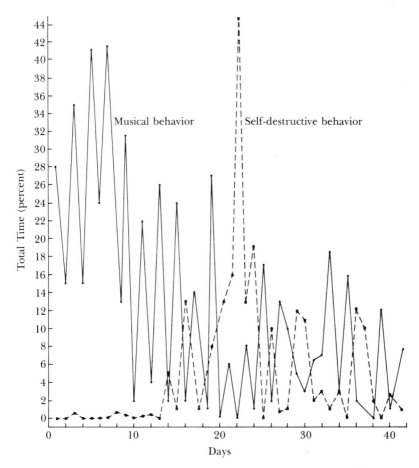

FIGURE 20-1
Changes in frequency of musical behavior (clapping and singing to music) and self-destructive behavior (banging the head and body against walls, sharp objects, etc.) by a nine-year-old girl in the extinction phase of an experiment designed to increase the frequency of the former and decrease the latter. (Lovaas *et al.*, 1975.)

from self-hatred, with hostile guilt feelings directed against the self. On such a view, reassuring the patient that she was not so bad should have reduced the frequency of the behavior. It did not; the frequency of the behavior increased, just as Laing and Lovaas would have predicted.

In another part of the study nondestructive behavior, e.g., singing and clapping to music, was given social reinforcement. Smiles and comments like "That's a good girl" were used. This resulted in a high rate of nondestructive behavior and a low rate of self-destructive behavior. When confirmation for nondestructive behavior ceased, the frequency of nondestructive behavior first increased then decreased, with self-destructive behavior mirroring these changes (Figure 20–1). Continued nonreinforcement of self-destructive behavior led to a decline in its frequency. When the investigators reinstated reinforcement for nondestructive behaviors, the frequency of self-destructive behaviors dropped effectively to zero. The study as a whole shows quite convincingly that, in this case at least, self-destructive behavior was a means of gaining confirmation and could be extinguished if it no longer served that end. Several other studies with single patients have found similar results (Ball, Dameron, and Lovaas, 1964; Williams, 1959; Wolf, Mees, and Risley, 1963). They constitute the most striking evidence of the power of social reinforcement, or personal confirmation as we will continue to call it.

WHAT DEVELOPS IN PERSONALITY DEVELOPMENT?

The literature abounds with studies showing that the personality-indexing behavior of children is plastic. However, none of these studies is particularly interesting; as we saw in the last chapter, the same behaviors are extremely plastic in adults as well. What we are looking for are forces that will produce long-term stable effects in development, the sort of forces or processes that produce the different world views we alluded to in the previous chapter. Above we mentioned that feeding schedules in infancy produce some, albeit weak, effects on behavior in the preschool age group. We interpreted these effects from the Laingian view of reinforcement. We did not really stop to consider what it was that was being reinforced. It certainly could not have been specific behaviors. The behaviors associated with feeding in infancy are not the behaviors associated with dependent or independent behavior in children 4–5 years old. However, something was reinforced that generated the dependent or independent behavior at age 4–5. That something must be, I would maintain, a conception or "theory" about the self and its relation to adults. This idea must be something of the form: "I must not initiate actions. I must do what I am told to do." Such a conception or "theory" would generate dependent behavior; its converse would generate independent behavior. Rigid feeding schedules could well provide the kind of experience that would generate such a "theory."

Consider one of the classic experiments on peer modeling (Bandura, Ross, and Ross, 1963). Children were shown a film of someone beating up a doll. They were then shown the real doll and left to themselves. Most of the children assaulted the doll. The film was more effective if the model was a child rather than an adult, and most effective if the model was a child of the same sex. However, in order for the subjects to imitate the behavior of the film model they must have a self-concept of the form: "I am a boy/girl. I should behave like other boys/girls. Since that boy/girl is bashing the doll, I will bash the doll." Given a self-concept of that kind, the experimental results are quite comprehensible. The real problem is how knowledge of that sort is generated. How does the child know he is a boy? How does one generate a self-concept, a concept that "I" exist and that "I" is different from "me"? There are numerous theories of this process, some of which have some supporting data.

Development of the self-concept

Some psychoanalytic theories assert that the distinction between "I" and "me" is accomplished very early, perhaps even in infancy. Two psycho-analytically oriented theorists have addressed themselves to these problems. Lacan (1972) describes a *mirror phase* in development during which the basic differentiation between "I" and "me" is made. The mirror-phase begins around six months of age or whenever after that the baby first sees himself in a mirror or other reflecting surface. The critical moment comes when the baby realizes that the reflection in the mirror is himself, as he appears to other people. A baby, just like an adult, sees only bits of himself—his nose, cheeks, part of his trunk, arms, and legs. In the mirror, however, he can see himself as he appears to others. At this point he realizes that he can see himself in a way that no one else can, that there is a public "me" and a private "I," that "I" can see "me" as no one else can.

According to Lacan, a child may refuse to accept that "I" and "me" are the same; he may feel that his body is not "his" body. Lacan cites cases of childhood psychosis in which the root problem seems to have been just that. If this is the case, then the child enters the world of language aware of a split between himself as he appears to himself and himself as he appears to others. As far as subsequent development is concerned, Lacan's theory seems similar to Laing's but less specified. We will thus turn to a consideration of Laing's theory of self-construction.

Like Lacan, Laing (1961) puts the beginning of the process of self-construction early in childhood, in the period of infancy. The process of self-construction has the same structure as the development of the object concept. Like Freud before him, and indeed like most parents, Laing is impressed by the pleasure and interest all children seem to take in making objects disappear and then recovering them. He has called attention to another common children's game that is formally very similar to the object-permanence games. This is the game in which the child makes himself disappear, either completely, so that the whole body is out of sight, or partially, as in peek-a-boo games, or even by asking or making the adult playmate close his or her eyes. The pleasure consists in being unseen but present in the vicinity of an adult. This is a common game in my experience. My youngest daughters, age four, still play it. In the course of it, one of them said, "You can't see *me* but *I'm* still here." This is a clear differentiation between "I" and "me," "I" being the private self and "me" the public person.

The enjoyment of this difference is, according to Laing, the motive for the enjoyment of these primitive hiding games. Laing argues that it is the experience of *being* without *being seen* that creates awareness of the differentiation between the self and the public person, a differentiation that is basic to all subsequent personality development. Some evidence in favor of this hypothesis is the relatively late development in blind children of the use of the pronoun "I" (Hawk, 1937; Maxfield, 1936). They arrive at an awareness of the dual selves by nonvisual means, which presumably takes longer.

There is current work on the acquisition of gender labels. Again it seems that the process is very early. By the age of 10 months or so babies can identify individuals of their own sex and will preferentially attend to them (Lewis and Brookes, 1974).

Moral development

The most detailed work on personality development in our sense is work on moral development. What develops in moral development are theories about social responsibility. The theories are often neutral as far as specific behavior is concerned. In the previous chapter we presented the classic Hartshorne and May study (1928) that indicated that moral behavior was situationally specific. This has been taken as evidence that moral judgement does not control behavior. This is too strong a conclusion. The extent to which behavior is situationally specific may be a function of the level of moral development of the individual in the situation. Kohlberg (1963, 1969) has proposed six stages of moral development, which fall into three levels.

I. *Preconventional level.* At this level the child is responsive to cultural rules and labels of good and bad and right or wrong, but interprets these labels in terms of action (punishment, reward, exchange of favors) or in terms of the physical power of those who enunciate the rules and labels. The level is divided into the following two stages.

Stage 1: *The punishment and obedience orientation.* The physical consequences of action determine its goodness or badness regardless of the human meaning or value of these consequences. Avoidance of punishment and unquestioning deference to power are valued in their own right, not in terms of respect for an underlying moral order supported by punishment and authority (the latter being Stage 4).

Stage 2: *The instrumental relativist orientation.* Right action consists of that which instrumentally satisfies one's own needs and occasionally the needs of others. Human relations are viewed in terms like those of the marketplace. Elements of fairness, of reciprocity, and of equal sharing are present, but they are always interpreted in a physical, pragmatic way. Reciprocity is a matter of "you scratch my back and I'll scratch yours," not of loyalty, gratitude, or justice.

II. *Conventional level.* At this level maintaining the expectations of the individual's family, group, or nation is perceived as valuable in its own right, regardless of immediate and obvious consequences. The attitude is one not only of *conformity* to personal expectations and social order but of *loyalty* to it, of actively *maintaining*, supporting, and justifying the order and of identifying with the persons or group involved in it. At this level, there are the following two stages.

Stage 3: The interpersonal concordance or "good boy–nice girl." Good behavior is that which pleases or helps others and is approved by them. There is much conformity to stereotypical images of what is majority or "natural" behavior. Behavior is frequently judged by intention—"he means well" becomes important for the first time. One earns approval by being "nice."

Stage 4: The "law and order" orientation. There is orientation toward authority, fixed rules, and the maintenance of the social order. Right behavior consists of doing one's duty, showing respect for authority, and maintaining the given social order for its own sake.

III. *Postconventional, autonomous, or principled level.* At this level there is a clear effort to define moral values and principles that have validity and application apart from the authority of the groups or persons holding these principles and apart from the individual's own identification with these groups. This level again has two stages.

Stage 5: The social-contract, legalistic orientation. Generally with utilitarian overtones. Right action tends to be defined in terms of general individual rights and in terms of standards that have been critically examined and agreed upon by the whole society. There is a clear awareness of the relativism of personal values and opinions and a corresponding emphasis upon procedural rules for reaching consensus. Aside from what is constitutionally and democratically agreed upon, the right is a matter of personal "values" and "opinion." The result is an emphasis upon the possibility of changing law in terms of rational considerations of social utility (rather than freezing it in terms of Stage 4 "law and order"). Outside the legal realm, free agreement and contract are the binding elements of obligation. This is the "official" morality of the American government and Constitution.

Stage 6: The universal ethical principle orientation. Right is defined by the decision of conscience in accord with self-chosen *ethical principles* appealing to logical comprehensiveness, universality, and consistency. These principles are abstract and ethical (the Golden Rule, the categorical imperative); they are not concrete moral rules like the Ten Commandments. At heart, these are universal principles of *justice*, of the *reciprocity* and *equality* of human *rights*, and of respect for the dignity of human beings as *individual persons*.

Consider this dilemma, already discussed in Chapter 17:

In Europe, a woman was near death from a very bad disease, a special kind of cancer. There was one drug that the doctors thought might save her. It was a form of radium for which a druggist was charging ten times what the drug cost him to make. He paid $200 for the radium and charged $2,000 for a small dose of the drug. The sick woman's husband, Heinz, went to everyone he knew to borrow the money, but he could only get together about $1,000, which is half of what it cost. He told the druggist that his wife was dying and asked him to sell it cheaper or let him pay later. But the druggist said, "No, I discovered the drug and I'm going to make money from it." So Heinz got desperate and broke into the man's store to steal the drug for his wife. Should the husband have done that? Why? (Rest, 1968.)

The quotations below are typical of answers of children at each of the six stages of moral development (Rest, 1968):

Stage 1
    Action is motivated by avoidance of punishment and "conscience" is irrational fear of punishment.

Pro: If you let your wife die, you will get in trouble. You'll be blamed for not spending the money to save her and there'll be an investigation of you and the druggist for your wife's death.
Con: You shouldn't steal the drug because you'll be caught and sent to jail if you do. If you do get away, your conscience would bother you thinking how the police would catch up with you at any minute.

Stage 2
    Action motivated by desire for reward or benefit. Possible guilt reactions are ignored and punishment viewed in a pragmatic manner. (Differentiates own fear, pleasure, or pain from punishment-consequences.)

Pro: If you do happen to get caught you could give the drug back and you wouldn't get much of a sentence. It wouldn't bother you much to serve a little jail term, if you have your wife when you get out.
Con: He may not get much of a jail term if he steals the drug, but his wife will probably die before he gets out so it won't do him much good. If his wife dies, he shouldn't blame himself, it wasn't his fault she has cancer.

Stage 3
    Action motivated by anticipation of disapproval of others, actual or imagined-hypothetical (e.g., guilt). (Differentiation of disapproval from punishment, fear, and pain.)

Pro: No one will think you're bad if you steal the drug but your family will think you're an inhuman husband if you don't. If you let your wife die, you'll never be able to look anybody in the face again.

Con: It isn't just the druggist who will think you're a criminal, everyone else will too. After you steal it, you'll feel bad thinking how you've brought dishonor on your family and yourself; you won't be able to face anyone again.

Stage 4

Action motivated by anticipation of dishonor, i.e., institutionalized blame for failure of duty, and by guilt over concrete harm done to others. (Differentiates formal dishonor from informal disapproval. Differentiates guilt for bad consequences from disapproval.)

Pro: If you have any sense of honor, you won't let your wife die because you're afraid to do the only thing that will save her. You'll always feel guilty that you caused her death if you don't do your duty to her.

Con: You're desperate and you may not know you're doing wrong when you steal the drug. But you'll know you did wrong after you're punished and sent to jail. You'll always feel guilt for your dishonesty and lawbreaking.

Stage 5

Concern about maintaining respect of equals and of the community (assuming their respect is based on reason rather than emotions). Concern about own self-respect, i.e., to avoid judging self as irrational, inconsistent, non-purposive. (Discriminates between institutionalized blame and community disrespect or self-disrespect.)

Pro: You'd lose other people's respect, not gain it, if you don't steal. If you let your wife die, it would be out of fear, not out of reasoning it out. So you'd just lose self-respect and probably the respect of others too.

Con: You would lose your standing and respect in the community and violate the law. You'd lose respect for yourself if you're carried away by emotion and forget the long-range point of view.

Stage 6

Concern about self-condemnation for violating one's own principles. (Differentiates between community respect and self-respect. Differentiates between self-respect for general achieving rationality and self-respect for maintaining moral principles.)

Pro: If you don't steal the drug and let your wife die, you'd always condemn yourself for it afterward. You wouldn't be blamed and you would have lived up to the outside rule of the law but you wouldn't have lived up to your own standards of conscience.

Con: If you stole the drug, you wouldn't be blamed by other people but you'd condemn yourself because you wouldn't have lived up to your own conscience and standards of honesty.

It is clear that the behavior of an individual in stage 2 would be different from the behavior of an individual at stage 6. We have already mentioned some of the data supporting this proposition. In Milgram's experiment (p. 358) subjects at stage 6 are much less willing than less-developed subjects to inflict shock. Cheating in various situations can also be predicted on the basis of levels of moral development; higher-stage subjects refuse the temptation to cheat (Krebs, 1967). Behavior in real-life situations, both trivial and serious, can also be predicted. Higher-stage subjects are more likely to fulfill a commitment to return a questionnaire than are lower-stage subjects (Krebs and Rosenwald, 1973). More seriously, Kohlberg and Freundlich (1977) have found that moral stage is a good predictor of the likelihood that a delinquent will return to delinquency after his release from a corrective institution. The released delinquent at a high moral stage is unlikely to become involved with the law again, despite being exposed to the same temptations and pressures as his peers at a lower stage, who are more likely to resume their old ways. The level or stage of moral judgement is thus an attribute of a person that does allow us to predict his behavior in real-life situations. It is one of the important "theories" by which we interpret our own actions and those of others, and so deserves our attention as an important attribute of personality.

Kohlberg and Piaget (1932) have both argued that moral judgement develops, that moral stage is a developmental variable. Kohlberg, in particular, has claimed that the sequence of moral development (as given above) is invariant and irreversible. An individual cannot go from stage 2 to stage 6 without passing through stages 3, 4, and 5. Second, an individual cannot retreat to a lower stage. It is this last claim, if accepted, that would qualify moral judgement as a developmental variable. Needless to say, both claims have been subject to severe criticism.

The Bandura and McDonald study

Some authors have argued that moral judgements are responses learned from adults, and that they can be shifted up or down by exposure to appropriate adult models. This claim, if valid, would completely negate both of the assertions about moral development that were given above. It is therefore a most important claim. It is based on an experiment by Bandura and McDonald (1963) replicated by Cowan and co-workers (1969). In these studies children were presented with pairs of stories. In one story a child brings about major negative consequences as a result of good intentions; in the other a child brings about minor negative consequences as a result of bad intentions. Piaget (1932) argued that there is a developmental shift from judging an action in terms of its consequences to judging an action in terms of its intentions. It was this shift that the experimenters attempted to manipulate. In a pretest, the children, ages nine to 12 years, heard 12 pairs of stories. They were asked to identify which child was naughtier in each pair. They were then given a score corresponding to the number of times they used intention as a criterion of naughtiness. Two weeks after this pretest, subjects who scored low on intention were then conditioned "up." Subjects who scored high on intention were then conditioned "down." The conditioning procedure was as follows.

> The experimenter explained that she wanted to find out what children and adults thought of the stories she was going to read, and so an adult (the model) would be working along with him. Twenty-four different item pairs were read, one to the model and then one to the subject. If the subject were to be conditioned up, the model would explain her answer by contrasting the intent of the children in each story; if subjects were to be conditioned down, the model contrasted the amount of negative consequences without referring to the intent. If the subject was in the low group all the judgements of the model were at a high moral level; the reverse was true for the high subjects. Both model and subject were given approval for answers in the desired direction.

The results of these studies are fascinating. It is important to differentiate between those predictions developmental theories would make and those made by learning theory. Neither theory would deny the possibility that a shift in the direction of the adult response could occur. The "good boy/girl" orientation alone would ensure some compliance. The only difference really lies in the detail of the predictions about (1) the effect the starting level of the child has on the conditioning experience, and (2) the effects of attempts to change subjects downward. The most important difference is the second one. A developmental theory would predict that it should be much easier to move a subject up. Even a compliant subject should have some internal resistance to giving judgments on a moral basis that he no longer held as valid. Learning theory, by contrast, would predict no difference, that it should be as easy to train subjects "down" as "up." As Figure 20–2 shows, the results definitely favor the developmental theory.

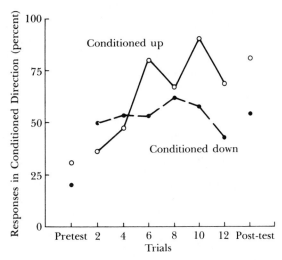

FIGURE *20–2*

Children who gave responses at a high moral level to stories on a pretest were conditioned down to a lower level by an adult. Children who gave responses at a lower level of morality on the pretest were conditioned up to a higher level. As the results of the experiment show, it was easier to condition children up to a higher level of moral thought than to condition them down to a lower one.

This experiment is not a conclusive test of the theories. Ideally for the developmental argument, it would be better to find no change as a result of downward conditioning. Given the age and stage of moral development of the subjects in this experiment, such a result could not have been obtained here, since concurrence with adult opinion was regarded as morally good by these subjects.

Turiel's study

A number of other studies have attempted to alter the stage of moral judgement in different ways. A model experiment of this kind is the study by Turiel (1966). Turiel assessed the moral stage of a group of subjects 12–13 years old. They were then exposed, by way of a role-playing situation, to moral arguments either one stage lower than their own, one stage higher, or two stages higher. For example, after hearing Kohlberg's moral conflict story (p. 416), a stage 2 subject would hear two people each present one of the following arguments based on stage 3 reasoning.

> 1. You really shouldn't steal the drug. There must be some better way of getting it. You could get help from someone. Or else you could talk the druggist into letting you pay later. The druggist is trying to support his family; so he should get some profit from his business. Maybe the druggist should sell it for less, but still you shouldn't steal it.

> 2. You should steal the drug in this case. Stealing isn't good but you can't be blamed for doing it. You love your wife and are trying to save her life. Nobody would blame you for doing it. The person who should really be blamed is the druggist who was just being mean and greedy.

The subjects were not therefore in a compliance situation like the one used by Bandura and McDonald. From the viewpoint of learning theory, there is no reason why subjects should change their responses in any of these situations. Nonetheless, change did occur in an upward direction in those subjects exposed to arguments one stage higher than their own stage of development (Table 20–1). While this study has been severely criticized, its main conclusions have been verified several times (Keasey, 1973; Tracy and Cross, 1973).

The most interesting result of this study and its various replications is that change occurs in an upward rather than a downward direction. Arguments based on one stage lower or two stages higher than the subject's own were relatively ineffective. This again would contradict a learning theory point of view. If moral judgements are simple learned habits, subjects should be equally moveable in any direction by any amount. It has been suggested that subjects reject arguments from lower stages because they have been through those stages and thus have already

TABLE *20–1*

After having been exposed to moral arguments one stage lower, one stage higher, or two stages higher than their assessed level of moral development, children were reassessed for any change in moral development and compared with a control group who had not been exposed to any arguments. The data here show the proportions of children who, under a particular condition, moved up one or two stages or showed no change. The highest proportions of subjects who moved up either one or two stages were those who had been exposed to arguments one stage higher than their original assessed level. (Turiel, 1966.)

	CHANGE IN STAGE		
CONDITION	0	+1	+2
One stage lower	28.3%	13.1%	5.7%
One stage higher	34.6	26.6	10.2
Two stages higher	37.4	14.5	9.9
Control	39.5	12.2	8.5

rejected the reasoning of those stages. By contrast, the arguments derived from two stages higher are ineffective because they are incomprehensible. A study by Rest (1968) found that subjects would "translate" arguments from a stage much higher than their own in terms compatible with their own stage of judgement. They simply did not understand the higher level arguments.

There is other data, from longitudinal studies, that may be taken as indicating that moral development is a developmental process. It has been found that moral development stops at about the age of 20 (Kohlberg and Elfinbein, 1975). This is the age, on average, by which the processes of gene expression are over. If advance in moral judgement does depend on gene expression, we would expect it to stop around the age of 20. The same studies have also shown the importance of experience in moral development. The range of stages at which subjects stopped ran all the way from stages two to six. That this is a matter of experiential differences rather than genetic differences should be clear from the studies cited above, all of which show that quite minimal exposure to the right kind of argument can produce change. Moral development is thus a function of experience affecting gene expression to produce irreversible changes in structure. Gene expression alone is not effective, nor is experience after the age at which gene expression is no longer possible. The nature of the relevant experience is not yet totally clear. As we argued earlier (pp. 348–359), it is probable that exposure to peers is critical for the early advances, while exposure to different moral systems is responsible for the later advances.

It is worth noting that moral judgement is, like the other developmental variables we have looked at, at least one step removed from actual behavior. The behavior will still be situationally specific. Only by sampling a range of situations could we determine the rules or "theories" that underlie a specific response in a specific situation. Saying that someone is at a particular moral level allows one to predict that the subject's behavior will fall in a certain class of behaviors. The specific behavior in any specific situation is less predictable.

THE PLASTICITY OF PERSONALITY

In the previous chapter we argued that many of the behaviors that index personality in adults are quite plastic. In this chapter we have been arguing that personality is the outcome of a developmental process, an irreversible process. There is a contradiction here, at least superficially, although it is a contradiction that will fade away, I think, if we look at the precise nature of what is developing in social development. Consider the specific behavior associated with sex labels. It seems that by the time a child is three years old the child has learned "I am a girl" or "I am a boy." That piece of learning is seemingly irreversible (pp. 365–366). But it is also very abstract; it contains third-level information, if we wish to compare it to cognitive acquisitions (pp. 221–226). The specific behaviors that are learned along with "I am a boy" or "I am a girl" are necessarily of a very different nature and necessarily very plastic. The "correct" masculine or feminine behavior for a four-year-old is very different from that of an eight-year-old, which in turn is very different from that of a teenager. In fact, specific behaviors may be "masculine" at one age and "feminine" at another (Kagan and Moss, 1962; Kagan, 1964). What does not reverse is the third-level knowledge of what sex one is. That knowledge is transduced into observable behavior by way of other information drawn from the cultural milieu, telling the child how to behave in accord with the persisting third-level information.

A similar process must occur in the formation of deep and shallow attachments. The deep intimate relations of an 18-month-old are very different, behaviorally, from the deep intimate relations an 18-year-old will have. The former is necessary for the latter, but it is not necessary in the sense that the baby acquires specific skills that the 18-year-old needs. Rather, the baby acquires the very abstract idea that it is possible to have deep intimate relations with people, an idea that will be translated subsequently into whatever behaviors are culturally permissible expressions of intimacy at a particular time of life.

The observed pliability of personality, i.e., the situational specificity we talked about in Chapter 19, need not mean therefore that "personality" does not develop. What does develop are rather abstract ideas about

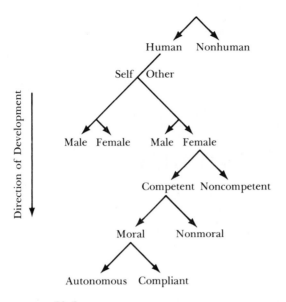

FIGURE *20–3*

Social development can be viewed as a series of successive differentiations. The initial differentiation is between human and nonhuman, and there is some evidence that this differentiation may be innate. The second differentiation, between Self and Other, may also be innate. The next step in the series is differentiation of gender, with the rest of the series following over time.

oneself in relation to others. These ideas become translated into specific behavior in specific situations. Our personality thus appears plastic in behavior, but the higher-order principles that generate specific behaviors stay the same. Since we do not all have the same principles or "theory," there will be individual differences in our responses to the same situation. Figure 20–3 is an epigenetic chart of the higher-order principles that make up personality. I hope this will help explain how it is we can develop in the world of people, remaining constant at one level while changing so drastically at another.

21

Development:
A Summary

We have been looking thus far at the development of the specific skills, abilities or characteristics that occurs during the first 20 years or so of a human life. It is now time to say something about development in general, something about the process that may (or may not) underpin all of the specific instances we have examined. In this chapter I would like to offer some account of development itself.

"Development" is the study of some age-related changes in psychological functioning. It seems to me that any theory of development must answer five questions. The first question that must be answered is which age-related changes are to be considered as developmental, part of our data, and which are to be left aside, as part of the province of, say, learning theory. Second, we must consider whether or not development is a single unitary process, with all of us advancing more or less speedily, more or less far down a single path of human development. This is a popular view; on the basis of such a view variations in human intelligence are expressed in a single number, the IQ; cultures which do not view the world as we do are labeled primitive; and so on. The alternative is to view differences in the outcome of development as the reflection of different possible paths of development, with some individuals proceeding down one path, others down another. On this view attempting to measure the quantitative superiority or inferiority of development would be a pointless procedure: there is no superiority or inferiority, merely difference.

Third, and intimately related to the second question, is the question of whether all of the age-related changes in function that constitute the data of development are of the same logical or scientific type. If we offer a theory of the emergence of walking, say, can we expect it to have any relevance to the emergence of formal reasoning; would a theory of formal reasoning have anything to say about the emergence of the affectionless character? Must we have micro-theories of each change, or can we formulate a general theory to account for all changes?

The previous two questions are "what" questions. If we can answer these, we must still answer the fourth question, "why?". Why do developmental changes occur; what is it that can make a change occur, or, perhaps more important, prevent it from occurring?

Lastly, any theory of development should offer an account of "how" these changes take place; by this I mean the theory should have something to say about the neural mechanisms that underlie the behavioral changes we can see.

The first question—what age related changes are to be taken as developmental—is surely the most fundamental. Earlier in the book I suggested that we should concentrate on those changes that are irreversible. As we have seen, there are few intellectual or social changes that never show any surface reversibility. I would therefore like to modify my original suggestion and propose that we concentrate on those changes that are irreversible or that have irreversible consequences. This suggestion seems paradoxical; how can any change that is not irreversible have irreversible consequences? I have written at length elsewhere about this seeming paradox (Bower, 1977c). Its solution in fact depends on answers to questions 2 and 3, the "what" questions. I would like to propose that development is a process of differentiation, occurring at many different levels.

Throughout the book I have argued that there are different levels or types of development. I have differentiated "levels" as "types" are differentiated in the Theory of Types. At present, rather than go through the logic of distinctions of levels, I would prefer to offer some empirical distinctions. For example, we have spent some time in the book on the development of gender-appropriate behavior. Gender-appropriate behavior changes from age to age. There is little consistency at a specifically behavioral level. However, there is consistency at a conceptual level; once the child has decided "I am a boy" or "I am a girl" there is very little possibility of change. It is that basic conceptual decision that generates the variable, gender-appropriate behavior seen at later ages. We can thus make a distinction between development of a concept and development of the behaviors generated by the concept. I hope it is clear what I mean when I say the behavior and the concept represent different *levels* of development.

If there is clearly a difference between behavior and the concepts that generate it, I trust it is equally clear that there can be differences of the same sort between concepts. Consider one of the problems of the formal operations period, the problem of what happens to popcorn when it is popped. Solution of that problem requires skills or concepts at many different levels. There are specifically behavioral skills involved, the skills of weighing popped and unpopped corn, for example. Awareness of the problem depends on concepts of volume and weight and a concept of their relation. A correct solution depends on a concept of density, a product of the other two. All of these concepts are different expressions of a concept of measure, which, for that reason, is a concept of a different type, or level. "Density" in addition requires a willingness to postulate an idea of the form, "Invisible events may be necessary for the explanation of visible events." Since that idea has many more expressions than the concept of density alone, it too, I would argue, is at a different level from the concept of density. But why formulate this last idea, that it may be necessary to postulate invisible events to explain visible events? The answer to that, I think, involves perception of visible paradoxes plus a very high-level concept of the form, "The world is a consistent and orderly place; every change has an explanation." (Along with these beliefs about the world, there must be, I think, a belief about the self—"I can solve problems.") I have been arguing that there are different types of levels of concept involved in this one problem. Each higher-order concept represents a common factor of several lower-order concepts. Thus, in representing the factors involved in the popcorn problem, we could produce a structure like this:

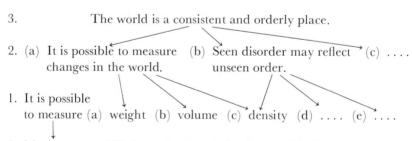

3.   The world is a consistent and orderly place.

2. (a) It is possible to measure   (b) Seen disorder may reflect   (c) ....
       changes in the world.   unseen order.

1. It is possible
   to measure (a) weight (b) volume (c) density (d) .... (e) ....

0. Measurement skills (e.g., the knowledge that $1 + 1 = 2$)

All of these levels must be involved in a problem-solving sequence; that sequence may vary from child to child but must eventually call upon all of these conceptual rules. Thus, one problem solver might go $1a \rightarrow 1b \rightarrow 1a \rightarrow 3 \rightarrow 2b \rightarrow 2a \rightarrow 1c$. Other orders would be possible.

There is nothing new or particularly unorthodox about the distinctions made above. What is unorthodox is the assertion that the higher levels precede the lower in the course of development and that the higher levels are necessary if the lower levels are to develop. This assertion is of some importance for the first question outlined above. Consider again the popcorn problem. Without the aid of a balance arm, one's first perception of this problem is likely to be erroneous. Because of the size-weight illusion, the popcorn is likely to be perceived as *lighter* than the unpopped corn. However, suppose we did not stop at this point but used a balance arm to equate the weights. How would one explain what had happened? A possible explanation, akin to several offered in the course of the history of science, might be that the popcorn had grown and had therefore become heavier but had simultaneously gained lightness during the heating process. What are the characteristics of this explanation? At the most abstract level it involves a willingness to explain a perceptible event by postulating an imperceptible characteristic to objects, the characteristic being lightness. Lightness is a property that is imparted by heating. It is a property that objects have to different degrees, so that objects of the same size can be of different weight. The explanation could be generalized to other situations, such as the boiling away of water. Water could be used to show the reversibility of the effect. Heated water becomes bigger and lighter, but cooling will reverse the change.

Let us contrast this erroneous interpretation with the correct interpretation.

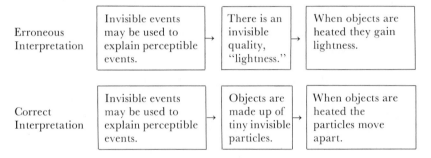

It must be obvious that it is only at the level of the *specific* solution that the two systems of explanation are qualitatively different. Both involve hypothetical explanations. Both involve "invisible" concepts. Both are susceptible to the same empirical validation. Is there any sense in which one is "better" than the other? What does "better" mean here? The correct solution is probably better in the scientific sense in that it allows generalization to more problems, such as the problem of what happens to sugar in hot water. Nonetheless, both are equally complex and equally internally coherent. The most obvious way in which the correct solution is better is that it is in accordance with ideas that are prevalent in our culture. A child faced with problems involving density can pick up these ideas from the cultural artifacts around him. Having worked out a solution, he can have it approved by the adults in his vicinity. If he lived in a culture where adults operated with a concept of "lightness," he might succeed in working out an atomic hypothesis, but he would not get approval for it from the social world around him. Scientific innovators, as we mentioned above (pp. 218–220), rarely gain instant approval.

What has this to do with a concept of development? I am suggesting that there is no one formal system of thought. I am proposing that every one in every culture will come to the point of attempting to explain the puzzles of the world as perceived by calling upon unseen powers, unseen events to explain the puzzles. The specific solution an individual uses will depend upon his cultural milieu. However, the effect of that cultural milieu is seemingly developmental. It seems clear that an individual is not likely to be able to change the specific concepts he uses to explain the world much past the age of 20. The evidence for this is not overwhelming. Indeed it is not psychological evidence at all, but rather the evidence from the history of science that was alluded to above. The little psychological data there is comes from cross-cultural studies indicating that adults in non-Western cultures are far less likely than are children to manifest "correct" solutions to problems (pp. 190–192). This, I would argue, occurs because the adults are already so far down one specific conceptual path that they cannot transfer to any of the alternatives.

It is important to note what I am denying. I am denying that those adults who offer incorrect solutions to formal problems do so because they are incapable of reasoning about unseen events. Any culture with myth, magic, or religion is capable of reasoning about unseen events. I am also denying that these individuals lack any of the mental operations that are required for the formal skills. As we saw in Chapter 6, two-year-olds will demonstrate these operations in the appropriate situation. Nor can it be said that an individual with a magical view of the world lacks concepts. At this level the concepts are clearly *different*, but not lacking. It is this difference that leads me to argue that cognitive development is a matter of differentiation rather than growth along a single scale.

Is there any evidence that development does follow this course of differentiation from higher to lower? The best evidence comes from the paradoxes of reversibility and irreversibility alluded to throughout the book. Throughout development changes occur that are reversible, indeed that do reverse; nonetheless, these changes, themselves reversible, seem to be responsible for irreversible effects, occurring many years later. For example, the sighted child during infancy learns a great deal about the structure of space. By the age of 16 months or so, the sighted child no longer shows any egocentrism in spatial problems (pp. 122–124). Egocentrism will of course recur. The child though has been learning more than that. He has learned something of the form, "The world is ordered in three dimensions," level-3 information that many years later will generate knowledge and understanding of the complexities of geometry. Even if the child goes blind at two years of age and is thereby cut off from any further direct information about the three-dimensional structure of the world, he can still formulate and understand the same geometrical concepts as a child who has never been blind. The child born blind is very different. It does seem that it is impossible to teach geometry to a child who has never been sighted. Why is this? Why does two years of differential experience at the beginning of life produce differential effects after 10 years of seemingly identical experience? The answer is, I think, that the experiences of the child born blind and the later-blinded child *cannot* be identical. The later-blinded child, like the sighted child, has learned a level-3 rule that states that the world is ordered in three dimensions; after that rule is formulated, all inputs will be seen through it, resulting in continuity of three-dimensional experience, despite lack of vision. By contrast, the child born blind can only formulate a rule that would say, "The world is ordered in time." Such a framework for experience would prevent the growth of three-dimensional knowledge; indeed, if sight were restored, it could militate against the very possibility of three-dimensional experience. With two very different frames with which to interpret the world, the experiences of those born blind and those blinded later cannot be the same. In this way the abstract, high-level attainments of infancy program the possibilities for development thereafter. Surely it is obvious that we are not dealing with failure of development but with two different paths of development.

A similar case can be made in the realm of social development. Normal children show strong attachment to a single individual plus fear of strangers around the age of eight months. These behaviors indexing attachment and fear disappear at some later point. A child raised in an impersonal institution may never develop either attachment or fear. The normal child, many years later, will develop deep attachments again, in marriage and parenthood for example. The institutional child may never be able to do so. These differences hold true even if the child from a normal home is institutionalized after babyhood and the institutional child fostered out to a warm and loving home. Again I would propose that these differences result from different level-3 rules acquired during infancy. The child from the normal home has learned that it is possible to have deep relations with people, given time; the institutional child has learned something quite different, that it is only possible to have shallow relations. Again, with different frameworks for the interpretation of information the children can never have the same psychological worlds. Despite similarities in the objective features of their world, the children will carry forward a continuity of individual and different experience from infancy, resulting in long-term differences in behavior. Here again, surely, we are dealing with two different paths of development, rather than failure of development.

The high-level abstract attainments we have been discussing can each generate many lower-level concepts. I have been referring to this as a process of differentiation. Unlike some other authors, I view development as a process of differentiation without loss; the initial high-level attainments persist along with their differentiated products, and will be referred to whenever the differentiated products fail in use.

Development then is a process of differentiation without loss. The child is born with or rapidly acquires some abstract, high-level framework for interpreting the world around him, both the physical and the social worlds, with himself in relation to these worlds a third enigma to be understood. Since these frameworks by their very nature cannot cope in detail with detailed, specific situations, more specific concepts or rules will emerge, the process continuing until behavior is adapted to every specific situation that occurs. The process of downward specification takes time. Its rate and direction will depend on the challenges posed by the environment; the environment that poses these challenges is not the "objective" environment that a Martian might describe; it is a psychological environment that is a function of the "objective" situation and the frameworks of interpretation that are brought to bear on it. This kind of differentiation without loss is universal within the developmental process. Whatever it is that produces intellectual development also produces social and personality development.

This brings us to the fourth question, the question of "why." Why do changes occur? Why do expected changes sometimes fail to occur? Why are some changes irreversible? "Why" questions are in part questions of motivation. What motives impel development? I have spoken of two, a motive to understand and a motive to commune with people. The two are closely intertwined; people present the growing child with many of the problems he must solve; solving these problems, as well as the problems of the physical world, will help unite the child more closely with the people around him. Of the two, I think the motive to understand is the more important, since, as with the affectionless character, changes in understanding can change the nature of the social motive itself. Motives of this kind are unfortunately hard to index; it would be difficult to measure them as we measure physiological needs like hunger or thirst. There is some evidence that the comprehension motive is triggered whenever the child finds he has two contradictory ways of interpreting the same event in the world. The contradiction inspires a search through higher-level interpretations to program an adjustment of the lower-level interpretation to produce a consonant non-contradictory view of the world. While this may be the universal trigger for the later phases of development, contradiction could hardly be responsible for the emergence of the earliest, most abstract formulations. While it is possible that some of these are innate, the possibility of alternative formulations, noted throughout this book, should caution us against such an easy explanation. It is more probable that the abstractness of the child's first descriptions of the world reflect the characteristics of the world. Consider one high-level description, "The world is ordered in three dimensions." The information supporting such a description is continually presented to the seeing child. No matter what variations of color, form, size, distance, and arrangement are present in the world he sees, that world always presents a three-dimensional organization. I would propose that abstract descriptions are formulated first because they are universally, or near universally, useful. The child early in life is exposed to many, many more situations where abstract descriptions will be useful than to situations where only a precise description will do. It seems reasonable that the child should pick up the abstract, general properties of the world first, simply because these general properties are more frequently presented. However, because abstract descriptions are just that, descriptive of the essence of many situations, they cannot be adequate for precise situations, and so must be specified or differentiated, raising then the possibilities for contradiction, transfer, and so on.

The frequency of utility of the high-level descriptions of the world may also have something to say about seeming irreversibility. A rule of the sort, "The world is ordered in three dimensions," is confirmed every time the child acts in the world. The rule, "The world is consistent and orderly," is reinforced every time the child makes sense of a problem. A self-description, "I am competent," will likewise be reinforced every time a problem is successfully solved. In addition, as was pointed out earlier, these high-level rules are essentially frameworks for interpreting the world. If the world cannot be interpreted save through these frames, information to contradict the frames can hardly be fed in. In those very rare situations where this is possible—as, for example, with the blind (pp. 205–206)—the lack of an alternative interpretational system will lead to retreat from the problem rather than a new development. The same may occur with descriptions of the self and the social world (pp. 413–414).

What of our fifth question, how does development take place? All of the above tends to make developmental processes sound like frequently reinforced learning processes. I suspect that this is inaccurate. The "how" of development may be different from the "how" of learning. Early in this book I proposed that in development the genes make new structures. Which genes are switched on and when depends on the environment, the psychological environment, the world as experienced, just as much as the physico-chemical environment—more so in the case of brain growth. Have we seen any evidence that developmental processes do result in differential patterns of brain growth? The best evidence remains the evidence from growth of the visual system (pp. 37–43). "Seeing" is an event in the psychological world, and what is seen determines the way the brain will grow. Hearing language is likewise something that belongs in the world of experience, and we have seen (pp. 86–91) that delayed opportunity to hear language can alter the way the brain grows; it would seem that areas of the brain normally used for language processing can be directed to other functions in the absence of linguistic input, provided that there is some competing function to switch on its own particular genes, to make its own particularly appropriate structures. Again, in brain growth we are not dealing so much with failures of development as with redirection of development, differential development as a function of differential demands from the psychological environment. It seems to me that we can advance as tentative hypotheses the propositions that (1) events in the psychological world switch on some of the genes that could be switched on; (2) these genes create permanent structures which prevent the formation of alternative structures; and (3) the permanence of the structures created results in the irreversibility of development. These hypotheses seem valid for a few aspects of development. Whether they are adequate for the rest will depend on a great deal more research.

OMISSIONS

This book has said nothing about the study of development in adulthood. There are currently many theorists who would argue that psychological development continues throughout the lifespan (Erikson, 1950; Loevinger, 1966). With respect, I feel that such claims do some violence to the idea of development. To be sure there are changes after 20 or so, but they are not changes resulting from gene expression, nor are they age-linked, nor indeed are they at all universal (with one exception—see below). Anyway, any such changes are, I feel, at the most differentiated end of psychological functioning. As such they are continuations of the abstract accomplishments of the growth phase of development. I know of no evidence indicating genuine developmental change in the adult's basic world view, whether of the self, of the social world, or of the physical world.* Indeed, what little evidence there is indicates that such changes do not take place (pp. 210–216). Rather, the adult becomes more and more rigidly fixed in his or her own world of experience (pp. 334–338), with all of the problems that creates between parent and child.

Death

One aspect of development in adulthood I would have liked to consider is death. Natural death, it would appear, is an epigenetic process *par excellence*. Events in the environment switch on lethal genes which destroy earlier

---

*A few individuals, for example, St. Paul, may have been exceptions to this rule.

accomplishments, resulting in death. Among the critical events to which we must give a role are events in the *psychological* world, events like sudden helplessness, sudden loss of competence, plus many other less usual accompaniments of aging (Seligman, 1975). Death provides one of the best instances of the argument presented in answer to our "how" question. It does seem to be the result of gene expression, the relevant genes being switched on by events in the psychological world of the individual. It would thus appear that there is a commonality between the processes that begin psychological life and those that end it. We are all ultimately at the mercy of our genes and the world that controls them.

References

Adby, P. R., and Dempster, M. A. H.
  1974 *Introduction to Optimization Methods.* London: Chapman and Hall.
Ahrens, R.
  1954 Beiträge zur Entwicklung des Physiognomie- und Mimikerkenntnis. *Zeitschrift für experimentelle und angewandte Psychologie,* **2**(3):414–454.
Ainsworth, M. D. S., and Wittig, B. A.
  1965 Attachment and exploratory behavior of one year olds in a strange situation. In *Determinants of Infant Behaviour,* Vol. IV, B. M. Foss, ed. London: Methuen.
Anastasi, A.
  1958 *Differential Psychology.* London: Macmillan.
Ambrose, J. A.
  1961 The development of the smiling response in early infancy. In *Determinants of Infant Behaviour,* Vol. I, B. M. Foss, ed. New York: Wiley.
André-Thomas, C., and Dargassies, St. A.
  1952 *Etudes neurologiques sur le nouveau-né et le jeune nourrisson.* Paris: Masson.
Aronson, E., and Rosenbloom, S.
  1971 Space perception in early infancy: Perception within a common auditory-visual space. *Science,* **172**: 1161–1163.
Argyle, M.
  1969 *Social Interaction.* London: Methuen.
Asch, S. E.
  1958 Effects of group pressure upon the modification and distortion of judgements. In *Readings in Social Psychology,* E. E. Maccoby, J. M. Newcomb and E. L. Hartley, eds. London: Methuen.

Ayllon, T., and Michael, J.
  1959   The psychiatric nurse as a behavioral engineer. *Journal of the Experimental Analysis of Behavior*, **2**: 323–334

Ball, T. S., Dameron, L. E., and Lovaas, O. I.
  1964   *Control of Self-destructive Behaviors in Mentally Retarded Children.* Unpublished manuscript, University of California, Los Angeles.

Ball, W., and Tronick, E.
  1971   Infant responses to impending collision: Optical and real. *Science*, **171**: 818–820.

Bandura, A., and McDonald, F. J.
  1963   The influence of social reinforcement and the behavior of models in shaping children's moral judgements. *Journal of Abnormal and Social Psychology*, **67**:274–281.

Bandura, A., Ross, D., and Ross, S. A.
  1963   Imitation of film-mediated aggressive models. *Journal of Abnormal and Social Psychology*, **66**:3–11.

Bandura, A., and Walters, R. H.
  1963   *Social Learning and Personality Development.* New York: Holt, Rinehart and Winston.

Bateman, K. G.
  1959   The genetic assimilation of four veination phenocopies. *Journal of Genetics*, **56**:445–474.

Bateson, G.
  1972   *Steps to an Ecology of Mind.* New York: Ballantine.

Bateson, G., Jackson, D. D., Haley, J., and Weakland, J. H.
  1956   Toward a theory of schizophrenia. *Behavioral Science*, **1**:251–264.

Bayley, N.
  1955   On the growth of intelligence. *American Psychologist*, **10**:805–818.

Beazley, L. D.
  1975   Factors determining decussation at the optic chiasma by developing retinotectal fibres in *Xenopus. Experimental Brain Research*, **23**:491–504.

Becker, W. C.
  1964   Consequences of different kinds of parental discipline. In *Review of Child Development Research*, Vol. I, M. L. and L. W. Hoffman, eds. New York: Russell Sage Foundation.

Berenda, R. W.
  1950   *The Influence of the Group on the Judgements of Children.* New York: King's Crown.

Bereiter, C.
  1972   An academic preschool for disadvantaged children: Conclusions from evaluation studies. In *Preschool Programs for the Disadvantaged*, J. C. Stanley, ed. Baltimore: Johns Hopkins University Press.

Berry, J. W.
  1966   Temne and Eskimo perceptual skills. *International Journal of Psychology*, **1**:207–229.
  1971   Ecological and cultural factors in spatial skill development. *Canadian Journal of Behavioral Science*, **3**:324–336.

Berry, J. W., and Dasen, P. R.

1974 *Culture and Cognition: Readings in Cross-Cultural Psychology.* London: Methuen.

Bever, T. G., Mehler, J., and Epstein, J.

1968 What children do in spite of what they know. *Science,* **162**:921–924.

Birdwhistell, R. L.

1971 *Kinesics and Context: Essays on Body-Movement Communication.* London: Allen Lane.

Bloom, B. S.

1964 *Stability and Change in Human Characteristics.* New York: Wiley.

Bower, T. G. R.

1966 The visual world of infants. *Scientific American,* **215**(6):80–92.

1971 The object in the world of the infant. *Scientific American,* **225**(4):30–38.

1972 Object perception in infants. *Perception,* **1**:15–30.

1974a *Development in Infancy.* San Francisco: W. H. Freeman.

1974b The evolution of sensory systems. In *Perception: Essays in Honor of J. J. Gibson,* R. B. MacLeod and H. L. Pick, eds. Ithaca: Cornell University Press.

1977a *The Development of Reaching in Infants.* Unpublished monograph, University of Edinburgh.

1977b Infant behavior with virtual objects. Unpublished manuscript, University of Edinburgh.

1977c Concepts of development. Paper read at 21st International Congress of Psychology, Paris. In *Proceedings of the 21st International Congress of Psychology, Paris,* Presses Universitaires de France, 1978.

1977d Blind babies see with their ears. *New Scientist,* **73**(1037):255–257.

1978 Visual development in the blind child. In *Clinic in Developmental Medicine: Vision,* A. Macfarlane, ed. Spastics International Medical Publications. In press.

Bower, T. G. R., Broughton, J. M., and Moore, M. K.

1970a Infant responses to approaching objects: An indicator of response to distal variables. *Perception and Psychophysics,* **9**:193–196.

1970b The coordination of vision and touch in infancy. *Perception and Psychophysics,* **8**:51–53.

1970c Demonstration of intention in the reaching behaviour of neonate humans. *Nature,* **228**(5272):679–681.

1971 Development of the object concept as manifested by changes in the tracking behavior of infants between 7 and 20 weeks of age. *Journal of Experimental Child Psychology,* **11**(2):182–192.

Bower, T. G. R., and Paterson, J. G.

1972 Stages in the development of the object concept. *Cognition,* **1**(1):47–55.

1973 The separation of place, movement and object in the world of the infant. *Journal of Experimental Child Psychology,* **1**(15):161–168.

Bower, T. G. R., and Wishart, J. G.

1972 The effects of motor skill on object permanence. *Cognition,* **1**(2):28–35.

1976 Compensation and conservation in the drinking behaviour of infants. Unpublished manuscript, University of Edinburgh.

Bowerman, C. E., and Kinch, J. W.
   1959   Changes in family and peer orientation of children between the 4th and
          10th grades. *Social Forces*, 1937:206–211.
Bowlby, J.
   1951   *Maternal Care and Mental Health*. Geneva: World Health Organization.
   1969   *Attachment and Loss, Volume I: Attachment*. London: Hogarth Press.
   1972   The social development of the child. Paper read at Department of
          Psychiatry, University of Edinburgh.
   1973   *Attachment and Loss, Volume II: Separation*. London: Hogarth Press.
Brackbill, Y.
   1958   Extinction of the smiling response in infants as a function of reinforcement
          schedules. *Child Development*, **29**:115–124.
Braine, M. D. S.
   1963   The ontogeny of English phrase structure: The first phrase. *Language*,
          39:1–13.
Brainerd, C. J.
   1973   Neo-Piagetian training experiments revisited: Is there any support for
          the cognitive developmental stage hypothesis? *Cognition*, **2**:349–370.
Bresson, F., Maury, L., Pieraut-le Bonniec, G., and de Schonen, S.
   1977   Organisation and lateralisation of reaching in infants: An instance of
          asymmetric function in hand collaboration. *Neuropsychologia*, **15**:311–320.
Bronson, G. W.
   1972   Infants' reactions to unfamiliar persons and novel objects. *Monograph of
          the Society for Research in Child Development*, Vol. 37, No. 3.
Brown, D. G.
   1956   Sex-role preference in young children. *Psychological Monographs*, Vol. 70,
          No. 14:1–19.
Brown, R., and Bellugi, U.
   1964   Three processes in the child's acquisition of syntax. *Harvard Educational
          Review*, **34**:133–151.
Bruce, R. W.
   1933   Conditions of transfer of training. *Journal of Experimental Psychology*,
          16:343–361.
Bruner, J. S.
   1968   *Processes of Cognitive Growth: Infancy*. Worcester, Mass.: Clark University
          Press.
Bruner, J. S., and Anglin, J. M.
   1973   *Beyond the Information Given*. Toronto: McLeod.
Bruner, J. S., and Koslowski, B.
   1972   Visually preadapted constituents of manipulatory action. *Perception*,
          1:3–15.
Bruner, J. S., Olver, R. R., and Greenfield, P. M.
   1966   *Studies in Cognitive Growth*. New York: Wiley.
Buber, M.
   1937   *I and Thou*. Edinburgh: T. & T. Clark. (Original German edition 1923.)
Bühler, C.
   1930   *The First Year of Life*. New York: Day.

Burlingham, D.
  1952 *Twins*. New York: International Universities Press.
Burwen, L. S., and Campbell, D. T.
  1957 The generality of attitudes towards authority and non-authority figures. *Journal of Abnormal Social Psychology*, **54**:24–31.
Bridges, K. M. B.
  1931 *The Social and Emotional Development of the Pre-school Child*. London: Routledge and Kegan Paul.
Byrne, D., and Griffith, W.
  1966 A developmental investigation of the law of attraction. *Journal of Personality and Social Psychology*, **4**:699–703.
Caro, F. G.
  1966 Social class and attitudes of youth relevant for the realization of adult goals. *Social Forces*, **44**:495.
Carpenter, G.
  1975 Mother's face and the newborn. In *Child Alive*, R. Lewin, ed. London: Temple Smith.
Cazden, C.
  1965 *Environmental Assistance to the Child's Acquisition of Grammar*. Doctoral thesis, School of Education, Harvard University.
Clark, E.
  1978 From gesture to word: On the natural history of deixis in language acquisition. In *Human Growth in Development*, J. S. Bruner and A. Garten, eds. Oxford: Clarendon Press.
Condon, W. S., and Sander, L.
  1974 Neonate movement is synchronized with adult speech: Interactional participation and language acquisition. *Science*, **183**:99–101.
Conger, J. J.
  1971 A world they never knew: The family and social change. *Daedalus*, fall issue, pp. 1105–1138.
  1973 *Adolescence and Youth*. New York: Harper & Row.
Cowan, P. A., Langer, J., Heavenrich, J., and Nathanson, M.
  1969 Social learning and Piaget's cognitive theory of moral development. *Journal of Personality and Social Psychology*, **11**:261–274.
Crandall, V. J., Orleans, S., Preston, A., and Rabson, A.
  1958 The development of social compliance in young children. *Child Development*, **29**:429–443.
Crutchfield, R. S.
  1955 Conformity and character. *American Psychologist*, **10**:191–198.
Curtiss, S., Fromkin, V., Krasken, S., Rigler, D., and Rigler, M.
  1974 The linguistic development of Genie. *Language*, **50**:528–554.
Dasen, P. R.
  1974 The influence of ecology, culture, and European contact on cognitive development in Australian Aborigines. In *Culture and Cognition: Readings in Cross Cultural Psychology*, J. W. Berry and P. R. Dasen, eds. London: Methuen.
  1975 Cross-cultural data on operational development: Asymptotic development curves. Paper read at Conference on Dips in Learning and

Development Curves, Saint-Paul-de-Vence. (To be published 1979, Lawrence Erlbaum Associates, Hillsdale, N.J.)

Dasen, P. R., and Christie, R. D.
1972   A regression phenomenon in the conservation of weight. *Archives de Psychologie*, **41**:145–152.

Day, R. H., and McKenzie, B. E.
1973   Perceptual shape constancy in early infancy. *Perception*, **2**:315–321.

De Lemos, M. M.
1969a Conceptual development in Aboriginal children: Implications for Aboriginal education. In *Aborigines and Education*, S. S. Dunn and C. M. Tatz, eds. Melbourne: Sun Books.
1969b The development of conservation in Aboriginal children. *International Journal of Psychology*, **4**:255–269.

Dennis, W.
1940   The effect of cradling practices upon the onset of walking in Hopi children. *Journal of Genetic Psychology*, **56**:77–86.

Drever, J.
1962   Perception in action. *Bulletin of British Psychological Society*, **45**:1–14.

Dunkeld, J.
1972a The development of representation. Unpublished manuscript, University of Edinburgh.
1972b *The Development of Imitation in Infancy*. Ph.D. thesis, University of Edinburgh.

Dunkeld, J., and Bower, T. G. R.
1978a Infant response to impending collision. *Perception*. In press.
1978b The effect of wedge prisms on the reaching behaviour of infants. Unpublished manuscript, University of Edinburgh.
1979   Infant smiling in different situations. Unpublished manuscript, University of Edinburgh.

Eibl-Eibesfeldt, I.
1971   *Love and Hate*. London: Methuen.

Eimas, P. D., Siqueland, E. R., Jusczyck, P., and Vigorito, J.
1971   Speech perception in infants. *Science*, **171**:303–306.

Eisenberg, L.
1958   School phobia: A study in the communication of anxiety. *American Journal of Psychiatry*, **114**:712–718.

Engen, T., and Lipsitt, L. P.
1965   Decrement and recovery of responses to olfactory stimuli in the human neonate. *Journal of Comparative Physiology and Psychology*, **59**:312–316.

Engen, T., Lipsitt, L. P., and Kaye, H.
1963   Olfactory responses and adaptation in the human neonate. *Journal of Comparative Physiology and Psychology*, **56**:73–77.

Erikson, E. H.
1950   *Childhood and Society*. New York: Norton.

Etzel, B. C., and Gewirtz, J. L.
1967   Experimental modification of caretaker-maintained, high-rate operant crying in a 6- and a 20-week-old infant (infans tyrannotearus): Extinction of crying with reinforcement of eye contact and smiling. *Journal of Experimental Child Psychology*, **3**: 303–317.

Eyferth, K.
1961   Leistungen verschiedener Gruppen von Besatzungskindern in Hamburg-Weschsler Intelligenztest für Kinder. *Archiv für die Gesamte Psychologie*, **113**:222–241.
Eysenck, H. J.
1971   *Race, Intelligence, and Education*. London: Temple Smith.
Faigin, H.
1958   Social behaviour of young children in the kibbutz. *Journal of Abnormal Social Psychology*, **56**: 117–129.
Festinger, L.
1957   *A Theory of Cognitive Dissonance*. Stanford, Calif.: Stanford University Press.
Ford, C. S., and Beach, F. A.
1951   *Patterns of Sexual Behaviour*. New York: Harper & Row.
Fraiberg, S.
1968   Parallel and divergent patterns in blind and sighted infants. *Psychoanalytic Study of the Child*, **23**:264–299.
Fraiberg, S., and Freeman, D. A.
1964   Studies in the development of the congenitally blind infant. *Psychoanalytic Study of the Child*, **19**:113–169.
Fraiberg, S., Siegel, B. L., and Gibson, R.
1966   The role of sound in the search behavior of a blind infant. *Psychoanalytic Study of the Child*, **21**:327–357'
Freedman, D. G.
1964   Smiling in blind infants and the issue of innate versus acquired. *Journal of Child Psychology and Psychiatry and Allied Disciplines*, **5**:171–184.
Freud, S.
1949   *An Outline of Psychoanalysis*. New York: Norton.
Freud, A., and Dann, S.
1951   An experiment in group upbringing. *Psychoanalytic Study of the Child*, **6**:127–168.
Furth, H. G.
1964   Conservation of weight in deaf and hearing children. *Child Development*, **34**:143–150.
1971   Linguistic deficiency and thinking: Research with deaf subjects, 1964–69. *Psychological Bulletin*, **76**:58–72.
Gaze, R. M.
1970   *The Formation of Nerve Connections*. London: Academic Press.
Gaze, R. M., Jacobson, M., and Székely, G.
1963   The retinotectal projection in *Xenopus* with compound eyes. *Journal of Physiology*, **165**:484–499.
Gergen, K. J.
1971   *The Concept of Self*. New York: Holt, Rinehart and Winston.
Gesell, A., and Thompson, H.
1929   Learning and growth in identical infant twins: An experimental study by the method of co-twin control. *Genetic Psychology Monographs*, **6**:1–125.
1934   *Infant Behavior: Its Genesis and Growth*. New York: McGraw-Hill.
Geschwind, N.
1972   Language and the brain. *Scientific American*, **226**(4):76–83.

Gibson, J. J.
    1966   *The Senses Considered as Perceptual Systems.* Boston: Houghton-Mifflin.
Gibson, J. J., Kaplan, G. A., Reynolds, H. N., and Wheeler, K.
    1969   The change from visible to invisible: A study of optical transitions. *Perception and Psychophysics,* **5**:113–116.
Goffman, E.
    1959   *The Presentation of Self in Everyday Life.* Garden City, N.Y.: Doubleday.
Goldberg, S., and Lewis, M.
    1969   Play behaviour in the year-old infant: Early sex differences. *Child Development,* **40**:21–31.
Goodson, B. D., and Greenfield, P. M.
    1975   The search for structural principles in children's manipulative play: A parallel with linguistic development. *Child Development,* **46**:734–746.
Gottesman, I. I.
    1974   Developmental genetics and ontogenetic psychology: Overdue detente and propositions from a matchmaker. In *Minnesota Symposium on Child Development,* A. D. Pick, ed. University of Minnesota Press.
Gouin-Décarie, T.
    1966   *Intelligence and Affectivity in Early Childhood: An Experimental Study of Jean Piaget's Object Concept and Object Relations.* New York: International Universities Press.
    1969   A study of the mental and emotional development of the thalidomide child. In *Determinants of Infant Behaviour,* Vol. IV, B. M. Foss, ed. London: Methuen.
Greenfield, P. M.
    1975   The grammar of action in cognitive development. In *Human Brain Function,* D. Walter, ed. Los Angeles: Brain Information Service/Brain Research Institute, University of California.
Greenfield, P. M., Nelson, K., and Salzman, E.
    1972   The development of rulebound strategies for manipulating seriated cups: A parallel between action and grammar. *Cognitive Psychology,* **3**:291–310.
Gunn, B.
    1964   Children's conceptions of occupational prestige. *Personnel Guidance Journal,* **42**:558–563.
Gurdon, J. B.
    1968   Transplanted nuclei and cell differentiation. *Scientific American,* **219**(6): 24–36.
Guttman, N.
    1963   Laws of behaviour and facts of perception. In *A Study of a Science,* Vol. 5, S. Koch, ed. New York: McGraw-Hill.
Hacking, I.
    1975   *The Emergence of Probability.* Cambridge University Press.
Halliday, M. A. K.
    1973   *Explorations in the Functions of Language.* London: Arnold.
    1975   *Learning How to Mean: Explorations in the Development of Language.* London: Arnold.

Hartshorne, H., and May, M. A.
　1928　*Studies in the Nature of Character, I: Studies in Deceit.* New York: Macmillan.
Hastorf, A.
　1965　The "reinforcement" of individual actions in a group situation. In *Research in Behavior Modification*, L. Krasner and L. P. Ullman, eds. New York: Holt, Rinehart and Winston.
Hatwell, H.
　1966　*Privation sensorielle et intelligence.* Paris: Presses Universitaires de France.
Hawk, S. S.
　1937　Moto-kinaesthetic speech training for children. *Journal of Speech Disorders*, **2**:231–237.
Heber, R., Dever, R., and Conry, J.
　1968　The influence of environmental and genetic variables on intellectual development. In *Behavioral Research in Mental Retardation*, H. J. Prehm, L. A. Hamerlynck, and J. E. Crosson, eds. University of Oregon Press.
Heber, R., and Garber, H.
　1970　An experiment in the prevention of cultural familial mental retardation. Paper presented at the 2nd Congress of the International Association for the Scientific Study of Mental Deficiency, Warsaw, Poland.
Heider, K. G.
　1974　*Dani Sexuality: A Low-energy System.* Unpublished manuscript.
　1976　*Ethnographic Film.* University of Texas Press.
Heinicke, C., and Westheimer, J.
　1966　*Brief Separation.* New York: International Universities Press.
Held, R.
　1965　Plasticity in sensory-motor systems. *Scientific American*, **213**(5):84–94.
Hilden, A. H.
　1949　A longitudinal study of intellectual development. *Journal of Psychology*, **28**:187–214.
Hoffman, M. L.
　1970　Moral development. In *Carmichael's Manual of Child Psychology*, Vol. II, P. H. Mussen, ed. New York: Wiley.
Hofsten, C. von
　1977　Binocular convergence as a determinant of reaching behaviour in infancy. *Perception*, **6**:139–144.
Holmes, M. A. M.
　1974　The academic dispositions of scientists and their seasons of birth. Paper given to the Anabas Conference, University of Edinburgh (March).
Honzig, M. P., MacFarlane, J. W., and Allen, L.
　1948　The stability of mental test performance between two and eighteen years. *Journal of Experimental Education*, **17**:309–324.
Horner, M. S.
　1970　Femininity and successful achievement: A basic inconsistency. In *Feminine Personality and Conflict*, J. M. Bardwick, E. Douvan, M. S. Horner, and D. Guttman, eds. Belmont, Calif.: Brooks/Cole.
Hovland, I. C.
　1937　The generalization of conditioned responses. The sensory generalization of conditioned responses with varying frequencies of tone. *Journal of General Psychology*, **17**:125–148.

Hudson, L., Jacot, B., and Sheldrake, P. F.
   1973   *Lieben und Arbeiten: Patterns of Work and Patterns of Marriage.* Occasional
          Paper 12, Centre for Research in the Educational Sciences, University of
          Edinburgh.
Hudson, L., Johnston, J., and Jacot, B.
   1972   *Perception and Communication in Academic Life.* Occasional Paper 8, Centre
          for Research in the Educational Sciences, University of Edinburgh.
Hull, C. L.
   1934   Learning II: The factor of the conditioned reflex. In *Handbook of General
          Experimental Psychology*, C. Murchison, ed. Worcester: Clark University
          Press.
Humphrey, T.
   1969   Postnatal repetition of human prenatal sequences with some suggestions
          of the neuroanatomical basis. In *Brain and Early Behaviour*, R. J. Robinson,
          ed. London: Academic Press.
Hunt, J. McV., and Uzgiris, I. C.
   1964   Cathexis from recognitive familiarity: An exploratory study. Paper
          presented at the Convention of the American Psychological Association,
          Los Angeles, California (September).
Hunt, R. G., and Synnerdale, V.
   1959   Social influences among kindergarten children. *Sociology and Social
          Research*, **43**:171–174.
Illingworth, R. S.
   1955   Crying in infants and children. *British Medical Journal*, **1**:75–78.
Inhelder, B., and Piaget, J.
   1958   *The Growth of Logical Thinking from Childhood to Adolescence: An Essay on the
          Construction of Formal Operational Structures.* New York: Basic Books.
          (Original French edition 1955.)
Inhelder, B., Sinclair, H., and Bovet, M.
   1974   *Learning and the Development of Cognition.* Cambridge, Mass.: Harvard
          University Press.
Iscoe, I., Williams, M., and Harvey, J.
   1963   Modification of children's judgments by a simulated group technique:
          A normative developmental study. *Child Development*, **34**:963–978.
Jacobson, M.
   1968   Development of neural specificity in retinal ganglion cells of *Xenopus*.
          Developmental Biology, **17**:202–218.
James, W.
   1890   *The Principles of Psychology*, 2 vols. New York: Holt.
Jencks, C.
   1972   *Inequality.* New York: Basic Books.
Jensen, A. R.
   1969   How much can we boost IQ and scholastic achievement? *Harvard
          Educational Review*, **39**:1–123.
   1972   *Genetics and Education.* New York: Harper & Row.
Kagan, J.
   1964   Acquisition and significance of sex typing and sex role identity. In
          Review of Child Development Research, Vol. I, M. L. Hoffman and L. W.
          Hoffman, eds. New York: Russell Sage Foundation.

1967   On the need for relativism. *American Psychologist*, **22**:131–142.

Kagan, J., and Moss, H. A.
1962   *Birth to Maturity*. New York: Wiley.

Kallman, F. J.
1950   The genetics of psychoses: An analysis of 1,232 twin index families. *International Congress of Psychiatry Reports*, **6**:1–27.

Kaye, H.
1965   The conditioned Babkin reflex in human newborns. *Psychonomic Science*, **2**:287–288.

Keasey, C. B.
1973   Experimentally induced changes in moral opinions and reasoning. *Journal of Personality and Social Psychology*, **26**:30–38.

Kelly, G. A.
1955   *The Psychology of Personal Constructs*, 2 vols. New York: Norton.

Kleist, K.
1934   *Gehirnpathologie*. Leipzig: Barth.

Kohlberg, L.
1963   The development of children's orientations towards a moral order, I: Sequence in the development of moral thought. *Vita Humana*, **6**: 11–33.

1964   Development of moral character and moral ideology. In *Review of Child Development*, Vol. 1, M. L. Hoffman and L. W. Hoffman, eds. New York: Russell Sage Foundation.

1965   Relationship between the development of moral judgment and moral conduct. Paper presented at Symposium on Behavioral and Cognitive Concepts in the Study of Internalization, Society for Research in Child Development, Minneapolis, Minnesota.

1969   Stage and sequence: The cognitive developmental approach to socialization. In *Handbook of Socialization Theory and Research*, D. A. Goslin, ed. Chicago: Rand-McNally.

Kohlberg, L., and Elfinbein, D.
1975   The development of moral judgments concerning capital punishment. *American Journal of Orthopsychiatry*, **45**(4):614–640.

Kohlberg, L., and Freundlich, D.
1977   Moral judgement in youthful offenders. In *Moralization: The Cognitive-Developmental Approach*, L. Kohlberg and E. Turiel, eds. New York: Holt, Rinehart and Winston.

Kohlberg, L., and Gilligen, C.
1971   The adolescent as a philosopher: The discovery of self in a post-conventional world. *Daedalus*, fall issue, pp. 1051–1086.

Koslowski, B., and Bruner, J. S.
1972   Learning to use a lever. *Child Development*, **43**:790–799.

Krafka, J.
1919   The effect of temperature upon facet number in the bar-eyed mutant of *Drosophila*, Part I. *Journal of General Physiology*, **2**: 409–432.

Krebs, R. L.
1967   *Some Relationships Between Moral Judgement, Attention, and Resistance to Temptation*. Ph.D. dissertation, University of Chicago.

Krebs, D., and Rosenwald, A.
 1973 Moral reasoning and moral behavior in conventional adults. Unpublished manuscript, Harvard University.
Kringlen, E.
 1967 *Heredity and Environment in the Functional Psychoses*. London: Heinemann.
Kringlen, E., and Jorgerson, K.
 1975 Personality development in twins. Unpublished manuscript, Center for
 Advanced Study in the Behavioral Sciences, Stanford.
Kuhn, T. S.
 1962 *The Structure of Scientific Revolutions*. Chicago: University of Chicago Press.
Lacan, L.
 1972 *Écrits*, 3 vols. Paris: Presses Universitaires de France.
Laing, R. D.
 1959 *The Divided Self*. London: Tavistock.
 1961 *The Self and Others*. London: Tavistock.
 1967 *Politics of Experience*. London: Penguin.
Lenneberg, E. H.
 1967 *Biological Foundations of Language*. New York: Wiley.
 1969 On explaining language. *Science*, **164**:635–643.
Leopold, W. F.
 1947 The study of child language and infant bilingualism. *Word*, **4**:1–17.
Lewis, M., and Brooks, J.
 1974 Infants' social perception: A constructivist view. In *Infant Perception:
 From Sensation to Cognition*, Vol. II, L. B. Cohen and P. Salapatek, eds.
 New York: Academic Press.
Lipsitt, L. P.
 1969 Learning capacities of the human infant. In *Brain and Early Behaviour*,
 R. J. Robinson, ed. London: Academic Press.
Loehlin, J. C., Lindzey, G., and Spuhler, J. N.
 1975 *Race and Intelligence*. San Francisco: W. H. Freeman.
Loehlin, J. C., Vandenberg, S. G., and Osborne, R. T.
 1973 Blood group genes and Negro-White ability differences. *Behavior Genetics*,
 26:400–411.
Loevinger, J.
 1966 The meaning and measurement of ego development. *American Psychologist*,
 21:195–206.
Lovaas, D. I., Freitag, G., Gold, V. J., and Kassorla, I. C.
 1965 Experimental studies of childhood schizophrenia: Analysis of self-
 destructive behavior. *Journal of Experimental Child Psychology*, **2**:67–84.
Maccoby, E., and Masters, J. C.
 1970 Attachment and dependency. In *Carmichael's Manual of Child Psychology*,
 3rd ed., Vol. II, P. H. Mussen, ed. New York: Wiley.
MacNaughton, A.
 1974 *Moral Development in Kibbutzim Children*. Master's thesis. Department of
 Psychology, University of Edinburgh.
Maratos, O.
 1973 *The Origin and Development of Imitation in the First Six Months of Life*.
 Ph.D thesis, University of Geneva.

Maratsos, M. P.
    1973   Decrease in the understanding of the word "big" in pre-school children. *Child Development*, **44**:747–752.
Maxfield, K. E.
    1936   The spoken language of the blind pre-school child: A study of method. *Archives of Psychology*, No. 201.
McDonnell, P. M.
    1975   The development of visually-guided reaching. *Perception and Psychophysics*, **18**:181–185.
McGraw, M. B.
    1940   Neural maturation as exemplified by the achievement of bladder control. *Journal of Paediatrics*, **16**:580–590.
McKinnon, J. W., and Renner, J. W.
    1971   Are colleges concerned with intellectual development? *American Journal of Physics*, **39**:1047–1052.
McLaren, A. P., and Bowman, P.
    1969   Mouse chimaeras derived from fusion of embryos differing by nine genetic factors. *Nature*, **224**:238–240.
Mead, M.
    1937   Public opinion mechanisms among primitive peoples. *Public Opinion Quarterly*, **1**:5–16.
Mehler, J., and Bever, T.
    1967   Cognitive capacity of very young children. *Science*, **158**:141–142.
Melzoff, A. N.
    1976   *Facial Imitation in the Newborn Period*. Ph.D thesis, Oxford University.
Melzoff, A. N., and Moore, M. K.
    1977   Imitation of facial and manual gestures. *Science*, **198**:75–80.
Milgram, S.
    1963   Behavioral study of obedience. *Journal of Abnormal and Social Psychology*, **67**:371–378.
    1974   *Obedience to Authority*. New York: Harper & Row.
Miller, G. A.
    1956   The magical number seven plus or minus two: Some limits on our capacity for processing information. *Psychological Review*, **63**:81–97.
Miller, N. E., and Dollard, J.
    1941   *Social Learning and Inhibition*. New Haven, Conn.: Yale University Press.
Milton, G. A.
    1957   The effects of sex-role identification upon problem-solving skill. *Journal of Abnormal and Social Psychology*, **55**: 208–212.
Mischel, W.
    1968   *Personality and Assessment*. New York: Wiley.
Money, J., and Ehrhardt, A. A.
    1972   *Man and Woman, Boy and Girl*. Baltimore: Johns Hopkins University Press.
Monnier, C.
    1977   *La genèse de l'experimentation: Exploration d'objects nouveaux par les bébés*. Ph.D thesis, Free University of Brussels.

Morgan, T. H.
    1927   *Experimental Embryology.* New York: Columbia University Press.
Morgan, G. A., and Ricciuti, H. N.
    1969   Infants' responses to strangers during the first year. In *Determinants of Infant Behaviour*, Vol. 4, B. M. Foss, ed. New York: Wiley.
Morse, S., and Gergen, K. J.
    1970   Social comparison, self-consistency, and the concept of self. *Journal of Personality and Social Psychology*, **16**:148–156.
Moss, H.
    1967   Sex, age, and state as determinants of mother-infant interaction. *Merrill-Palmer Quarterly*, **13**:19–36.
Mounoud, P., and Bower, T. G. R.
    1974   Conservation of weight in infants. *Cognition*, **3**:29–40.
Mowrer, O. H., and Mowrer, W. N.
    1938   Enuresis: A method for its study and treatment. *American Journal of Orthopsychiatry*, **8**:436–459.
Mundy-Castle, A. C.
    1970   The descent of meaning. *Social Psychology Information*, **9**:125–141.
Murphy, L. B.
    1962   *The Widening World of Childhood.* New York: Basic Books.
Mussen, P., and Rutherford, E.
    1963   Parent-child relations and parental responsibility in relation to young children's sex-role preferences. *Child Development*, **34**:225–246.
Neilson, I. E.
    1978   *A Reinterpretation of the Development of the Object Concept in Infancy.* Ph.D. dissertation, University of Edinburgh.
Newson, J., and Newson, E.
    1963   *Infant Care in an Urban Community.* London: Allen and Unwin.
Noirot, E.
    1978   Développement de pointe de vue éthologique. Paper read at the Biannual Round Table on Cognitive Development in Infancy, Paris (March).
O'Connor, N., and Hermelin, B.
    1972   Seeing and hearing in space and time. *Perception and Psychophysics*, **11**:46–48.
Oléron, P.
    1953   Conceptual thinking of the deaf. *American Annals of the Deaf*, **98**:304–310.
Oléron, P., and Herren, D.
    1961   L'acquisition des conservations et le langage: Étude comparative sur des enfants sourds et entendants. *Enfance*, **14**:203–219.
Osborne, R. T., and Suddick, D. E.
    1971   Blood type, gene frequency, and mental ability. *Psychological Reports*, **29**:1243–1249.
Page, E. B.
    1972   Miracle in Milwaukee: Raising the IQ. *Educational Researcher*, **1**:8–16.
Pages, J.
    1949   *Abnormal Psychology.* New York: McGraw-Hill.

Papousek, H.
    1967   Experimental studies of appetitional behavior in human newborns and
            infants. In *Early Behavior*, H. W. Stevenson, E. H. Hess, and H. L.
            Rheingold, eds. New York: Wiley.
    1969   Individual variability in learned responses in human infants. In *Brain
            and Early Behaviour*, R. J. Robinson, ed. London: Academic Press.
Pavlov, I. P.
    1927   *Conditioned Reflexes*, translated by G. V. Anrep. Oxford University Press.
Piaget, J.
    1926   *The Language and Thought of the Child*. New York: Harcourt Brace
            Jovanovich. (Original French edition 1923.)
    1929   *The Child's Conception of the World*. New York: Harcourt Brace Jovanovich.
            (Original French edition 1926.)
    1932   *The Moral Judgment of the Child*. New York: Harcourt Brace Jovanovich.
            (Original French edition 1932.)
    1950   *The Psychology of Intelligence*. London: Routledge and Kegan Paul.
            (Original French edition 1947.)
    1951   *Play, Dreams and Imitation in Childhood*. New York: Norton. (Original
            French edition 1946.)
    1954   *Origins of Intelligence*. New York: Basic Books. (Original French edition
            1936.)
    1955   *The Construction of Reality in the Child*. London: Routledge and Kegan
            Paul. (Original French edition 1937.)
    1967   *On the Development of Memory and Identity: Heinz Werner Lectures, Clark
            University, Worcester, Vol. 2*. Barre, Mass.: Barre Publishers.
    1971   *Biology and Knowledge*. Chicago: University of Chicago Press. (Original
            French edition 1967.)
    1972   Intellectual evolution from adolescence to adulthood. *Human Development*,
            15:1–35.
Piaget, J., and Inhelder, B.
    1956   *The Child's Conception of Space*. London: Routledge and Kegan Paul.
            (Original French edition 1948.)
    1972   *Memory and Intelligence*, translated by A. J. Pomerans. New York: Basic
            Books. (Original French edition 1968.)
    1974   *The Child's Construction of Quantities: Conservation and Atomism*. New York:
            Basic Books. (Original French edition 1941.)
    1975   *The Origin of the Idea of Chance in Children*. New York: Basic Books.
            (Original French edition 1951.)
Piaget, J., and Szeminska, A.
    1952   *The Child's Conception of Number*. New York: Humanities Press. (Original
            French edition 1941.)
Piaget, J., Inhelder, B., and Szeminska, A.
    1960   *The Child's Conception of Geometry*. New York: Basic Books. (Original
            French edition 1948.)
Price-Williams, D. R., Gordon, W., and Ramirez, M.
    1969   Skill and conservation: A study of pottery-making children. *Developmental
            Psychology*, **1**:769.

Ramey, C. T., Campbell, F. A., and Nicholson, J. E.
  1973   The predictive power of the Bayley scales of infant development and the
          Stanford-Binet Intelligence Test in a relatively constant environment.
          Child Development, **44**:790–795.
Rebelsky, F., and Hanks, C.
  1971   Fathers' verbal interactions with infants in the first three months of life.
          Child Development, **42**:63–68.
Reiss, B. F.
  1940   Semantic conditioning involving the galvanic skin reflex. *Journal of
          Experimental Psychology*, **26**:238–240.
Rest, J.
  1968   *Developmental Hierarchy in Preference and Comprehension.* Ph.D. dissertation,
          University of Chicago.
Reynolds, M. M.
  1928   Negativism of preschool children. *Teachers College Contributions to Education*,
          No. 288.
Rheingold, H. L.
  1969   The effect of a strange environment on the behaviour of infants. In
          Determinants of Infant Behaviour, Vol. 4, B. M. Foss, ed. London: Methuen.
Rheingold, H., Gewirtz, J. L., and Ross, H. W.
  1959   Social conditioning of vocalization in the infant. *Journal of Comparative
          Physiology and Psychology*, **52**:68–73.
Robinson, H., and Robinson, N.
  1971   Longitudinal development of very young children in a comprehensive
          day care program. *Child Development*, **42**:1673–1683.
Rock, I.
  1958   Repetition and learning. *Scientific American*, **199**(2):68–72.
Rosenthal, M. K.
  1965   *The Generalization of Dependency Behaviors from Mother to Stranger.* Ph.D.
          dissertation, Stanford University.
Rosenthal, K., and Jacobson, L.
  1968   *Pygmalion in the Classroom.* New York: Holt, Rinehart and Winston.
Rutter, M.
  1972   *Maternal Deprivation Reassessed.* Harmondsworth, England: Penguin.
Sander, L. W.
  1969   Regulation and organisation in the early infant-caretaker system. In
          Brain and Early Behaviour, R. J. Robinson, ed. London: Academic Press.
Sankoff, G., and Laberge, S.
  1973   On the acquisition of native speakers by a language. *Kivung*, **6**:32–47.
Sansom, W.
  1960   *Collected Stories.* London: Hogarth.
Schaffer, H. R.
  1963   Some issues for research in the study of attachment behaviour. In
          Determinants of Infant Behaviour, Vol. 2, B. M. Foss, ed. London: Methuen.
  1966   The onset of fear of strangers and the incongruity hypothesis. *Journal of
          Child Psychology and Psychiatry*, **7**:95–106.
  1971   *The Growth of Sociability.* Harmondsworth, England: Penguin.

Schaffer, H. R., and Emerson, P. E.
  1964   The development of social attachments in infancy. *Monograph of the Society for Research in Child Development,* **29**:3.
Schonen, S. de, and Bower, T. G. R.
  1978   The understanding of spatial relations. Paper read at the Biannual Round Table on Cognitive Development in Infancy, Paris (March).
Schutz, R.
  1965   Homosexualität und Prägung. *Psychologie Forschung,* **28**:439–463.
Sears, R. R.
  1951   A theoretical framework for personality and social behaviour. *American Psychologist,* **6**:476–488.
Sears, R. R., Maccoby, E. E., and Levin, H.
  1957   *Patterns of Child Rearing.* Evanston, Ill.: Harper & Row.
Seligman, M. E. P.
  1975   *Helplessness.* San Francisco: W. H. Freeman.
Sheeran, L.
  1973   Vertical décalage in weight conservation between sensori-motor and conceptual levels. Master's thesis, University of Edinburgh.
Sherif, M., and Sherif, C. W.
  1964   *Reference Groups: Exploration into Conformity and Deviation of Adolescents.* New York: Harper & Row.
Shirley, M., and Poyntz, L.
  1941   The influence of separation from the mother on children's emotional responses. *Journal of Psychology,* **12**:251–282.
Silberbauer, G. B.
  1965   *Report to the Government of Bechuanaland on the Bushman Survey.* Gaberones: Bechuanaland Government.
Siqueland, E. R., and Lipsitt, L. P.
  1966   Conditioned head-turning in human newborns. *Journal of Experimental Child Psychology,* **3**:356–376.
Skinner, B. F.
  1938   *The Behavior of Organisms.* New York: Appleton-Century-Crofts.
Smedslund, J.
  1961   The acquisition of the concept of substance and weight in children. *Scandinavian Journal of Psychology,* **2**:71–87.
Sontag, L., Baker, C., and Nelson, V.
  1958   Mental growth and personality: A longitudinal study. *Monograph of the Society for Research in Child Development,* **2**:1–143.
Spemann, H.
  1938   *Embryological Development and Induction.* New Haven, Conn.: Yale University Press.
Sperry, R. W.
  1956   The eye and the brain. *Scientific American,* **194**(3):48–52.
Spitz, R. A.
  1950   Anxiety in infancy: A study of its manifestations in the first year of life. *International Journal of Psychoanalysis,* **31**:138–143.
Springer, S. P.
  1971   Ear asymmetry in a dichotic detection test. *Perception and Psychophysics,* **10**:239–241.

Starkweather, E. K.
    1964   *Conformity and Nonconformity as Indicators of Creativity in Preschool Children.* Cooperative Research Project No. 1967, United States Office of Education.

Strauss, S.
    1972   Inducing cognitive development and learning: A review of short-term training experiments. I: The organismic-developmental approach. *Cognition,* **1**:329–357.

Super, D. E., and Overstreet, P. L.
    1960   *The Vocational Maturity of Ninth Grade Boys.* New York: Teachers College Bureau of Publications, Columbia University.

Tanser, H. A.
    1939   *The Settlement of Negroes in Kent County, Ontario and a Study of the Mental Capacity of Their Descendants.* Chatham, Ontario: Shepherd.

Taylor, J. G.
    1962   *The Behavioral Basis of Perception.* New Haven, Conn.: Yale University Press.

Thigpen, C. H., and Cleckley, H. M.
    1957   *The Three Faces of Eve.* New York: McGraw-Hill.

Thorpe, W. H.
    1956   *Learning and Instinct in Animals.* London: Methuen.

Tienari, P.
    1963   Psychiatric illnesses in identical twins. *Acta Psychiatrica Scandinavia,* Supp. 171.

Tracy, J. J., and Cross, H. J.
    1973   Antecedents of shift in moral judgement. *Journal of Personality and Social Psychology,* **26**:238–244.

Trevarthen, C.
    1975   Early attempts at speech. In *Child Alive,* R. Lewin, ed. London: Temple Smith.

Trevarthen, C., and Tursky, B.
    1969   Recording horizontal rotation of head and eyes in spontaneous shifts of gaze. *Behavioural Research Methods and Instrumentation,* **1**:8.

Turiel, E.
    1966   An experimental test of the sequentiality of developmental stages in the child's moral judgements. *Journal of Personality and Social Psychology,* **3**:611–618.

Turkewitz, G., Birch, H. B., Moreau, T., Levy, L., and Cornwell, A. C.
    1966   Effect of intensity of auditory stimulation on directional eye movements in the human neonate. *Animal Behavior,* **14**:93–101.

Turner, M. E.
    1957   *The Child Within the Group: An Experiment in Self-Government.* Stanford, Calif.: Stanford University Press.

Urwin, C.
    1973   The development of a blind baby. Unpublished manuscript read at University of Edinburgh.

Utech, D. A., and Hoving, K. L.
    1969   Parents and peers as competing influences in the decisions of children at differing ages. *Journal of Social Psychology,* **78**(2):267–274.

Uzgiris, I. C., and Hunt, J. McV.
  1975   *Assessment in Infancy*. Urbana, Ill.: University of Illinois Press.
Verplanck, W. S.
  1955   The control of the content of conversation: Reinforcement of statements of opinions. *Journal of Abnormal and Social Psychology*, **51**:668–676.
Vygotsky, L. S.
  1962   *Thought and Language*, edited and translated by E. Hanfmann and G. Vakar. Cambridge, Mass.: M.I.T. Press.
Wahler, R. G.
  1967   Infant social attachments: A reinforcement theory interpretation and investigation. *Child Development*, **38**:1079–1088.
Washburn, R. W.
  1929   A study of smiling and laughing of infants in the first year of life. *Genetic Psychology Monographs*, **6**:1.
Watson, J. B.
  1925   *Behaviorism*. New York: Norton.
Watson, J. S.
  1966   The development and generalization of "contingency awareness" in early infancy: Some hypotheses. *Merrill-Palmer Quarterly*, **12**:123–135.
  1972   We assess lawfulness, but God knows what the law is. *Proceedings of APA 80th Annual Convention*, pp. 139–140.
  1973   Smiling, cooing, and "the game." *Merrill-Palmer Quarterly*, **18**:323–339.
Wertheimer, M.
  1961   Psycho-motor coordination of auditory-visual space at birth. *Science*, **134**:1692.
Wesman, A. G.
  1952   Faking personality test scores in a simulated employment situation. *Journal of Applied Psychology*, **36**:112–113.
Wheeler, L. R.
  1932   The intelligence of East Tennessee mountain children. *Journal of Educational Psychology*, **23**: 351–370.
White, B., and Held, R.
  1966   Plasticity of sensory-motor development in the human infant. In *The Causes of Behavior*, J. R. Rosenblith and W. Allinsmith, eds. Boston: Allyn and Bacon.
Williams, C. D.
  1959   The elimination of tantrum behaviors by extinction procedures. *Journal of Abnormal and Social Psychology*, **59**:269.
Wilson, R. S.
  1972   Twins: Early mental development. *Science*, **175**:914–917.
Wishart, J. G., and Bower, T. G. R.
  1977a   The comprehension of spatial relations in infancy. Unpublished manuscript, University of Edinburgh.
  1977b   Conservation of number in infancy. Unpublished manuscript, University of Edinburgh.
Wishart, J. G., Bower, T. G. R., and Dunkeld, J.
  1978   Reaching in the dark. *Perception*, **7**:507–512.

Wohlwill, J. F.
    1973   *The Study of Behavioral Development.* New York: Academic Press.
Wolf, M., Mees, H., and Risley, T.
    1963   Application of operant-conditioning procedures to the behavior problems
            of an autistic child. Paper delivered to Western Psychological Association,
            Santa Monica, Calif.
Wolff, P. H.
    1963   Observations on the early development of smiling. In *Determinants of
            Infant Behaviour*, Vol. 2, B. M. Foss, ed. New York: Wiley.
    1969   Motor development and holotelencephaly. In *Brain and Early Behaviour*,
            R. J. Robinson, ed. London: Academic Press.
Zax, M., and Stricker, G.
    1963   *Patterns of Psychopathology.* New York: Macmillan.
Zeeman, E. C.
    1976   Catastrophe theory. *Scientific American*, **234**(4):65–83.
Zimbardo, P. G.
    1972   The pathology of imprisonment. In *Social Psychology in the World Today*,
            E. Aronson and R. Helmreich, eds. New York: Van Nostrand.

Subject Index

Name Index